Lucy Goodison gained her doctorate for research into female religious symbolism in ancient Crete. She researched and directed historical and archaeological films for BBC Television. Active in community-based politics and the women's movement, she trained in massage and now teaches self-help therapy skills and runs bodywork, dream and dance groups at the Women's Therapy Centre in London. As a freelance journalist she specializes in issues of mental health and learning difficulties.

Lucy Goodison

MOVING HEAVEN AND EARTH

Sexuality, Spirituality and Social Change

Pandora
An Imprint of HarperCollins*Publishers*

Pandora Press
An Imprint of HarperCollins*Publishers*
77-85 Fulham Palace Road,
Hammersmith, London W6 8JB

First published by The Women's Press 1990
This revised edition published by Pandora Press 1992
10 9 8 7 6 5 4 3 2 1

A catalogue record for this book
is available from the British Library

ISBN 0 04 440 861 7

Typeset by Harper Phototypesetters Limited,
Northampton, England
Printed in Great Britain by
Mackays of Chatham, Kent

CONTENTS

For my friends,
who helped me

ACKNOWLEDGEMENTS

Over the years many people have helped me to produce this book. Many friends have read chapters and given valuable comments and criticism, in particular (Introduction) Jane Foot, Stef Pixner; (Chapter 1) Alan Colley, Linda Dove, Alison Fell, Stef Pixner, Joanna Ryan; (Chapter 2) Nikos Efstratiou, Jan Elson, Joanna Ryan; (Chapter 3) Joanna Ryan, Margaret Williamson; (Chapter 4) Inga Czudnochowski, Sheila Ernst, Marie Maguire; (Chapter 5) Patti Howe, Penny McEwan; (Chapter 6) David Boadella, Sue Cowan-Jenssen, Diana Dantes, Ann de Boursac, Judith Griffies, Paul Morrison, Victor Seidler; (Chapter 7) Jane Foot, Carlos Guarita, Stef Pixner, Beth Shaw. I am thankful to them all for their time and thought.

For kindly sharing their knowledge, ideas or experience with me on specific points I am also grateful to Lyn Agley, David Boadella, Ann de Boursac, Diane Burski, Michael Channon, Penny Cloutte, Diana Dantes, Sophie Dicks, Linda Dove, Sheila Ernst, Mike Falk, Jenny Fasal, Stephen Frank, Judith Griffies, Firmo and Jacinta Guarita, Keith Horn, Patti Howe, Jenny Kuper, Louise London, Marie Maguire, Isis Martins, Barbara Morrison, Joyce Morrison, Kathy Nairne, Will Parfitt, Sally Potter, Lynne Prather, Jenner Roth, Beth Shaw, Di Steeds, John Steeds, Sara Thomas, Emma Wilkinson.

Some individuals played an especial part in shaping the ideas in this book or in helping me through the writing process. As supervisor of the PhD thesis which forms the basis of Chapter 7, Alan Griffiths helped me through over 15 years of research with consistent good humour, encouragement and positive criticism. Many years ago, Paul Jordan steered me off the slippery slopes of mysticism. Members of the Red Therapy group developed important understandings about the relationship between the personal and political, and continued to provide a pool of strength. Ann Parks through her massage training showed that touch can be spiritual as well as sensual, and taught many of the basic meditation techniques which are described in this book. I am indebted to Bob Moore's empirical and compassionate teaching about 'subtle' energy at regular courses since 1978. Jenner Roth's warmth and wisdom has guided me through many tangles. Discussions with Patti Howe, Anna Ickowitz, Paul Morrison and Victor Seidler helped me to reconcile the apparent 'spiritual/political' split, and they also gave valued personal support. In recent years Stef Pixner was unfailingly generous in her encouragement and gave wise help with everything from despair to spelling.

Writing a big book over nineteen years draws heavily on human resources and takes a toll. I am grateful to Joanna Ryan for invaluable personal support which helped to keep me going and working through some difficult years. Since the beginning, Paul Morrison encouraged me to value my work and has been unwavering in giving whatever moral and practical support he could. I am grateful to my parents for bringing me up to believe that I could accomplish something, and for generously helping me by looking after my daughter Corey on many occasions to free me to write. I must thank Corey for good-naturedly enduring my preoccupations and the mountains of papers, and for her sustaining affection. Carlos Guarita kept his sense of humour in the face of overwhelming odds, and gave me the heart to finish. I have been grateful for Jane Foot's friendship, for her willingness to remind me that I could always put it on the bonfire, and for her alternative title suggestions, especially the rather apt *Costing Body and Soul*. For their support and friendship I must also thank Jane Armitage, Sue Cowan-Jenssen, Eileen Pembridge, Tom Weld, and my dream group.

During the original process of preparation the book was blessed with two wonderful editors. Over the final three years Sue Geary's precision and clarity helped to give style and shape to what was embryonic, and I was consistently grateful for her calm and sympathetic presence through the struggles of rewriting. I owe a special debt of thanks to Stephanie Dowrick who created the original opportunity for the book and steered it from its conception through to first draft with warmth, wit, acumen and inspiring encouragement; without her, there would have been no book.

Grateful acknowledgement is given to the following for permission to reproduce copyright material:

Text: Allison and Busby for permission to quote from 'Marxist Cultural Theory: the Althusserian Smokescreen' from *One-Dimensional Marxism* edited by Kevin McDonnell and Kevin Robins, 1980; Barrie and Jenkins for permission to quote from *Natural Symbols: Explorations in Cosmology* by Mary Douglas, 1970 and Pantheon Books, a division of Random House, Inc. copyright © 1970, 1973; Beacon Press for permission to quote from *Dreaming the Dark: Magic, Sex and Politics* by Starhawk, copyright © 1982 Miriam Simos; Cambridge University Press for permission to quote from *Themis: a Study of the Social Origins of Greek Religion* by Jane Ellen Harrison, 1927 and Merlin Press, 1977; Collins Publishers for permission to quote from *Memories, Dreams, Reflections* by C. G. Jung, recorded and edited by Aniela Jaffe, translated by Richard and Clara Winston, Collins Fount Paperbacks, 1977 and Pantheon Books, a division of Random House, Inc.; Country Women for permission to quote from 'Of Cabbages and Kings' by Harriet Bye, published in *Country Women*, 1977; The C. W. Daniel Company Ltd for permission to quote from *Radionics and the Subtle Anatomy of Man*, David V. Tansley, 1972; J. G. Ferguson Publishing Co. for permission to quote from *Man and his Symbols* edited by C. G. Jung, Aldus Books, 1964; Harper and Row, Publishers, Inc. for permission to quote from 'Theology in the Politics of Appalachian Women' by Sheila Collins in *Womanspirit Rising: a Feminist Reader in Religion*, copyright © 1979 edited by Carol P. Christ and Judith Plaskow; Heresies for permission to quote from 'Why Women Need the Goddess' by Carol P. Christ and 'A Hersterical Look at Some Aspects of Black Sexuality' by Sylvia Witts Vitale, both published in *Heresies*, 1978 and 1981 respectively; The Hogarth Press, publishers, and The Masters and Fellows of Darwin College in the University of Cambridge for permission to quote from *Early Greece: the Bronze and Archaic Ages* by M. I. Finley, 1981; Sheila Jeffreys for permission to quote from 'Male Sexuality as Social Control' published in *Scarlet Woman*, 1977; Jonathan Cape Limited for permission to quote from *Genesis as Myth* by Edmund Leach, 1969; Evelyn Fox Keller for permission to quote from 'How Gender Matters, or, Why it's so hard for us to count past two' in *Perspectives on Gender and Science* edited by Jan Harding, The Falmer Press, 1986; Jacky Lansley for permission to quote from 'Women Dancing' in *New Dance*, 1978; The MIT Press for permission to quote from 'Anthropological Aspects of Language: Animal Categories and Verbal Abuse' by Edmund Leach in *New Directions in the Study of Language* edited by Eric H. Lenneberg, 1964; New Directions Publishing Corporation for permission to quote from *The Colossus of Maroussi* copyright © 1941 by Henry Miller; W. W. Norton for permission to quote from *Of Woman Born: Motherhood as Experience and Institution* by Adrienne

Rich, 1976 and Virago Press Ltd, 1977 copyright © W. W. Norton and Company Inc.; Oxford University Press for permission to quote from *Divinity and Experience: the Religion of the Dinka* by Godfrey Lienhardt, 1961; Brian Pearce for permission to quote from his translation of *Class and Art: Problems of Culture under the Dictatorship of the Proletariat* by Leon Trotsky, a Fourth International Pamphlet, New Park Publications Ltd, 1968; Helen Poynor for permission to quote from 'To Live is to Dance' in *Human Potential Resources*, 1982; Princeton University Press for permission to quote from *The Collected Works of C. G. Jung*, translated by R. F. C. Hull, Bollingen Series XX, Vol. 9, 1: *The Archetypes and the Collective Unconscious*, copyright © 1959, 1969 by Princeton University Press and Routledge and Kegan Paul, 1959; The *San Francisco Examiner* for permission to quote from 'Dropping out from a life of spiritual quest', Lawrence David Hooper interviewed by Caroline Drewes, copyright © 1980 The *San Francisco Examiner*; Sigo Press for permission to quote from *The Inner World of Childhood: a Study in Analytical Psychology* by Frances G. Wickes, Sigo Press, 1988; Simon and Schuster for permission to quote from *The Nature of Personal Reality* by Jane Roberts, Prentice-Hall, Inc., Englewood Cliffs, NJ, 1974; Monica Sjöö for permission to quote from *The Great Cosmic Mother of All*, 1975, and *Women are the Real Left!*, 1979; Berta Stjernquist of Kungl. Humanistiska Vetenskapssamfunet i Lund for permission to quote from *The Minoan-Mycenaean Religion and its Survival in Greek Religion* by Martin P. Nilsson, C. W. K. Gleerup, Lund, 1950; Suhrkamp Verlag for permission to quote from *Öffentlichkeit und Erfahrung. Zur Organisationsanalyse von bürgerlicher und proletarischer Öffentlichkeit* by Oskar Negt and Alexander Kluge, 1974; University of Chicago Press for permission to quote from *Sowing the Body: Psychoanalysis and Ancient Representations of Women* by Page duBois, 1988; Verso for permission to quote from *Problems in Materialism and Culture* by Raymond Williams, published by Verso, 1980; Walter de Gruyter & Co. for permission to quote from *The Origins of Greek Religion* by B. C. Dietrich, published 1974, Walter de Gruyter & Co., Berlin and New York; William Morrow and Co., Inc. for permission to quote from *The Dialectic of Sex* by Shulamith Firestone, The Women's Press, 1979. Every effort has been made to contact the holders of copyright material and if any have been omitted the author regrets this fact and apologises.

I

INTRODUCTION
The Revolution of the Imagination

Good/bad; mind/body; pure/impure; white/black; male/female; active/passive; sun/moon; up/down; spirit/matter; culture/nature; spirituality/sexuality. This book is about divisions in our thought and society – and about exploring possibilities of connection.

The inequalities and splits in our society are echoed in a series of symbolic divisions which shape the way we think and imagine. Society is split between the haves and have-nots, dominant and oppressed races, leaders and followers; and we recreate those splits inside ourselves. We think of one side of ourselves as intelligent, godlike, divine, while the other half is sensual, human, mortal: 'the spirit is willing but the flesh is weak'. One side of the division is 'light', 'high', and 'pure', while the other is 'dark', 'low' and 'dirty'. We are so used to this polarisation of spirituality and sexuality that we rarely notice how it restricts our view of both. Nor do we often notice how, with the downgrading of sexuality, it parallels the polarisation of the 'male' and 'female' in our society, with the downgrading of the 'female'. We have lived with this split for so long that we rarely question it. It passes for a 'natural order', so that men are 'rational' and women 'earthy'. Members of one class work with their minds, another class with their bodies. The split fuels racist stereotypes so that black people are seen as 'sensual' or to 'have rhythm'. Such symbolic associations are seen as inevitable, as archetypal. They are part of a system of symbols which we have inherited, which we take for granted, but which drastically limit the way we perceive.

I hope this book can open some doors to change. I will argue that symbols are not universal or inevitable, but are the product of a particular society at a particular time; and that they serve to validate and perpetuate the status quo in that society. The symbolic split between mind and body has a particularly devastating effect on our attempts to envisage a world that is less traumatically divided by class, sex, race and wealth. Before we even leave the boundaries of our own being, we think in terms of superior and inferior: the mind 'superior' to the body, the 'rational' in us which must subdue the 'irrational'. But the mind/body split is an idea with a specific history, an idea which first appeared in western civilisation at a particular time and place.

Some twentieth-century theories have seen the classical world as the repository of elements of the modern unconscious mind. Freud's Oedipus and other mythological characters have become bywords for patterns of feeling and behaviour assumed to be intrinsic to human nature. Jung cited classical sources for his allegories of the sun-hero, his symbolic theory of the 'archetypes' and his search for the 'Eternal Feminine'. But tracing the early roots of classical ideas reveals a tradition which is socially determined and changes drastically over time, reflecting shifting preoccupations and values. Fifteen years of research into prehistoric Crete convinced me that there was a society with a radically different symbolism, where they celebrated a female sun and a creative 'Pandora's Jar'; where women were linked with symbols of power and growth; where the divine was immanent in the physical; and where the spirit/matter split did not appear to exist.

Some writers have cast their eyes back longingly across the centuries to ancient Crete hoping to reinvent a society where contemporary social injustices were inverted, where a Goddess reigned and women had power over men. My empirical work on the evidence in engravings, ruins, pottery and bones did not reveal a monotheistic 'Mother Goddess', or a matriarchy, or any kind of inversion of our contemporary splits. I found something more exciting – a completely different way of living and of seeing life which apparently did not include those splits at all.

Over the millenia since then, these splits have become part of our cultural heritage. We assume the polarisation of spirituality and sexuality, and their placing as private and intimate concerns outside the margins of the social arena. Thus we may find it hard to recognise that both sexuality and spirituality are potentially subversive and liberating forces. Both make us keenly aware of our bonds with other people. Both mobilise energy and passion which our society has relegated as 'unconscious' or 'irrational', but which could add muscle and verve to the movement for a more equal world.

Traditionally these areas of experience have been successfully exploited by reactionary forces. In recent years fear of sexuality, fear of the irrational, lack of identity and the search for a sense of belonging seem to have provided the fuel for 'moral' and religious crusades, whether in anti-abortion or 'law and order' campaigns or in persecuting AIDS sufferers. But both sexuality and spirituality, harnessing strong, wordless forces, can instead generate activity and visions capable of challenging the existing institutions of society.

In Germany in the 1930s Wilhelm Reich pointed out how unexpressed emotion and sexuality were exploited by Fascism to fuel prejudice, fear and hatred, and how they could serve instead as a powerful progressive force for social change. The women's movement has offered imaginative possibilities for integrating the personal (including emotional and sexual issues) with the political in a way which could expand our view of what is political. The ecology movement has also opened horizons by connecting human society with the broader context of the planet on which we live.

Spirituality does not happen only in churches, synagogues and mosques. As these recent movements have suggested, it is about the feelings in the self which link us to the world, the individual as part of a larger whole. Spirituality has its place, often unrecognised, in work and play, on the streets and in struggle. As the faculty which allows us to feel our connection with other humans, the natural environment and a wider sense of the universe, it has an important role to play in the movement towards a more just society.

If this book is not itself to reflect those damaging divisions I describe, it needs to include both theory and practice, looking at ways in which people can and do reconcile these splits in their daily lives. If there is no such thing as a 'universal' symbolism, if the symbolic divisions I have described are socially created and subject to change, how does this affect the way we live? A revolution of the imagination is needed to free us from what is a highly complex symbol system continuously reiterated and endorsed by our cultural heritage, by advertisements and the media as well as in schools and churches, in psychology and history books. Parallel with social and economic changes we may wish to see, parallel with external changes we may hope to make in our lives, we need to reclaim our imaginative life and allow changes to take place in the way we perceive and symbolise the world. This means questioning inherited symbolic systems – whether zodiac signs, Jungian archetypes, or patriarchal Greek myths – and finding new ways to use them. The book suggests practical methods for working with symbols to empower ourselves and bridge the mind/body split.

This volume is shorter than the original hardback and has been rearranged. Chapter 2 introduces some influential theories about how symbol systems are shaped and how they can change. In Chapters 3 to 6 I touch – in a critical and investigative spirit – on a number of techniques and disciplines including dream work, meditation, visualisation, astrology, alchemy, massage, healing and 'chakra' work, and show how these approaches can be used to influence a variety of life experiences from gardening and sex to writing and campaigning. Finally, Chapter 7 offers hope from history, describing the early Cretan society where heaven seems to have been no more holy than earth, until the advent of patriarchal social relations divided the two.

Readers may be disconcerted at the way the empirical and the esoteric rub shoulders in these pages. The book is scholarly and also contains practical sections about liberating the intuition and imagination from the very splits I am identifying. In writing it I have drawn on my academic research as well as on my training and practice in massage and healing and on experience from years of involvement with feminism and left-wing politics. Detailed work does not need to be dry: knowledge can be fed by experience, writing can spring from both thought and passion. This book is about bridging the gap between body and soul. I hope that I have also been able to bridge the gap between insight and enquiry, between head and heart, in the way that I have written it.

The soul/body split is a deep scar within us, which we cannot wish away. However, recognising it and working with it can transform it. Spirituality does not need to be divorced from sexuality and from daily material life; even now there are things that can be done to start healing that split, to use both those energies to change our everyday world for the better.

2

SYMBOLS:
God-given, Man-made or Woman-made?

We have inherited a divided world. Its splits show not only in the external fabric of our society, but in the symbols with which we spin our sentences and fantasies. They are apparent in the images held in circulation by politicians, scientists, pop songs, advertisements and television programmes. We may blot them out, analyse them, wince, weep or laugh at them, but those images are omnipresent. They incessantly carve out a contrast between 'male' and 'female', a polarisation which draws in its train a series of other divisions: between active and passive, subject and object, culture and nature.

To give an idea of the insistence and ubiquitousness of such symbolism, let's take the example of an afternoon's television. Our children, on their return from school, witness a feast of symbols which are crammed with meaning, even when the context seems trivial. Pet food advertising is a case in point. Dog food bears male names and is usually promoted through a boisterous outdoor image. In contrast, cat food bears female names, and the commercials often feature intimate and physically specific interior shots – soft fur, sensuous stretching, fastidious eating, satisfied purring. Despite many exceptions, this male/female symbolism is also evident in common speech with expressions such as 'sex-kitten', 'sea-dog', 'catty' and 'pussy-hunting'. Edmund Leach, in 'Anthropological Aspects of Language', has noted that cat and dog 'are paired terms, and seem to serve as a paradigm for quarreling husband and wife'. Do our children ignore such commercials, or do they unconsciously learn something about how activity and softness are apportioned to men and women in our society?

After the adverts, a programme: perhaps an episode of the caped crusader *Batman*, a favourite whose heroic deeds and rescues I often used to hear my daughter re-enacting with teddies in her bedroom.

The larger-than-life adventures are colourful, witty, entertaining. Do our children also notice the values embodied by such super-heroes: 'Stupid, rigid, unquestioning obedience to patriarchal law and order, asexual, never born by a mother and even clothed in rigid armour – totally a product of big cities and sky scrapers, mechanisation and no vegetation anywhere' (as Monica Sjöö has described them in *The Great Cosmic Mother of All*)? Do our children notice that these heroes, who triumph so spectacularly over nature, are always white and male?

Black people appear advertising products like crisps or muesli, where the image is 'cool', funny or outrageous, but rarely advertising a clean wash or a computer, rarely embodying the qualities of citizen or superhero. Nor will the afternoon's television offer a female version of the superhero. Fictional heroines like She-Ra and Wonder Woman always ultimately have a man to turn to, as do those other daring women who advertise a wild hair colour or a dangerous perfume. Most of television's images tell a rather different story: of women whose role is to be looked at, to be consumed. Of the identification of women with food for consumption (as in 'dish', 'tart', 'sweetheart'), Rosalind Coward has pondered in *Female Desire*:

> what are we to make of the particular kind of food by which women are described as objects of desire – the sugars, sweets and confectionery? . . . Nourishment, possession, inessential luxuries. With a startling precision, our language makes links between the attitudes which place women under the domination of men in this society.

Woman as nourishment is embodied in the symbol of the ideal mother who is paraded before us in so many commercials: cooking, washing, caring, touching immaculate babies, loving, radiantly happy. Rosalind Coward describes how female dissatisfaction is recast as desire, displaced into a desire for the ideal.

Luckily our children will be asleep by the time they show what happens on television to those other women, those who are single, sexual, who live alone, those whose murder or violation provide the spice for so many drab crime series and thrillers. Vulnerable, the female victim waits undefended in her home while the male aggressor moves in unerringly to invade the house and her, to rape or kill; if she is lucky another man will rescue her. Children know fairy tales about Red Riding Hood and St George and the Dragon, but as they grow older the stories of male aggression and rescue impinge ever

more closely. Susan Griffin in 'Pornography and Silence' has written
of pornography as arising from men's pursuit of the illusion of control
over their sexuality, the compulsion ritually to murder the part of
themselves which the woman arouses and represents. She suggest that
whereas human *needs* are satiable, the compulsion to deny the
existence of a part of ourselves is insatiable; it can never completely
succeed. So the woman must be murdered again and again. In this
scenario of aggression, the driving force of rigid masculinity is
expressed in its most condensed form in the symbol of the hard (but
desexualised) penis, often referred to consciously as a 'tool' or
'weapon', and understood less consciously as a mark of status and
power. Fictional heroes, from James Bond to Rambo, are involved with
sexual conquest rather than the erotic; some are symbiotic with
machines, and Superman in his hero aspect cannot consummate his
love for Lois Lane. As Sheila Jeffreys has pointed out in her paper on
'Male Sexuality as Social Control':

> By grasping the symbolic significance of the penis we can
> understand what is going on in the bedroom and on the streets
> and on the walls of public lavatories . . . It is that which
> distinguishes one class from another and to males it is a badge
> of office . . . When the adolescent youths I teach . . . draw very
> large, erect penises on the blackboard to greet me as I come into
> the classroom, they are saying that though I am a teacher, they
> are members of a more powerful class . . . It is not sex which
> is at issue but power.

Power is a crucial element in the subject/object duality which lies at
the heart of the consumer relationship. We buy in order to own, to
possess not just a consumer goody but the lifestyle, the glamour, the
pleasure, the happiness, that seem to be sold with it. As Rosalind
Coward has put it, 'Pleasure is this society's Permanent Offer.' The
Coca Cola advert shows girls in flared skirts and boys in blue jeans
having fun, fizzy with the sparkling spray shooting out of the opening
cans: bright young healthy people, laughing, with friends, cheerful,
excited, kissing, in love. The advert is watched by the ageing, the ill,
the isolated, the slow, the bored, the plain, the out of love. 'We were
trained to create a sense of inadequacy in the consumer,' said film-
maker David Puttnam talking in an interview about his work in
advertising. Out of the feeling of inadequacy comes the compulsion
to buy to feel better, as if we could purchase joy, or dignity, or

satisfaction. As Trevor Blackwell and Jeremy Seabrook have put it in *The Politics of Hope*, we are confronted with the necessity 'of buying back, redeeming through money, that which is, ought to be, ours by right, by virtue of our humanity'. Consumerism becomes a model for personal relationships, and sexual interactions resemble financial transactions. Ros Coward has pointed out how the language of the emotions resembles economic activities: we talk in terms of 'commitment' or 'investment' in a relationship, 'returns', 'security' and 'possessiveness'. Often advertisements suggest that objects are more satisfying and reliable than people, like the colour magazine advert with the slogan 'I'd give up everything I own just to have you back again'; the photograph shows a beautiful young man standing alone in a stripped room gazing lovingly at a stereo system.

The bombardment of symbols emanates not only from television and newspapers. A children's workbook found at a local newsagent reiterates the same divisions (see opposite). The child is asked to fill in the second part of a list of pairs. At the top the pair 'boy/girl' shows the idea; underneath we find 'man/woman'; 'bat/ball'; 'men/women'; 'on/off'; 'up/down'; 'dog/cat'. It is interesting that underneath 'man' we find 'dog', 'on' and 'up', while underneath 'woman' we find 'cat', 'off' and 'down'. In a study of 'Gender Advertisements', Erving Goffman found that advertising photographs more often pictured women on the floor, the 'less exalted' part of the room, or in recumbent, vulnerable positions. He suggests that in western society 'high physical place' symbolises 'high social place', and points out that in adverts men are recurrently placed higher in the frame than women, even if some contortion is required. Men are 'up' while women are 'down', and here the symbols of the two sexes link in with a wider world view of spirituality and matter, God and sin, good and bad, and the symbols of advertisements and education dovetail with those of religion.

We speak of 'Mother Earth' and 'Mother Nature', and of women as childbearers being 'closer to nature' than men. Even those who do not belong to the Christian church are often influenced by its concepts, which include a God described as the 'Lord most High' who lives 'up' in Heaven. 'Up' is better and purer, and to attain spiritual worthiness, the Prayer Book instructs worshippers to 'Lift up your Hearts'. Parallel with the contrast between high and low in religious symbolism is that between light and dark. God is 'God of God, Light of Light', in contrast to 'us, miserable sinners, who lay in darkness and the shadow of death'. Thus white is seen as good and black as bad, a symbolism that has reverberations through a series of metaphors in common use, such

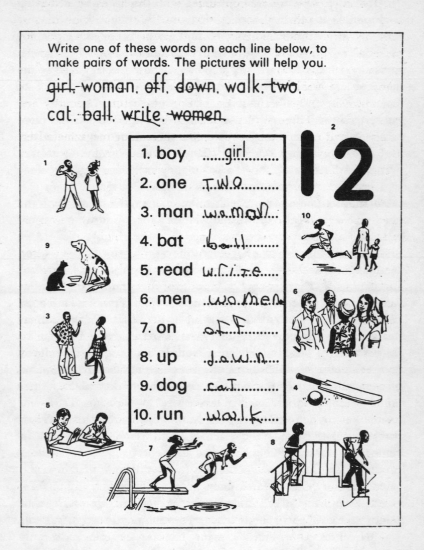

Write one of these words on each line below, to make pairs of words. The pictures will help you.

girl, woman. off. down. walk, two. cat. ball. write. women.

1. boy .....girl.......
2. one ..T.W.O........
3. man ..wa.man...
4. bat ..ball........
5. read ..write....
6. men ..women..
7. on ..off.........
8. up ..down...
9. dog ..cat.........
10. run ..walk.....

From childhood onwards we learn that the world divides into paired opposites.

Source: The Ladybird Sunstart Reading Scheme Workbook B, Ladybird Books, Loughborough, 1975, p.3.

as 'black sheep', 'blacklist', 'a black day'; black people have pointed out how such language fuels white racism. God is associated with height and light and virtue, while the mortal world is linked with sin, darkness and death. God is day, not night. He is purity, while wickedness is dirty, the 'spot of sin'. While spirit is abstract and pure, physical matter is less well regarded: 'our sinful bodies' need to be chastised and 'washed'. In Christianity the spirit is male (Father, Son and Holy Ghost), while the lower aspects of earth and sexuality are female (it is Eve who eats the apple and misleads Adam, while in her purity Mary is alone of all her sex). We begin to see how individual symbols link up along either side of a great divide: high/low, light/dark, day/night, white/black, good/bad, mind/body, male/female, spirituality/ sexuality. Sherry Ortner, in *Woman, Culture, and Society*, sees the devaluation of women as a result of an all-pervasive binary logic in which man represents culture and women nature, and where nature is seen as a lower order of existence.

In this way symbols come together to form a scheme or pattern for classifying the world, a kind of grid through which people see things, sometimes called a 'symbolic' or 'classificatory' system, providing 'the categories and concepts through which people impose meaning on their experience and make sense of their situation', as Graham Murdock has described it in 'Mass Communication and the Construction of Meaning'. Hélène Cixous in 'La Jeune Née' has lined up the pattern of oppositions she sees in patriarchal thought as follows: activity/passivity, sun/moon, culture/nature, day/night, father/ mother, head/emotions, intelligible/sensitive, logos/pathos. These can broadly be grouped around two poles: the feminine-negative-passive-material and the male-positive-active-spirit, which Monica Sjöö in *Women are the Real Left!* has described as 'the language of oppression. In our society the boy has in a sense to be trained "to be" and the girl to "not be"'. Our children, bombarded with symbols from books, advertisements and television programmes, have many more years of training ahead of them. Individuals' receptivity and susceptibility to symbols varies according to many factors, including not only temperament but class, age and material situation. But such symbols, continuously presented to us by the media and interwoven in our daily language do, at some level, insidiously affect the way we think, feel, dream and act. These splits run through the whole symbolic system which we use to experience and understand the world. They affect our deepest sense of ourselves; they influence our view of the possibilities open to us as women and as men; they colour the way we treat and care for our bodies and the way we make love; they shape our idea of what it means to be spiritual. They are the subject of this book.

Where Do Symbols Come From?

Where do such symbols come from? Why are women seen as 'lower' than men, and black people symbolically aligned with the 'powers of darkness'? Are these symbols part of a universal coinage or are they only a local currency? Do they tell us fundamental truths about how things have to be, or are they largely fabrications reflecting our society's behaviour and values? In this book I will take issue with those who would derive symbols from a universal, absolute or primordial language or from innate patterns in the human mind. I am more interested in exploring the relationship between symbols and the power structures in a society. I will suggest that it is no coincidence that relatively powerless groups in our society are associated with less powerful, or negative, symbols. I will suggest it is a mistake to confuse patriarchal symbols with universal symbols.

Even in the few examples which might emerge from an afternoon's television, there are several striking connections that could be made to social factors – whether of the actual conditions of our society (men do rape women) or of its ideology ('men are better than women'). But it is not just the symbols themselves which are informative. It is also the relationships between them, the patterns in which they are structured. Thus many of our society's symbols are structured hierarchically. Traditional symbols like the national flag and the cross command our reverence and obedience: they are set up to have power *over* us. Many of the symbols in advertisements are asking us to own or consume them: the car, the Coca Cola drink, exist as condensed symbols of certain qualities which we are led to believe we can acquire if we possess or imbibe the object. In all these cases the symbols do not expand or open out our experience; rather they act as a funnel, focusing aspirations or feelings down into a cul-de-sac (the car, the soft drink). The part stands for the whole, the penis for the man, the skin colour for the person. Instead of helping us to appreciate an experience in its totality, or to see illuminating connections between things, these symbols fetishise one small item, objectify it, and cram into it a much wider range of meaning. Our perceptions of the world are reduced, narrowed down. As Raymond Firth explains it in *Symbols, Public and Private*, the objects become magical carriers of more power

than they can rightly bear, and concentrate on themselves the feeling
and fervour which properly belong only to the wider reality which
they symbolically represent. Instead of images and myths which extend
and clarify experience, we have ones which substitute and limit it.

Objects dominate our imaginative horizons. Whatever the specific
symbol, a subject/object power relationship is usually implicit. The
mode of control and domination prevails even where the symbols
concerned are not objects. The passive woman, for example, is seen
as a 'thing' waiting to be consumed or controlled, compared to a new
country awaiting invasion, or photographed draped over a new car
as if she were for sale with it. Thus the prevailing imaginative model
of sexuality is of aggression, domination, imperialism.

It is possible to understand such modes of symbolising as reflections
of the way our civilisation is organised economically and socially. In
a social structure where control rests in the hands of (predominantly)
male authority figures, it is hardly surprising that we generate
hierarchical symbols, as Monica Sjöö points out: 'God the Father
legitimises all earthly patriarchs, Fathers, male-controlled institutions
and professions of church, state, university, law, medicine, army, that
capture and reify process' (*The Great Cosmic Mother of All*). In a society
where wealth and power are concentrated in the hands of the few
and withdrawn from the many, it is hardly surprising that our symbols
condense and rigidify meaning into symbolic culs-de-sac, rather than
making connections, opening doors and extending meaning into
wider areas. In a society where the relationships of work are those
of control and money exchange (the buying of labour), it is hardly
surprising that most relationships are symbolised as ownership or
consumption. In a society where people need to buy to keep the
wheels of the economy turning and where industry continually has
to find new markets to invade with its commodity ethic (not just our
labour but our leisure, feelings, sexuality), it is hardly surprising that
the prevailing mode of our mass dreams is of objects to be consumed,
and that even people become symbolised as objects. In a mechanistic
society, it is hardly surprising that people are seen as machines. In
a society where the resources of the natural world are approached
with a view to taming them, exploiting them and producing profits
from them, it is hardly surprising that everything natural and earthy
in ourselves is seen as inferior to the organising intelligence. In a
society which rests on the sexual division of labour, on men and
women being clearly differentiated and assigned to different roles, it
is hardly surprising that our imaginative world is also split in two. In

a society which rests on a series of powerful divisions between rich and poor, between white people and black people, where (as Adrienne Rich puts it in *Of Woman Born*) 'the powerful (mostly male) make decisions for the powerless: the well for the sick, the middle-aged for the ageing, the "sane" for the "mad", the educated for the illiterate, the influential for the marginal', it is hardly surprising that the corresponding cleft in our imaginative life and in our dreams is so deep that our sense of identity is often experienced as torn in two. As Adrienne Rich describes it:

> The dominant male culture, in separating man as knower from both woman and from nature as the objects of knowledge, evolved certain intellectual polarities which still have the power to blind our imaginations. Any deviance from a quality valued by that culture can be dismissed as negative: where 'rationality' is posited as sanity, legitimate method, 'real thinking', any alternative, intuitive, supersensory, or poetic knowledge is labeled 'irrational'.

Reason, God, light, day, technical knowledge, the male are irrevocably separated from intuition, earth, sex, darkness, night-time, the female; and never the twain shall meet. Much of our inner life is denied. Half of our power and half of our possibilities as individuals and as a society are relegated to a twilight world.

These, then, are some of the connections that can be made between our society and its symbols. But not all those who have thought and written about symbols in this century have emphasised these social connections. Many have taken a very different approach. Let's see what such theorists have to offer.

What is a Symbol?

The word 'symbol' comes from the ancient Greek word 'συμβολον' (in Modern Greek pronounced 'seemvollon'), meaning something which is *put together*, an agreement, connection, comparison or link. I *put* 'cat' and 'woman' *together*, implying that they have something in common. I might use the word 'cat' to stand for 'woman', perhaps because I am scared to mention 'woman', or because I want to add all the associations of cat to the idea of woman or simply because the word 'cat' is shorter. Language is itself nothing but a set of symbols, the five letters of the word 'woman' in themselves making up for us a symbol standing for the physical reality of a woman. As the anthropologist Mary Douglas points out in *Natural Symbols*, 'All communication depends on use of symbols, and they can be classified in numerous ways, from the most precise to the most vague, from single reference signs to multi-reference symbols.' Thus at one end of the scale is a sign like the '+' sign used in arithmetic, at the other a complex and stirring dream symbol like a drowning sea, which could variously suggest external forces sweeping you away, internal chaos, a childhood memory, passion, or death.

The philosopher Ernst Cassirer provides a useful framework in which he classifies symbols by category, dividing them according to subject matter into symbols of science, language, art and religion. Whereas mathematical symbols are lucid and precise, Cassirer points out that the other areas are increasingly vague and equivocal. Language, midway on the scale, can be precise or suggestive. At the far end of the scale are the symbols of dream, myth and neurosis, whose meaning is the hardest to pin down: we could say that they stand for the partly known and the unknown. Cassirer defines man as the 'symbolizing animal'; he believes that the symbol pervades all human activities and underlies all human expression and culture.

This book is concerned with the relationship between symbols – mostly those of dream, myth, art and religion, the vision of body and soul – and the society in which they have currency; so I will be investigating who creates symbols, when and how. In what situations do we choose to use a particular language of picture and image? What is the process whereby we make these connections between animals and colours and people and moral qualities? Why do we link certain parts of our experience with others? Why does a certain picture of the world, a certain classification system or set of connections, prevail in any one culture? How do the kind of social factors I have outlined exert pressure? As important, when may an individual create an original symbol which does not conform to those normally used in her society? How does the meaning and structure of symbol systems change?

Some of the most influential theories about symbols have been put forward during this last century, and I shall touch very briefly on the work of a selection of psychoanalysts, psychologists and anthropologists who have made a major contribution to our understanding of how symbolism works. Most of them have claimed, directly or indirectly, that symbols are 'universal'; and none of them has put forward a model for understanding how the meaning of symbols can change. It is on this limitation in their work that I shall be focusing, to provide a background against which different ideas might be spelled out. Through the last part of the chapter, I shall discuss alternative theories about the social origin of symbols and the possibility of developing new symbolic languages. I shall also review the ideas of some political thinkers, including Marx, about how symbol systems are created, perpetuated, and – most importantly – how they can change.

First, Freud.

Freud and Dream Symbols

Sigmund Freud's writings about symbols gravitate around the idea that the symbol is a disguise for repressed unconscious material. Freud states in his *Introductory Lectures on Psychoanalysis* that a dream is 'the distorted substitute for something else, something unconscious', and that the task of dream interpretation is 'to discover these unconscious thoughts'. For example, a male patient dreams about a gun. Really he is dreaming about his penis, but he avoids and censors the picture of a penis and substitutes a gun in its place. His feelings about his penis arc being displaced and transferred on to the gun. Freud proposes a distinction between the 'manifest content' of a dream and the 'latent thoughts' lying beneath the surface. Behind the symbol of the gun there is a disguised statement about the penis, a hidden dream-thought which the analyst aims to track down. The thought, and whatever problem about his penis concerns the patient, can usually be traced back to formative experiences in his childhood. This example is simple but several themes clearly emerge. Freud's method suggests that the symbol is misleading and is the result of displacement, and is therefore in some way not to be trusted. It looks for the dream symbols' connection with childhood and with problems stemming from that time. As a dream theory, it was developed in the context of understanding neurosis and attempting its cure.

Freud's theory of dream symbols was revolutionary in his time, and provided insights which have influenced most thinkers since. Within the psychoanalytic context it is still the basis of dream interpretation methods. However, within a wider life context there are obviously many areas of symbol use which it does not cover, for we cannot expect this partial and specific theory to stretch into a general theory of symbolism.

Freud did also state that some simple symbols are the result of the mind blending images in an eonomical way without the involvement of any process of censorship (for example, gun = penis as a 'condensation' or shorthand method of communicating several ideas about the penis). However, he does not discuss situations where symbols might be understood as illuminating or enriching, be they in dreams, speech or poetry. The emphasis of Freudian psychoanalysis is rather on the function of symbols to distort and repress, assisting in what R. H. Hook has described in *Fantasy and Symbol* as 'the binding and discharge of psychic energy'. The theory is that this energy might otherwise cause great anxiety or might break out into socially undesirable behaviour, if, for example, the man dreamed about his penis directly.

Freud also separated symbolic thought (like the man dreaming of the gun) very sharply from rational thought. Symbolic thought was seen as a world apart, and was believed to work in a way diametrically opposed to logical thought. From where did this world apart derive its symbols? Freud noticed that certain symbols occurred repeatedly in his patients' dreams, standing for certain things: a weapon representing the penis was repeated time and again, for example. (His lists reflect a predominance of sexual symbols, with not only guns, but knives and snakes emerging as phallic symbols also.) Similarly a house often symbolised the body, water symbolised birth, vermin children, cupboards or rooms the uterus and so on. He might have presented these symbolic links simply as data culled from the individual imagination of his patients. He might have related the choice of symbol to his patients' social context. But the social dimension of their lives remained of secondary interest to Freud. He came to the conclusion that such symbols derived, like folklore, myths and fairy tales, from 'an ancient but obsolete mode of expression', a kind of primordial language of which we all have unconscious memories. What were the specific social origins of this primordial language? Where? When? Freud does not specify, but states that these basic symbolic comparisons are 'ready to hand, *perfect for all time*' (my italics). In other words, the dream experiences of his patients are seen as an expression of symbolic structures which have a mysterious independent existence, having sprung out of nowhere and being fixed for all time. Thus, as Kevin McDonnell and Kevin Robins point out in *One-Dimensional Marxism*, his empirical data become elevated, abstracted and fixed as structures of the unconscious, as if the penis has always been symbolised as a weapon, all over the world since the beginning of time. This is inferring too much from too little: to substantiate such a notion we would need further evidence of a variety of kinds. But Freud, whose dream theory was such an eye-opener when he put it forward, did not get as far as addressing this particular problem: he never tackled the empirical work of tracking down and establishing the existence of his primordial universal language.

The result of such an approach can be seen in Freud's treatment of the Oedipus myth. This myth, which originates in ancient Greece, tells how Oedipus killed his father and married his mother. Freud coined the term 'Oedipus complex' to describe certain patterns which he discovered in the emotional development of small male children, such as their erotic desire for their mother and rivalry with the father for her love. The antiquity of the Oedipus story served to validate the theory that such patterns are innate in human beings and are a universal phenomenon. In *Sowing the Body*, Page duBois has questioned Freud's procedure of drawing on a classical text or authority to justify previously made theoretical or clinical findings. She comments that:

> The desire to assimilate ancient and future cultures into our own, to assume a universal ahistorical version of socialization . . . seems to me naive and ideologically suspect. The conservatism of the psychoanalytic tradition, with some exceptions, leads to a view of the world as immutable . . .

As the 'cradle' of western civilisation, ancient Greece has been pillaged not only of precious art works like the Elgin Marbles, but of stories and symbols which are dragged into the present to confirm patriarchal values, at whatever violence to the actual context of their origin.

The Oedipus story was created at a particular point in Greek history. It may be true for a society where a male child knows his father; where the two parents are the main focus in his upbringing; where sexual love is exclusive; where love is predominantly heterosexual; where eroticism in children is suppressed. In another context, the story would be meaningless. In the journal *Psyche* in 1924, the anthropologist Malinowski pointed out to Freud that on the Trobriand Islands, where uncles acted as fathers, completely different tensions surfaced between family members. The Oedipus story is a product of time and place, and needs to be seen in relation to the material background of its creation. As Roland Barthes puts it in 'Myth Today', 'Bourgeois ideology continually transforms the products of history into essential types . . . myth has the task of giving a historical intention a natural justification.' Ancient Greek society has its own specific history and cannot be colonised as a repository of 'primordial' or unconscious elements of twentieth-century western civilisation. My own study of the earlier, prehistoric period of Greece unearthed some symbols of a completely different kind, which I describe in Chapter 7. The case for a 'primordial language' of symbol remains unproven.

Freud's sharp distinction between rational and symbolic thought has also been effectively challenged. The French psychologist Jean Piaget sees symbols in a much more positive way, as part of a continuum of the thought process.

Piaget believes that we use symbols to assimilate our experience so that we can make sense of it and learn from it. He also suggests that there is a continuity between dream symbols and the more conscious symbols which we use in daily life. Symbols are not seen as a world apart but as tools the mind uses when in a particular state. In this state the ego drops its barriers and resistance to the external world, and becomes especially open to seeing connections between things inside and things outside. This state, which Piaget calls 'egocentricism' is found in playing children and in both children and adults when they are dreaming or daydreaming.

Piaget thought the ability to symbolise was a very valuable function of the human mind. While Freud draws a sharp contrast between conscious, rational, intellectual thought and unconscious, emotionally fuelled symbolism, Piaget points out that intellectual as well as emotional activity can be expressed in dreams. He cites cases where symbolic thinking helped to solve scientific problems: the geologist Agassiz, for example, who dreamt about fossilised fish, and Kékulé, who was helped by a dream to realise the molecular structure of benzine. In both these cases rational researches were advanced by insights emerging from the unconscious during dreams. Piaget sees symbolising as a process of assimilating past experiences to present ones, which fuels both our emotional and our intellectual development: 'Even when intelligence is at its most lucid the inner mechanism of assimilation is outside awareness.' Piaget thus unites Freud's split between conscious and unconscious, rational and irrational, mind processes. Both intellectual and emotional thought have their unconscious symbolic aspects as well as their conscious ones, and while symbolic thought may belong to a more primitive level of thought, it too 'contains an element of logic, a pre-logic . . . comparable to intuitive pre-logic'. So far from simply leading us back into the childhood past, symbolic thought can help us to relate past experiences to the present and can enhance serious thought in our immediate adult life.

Jung and the Eternal Archetypes

If we turn to the ideas of Carl Jung we find someone who, like Freud, sees symbols as a language apart, separate from waking life and the daily world of reason and activity. They are seen as part of our psychic life, which is a different world. Jung, who trained as a psychoanalyst with Freud but later developed his own theories, believed that symbols are the natural language of the unconscious, and express inner realities which can only inadequately be expressed consciously or in words. For this reason he did not try to place a literal interpretation on his patients' dreams, as Freud did, but rather saw them as messages in a more subtle language which could only be partly decoded. He understood symbols as having many possible meanings. If one of his patients dreamed about a gun, he would not assume that it could be mechanistically translated as signifying the penis, but would look at the texture of the symbol and the qualities it carried. As he explains in *Man and his Symbols*:

> A man may dream of inserting a key in a lock, of wielding a heavy stick, or of breaking down a door with a battering ram. Each of these can be regarded as a sexual allegory. But the fact that his unconscious for its own purposes has chosen one of these specific images . . . is also of major significance. The real task is to understand why the key has been preferred to the stick or the stick to the ram. And sometimes this might even lead one to discover that it is not the sexual act at all that is represented, but some quite different psychological point.

The unconscious mind for Jung contained not only painful memories and repressed forbidden desires from childhood, as Freud believed, but also treasures of joy and understanding, wisdom and healing energy. While Freud's patients dream anxiously about their penises or wish they had killed their little sisters, Jung's patients might also dream joyfully about reaching the top of a mountain or bathing in golden light.

To illuminate the difference between a Freudian and a Jungian approach, David L. Miller, in *Myths, Dreams, and Religion*, takes a hypothetical example. A man dreams he is a little boy, unable to swim, being carried across a river by a frightening man; the little boy panics, jumps into the water, and although afraid of drowning manages to swim to the other side. Miller points out that to a Freudian this dream would be taken as a symptom of sickness, reflecting an original family plot-action, specifically the dreamer's past anxiety-producing dependency on someone he thinks he should love but really feels ambivalent about. To a Jungian, on the other hand, the dream would be taken as an image of health, pointing optimistically towards a future vocational drama, a future plot-action that will resolve present dilemmas. The message is that if the dreamer will swim for himself through the waters of everyday life and of his deepest inclinations, then however frightening the waters at first appear, all will be well. Freud's emphasis on disguise, difficulty and ambivalence and Jung's on unconscious wisdom, hope and healing, each stress important, and complementary, aspects of human life. Jung's appreciation of the complexity, polyvalence and healing power of dream symbols extended the work of Freud and has added enormously to our understanding.

However, Jung too traced his patients' dream symbols back to a universal source. He suggested that when focused thinking ceases, a modern individual regresses to an archaic way of thinking, peculiar to children and primitive people, and in this way can be regenerated by reconnecting with 'primordial images' which have an instinctual base. In his patients' dreams, Jung saw certain figures or elements recurring which he called 'archetypes'. Among these he identified a number of dominant types to which he gave names such as the 'persona' or mask, the 'shadow', the 'anima' and 'animus', the 'earth mother', the 'wise old man' and the 'self'. He believed that the unconscious mind of any individual floats in a sea which is the 'collective unconscious' of humankind, so that an individual's dream symbols derive not only from her own experience but from the whole history of the human race. Thus if a patient dreamed that an old woman helped her, this could be seen not only as a childhood memory and symbol of her own mother, but as an expression of the 'archetype' of the 'earth mother' which has been universally present in the minds of humans at all times, as part of our instinctual heritage. Beyond the real mother lies the 'Eternal Feminine'. He researched the myths and rituals of ancient, distant and primitive societies for similarities with the content of his patients' dreams.

For Jung the 'archetype' is a 'universal and inherited' mode of psychic functioning, like a pattern of behaviour with a biological basis. These 'pre-existent, innate patterns' can create in widely differing people identical ideas which cannot be derived from their individual experience. Moreover, the archetypes are autonomous, and with a more or less spontaneous manifestation can, as Jung describes in *Symbols of Transformation*, 'mould the destinies of individuals by unconsciously influencing their thinking, feeling, and behaviour'. The archetype can in fact 'seize hold of the ego and even compel it to act as it – the archetype – wills'. They can also shape society at large. Jung claims, in *Man and his Symbols*, that 'the archetypes have their own initiative and their own specific energy' and can 'create myths, religions and philosophies that influence and characterize whole nations and epochs of history'. This represents a rather big step from Jung's empirical observation of similarities in his patients' dreams.

I would prefer to look at those similarities in a different way. We could very fruitfully understand these recurring forms or archetypes as psychological constructions which the patients had built out of their own experience of life. We could see them as patterns created in people's minds and behaviour from their participation in the workings of the real world. Thus I might see the 'persona' simply as the social front which we are encouraged to present to the world; the 'shadow' as our forbidden or unexpressed side; the 'anima' and 'animus' as our 'male' and 'female' qualities or aspects; the 'earth mother' as our intuitive and nourishing energies; the 'wise old man' as our knowledge and unconscious wisdom; the 'self' as our most central sense of identity. We could conclude that these basic elements, aspects or character formations are present in the human make-up characteristic of many people in twentieth-century western society. We could suggest that Jung's patients clothed these elements in these particular recurring symbols because of the social formulations and values of the culture they lived in. Thus 'black is bad', so the negative is a shadow; 'men are clever', so wisdom is an old man; 'women look after people', so nourishment takes the shape of a female symbol; the public/ private split in social life contributes to the persona/shadow division; and experience of two parents with highly differentiated sexually stereotyped roles leads to the emphasis on the contrasting 'animus' and 'anima'. We could approach dreams in an enquiring spirit and draw out a very interesting and rich empirical description of the kind of dream symbols used by patients and end up with a map which would be very useful within the context of their culture. Sheila Rowbotham has stressed the role of theory as a map to help us explore, rather than something 'fixed, hanging above us in a kind of ahistorical space'. She suggests that 'each effort of abstraction must be constantly re-examined, criticised, dipped back into experience, merge and be born again' (*Beyond the Fragments*). By seeing his archetypes as more than a map, and setting them beyond such scrutiny, Jung, despite his best intentions, has left us with something closer to a religion.

This is sad, because Jung was also committed to exploring religious ideas empirically, and compared Christianity with other religions in an illuminating fashion, suggesting that the symbols of each fulfil a primarily psychological need. He points out the pitfalls of 'blind faith'. Ultimately, however, he does ask for a belief in the archetypes, and when he says that 'in God we honour the energy of the archetype' he seems to have substituted the one for the other.

The problem seems to arise when he switches from being descriptive to being prescriptive. We would be foolish to assume that a road map of Geneva would be useful in Manila or Dar es Salaam, or that symbols used in one context will be applicable everywhere. The evidence Jung provides for the universal relevance of the archetypes and their prevalence in all cultures throughout history is questionable. Approaching ancient and primitive myths 'en masse' with western humanistic values and the psychotherapeutic preoccupations of his professions, he sometimes ends up straining the material to fit his categories and runs into difficulties, for example in explaining how the tree can be both a universal mother symbol and a phallic symbol, how the 'Terrible Mother' can appear in the form of a male magician, or how the Logos or 'spermatic Word' becomes a cow. In several passages of *Symbols of Transformation* he admits 'contradictions' or resolves inconsistencies with the catch-all that 'all the figures are interchangeable', a reductionism which leaves very little of his theory to prove or disprove. Such inconsistencies undermine the validity of his claim that the archetypes are based in a universal human biology. And without biology we are left with no other possible basis or source for the archetypes, because Jung consistently neglects physical and material factors. His thinking is limited for us by his tendency to see symbols and the unconscious as separate from daily life. In his survey of other cultures' myths, he lacks the theoretical and practical tools to approach such societies on their own terms and make the full investigation of the culture as a whole which would be necessary to fathom the meaning of its symbols. He never asked how such symbols and myths may have related to the specific social conditions and material lives of the peoples who created them at various places and times. In his wish to syncretise myths to a common pattern, he overlooks local differences and peculiarities; in his search for the general and universal, he omits the particular. Because he does not look for the possible sources of his archetypes on the ground, they seem to appear out of thin air. In this way Jung has turned things upside down. As Barthes comments of myth generally: 'A conjuring trick has taken place; . . . it has removed from things their human meaning so as to make them signify a human insignificance'.

Jung argues that psychological truths and metaphysical truths are realities because they '*work*'. I know many people who have found the archetypes useful and relevant symbols to work with as tools. But there is a difference between symbols with a local, as distinct from a universal, validity. There is also a difference between symbols which people use, and symbols which use people. It is a big step to believe that the imaginary (the 'archetype') has power and influence over all human life, the unreal over the real. It involves downrating the physical world for an unevidenced and therefore in some way mystical conception. As with traditional religion, the possibility of our creating our own worlds of event and imagination is thereby denied: we are dwarfed by powers greater than ourselves. Inevitably, the material realities of our day-to-day lives are in some way downgraded as pale reflections of higher truths, while our bodies, with all their power, beauty and capacity for feeling, are neglected for the shadows of another world. The view of the world presented is mystifying and, with unchangeable archetypes, ultimately deeply reactionary.

Jung made an enormous contribution to symbol theory. If I have been overly critical of him here, it is because I found his ideas very seductive. It is also because I am concerned about the effects of an uncritical acceptance of his ideas. Feminists who have adopted his theories have taken on, along with his insights, many of his limitations. Some of these are epitomised in the writings of Esther Harding, who looks into religious and mythic traditions to celebrate *Woman's Mysteries: Ancient and Modern*. There is an emphasis on rehabilitating 'the feminine principle' with all its associations of the moon, intuition, 'natural' mothering, mystery, the inner life, love, instinct, feelings and relationships. This 'feminine principle' has fallen upon what Esther Harding describes as 'evil days of neglect and decay', not only at the hands of modern male scientific society, but also as a result of the too-masculine orientation of 'emancipated' women.

Now an appreciation of those aspects of human life, downgraded by patriarchy, is long overdue. But I am puzzled by the eagerness of some women to embrace those qualities which a male world view has relegated as 'feminine'. It seems rather like settling for the half of human experience which men have assigned to us. Many of those qualities are based on biological assumptions which have long been suspect to feminists. Many Jungians stress that Jung believed every person to contain both a male and a female principle; but they give little space to question which qualities are ascribed to each of those principles. Because, for example, patriarchal misuse of logic has made it a dirty word for us, are women to believe it alien to our essence? Because patriarchal men do not know how to be tender, does that mean women accept it as less natural for men to care? It could be seen as a lack of imagination to accept any external and static definition of what is essentially 'feminine'. There is a danger here of deepening the sex role polarisation which splits our society. To the sceptical, Jung's archetypes could be seen as lending a mystical and questionable endorsement to our social prejudices about the 'natural' differences between the sexes. As Monica Sjöö comments of the search for female and male life-principles, 'There might be differences but it will take us long ages of undoing the indoctrination of women by men before we will be able to define ourselves freely and know who we are' (in *Women Are the Real Left!*).

It is rewarding to recover and appreciate women's traditions from ancient and primitive societies, and many feminists stress that they view the archetypes as *enabling* rather than as prescriptive or binding images. But reading authors like Esther Harding, the fear remains that a belief in male/female stereotypes as 'laws or principles . . . inherent in the nature of things' which 'function unerringly and inevitably' will blinker our vision of other possibilities.

Anthropology and the Great Divide

In the last hundred years, anthropology has produced a wealth of evidence about the symbols of other cultures very different from our own. Potentially this could allow us to see that symbols are not a universal order, that our symbolic map of the world is only one of many maps. We could see our culturally shaped view in perspective and understand that it is not absolute. But anthropologists have often been unwilling or unable to do this: they have tended to assume that western culture is superior to those under investigation, which are seen as more 'primitive', and which would come to see the world our way if only they were more 'intelligent' or 'developed'. This kind of cultural snobbery applies standards to our own culture which are different from those applied to other cultures: as Leach points out in *Genesis as Myth*, the idea of virgin birth among the Pacific Trobrianders can be attributed by anthropology to the islanders' ignorance, while the Christian doctrine of the virgin birth of Jesus is seen as a wholly acceptable and tenable religious belief. This is but one example of the way the academic establishment has been able to maintain the myth of its own 'objectivity', which disguises the fact that the act of perception, investigation and description is an active one. There has been a tendency among anthropologists to look for what they know, for what is similar to their own world view; they have often failed to see, to recognise or to value what is different or challenging. This may mean that only certain kinds of information are gleaned: for example by field-workers speaking mainly to one section of the population, often to men rather than to women. As the anthropologist Edwin Ardener points out, 'Those trained in ethnography evidently have a bias towards the kind of model that men are ready to provide . . . rather than towards any that women might provide. If the men appear "articulate" compared with the women, it is a case of like speaking to like.' How are we to value research based on evidence from only one half of the population? Another, less obvious, process is when anthropologists 'read into' the data they have collected structures which reflect their own world view; they may then conclude that these symbolic structures carry a 'universal' truth. Perhaps one example of this is the way Lévi-Strauss and the structural anthropologists look everywhere for two-way splits or binary oppositions.

In western society, as I pointed out earlier in this chapter, we tend to divide the world into opposing pairs like heaven and earth, male and female, right and left, light and dark. This 'great divide' is one of the most deeply ingrained of our symbolic models and has proved one of the hardest to shake off. Writers who accept that much symbolism is socially determined will still claim that there is something 'natural' about a dualistic view of the world. Much academic work has been done, using allegedly objective techniques to support what one suspects are unconscious emotional beliefs, to prove that this tendency of ours to split the world in two carries a universal validity. Thus the French anthropologist Lévi-Strauss has found in the myths of primitive cultures many series of paired contrasts between culture and nature, cooked and raw food, life and death, summer and winter, north and south, fire and water, right and

left, sky and land, family and non-family, and so on. This approach
proved attractive to many anthropologists and led Leach, for example,
to state in *Genesis as Myth* that:

> Binary oppositions are intrinsic to the process of human thought
> . . . An object is alive or not alive and one could not formulate
> the concept 'alive' except as the converse of its partner 'dead'. So
> also human beings are male or not male, and persons of the
> opposite sex are either available as sexual partners or not available.
> Universally these are the most fundamentally important
> oppositions in all human experience.

The gross masculinist assumptions betrayed in the very wording of
this statement would seem to disqualify any claims it might make to
objectivity.

Few would question the struturalists' contribution in pointing out
that beneath the surface phenomena of a society, whether of its myths,
language or marriage customs, there are underlying structures. What
is questionable is whether the relations between these structures can
all ultimately be reduced to binary oppositions. As Michael Lane
points out in his reader on structuralism, this is one of the untested
assumptions for which the structuralists have been criticised. Other
untested assumptions include the notion that humans have a
genetically based and innate mechanism to structure their experience
in a certain way, and that all patterns of human social behaviour are
codes, like languages. Structuralists have also been accused of turning
a method into a theory. In other words, it is one thing to cut an apple
in half and to suggest that this is a useful method if you want to eat
the apple or look inside; but it is another thing to turn that method
into a full-blown theory, claiming that the apple or the cutter are
essentially binary in nature. Thus one could suggest that structuralist
models are simply an aid to understanding; that society is not as the
structuralists describe it, although their models can make it seem
more intelligible. The structuralist model also makes the world seem
tidier. Critics have suggested that the theory's architectural
equilibrium, internal coherence and elegance become their own
justification, and Leach himself admits in *Genesis as Myth* that 'To some
extent the pleasure which can be derived from structural analysis is
aesthetic.' We are offered an attractively neat system to impose on the
sprawling multicoloured experience of daily life. In their search for
a psychic unity of mankind, a timeless and universal logic linking all

humans ancient and modern, civilised and primitive, the structuralists ignore history, the passage of time, and laws of cause and effect. They also leave us eternally trapped in dualism.

It is important to remember that though our western symbolic view, and maybe some others, see the world as divided in two between life and death, male and female and so on, it is another matter altogether to suggest that these splits are fundamental to all human experience. An open-minded perusal of the evidence shows that these splits are by no means universal. To us in our society life/death may seem a clear polarisation, but for a society which believes in reincarnation, life and death may be seen in terms of cycles or of a revolving wheel. In cultures where people believe they communicate with spirits or leave their inert bodies for astral travel during dreams or trance, the line between life and death is also by no means so clear-cut or oppositional. World views can come in triangular, fourfold, or a multitude of shapes and patterns. For example, Rodney Needham in *Symbolic Classification* gives an example of the traditional symbolic world view of Java, which divides society and nature into five classes shaped round the four points of the universe and the centre. To each of these classes belongs a colour, a metal, a day of the (five-day) week, a character, profession, certain natural phenomena, qualities, goods and architectural items. Thus east is linked with white, the metal silver, reservedness, farmer, food, garden, verandah, wind, water, cool, propitiousness; north is linked with black, iron, stiffness, butcher, meat, broken, stable, and fire, and so on.

In a culture where rain comes from the west, the west may be seen as 'wet'. If rain comes from the east, people may see the east as 'wet'. One is no more 'naturally' linked with water than another. Similarly all elements of colour, minerality, sex, food, will have different meanings for people in different material situations. They reflect the many different ways in which the natural world offers its face to people at various places and times. The evidence for binary classification is not overwhelming; perhaps structuralists find it because of the nature of their method. To return to my earlier metaphor: if you slice an apple down the middle, you will see it in two halves.

Where similarities between the actual symbols of different peoples can be demonstrated, this can to some extent be understood as the result of humans trying to make sense of roughly similar phenomena in the natural world around us. Again, some similarities in these processes can be traced to the physical basis of human life. Part of our physical make-up comprises a dual system with two roughly symmetrical sides, two arms, two legs, two eyes, two ears and so on. Our brains are apparently structured in two parts as well. The champions of binary thought might suggest that because we have two of each limb, it is natural for us to think in twos. However, one could also suggest that both our emphasis on the duality of our bodies and our tendency to think in twos are fostered by our social environment. There are several possible views of the body other than the twofold. There are different patterns and structures in the body which could equally influence the way in which we perceive the world. One such is the model of the digestive system (taking in, processing and putting out), another the blood (circulation), or the principle of balance, and so on. In some cultures the basic shape of the body is seen as egg-shaped, with an energy field surrounding it; in others our outstretched limbs are seen as marking out the diagonals of a wheel or circle. Our two spread legs and head can mark out a triangular structure, or we can emphasise the process whereby we grow from the ground upwards (like plants). The fact that the duality model predominates in our culture is the result of the twofold aspect of our bodies being preferred over other possible models.

Similarly, physical difference exists between male and female, but our society has chosen to polarise that difference into a far more extreme form than it might otherwise have taken; thus the many millions of people with a homosexual, lesbian or bisexual orientation are seen as 'abnormalities' because they do not fit neatly into these rigid categories. Even the physical differences on which the male-female distinction is based are not as definitive as we tend to assume, and our society has further attached to definitions of 'male' and 'female' a whole series of additional differentiations around work, parenting, sexuality and so on, which are not necessarily appropriate at all. There is an arbitrariness at work here: certain physical facts exist but the question is what we make of them and how we elaborate on them. *The Cultural Construction of Sexuality,* edited by Pat Caplan, recently sampled the incredible variety of such elaborations in different cultures. As the anthropologist Shirley Ardener puts it in *Perceiving Women:* 'We do not really understand how supposedly measurable biological differences are related to those we cannot yet easily analyse, such as emotional and intellectual processes'. A passage in *The Nature of the Psyche,* one of Jane Roberts' 'Seth' books, humorously points out that the hand and foot have different functions, and that if we placed the same emphasis on the differences in their behaviour as we place upon the differences between male and female, we could build an entire culture based on their diverse functions, capabilities and characteristics. (These interesting books, which deal a lot with symbols and the unconscious, were dictated by Jane Roberts in a state of trance, 'Seth' being the name of a spirit guide; see Chapters 3-6.)

The fact that our culture tends to see things in twos does not imply that this is the only way human beings can think; and it certainly does not mean that it fits the phenomena of the natural world we are trying to apprehend. Perhaps what the structuralists describe as a universal and innate mode of thought is simply the system of pigeon-holing most current at this time in western society.

In addressing the question 'Where do symbols come from?', some anthropologists have been more inclined than the structuralists to recognise the role a society plays in shaping the symbols used by its members. One of the founders of anthropology, Emile Durkheim, argued that all symbolic divisions and classifications are based on divisions within society. His argument is that the first categories which humans made were social categories, and the first groupings or classes of things were classes of people. These categories were then transferred to nature, and nature was seen through the same model, as falling into the same groupings as the society they knew. The social order is in turn strengthened and validated by its reflection in the natural world. Social divisions and classes are endorsed by appearing to be part of a vast metaphysical scheme of things. Symbols are thus a collective creation, a collective representation which reflects and endorses the unity of the group.

Durkheim added an important piece to the jigsaw; while the other theories I have discussed trace symbols and symbolising to innate processes in the brain, he provides a social dimension. Looking at symbols in a social framework, he comes up with different answers to those of Freud, for example, who studied symbols on an individual and psychological level. But while Freud omits the social context, Durkheim's emphasis on the social role of symbols also leaves gaps. His view of a society and its symbols tends to be rather static. This is partly because he did not ask *where* the different social groupings, and the dominant social values, originated in the first place. What is lacking here is Marx's dynamic view of the way that economic factors contribute to the shaping of social classes. As external conditions change, or advances are made in technology, different social groupings may slowly form to meet new situations, and these may in turn be reflected by new symbols, new world views, new collective values. Durkheim presented a strong case for seeing the match between a society and its symbols, but by seeing symbols largely as a means of endorsing certain social groupings, he ignored other important factors, including material ones. Because of this, social groups are seen as rather static, eternally married to their matching symbols, and there is no strong model for non-conformity or change in either a society or its symbols.

A 'Universal' Language?

It becomes clear that some of the best-known theories about symbolism share certain limitations. They tend to view symbols as static, as a separate, pre-ordained and 'universal' language. Historical research and empirical evidence tend to be sacrificed to a theory's coherence and elegance. Though each of these theorists illuminates one aspect of the symbolising process – the psychic structuring, the social shaping – each tends to see their analysis as a comprehensive explanation of the whole process. We need to understand symbols at all these different levels, and build links between these different areas, rather than collapsing the social into the psychological or vice versa. To do justice to what is valuable in each theory, we need a model allowing these different aspects or factors to interact dynamically in the creation of symbols.

So I will now turn to those theories which recognise and allow for the possibility of change, which suggest that making symbols weaves in and out of other human processes such as thinking, talking, imagining, and assimilating experience. Like those other processes it is closely linked with the everyday life of human beings, their specific material conditions, psychological states and social organisations. Somewhere in that melting pot, symbols are created. Trying to understand this process is a much more messy and contradictory affair, and much less inviting. All kinds of questions are raised and there are no elegant answers: it is like dipping a jam-jar into a pond and coming up with a muddy tangle of insects, water plants, teeming fish and wriggling worms. But I believe that it is only by looking into that jam-jar that we will understand why certain plants die or live, and how tadpoles turn into frogs. The living does not stand still.

Being Taught to 'See Straight'

To start with what is, for each of us as individuals, the beginning of that messy process, we need to ask how members of a society learn to use its symbols. How are our imaginations first ensnared?

The early stages of learning to talk and use symbols are a process of coming to terms with an apparently random, confused and unruly universe, giving it sense and meaning by defining, classifying, delimiting and packaging the world. It has been suggested that a child initially approaches the world with few preconceptions and then, in each society, gradually learns which terms are generally agreed upon for describing her experience. Thus Leach, in an article on 'Anthropological Aspects of Language', postulates:

> the physical and social environment of a young child is perceived as a continuum. It does not contain any intrinsically separate 'things'. The child, in due course, is taught to impose upon this environment a kind of discriminating grid which serves to distinguish the world as being composed of a large number of separate things, each labeled with a name. This world is a representation of our language categories, not vice versa.

Thus the child acquires a set of filters for monitoring her experience, which vary from one society to another. One language discriminates between 'tree' and 'bush' while another does not; in one language hair is seen as one unit 'hair' while in others it is seen as many *(les cheveux)*. The classification of space, time and colour varies in different societies, and with these different processes of naming come a host of connections, symbols, comparisons and value judgments. A child may be encouraged not to use her left hand and at the same time may learn that 'right' means correct and that a 'right-hand man' is a good chap. She may read stories at nursery about 'black sheep' who are difficult or rejected. It is hard for us to recognise the arbitrariness of the classifying system whereby we continuously make order out of the world around us.

The symbolic indoctrination, begun in childhood, continues throughout adult life. Rarely does it appear as a conspiracy, or conscious deliberate effort, by forces within the society to teach individuals to conform. The models of language and symbol are passed on by parents, teachers and journalists, who are often unconsciously communicating their own deeply held classifications and values. Individual makers of TV programmes or commercials, whose aim is to attract viewers or to sell products, often simply provide the viewer with what Goffman describes as '. . . an opportunity to face directly a representation . . . a mock up of what he [sic] is supposed to hold dear, a presentation of the supposed ordering of his existence'. It may only be when a threat is posed to this process of teaching and reinforcing a symbolic system with appropriate values that its workings and organisation become clear. During my own years of experience in broadcasting, it became evident that most censorship happened invisibly through self-censorship, as broadcasters learned what was acceptable. It was only very rarely, when a broadcaster accidentally or deliberately broke the unwritten rules or consensus, that the chain of command would become visible, right up through the echelons of the organisation and sometimes even to the point of government intervention, as it mobilised to prevent the transmission of a programme deemed to be too politically or socially controversial. To take another example, when a homosexual teacher is sacked as a 'threat to children's morals', the bones of power are suddenly laid bare: the school and local government are dramatically revealed as those with the authority to hire and fire; newspapers with right-wing owners are usually the ones to scream scandal and whip up public feeling most fervently; and ultimately the law, which discriminates against sexual orientations other than the heterosexual, has the power to endorse sanctions or punishments based on dominant values. But when the process is running smoothly, it requires little overt management, and is self-perpetuating, ubiquitous and invisible.

Our classification system is communicated to us through the whole structure of our experience within society. In *Problems in Materialism and Culture*, Raymond Williams stresses that the process does not take place at the level of 'mere opinion or mere manipulation', but involves the processes of education and of wider social training within institutions like the family as well as the definition and organisation of work. Our consciousness is accordingly 'saturated', and the extent to which we have assimilated our society's models, classifications and symbols goes deeper than our daily waking life. Thus similar dreams and fantasies can be shared by millions of people in the same society. As Leites and Wolfenstein put it in *Movies: A Psychological Study:* 'where a group of people share a common culture, they are likely to have certain daydreams in common. We talk, for example, of the American dream . . . and the acquisition of gleaming cars and iceboxes . . .' It is common to think of the unconscious as a world apart with its own life, and to fail to appreciate how our particular time, place, history and social experience permeate the unconscious and affect its workings. Psychotherapists note with surprise how the patients of Freudian analysts tend to produce dreams with Freudian forms and structures, while Jungian patients have Jungian dreams. As Joseph Chilton Pearce points out in 'Don Juan and Jesus', in trance religions a strict protocol controls the context of seizures: the possessed can be relied on to contact the expected spirits of their culture, not those of another society a hundred miles away. Given, then, the extent to which we imbibe and deeply experience the symbol system of our society, it is hardly surprising that to most people it appears 'absolute', 'natural' or 'real', and no alternative view seems possible. In *Problems in Materialism and Culture*, Raymond Williams describes it as a central, effective and dominant system of meanings and values, which are not simply abstract but lived, and appear as reciprocally confirming: 'It thus constitutes a sense of reality for most people in the society, a sense of absolute because experienced reality beyond which it is very difficult for most members of the society to move, in most areas of their lives.'

But however powerful our symbols appear, they are not supernatural or fixed. They can and do change. To understand how, and to demystify what they are, we need to understand not only how they are communicated to us but also why they take the shape that they do. We need to trace the process by which they are made back, as it were, to the factory floor, to find the moulds which determined their form.

According to Marx, the factory floor is in fact the very place where we should look. The means of production of food and other necessaries in any society, as well as its trade, exchange of money and organisation of labour, were for him the 'economic base' or bedrock on which were founded all other social institutions, groupings, and ideologies (the 'superstructure'). The material subsistence of a society was seen as the most important factor in its survival and everything else to some extent followed, forming structures which fitted in, reflected and endorsed it. Thus we might argue that the extended family unit has been transformed into the nuclear family unit in response to industry's needs for a more mobile workforce; that laws and values around sexuality serve the function of preserving the stability of that family unit; that certain sexual or consumer fantasies offered by the media serve to channel away energy that might otherwise become restless, and perhaps compensate for the boredom of mechanised and often isolated labour, and so on. Earlier in this chapter I suggested other ways in which our symbols both in themselves (the Hero, the Woman Victim) and in their structure (hierarchical, consumerist) represent a mirror image of our society's organisation, to some extent endorsing it and perpetuating it. The relationship between the economy, social institutions and symbols is not, however, an obvious or straightforward one, and has been much debated by theorists.

The Marxists' suggestion is not that the 'economic base' totally determines the 'superstructure' in a predictable and static way. As Raymond Williams points out, interpreting the superstructure as *simple* reflection or ideological expression of the base leads to a mechanistic reductionism. While the economic base plays an important shaping role, the most convincing view is that of society as a totality in which all the different elements of our way of life affect one another, in what Williams describes as a 'field of mutually if also unevenly determining forces'. This is not a mechanistic process in which the human factor is omitted. As Williams makes clear, none of the elements in this interaction are static but reflect the continuing activities of human beings 'in real social and economic relationships, containing fundamental contradictions and variations and therefore always in a state of dynamic process.' This model would explain why symbol systems are themselves complex and often contain internal contradictions. A culture may overwhelmingly classify dogs as 'unclean' and yet have one lone area where they are celebrated. A symbol may reflect not what exists in a society, but precisely what is missing. Thus we see a cult of individuality flourishing in a society whose conditions consistently dehumanise and de-individualise its members. Mass consumerism, TV shows programmed to reach millions, high-rise buildings and monster housing estates, the conditions of travel in big cities, all impress on us how little any of us signifies in the whole. No wonder advertisements tell us that we will be a little special or different if we buy a particular brand of car or perfume: the symbol offers us an escape from feeling so small and insignificant. No wonder we fantasise about tropical islands, and no wonder the myth of the free/natural man like Robinson Crusoe has such appeal. A symbol can represent the 'big lie': it can be an out-and-out contradiction of the truth, like the historic tourist advertisements, showing bathers sporting on golden beaches, which urged us to 'Feel Free – Come to Spain' during Franco's dictatorship.

There may also be a time-lag, in which a once powerful and highly loaded symbol may survive in desiccated form as a pale reflection of an earlier era. The metaphors of the English language are full of symbols ('he'll fleece you', 'it came out of the blue', 'take the bull by the horns') which draw their power from a closeness to country and agricultural life which most of the population no longer experience.

Our twentieth-century fairy stories and nursery rhymes are full of kings and queens, who no longer have the material power in contemporary society they once had. Our religious festivals are full of symbols which have a curious tenacity. These examples show that some symbols, once generated in a culture, have a relatively independent life span, and may survive as residual elements in a society where the dominant culture organises around very different symbols. Many of these residual symbols (like the maypole, the Hallowe'en Jack O'Lantern) derive from the rural past and carry values which continue to co-exist with newer values, as long as they do not threaten them.

Within a society there can also exist certain 'alternative' cultures and symbol systems, which do not conform to the norm, but which are tolerated. Very often these alternative models have not been developed completely independently of the dominant culture, but have to some extent been shaped by it. Thus in western countries various eastern religious sects flourish, where members follow a guru who becomes another male authority symbol, like the Christian God. Astrology is an alternative belief and symbol system which is tolerated and is awarded a few column inches in newspapers. As popularly practised, it is not threatening: it addresses itself to 'normal' concerns like money and travel, and its internal structure of symbols and classification shows a familiar male-female, active-passive, positive-negative polarisation. It is a different matter when these alternative systems take a proselytising attitude and directly threaten certain values or institutions deemed central to society. There is a difference between alternative and oppositional. For example, various dubious activities of the Scientology cult were long overlooked in Britain, but legal action was taken against it after reports that its initiates regularly severed all ties with their families.

How Do Symbols Change?

Here we come to symbols and cultures of opposition, those which are directly opposed to the dominant culture in a society. A prominent feature of western capitalist society is that its economic structure is organised to favour one section of the population over another. There are those who make profit and those who do not. The dominant group tends to control the means of communication. Correspondingly its symbol system may serve the interests of one group in society rather than another. Blatant examples of this are the myth of the 'national interest' ('We're all in one boat together') to mask measures such as a wage freeze primarily affecting blue-collar workers, or the still dominant symbol of the white male newsreader as the objective, rational one-who-knows. However, it more often works at infinitely more subtle and indirect levels. Those who belong to racial, sexual or economic groups whose interests are to some extent at odds with those of a dominant class, may develop their own alternative symbolic structure.

Thus women may develop their own view of the world. But such a view can be very difficult to form and to articulate in society as a whole. As dancer and choreographer Jacky Lansley points out in 'Women Dancing', many women '"know what they mean" but are unable to express it in any organised so-called rational way because their meaning cannot be expressed through the pre-determined formulas of language and action that have been prescribed by the patriarchal power structures'. As a result women's experience, like that of other relatively powerless groups, may die unspoken. Shulamith Firestone writes, in her feminist classic *The Dialectic of Sex:*

> Women have no means of coming to an understanding of what their experience *is,* or even that it is different from male experience. The tool for representing, for objectifying one's experience in order to deal with it, culture, is so saturated with male bias that women almost never have a chance to see themselves culturally through their own eyes. So that finally, signals from their direct experience that conflict with the prevailing (male) culture are denied and repressed.

The miracle then is that oppressed groups and newly emerging classes ever do manage to create the new language that does not yet exist, the new culture and symbols which articulate a new experience, new perceptions and new values.

Raymond Williams stresses the role of the emerging class and the excluded in contributing to such transformation of language, symbols and culture. It is those whose voice has been drowned out by the dominant culture who will have the impetus to develop a new language and new symbols: ethnic minorities and young people as well as women. In addition, individuals from any grouping may respond to their experience in new ways, or in ways which transcend the specific social context in which they live. Some write it large with words or on canvas and are called artists or visionaries; for others it is a collective process which does not produce physically enduring artefacts. I have argued here for the importance of social factors in shaping symbols because those factors are so often ignored or underestimated. But this is not to say that they explain everything. Some individuals are able to perceive things with a vision broader than that usually permitted by their specific historical and social situation.

In his speech on 'Class and Art', delivered in 1924 to jeers from other Communist Party members, it is surprising to see Trotsky affirm that certain fundamental human experiences, and certain great writers, may find expression in symbols which cut across time and class positions. He suggests that if we approach the 'Divine Comedy' as a source of artistic perception:

> this happens not because Dante was a Florentine petty bourgeois of the 13th century but, to a considerable extent, in spite of that circumstance. Let us take, for instance, such an elementary psychological perception as fear of death . . . In different ages, in different social milieux . . . men have feared death in different ways. And nevertheless what was said on this score not only by Shakespeare, Byron, Goethe, but also the Psalmist, can move us.

The ability to transcend socially defined perceptions is most often understood as being part of the artistic process. As Jacky Lansley writes of her creative work in dance:

> My consciousness of the oppression of women in society at large and in an art/dance context has certainly influenced my aesthetic criteria and helped me to understand and situate my personal experience as a woman but in no way does this analysis totally determine my aesthetic sensibility as either an artist or as a member of the audience . . . Art reflects the social, political, and psychological environment in which it evolves, but it also *has the function* of transcending or elevating our fragmented experience of reality.

From where, then, do we derive this ability to go beyond, to see further than our agreed social reality? Raymond Williams argues that the very narrowness of the dominant culture and symbols leaves us space for manoeuvre. He suggests that:

no mode of production, and therefore no dominant society or order of society, and therefore no dominant culture, in reality exhausts the full range of human practice, human energy, human intention (this range is not the inventory of some original 'human nature' but, on the contrary, is that extraordinary range of variations, both practised and imagined, of which human beings are and have shown themselves to be capable) . . . it is a fact about the modes of domination that they select from and consequently exclude the full range of actual and possible human practice.

Just as the structure of our society's economic organisation leaves some small chinks and openings through which women, for example, have developed a movement with its own organisations and structures (women's centres and refuges, women's bookshops and publishers, support networks, demonstrations and street actions, collective living and shared childcare); so, too, in the area of symbols and culture there is a space in which we can start the work of reclaiming our imaginative life, creating a new symbol language for our thoughts, dreams and fantasies. Traditionally the work of artists, it is also a project for anyone who wishes to clear away the mists of socially agreed preconceptions and see their experience with a different eye. As Geoff Nuttall put it pithily in a television discussion: 'The human individual imagination will not pack up, and it will incur change.' The ability to articulate new symbols rises both from the different quality of an individual's or group's experience, unrecognised by society as a whole, and from a leap of imaginative powers not totally colonised by that dominant culture. We have here a model, however tentative, for changing symbols.

The Struggle for Our Own Symbols

Like all practices set up to challenge or oppose the mainstream of society, the project of creating our own culture is tolerated or overlooked as long as it does not seem to pose a direct threat to the status quo. Sometimes the dominant culture will, because of its very limitations, not recognise a threat. Where the opposition and confrontation is very overt, the dominant culture will move in to incorporate, to discredit or to stamp out.

It is worth the struggle? There are women in the women's movement, women and men in the socialist movement, who believe that symbols as such are irrelevant, that the important changes in society are those effected in the 'economic base' from which other, secondary, changes will automatically follow. But, as we have seen, it is not that simple. Our culture and symbols are not just icing on the cake but deeply saturate our lived experience in capitalist society. We have also seen that symbols may accumulate power and develop a certain momentum, and often survive a considerable time from their point of creation. The symbol of the 'strong leader' may linger into a socialist society and hinder efforts to create new structures of power. Old symbols may blinker our vision if they are not consciously questioned; they may hold us back, may lead us to reshape the new in the form of the old, or to slip back into old oppressions under new names. Symbols are deeply a part of our experience; they are part of the language and fabric of our society, and any movement for change must address every such issue.

It has been one contribution of the women's movement to remind socialists that the personal is political, that we need to reclaim our imaginations just as we need to reclaim our sexuality and relationships from the restricting stereotypes into which they have been cast. This has not been to deny the importance of changes in the distribution of wealth, the organisation of factory and other working practices, and family and social institutions, but rather to see the transformation of culture as a necessary part of that wider movement. As Sherry Ortner comments in *Women, Culture, and Society*, 'Efforts directed solely at changing the social institutions . . . cannot have far-reaching effects if cultural language and imagery continue to purvey a relatively devalued view of women.'

Within the women's movement one of the first and most essential steps has been to 'deconstruct' the current male culture. Women have needed to name and analyse the old symbols and become aware of how destructive they are to us, as well as creating new symbols and values. This deconstruction and recreation is a project which has been tackled with gusto through a variety of creative channels. Writers like Dale Spender in *Man Made Language* have analysed the male monopoly over naming and defining the world. The vocabulary with which male terms are used to denote the whole human race has been questioned, so that many people now feel uncomfortable using words like 'chairman', 'spokesman' or the generic 'he'. In *Gyn/Ecology*, Mary Daly raged at the terms that trap us, and mocked at euphemisms like 'homemaker' and 'the natural look'. The male bias of historians and the resulting invisibility of women's contribution to history has been analysed; much has been written on women's unsung achievements in literature and art, challenging the long reign of the symbol of the male 'artist' and 'genius'. The neglect of women's activities and crafts has also been exposed, as in Rozsika Parker's book about embroidery, *The Subversive Stitch*. Our cultural myopia about the serious artistic potential of needlework was also confronted by Judy Chicago's monumental art work of dinner plates with embroidered runners dedicated to significant women, 'The Dinner Party'. Spiritually inclined feminists have used rituals to confront male taboos and to honour precisely those aspects of female life which have been most shunned by patriarchy. The same project of deconstruction has been tackled through theatre, street events and dance. Jacky Lansley tells how, in a dance performance called 'Bleeding Fairies', 'we worked with archetypal images of women like the witch, the whore, the fairy, Mother Earth etc., images which reflect society's moral/religious distinctions between good and bad women'. She describes how the chaotic, aggressive quality of the performance attempted to express a destruction of the patterns and modes of behaviour that condition those archetypes. As we recognise existing oppressive symbols and defuse their power over us, the way does become clear to start creating alternatives.

Towards a New Language of Symbol

The project involves developing a use of symbols which does not disguise meaning or offer dead ends, but rather opens imaginative doors. There is not general agreement that this is possible. Some people, seeing the fetishised dominant symbols in our society as a reactionary force, funnelling energy away from our lived human experience, believe not just that symbols follow economics but that we would be better off without symbols altogether. We are urged to strip away symbols and images to face a more vibrant 'reality'. The argument runs something like this: if someone dreams about their mother as a dragon, this is because they are 'blocking', because they can't dream about her as herself. A healthy person in a healthy society will see a mother as a mother and nothing else. This is similar to Freud's view of symbols as a disguise. The founder of primal therapy, Arthur Janov, has also suggested that symbols are a device to avoid experiencing emotions, especially pain, directly. After treatment through primal therapy, the patient may move out of a 'symbolic never-

never land' and will have less symbolism in her dreams. The assumption is that a healthy person and a healthy society see the world in a completely literal, unimaginative and one-dimensional way. But this ignores the function of symbols to make connections: we may not want to abandon the faculty of making links between different areas of experience. Fantasy and symbols are escapist and distorting only if they are a replacement of reality, not if they are an extension of it. Symbols can mystify meaning; but they can also express it. Thus one could see *both* the mother *and* the dragon as an extension of her, perhaps as the expression of certain of her qualities (her rage, her majesty) which might have been frightening in childhood. One might have many other symbolic ideas of her: as a cool pine wood, as the colour blue. In the way the view of the mother is enriched and enlivened, rather than being distorted and blocked by the symbol of a dragon as a mask and cul-de-sac.

The argument that we should get away from symbolism and contact our 'real' experience and our 'real' selves presupposes that our 'real' selves do not have an aptitude for using symbols. Symbolising is one of the brain's faculties, one of its possibilities, and seeking to legislate against it is fruitless. I prefer to see symbolism as a richness, as a kind of language different from our spoken one, that is available for us to use, play with and learn from as a tool for discovering more about the world. Our symbolising faculty can be seen as an ability which needs to be actively used, for if it is denied it may turn sour and end up working against us.

It also seems fundamentally important, in evolving new ways of using symbols, to recognise that the power we attribute to a symbol is our own. If I dream about a dragon, the power of the dragon embodies *my* fear, *my* awe, attributed to that symbol and expressed through it. This leaves the road open for me to withdraw my energy from that symbol, or to change it. When I forget that I can do this, the symbol appears to have power over me and may end up tyrannising me. The difference between a symbol which expresses and one which can tyrannise is shown by the way a national flag may be used to stir up chauvinism. A flag can become the channel for emotions which have nothing to do with the flag itself. At different times we are told that 'our lifestyle' or 'our values' or 'our national character' are represented in the flag as a national identity; and that this identity is being threatened by another country or even a minority culture within our country. In such cases, the feelings that are being appealed to – pride and joy, the desire to protect family and loved ones – are all real feelings which people experience. What is not real is the link to the flag. The flag may in fact be serving the purposes of certain business interests to wage war on a distant country. It may be serving to divide artificially the loyalties of different races within the country whose material interests are the same. It may be serving to fuel the real fears people hold about their housing and job security against an imagined scapegoat. But it appears to have a power and authority of its own; it appears an objective symbol of nationhood, and when people feel a tear in the eye or a surge in the chest at the sight of that piece of cloth fluttering, it seems that this response is elicited by the flag itself. Thus we can be manipulated into giving our power away. If we recognise that our pride is our pride and our fear our fear – arising from our specific actions and experience – we become more aware of how easily these feelings can be kidnapped and pinned to a symbol like a flag.

In *Society of the Spectacle*, which served as a manifesto for the radical situationist movement in the 60s and 70s, Guy Debord describes how in our society the more the individual is conned into believing the images of his feelings that are fed to him [sic], the less he understands his own existence and his own desires: 'his own gestures are no longer his but those of another who represents them to him . . .' He becomes a 'prisoner of a flattened universe, limited by the *screen* of the spectacle behind which his own life has been deported' and concrete objects become 'automatically the masters of social life'. It is our own energy which is funnelled into the flag, taken away from us and labelled patriotism; it can then be used to encourage subservience, passivity, fear, hatred and racism, or its emotive power can be used to lead volunteers to be massacred on the battlefield. The state can take our energy, mis-name it, and use it against us. The symbol can serve to cloak, confuse and manipulate.

An alternative is not solely to approach the world in a more realistic minute-by-minute way, assessing and understanding each situation (the war . . . the loss of jobs . . .) on its own terms. There is also a different way to use symbols and symbolic objects. To make this point clearly, it may help to take an example from a society with a very different approach to symbols. *Divinity and Experience* is a fascinating practical account, by the anthropologist Godfrey Lienhardt, of the religion of the Dinka people in the Central Nile basin. Among the most important symbolic objects for the Dinka are sacred fishing-spears which are used for invoking divinity. Lienhardt comments, however, that although the older spears are venerated, their qualities and power are not thought to be intrinsic: 'The reputed strength of sacred spears derives from their association with the generations of ancestors who have invoked with them. It is the invocations which consecrate the spear, rather than the spear which guarantees the invocation.' Lienhardt points out that a sacred spear is thought to be ineffective in the hands of people who are not its proper owners: 'The power inherent in the spears is thus really a reflection of the power inherent in the descent-groups which own them, and members of those descent groups may be thought to invoke effectively, even with a stick.' Here the symbolic object, the fishing-spear, is understood as a carrier of human power but is not an independent embodiment of it. It reflects human feeling; it does not become master of it. It is a tool, not a tyrant.

In another example, from our own society, we could compare the example of the national flag with the emergence in the peace movement of the symbol of the web. At Greenham Common women's peace camp it has taken many forms, whether embroidered on the perimeter fence, or created in rope, larger than life, with human figures entwined in it. It is used without mystification (it is not seen as magical). It is open to adaptation, and it is open to question and change.

The issue of who articulates symbols and who can change them is crucial. Like elected representatives, they need to be subject to immediate recall. As long as the control of symbolic representations is centralised, and articulated by a minority for the majority, expressing the interests of one group or groups within a society, they are likely to ossify around that group's interests. It can be different when symbols grow out of a changing communal situation and experience. Women have been concerned recently to rescue and reinstate traditional female symbols: the moon, the egg and the witch have been offered as positive images for us to identify with in our struggle to affirm our own power and beauty. Some women in the movement have found the Goddess a strengthening symbol to rally round. Individuals like Bob Dylan and Che Guevara became symbols which served as rallying points for different movements. But there is a danger that these symbols too may become fixed and reified. It is not a question of substituting one set of fixed symbols for another. It is a question of thinking about a truly 'mass' culture which is mass not only in the way it is consumed (millions of people watching the same television programme) but also in the way it is created: where each person and group in the mass population are involved in a continuing creative process.

Just as it is hard for us to envisage mass participation in control of the economic sphere, so it is hard for us to believe that our imaginations could crawl out of the closet to play an active part in the creation of a mass culture. Perhaps the most we can contemplate is enlarging our corners of freedom. Much of this book is about the possibility of understanding and using symbols in a new way through practical activities and work with our own dreams and fantasies, our own bodies and feelings. It is not a quick or easy process; nor is it a project that can be undertaken voluntaristically. We cannot just 'change our symbols' as a matter of will. Any such changes need to develop in parallel with social changes. But we do have some room for manoeuvre.

Book References

Page numbers relate to passages I have referred to or quoted, listed in most cases in the order in which they have been used. Where there are numerous references to the same text, or where the context may not be obvious, I have indicated the subject matter.

Ardener, Edwin, 'Belief and the Problem of Women', in Shirley Ardener (ed.) *Perceiving Women*, p. 2.

Ardener, Shirley (ed.) *Perceiving Women*, J.M. Dent, London, Toronto and Melbourne; Halstead Press, New York, 1977, pp. xviii, xii. (See also Judith Okely, 'Gypsy Woman: Models in Conflict' in the same collection.)

Barthes, Roland, 'Myth Today', in Susan Sontag (ed.) *Barthes: Selected Writings*, Fontana/Collins, 1983, pp. 93-149; I quote pp. 145, 130-1.

Blackwell, Trevor and Jeremy Seabrook, *The Politics of Hope: Britain at the End of the Twentieth Century*, Faber and Faber, London and Boston, 1988, p. 32.

Caplan, Pat, (ed.) *The Cultural Construction of Sexuality*, Tavistock, London and New York, 1987.

Cassirer, Ernst: see Donald Phillip Verene (ed.) *Symbol, Myth and Culture: Essays and Lectures of Ernst Cassirer 1935-1945*, Yale University Press, New Haven and London, 1979.

Chicago, Judy, *The Dinner Party: a Symbol of our Heritage*, Anchor Press/Doubleday, New York, 1979.

—— *Through the Flower: My Struggle as a Woman Artist*, The Women's Press, London, 1982 (first publ. Anchor Press/Doubleday, New York, 1975).

Cixous, Hélène, see, most accessibly, Toril Moi, *Sexual/Textual Politics*, pp. 102-126, where she quotes 'La Jeune Née'. See also Elaine Marks and Isabelle de Courtivron (eds) *New French Feminisms*, Harvester Press, Brighton, 1981, pp. 90-8 and 245-64 for some writings in translation. (First published by the University of Massachusetts Press, 1980).

Coward, Rosalind, *Female Desire*, Paladin/Granada, London, 1984, pp. 90-1, 13.

Daly, Mary, *Gyn/Ecology: The Metaethics of Radical Feminism*, The Women's Press, London, 1979, especially pp. 331, 315ff. (First publ. Beacon Press, Boston, MA, 1978).

Debord, Guy, *Society of the Spectacle*, 'a Black and Red translation unauthorized,' *Radical America* 4, (5), and Black and Red, Box 9546, Detroit, MI, 48202, USA, 1970, paragraphs 30, 218, 216.

Douglas, Mary, *Natural Symbols*, Penguin, Harmondsworth, Middx., 1973, p. 29 (first publ. Barrie and Rockliff, 1970).

duBois, Page, *Sowing the Body: Psychoanalysis and Ancient Representations of Women*, University of Chicago Press, 1988, pp. 16-17.

Durkheim, Emile and Marcell Mauss, *Primitive Classification*, trans. and ed. R. Needham, University of Chicago Press, 1963 (also publ. Cohen and West, London).

Firestone, Shulamith, *The Dialectic of Sex: the Case for Feminist Revolution*, Paladin, London, 1972, p. 142 (also publ. The Women's Press, London, 1979).

Freud, Sigmund, *Introductory Lectures on Psychoanalysis*, trans. J. Riviere, Allen and Unwin, London, 1922, pp. 95, 100 (both on function of dream symbols), 128-39 (recurrent symbolism), 140 (ancient mode of expression, 139 (comparisons perfect for all time). (Also publ. Pelican Freud Library Vol. 1, trans. J. Strachey, Penguin, Harmondsworth, Middx, 1974).

Goffman, Erving, 'Gender Advertisements', *Studies in the Anthropology of Visual Communication*, 3 (2) Fall 1976, publ. Society for the Anthropology of Visual Communication, Washington, DC, pp. 111-12 (see also related photograph samples in his section V-2 and V-3).

Griffin, Susan, 'Pornography and Silence', in *Made from this Earth: Selections from her Writing*, 1967-1982, The Women's Press, London, 1982, pp. 110-160.

Harding, M. Esther, *Woman's Mysteries: Ancient and Modern*, Harper and Row, New York, 1976, p. 20, 16 and passim (first publ. C.G. Jung Foundation for Analytical Psychology, 1971).

Janov, Arthur, *The Primal Scream, Primal Therapy: the Cure for Neurosis*, Sphere, London, 1973, p. 99.

Jeffreys, Sheila, 'Male Sexuality as Social Control', *Scarlet Woman*, 5, 1977, pp. 13-15.

Jung, Carl G., (ed.) *Man and his Symbols*, Picador/Pan Books, London, 1978, pp. 13-14, 68 (first publ. Aldus, London, 1964).

—— *Symbols of Transformation*, trans. R.F.C. Hull, Routledge and Kegan Paul, London; Princeton University Press, NJ, 1956 (Vol. V of *Collected Works* and a rewriting of an earlier publication), pp. 23, 25 (both on dreams linked to archaic or childlike thought), 408 (collective unconscious), 391 (lists archetypes), Foreword xxix (archetypes omnipresent), 330 (on 'Eternal Feminine'), 228 (archetypes universal and inherited), 313 (archetypes pre-existent), 308 (their spontaneous manifestation), 309 (they mould destinies), 66 (can seize the ego), 221, 424, 219 (all on confused tree symbolism), 351 ('Terrible Mother' as male magician), 359 (Logos as cow), 222 ('contradictions'), 390 (all the figures interchangeable), 231 (psychological truths 'work').

Lane, Michael (ed.) *Structuralism: a Reader*, Jonathan Cape, London, 1970, p. 18.

Lansley, Jacky, 'Women Dancing', *New Dance*, Spring 1978, publ. New Dance, X6 Dance Space, Butlers Wharf, Lafone Street, London SE1, pp. 10-11.

Leach, Edmund, *Genesis as Myth*, Jonathan Cape, London, 1969, pp. 85-113 (on the virgin birth), 9-10, 40-1.

—— 'Anthropological Aspects of Language: Animal Categories and Verbal Abuse', in Pierre Maranda (ed.) *Mythology*, Penguin, Harmondsworth, Middx. 1972, pp. 39-67; I quote pp. 56, 47.

Leites, N. and M. Wolfenstein, *Movies: A Psychological Study*, The Free Press, Glencoe, ILL., 1950, quoted by Sol Worth in his introduction to Goffman, 'Gender Advertisements'.

Lienhardt, Godfrey, *Divinity and Experience: the Religion of the Dinka*, Clarendon Press, Oxford, 1961, p. 254.

Lévi-Strauss, Claude, *Structural Anthropology*, trans. C. Jacobson and B. Grundfest Schoepf, Penguin, Harmondsworth, Middx, 1968.

McDonnell, Kevin and Kevin Robins, 'Marxist Cultural Theory: the Althusserian Smokescreen', in *One-Dimensional Marxism*, Allison and Busby, London and New York, 1980, pp. 157-231; I quote pp. 201-2 (Freud's abstraction of empirical data).

Malinowski, B., 'Psycho-analysis and anthropology', *Psyche*, Vol, IV, no, 4, 1924, pp. 293-332, incorporated into his *Sex and Repression in Savage Society*, Kegan Paul, London; Harcourt, Brace, New York, 1927. See also his 'Mutterrechtliche Familie and Oedipus-Komplex. Eine Psychoanalytische Studie', *Imago*, 10, 1924, pp. 228-76.

Marx, Karl, see, most accessibly, David McLellan, *Karl Marx*, Penguin, Harmondsworth, Middx, 1975. See also David McLellan, *The Thought of Karl Marx: an Introduction*, Macmillan, London, 1980, and Tom Kemp, *Karl Marx's 'Capital' Today*, New Park Publications, London, 1982.

Miller, David L., 'Orestes: Myth and Dream as Catharsis', in Joseph Campbell (ed.) *Myths, Dreams, and Religion*, E. P. Dutton, New York, 1970.

Moi, Toril, *Sexual/Textual Politics: Feminist Literary Theory*, Methuen, London and New York, 1985.

Murdock, Graham, 'Mass Communication and the Construction of Meaning', in *Reconstructing Social Psychology*, Penguin, Harmondsworth, Middx, 1974, pp. 205-20.

Needham, Rodney, *Symbolic Classification*, Goodyear, Santa Monica, CA., 1979, p. 11 (referring to the work of J.Ph. Duyvendak).

Nuttall, Geoff, in the discussion programme *UK Late* on Channel Four Television, 17 July 1987.

Okely, Judith, 'Gypsy Women: Models in Conflict', in Shirley Ardener (ed.) *Perceiving Women*, pp. 55-86.

Ortner, Sherry B., 'Is Female to Male as Nature is to Culture?', in Michelle Z. Rosaldo and Louise Lamphere (eds) *Women, Culture, and Society*, Stanford University Press, Stanford, CA, 1974, pp. 67-87; I quote p. 87.

Parker, Rozsika, *The Subversive Stitch: Embroidery and the Making of the Feminine*, The Women's Press, London, 1984.

Pearce, Joseph Chilton, 'Don Juan and Jesus', in Daniel C. Noel (ed.) *Seeing Castaneda*, G.P. Putnam's Sons, New York, 1976, p. 205.

Piaget, Jean, *Play, Dreams and Imitation in Childhood*, trans. C. Gattegno and F.M. Hodgson, Heinemann, Melbourne, London and Toronto, 1951.

Puttnam, David, interviewed on *The South Bank Show*, ITV, London, 23 November 1988.

Rich, Adrienne, *Of Women Born: Motherhood as Experience and Institution*, Virago, London, 1977, pp. 64, 62 (first publ. W.W. Norton, USA, 1976).

Roberts, Jane, *The Nature of the Psyche: Its Human Expression*, A Seth Book, Prentice-Hall, Englewood Cliffs, NJ, 1979, p. 56.

Rowbotham, Sheila, Hilary Wainwright and Lynne Segal, *Beyond the Fragments: Feminism and the Making of Socialism*, Newcastle Socialist Centre and Islington Community Press, 1979, pp. 27-8 (also Merlin Press, London, 1979).

Sjöö, Monica, *The Ancient Religion of The Great Cosmic Mother of All*, self-published, Bristol, 1975, pp. 35, 33. See also revised edition, Monica Sjöö and Barbara Mor, *The Great Cosmic Mother: Rediscovering the Religion of the Earth*, Harper and Row, San Francisco, 1987.

—— *Women are the Real Left!*, Matri/anarchy Publications, 29, Milford Street, Bristol 3, 1979, p. 4.

Spender, Dale, *Man Made Language*, Routledge and Kegan Paul, London, Boston, Melbourne and Henley, 1985 (first publ. 1980).

Trotsky, Leon, *Class and Art: Problems of Culture under the Dictatorship of the Proletariat, Speech by Trotsky during discussion, May 9, 1924, at a meeting convened by the Press Department of the Central Committee of the Russian Communist Party (Bolshevik) on Party Policy in the Field of Imaginative Literature*, trans. B. Pearce, a Fourth International Pamphlet, New Park Publications, 186A, Clapham High Street, London SW4, 1968, pp. 11, 10 (reprinted from *Fourth International*, July 1967).

Van Baal, J., *Symbols for Communication: an Introduction to the Anthropological Study of Religion*, Van Gorcum/H.J. and H.M.G. Prakke, Assen, 1971. (This contains readable sections on Cassirer, Freud and Jung).

Williams, Raymond, *Problems in Materialism and Culture: Selected Essays*, Verso and New Left Books, London, 1980, pp. 39, 38 (power of dominant culture), 19, 20, 34 (all on base and superstructure), 44 (the emerging and excluded), 43 (no social order exhausts full human range).

3

THE STUFF THAT DREAMS ARE MADE OF
Symbols of Sleep, Fantasy and Meditation

'Human beings see selectively, not empirically. They see what the conceptual structure of their culture permits them to see, and they only see new things when that existing cultural model is broken.'
Vincent Scully, *The Earth, the Temple and the Gods*

If our existing cultural model is not god-given and timeless, but man-made, then it can be broken. How we can tackle that breaking, and how we can learn to see new things, is the subject of this book. For each of us our cultural symbols show up most strongly in our internal world of dreams and fantasy; this is the area where they most intimately affect our waking and sleeping lives, and where we can start to set in motion the delicate process of questioning, deconstructing, and reconstructing.

The project is urgent: all the more so as the prevailing fantasies of our culture paralyse our efforts to claim pleasure and power in our lived physical existence. In advanced western capitalism, as one situationist leaflet put it, 'Real experience is replaced by fantasy. The consumers, isolated together, are rendered helpless by impossibly remote longings . . .' What we cannot afford becomes more desirable than what we have. Images are substituted for reality, and the unattainable can dwarf our everyday experience. The film star or pop singer is presented as more desirable than any flesh-and-blood man or woman we are ever likely to meet. The image of the perfect mother overshadows our every effort to care for our children. Stereotyped and ubiquitous symbols distract us from seeing what is wrong in the present and from acting to change it. As Rosalind Coward has put it in *Female Desire*, 'So many of the promises tell us that women can improve their lives without any major social changes. I don't believe that.'

To loosen the grip of these debilitating daydreams, any movement for social change requires a revolution of the imagination. Rather than dismissing the experience of fantasy and symbol as an irrelevance, we need to be reminded of the radical potential of the imagination: its ability to make intuitive connections, to recognise oppression, to penetrate deceptions, to question and transform social relations. The current problem arises not from the *utilisation* but from the *restriction* of the imagination. In *Öffentlichkeit und Erfahrung*, Oskar Negt and Alexander Kluge have traced the historical process through which bourgeois society has successfully sought to separate off fantasy and imagination, making them marginal rather than central to human thought and the organisation of life. Negt and Kluge suggest that this has been a means of diverting the potentially subversive effect of the imagination:

> From the viewpoint of utilization, all that which appeared to be especially difficult to control – the raw work, the leftover potential of undeveloped wishes, conceptions, the brain's own laws of motion which could not be placed in bourgeois categories – was represented as fantasy, as the gypsy, as the unemployed among the intellectual faculties.

As an example of the marginalisation of fantasy, Jack Zipes in *Breaking the Magic Spell* discusses the folk tale as originally part of a pre-capitalist people's oral tradition, expressing their wish to attain better living conditions through a depiction of their struggles and contradictions; he describes how from the eighteenth century onwards it was appropriated, with the 'bourgeois coinage' of the term 'fairy tale', as a new literary form to delight and entertain, divorced from any social context. I am reminded too of a modern example, shown in Michael Channon's film *New Cinema of Latin America, Part 2:* he tells how two independent Colombian film-makers, Jorge Silva and Marta Rodríguez, set out to make a non-fiction realistic documentary showing the exploitation suffered by a community of Colombian peasants, as the peasants themselves experienced it. Arriving on location, they were disconcerted to find that the peasants' radical grasp of their situation was mediated through a rich series of stories and symbols, such as the Devil appearing in the form of the top-hatted landowner whose clip-clopping horse's hooves haunted them at night. As Jorge Silva puts it:

We realized that this magical universe was something more than strange stories, . . . through these stories they were representing . . . the forms of domination which had become symbols for them from the time of the Conquest until today. This magical universe wasn't something set apart from concrete reality.

To reflect the peasants' experience accurately, the resulting film needed to be based – contrary to the film-makers' expectations – not only on *vérité* but on such fantastic symbols which had not become marginalised but were central to the community's radical perceptions.

Such examples are consistent with Negt and Kluge's suggestion that the unconscious world of fantasy is not separate from material life: if you want to change the world, you need imagination on your side. I am reminded here of Piaget's understanding of the imaginative symbolising process as a crucial part of humans connecting with the world, arranging and rearranging it (see Chapter 2). Without the imagination to move beyond stereotyped ways of thinking, it is unlikely we would have the impetus or the direction to struggle for change.

So in this chapter I will look at some of the ways in which the dualistic world view is expressed in our dreams and fantasies, and suggest some small beginnings that can be made in the process of questioning those stereotyped symbolic splits. The divide between soul and body underlies a number of other splits, and I will tackle four of these in turn: the split between active and passive; between inner and outer; between black and white; and, lastly, between conscious and unconscious. Since these splits exist in our vocabulary and thought patterns, we cannot deny or try to discard them – our only option is to work with them. Through looking deeply into them, we may be able to draw out new meanings and seeds of change: our imaginations are never completely ensnared. We can learn to recognise fantasies which can transform and dreams which represent a creative force; and we can learn techniques to help the seeds of change to flower.

One such technique described in this chapter is the dream method of Gestalt therapy, which, by encouraging the dreamer to act out elements in a dream, enables them to draw out the passion and perception embedded in that dream. Another method I will describe is meditation, which can be a way of opening a door to that creative part of the brain, and allowing a dialogue with it. The unconscious often expresses itself in symbols, and so Roberto Assagioli, founder of the Psychosynthesis method, suggests that symbols are especially effective for transforming the unconscious. (See his book *Psychosynthesis* and his pamphlet, 'Symbols of Transpersonal Experiences', as well as Piero Ferrucci's more recent book on the techniques of Psychosynthesis.) I include some 'guided fantasies', such as are used in Psychosynthesis, which provide certain imagery to feed to the receptive mind both to stimulate and channel the imagination. For each section I will also include other relevant exercises.

There is one crucial difference between a dream or fantasy which serves as a pacifier or safety valve, and one which has a transforming effect: that difference lies in the relationship between the dream world and the *physical* world. The link between fantasy and action lies in the body: in the thoughts, feelings and sensations which it incurs in its daily interaction with the world. Only through the body can images feed into daytime reality. Perhaps we could say of the creations of fantasy what Alexander Lowen, in *The Betrayal of the Body*, states concerning all creative effort: 'In all cases where the creative effort is a substitute for the life of the body, it provides only an image, not a self. Creative activity is satisfying and meaningful only when it enriches and enhances the life of the body from which it draws its inspiration.' Our physicality is crucial as the link between the imagination and the realm of action in the material world; so in this chapter, whatever the theme, method or symbolic vocabulary being discussed, we will never stray far away from the life of the body.

Active and Passive: the 'Empty' Vessel and the 'Powerful' Penis

We start with themes of emptiness and fullness, active and passive, and the way in which these tally with our notions about sex and gender. In ancient Greece the vessel, originally a positive symbol of the female body associated with fertility, creativity and transformation, slowly developed under the influence of patriarchy into a symbol with sinister qualities: Pandora's jar, the source of every evil unleashed upon the world of men. The legacy of the vessel or container as a female symbol is still with us. In Chapter 2 we saw that Freud's list of universal symbols included the suggestion that containers in dreams usually represent the uterus. Slang refers to women as various kinds of containers, as in 'she's an old bag' or 'I've got a bun in the oven'. In the USA 'box' is used to refer to the female genitals. Unlike the vessels which were so important in Early Cretan religion, made in the shape of women and described by archaeologists as 'vessel-goddesses', these modern containers receive little respect. If they are not passively empty, waiting for another to fill them, they play a negative role. Jung, in *Symbols of Transformation*, devotes many pages to the problem of how the son can tear himself from the ark, chest, casket, barrel, ship or other vessel which represents the 'enveloping womb' or 'voracious maw' of the devouring 'Terrible Mother'.

What does the prevalence of this kind of symbolism mean for the dreams of twentieth-century women? I will look at some examples of dreams about containers and emptiness; these, and others in this chapter, are mostly from workshops run by Marie Maguire and myself at the Women's Therapy Centre in London, and were explored through the Gestalt method.

The basic idea of this method, pioneered by Fritz Perls, is that everything in the dream, whether characters, buildings or objects, represents a part of the dreamer's psyche. The dream symbol of a lion might represent unexpressed anger or power; a fairground, a fragile façade of jollity; a broken telephone, problems with communication. You will only discover what a specific dream means for you by *acting out* the different elements in it and developing dialogues between them. These dialogues usually reveal conflicts or contradictions within your personality. This method may at first appear strange and it is hard, simply from reading examples, to gain a sense of how strongly people can identify with dream elements, and how vivid the role-playing can be. A fuller introduction to the method can be found in Perls' *Gestalt Therapy Verbatim*; and in *In Our Own Hands* Sheila Ernst and I gave a brief guide for use of the method at home, alone or with friends in a group. Here, however, our interest is in showing how Gestalt can help us explore unconscious symbolism, and move towards changing it.

Here is an example of the method in action:

Sarah has a dream in which there are penguins standing on a distant shimmering mountain. Near the road where she is standing, a group of boys cluster round a ferret in a cage.

Even a short dream like this can illuminate significant themes in the dreamer's life. At first sight it appears to bear little relation to containers or passivity, but it is impossible to foretell what meaning will emerge when the dreamer allows feelings and associations to emerge spontaneously.

Sarah starts by developing a dialogue with the penguins. A different cushion can represent each element in the dream. First she sits on one cushion to act the penguins: 'We are calm and happy because we don't have to deal with the world.' She then moves to another cushion to reply to them as herself in the dream; 'It's all right for you,' she responds resentfully. Group members notice that Sarah is holding her hand over her eyes. Body gestures often reflect an unconscious feeling or conflict stirred up by the dream. So it is suggested that she exaggerate the gesture. What is the hand saying with that gesture? She gives the hand a voice: 'I'm strong, I'll protect you.' When asked what she imagines the face would say in reply, she speaks as the face: 'I am vulnerable. I can't cope with the harshness of the world. I don't want people looking at me.' This reminds her of the ferret in the cage who, she says, does not want to be stared at by the crowd of boys. The group suggest that she sits on another cushion to act the ferret. Sitting hunched up, she speaks as the ferret and tells the crowd of ogling boys to go away: 'I bite!' Group members ask how she could get out of the cage and she replies: 'By biting.' They give her a cushion to represent the bar of the cage, and she gnaws and tears at it with her teeth, letting out deep angry sounds. When she becomes self-conscious, group members encourage her to stay with the feeling and its expression. Eventually she feels she has got through the bars and out of the cage. She jumps up, now straight and unhunched, and moves around the room with eyes up and looking around her. She recalls her first part of the dream and experiences the 'shimmering' quality of the mountains: 'It's in me! It's in my bones and skin!'

Even in this small excerpt, summarising a process which lasted over an hour, it is easy to see the themes of helplessness, vulnerability, restriction, and of being the object of aggressive gazes, which are common aspects of the experience of women. The container is a trap in which she feels at the mercy of a group of boys. Through noticing her usual response of hiding her face and holding her anger in her jaw, Sarah has the opportunity to experiment with an alternative: releasing the anger in her jaw and finding that this enables her to raise her gaze to meet the world. The seeds of that possibility are there in the dream, in the penguins and the 'shimmering' mountain, symbols of calm and strength which are present, though very distant, at the start. Unlocking her held-in anger is the key to bringing that sense of well-being closer. Through the dream work, she realises the possibility of transforming the cage: from a goldfish in a bowl, she becomes a genie in a lamp who gets out. The theme, as so often in Gestalt dream work, is that of re-owning our personal power; this allows us to confront the inequalities of power in society more effectively. The accompanying increased bodily sensation, which Sarah reports, reveals how much the way she held her body had been repressing her capacity to feel; this body change in turn creates the possibility and desire for a different kind of behaviour.

Sarah's dream was about a caged animal who managed to escape. The next dream – also explored in a women's dream group – directly addresses the theme of emptiness and passivity as expressed in the symbol of the hole:

> Claire dreams that she is driving along a rough road. A man sitting in the back seat is telling her to go faster. The road becomes steep and mountainous and there are very large holes in it, which she tries to avoid.
>
> In the dream work Claire develops a dialogue between herself and the man, acting both parts. The man is critical and says he could do it better. She gets angry. Speaking 'to the cushion', she shouts at him to 'Shut up!' and hits the cushion hard with a burst of energetic movement.
>
> Then she speaks as the holes in the road: 'I'm frightening . . . If you fall in me you'll fall into the void and disappear . . . You'd better avoid me or you'll be in trouble . . .' She changes cushions to speak again as herself replying to the holes: 'I'm scared of you . . . I've either got to drive the car properly or I'll fall in and die . . .' And so on: she develops a dialogue backwards and forwards. During the dialogue the hole gradually changes. As she plays the role, she finds her tone gradually changing from 'I'm frightening' to 'I'm big and powerful, you could rest in me.' The group ask her to represent the hole with her body and she makes as big a circle as she can with her arms, like a huge embrace. The group suggest that she imagines lying in the hole, and she rests, breathing deeply and evenly, until she is quite calm.

Afterwards Claire talked to the group about her life, and about the conflict between the pushy, driven part of herself (symbolised by the man) and a passivity which she feared could engulf her. Thus, in the dream, speed, purpose and insensitivity were contrasted with a cavernous and dangerous hole. However, her experience of entering into the dream symbol of the hole allowed her to realise that it could be seen not as an emptiness, but as a source. She talked to the group about her frenetic tempo of work, her fear that if she wasn't 'doing' something she didn't exist, and her inability to pace and replenish herself with the rest and space she needed. Like Sarah, by connecting the fantastic creations of the dream to their associated feelings and to her own body, she made a bridge which could lead to different behaviour in the world.

Claire's dream is interesting because at first sight it fits in so neatly with the traditional symbolism both of everyday usage and of psychoanalysis. In conventional dream interpretation, the hole in the road would be taken as a female sexual symbol. Freud, in *Introductory Lectures on Psycho-Analysis*, states that:

> The female genitalia are symbolically represented by all such objects as share with them the property of enclosing a space or are capable of acting as receptacles: such as *pits, hollows and caves*, and also *jars and bottles*, and *boxes* of all sorts and sizes, *chests, coffers, pockets*, and so forth.

The hole in the road might seem a perfect symbol for women's so-called sexual passivity. However, many Freudians no longer adhere to such mechanistic translations. There is nothing inevitable about the association of the female sexual organs with passive receptacles and holes. Claire makes no sexual associations with the symbol. And although at first she experiences the hole in the road as a pit of nothingness, into which she might disappear or perish, the symbol is revealed as having other qualities, becoming a place to rest in, a source of calm and strength. A hole is not intrinsically male or female, and the qualities we ascribe to it are the result of our cultural conditioning. Investigating the feelings carried by dream symbols can take us beyond such stereotypes to reveal quite other qualities.

Alongside the womb as receptacle, the fact that we have an 'empty hole' or passage in the vagina is another feature of women's anatomy which is used to represent, and endorse, women's so-called passivity. Women are called empty, negative, passive receptacles waiting to be filled by the active penis. This symbolic view is used as a 'biological' or 'natural' justification for a socially constructed fabric of sexual oppression and constraint. In early Crete, the womb was viewed quite differently: as a powerful creative force, symbolically associated with the sun. There is nothing *inevitable* about perceiving receptacles and holes as passive: they have other qualities and potential associations which are rarely allowed full flowering in our androcentric society, with its dominant phallic symbolism. There are other symbolic links latent in the unconscious, which has a far broader bank of experience to draw on than the conscious mind, as Claire's dream work showed. Here is another example of how, even staying with patriarchy's primary female sexual symbol of the 'hole', we can sometimes draw out latent qualities in that symbol and unearth possibilities waiting to be realised:

> Ruth, in a self-help therapy group, retells the following dream: 'My bedroom is small, boxy and neat. I come back to it and there is a huge hole in one corner. All around the hole there is rubble and mess, and mice can run in and out of it.' Ruth feels disgusted about this hole in her bedroom. But when she acts it out, things change. She speaks as the hole, 'I am big, dirty and disruptive. I am rude and sexual and I upset Ruth's tidy little world. I frighten Ruth. I've got a big voice and a big laugh.' Acting the hole, Ruth spreads her legs and opens her mouth wide and lets out some broad throaty laughs, 'Ha ha ha ha ha'. After the dream work, Ruth discusses her fear of this part of herself, and acknowledges how much she is missing by denying it a place in her life.

Calm and powerful in Claire's case, crude and outgoing in Ruth's case, it is clear that the hole as symbol does not have to represent passivity, fear, vulnerability and pain. We can stress penetration or enclosure, we can stress the womb's role of waiting or of creating: it all depends on our cultural model. Exploring symbols in depth helps us to see how relative such cultural models are.

Underlying this particular set of stereotyped symbols is the fear of the void. It is a feature of western culture, not shared by eastern culture, that we learn to abhor a vacuum. While eastern art can be minimalist and contemplative, leaving empty spaces, western canvases tend to be busy with detail. Why have silence when you can have the television on? Why sit still when you could be moving at speed with the illusion of technological progress? But just as the womb, portrayed as passive, is the place within which human life is created, so also the hole or void can be seen symbolically as a *source*. Thus we read in Lao-Tzu's *Tao Te Ching*:

> The Tao is an empty vessel; it is used, but never filled.
> Oh, unfathomable source of ten thousand things!

In *The Reproduction of Mothering* Nancy Chodorow has suggested that males in our society have to build their identity on a void, based on the tenuous model of an absent working father, and to achieve maleness have to deny the emotionality of their strong early bond with their mother, thus cutting themselves off from the ground they stand on. Is this why our androcentric society has such terror of the void, projecting it on to women as a negative quality?

The point has been taken up in some of the new western psychotherapies. For example, in *Gestalt Therapy Verbatim* Fritz Perls comments, 'If you avoid your emptiness and fill it up with phony roles and dummy activities, you get nowhere . . .' He suggests that 'when we accept and *enter* this nothingness, the void, then the desert starts to bloom. The empty void becomes alive, is being filled. The sterile void becomes the fertile void.'

Here is an example of how one woman experienced the difference between the two kinds of void within her own body:

> I was depressed. I felt as if all there was of me was a column in my body running down from my neck to my groin. It felt smoky, white, hollow and empty as if everything had drained out of it. I relaxed and took some time to breathe deeply down into the column and up out again. I started to become aware of sensations in my body and instead of inner emptiness I began to have a deep feeling of yearning. I thought: that shaft *is* hollow but that also means things can come *up* it. Imperceptibly the image shifted to one of a dark deep well shaft. I did not want to dip into the well to touch the source or bring water up. I was yearning for someone to do it for me. It became a sexual image as if the well was my vagina and I wanted a man to enter me to draw me out. It linked with a sense of a lot of creative potential being locked in my womb. I gradually realised that it was *my* life force into which I could dip and bring up whatever I needed from the very depths.

It is only when this woman stops, relaxes, takes time to breathe deeply, and *accepts* her depression by letting herself focus on the 'drained' sensation associated with the column, that the emptiness turns into a creative potential. Many writers have stressed that it is only by accepting our painful feelings, especially those of loss, that we can contact our creative potential as human beings. As Norman O. Brown advises in *Love's Body*, 'Admit the void; accept loss forever . . . blessed are they that mourn'. And again: 'Creation is out of nothing . . . A pregnant emptiness . . . Object-loss, world-loss, is the precondition for all creation. Creation is in or out of the void; *ex nihilo.*'

Silence is important here. If our conscious life is crowded with words, they drown out the void and leave no space to listen to the creative impulses of the unconscious. Many people find they benefit from letting their mind rest in neutral gear, out of harness – lying in bed on a Sunday morning, for example. Meditation is a good way of learning to leave such spaces. In the simplest terms, it is a way of sitting and listening to one's own silence. Some forms of meditation focus on stilling the mind's busy-ness and letting it empty; others encourage you to become aware of body sensations; other forms of meditation create the possibility for symbols to come forward from the unconscious, like the symbol of the well in the example above. Such symbols can then be explored and worked with just like dream symbols. Different kinds of meditation are discussed by Naranjo and Ornstein in *On the Psychology of Meditation*. Taking time to meditate regularly could be very useful for a woman like Claire (above), whose dream about the holes in the road shows that she fears her own stillness. Meditation could show her that things can grow in silence and give her a different sense of identity, helping her to contact a part of herself that does not always have to be 'doing' to exist. It would also provide a way for her to replenish herself, and put her in touch with resources she is unaware of having. As the Japanese Master Okada Torajiro explains, meditation – or 'sitting', as he terms it – can be a very nourishing experience. 'When one sits, a good meal and a good bed are being prepared. The good cook and the good mattress are within oneself. When one sits, a lovely cool wind blows in summer, and in winter a cosy fire burns on the hearth. The cool wind and the warm hearth are within oneself' (quoted in Von Dürckheim, *Hara*). At the end of this section I will give some simple meditative exercises, and more such exercises will follow throughout the rest of the book.

So much for the 'empty' vessel, the 'passive' hole. What of its complementary partner in our society's stereotypical imagery, the 'active', 'penetrating' penis? Feeling our way into the elements of our dreams and fantasies enables us to realise alternative associations: just as we can do this with the vaginal 'hole', so we can do it with the penis. Through this kind of work the penis can be divested of the distorting symbolic associations with which it has been invested. Our society attaches power to symbols of masculinity, and as we grow up we internalise such symbols. But, as Esther Harding has put it in *Women's Mysteries*, 'When the value represented by the symbol has been

entirely explored and made conscious its power leaves it, and the
object which held the meaning of the symbol becomes only a natural
object once more.' If people can see the penis for what it is, simply
a part of the male body, the way is clearer in personal and political
life to use adult strength to confront the real problems of inequalities
in power, control and authority between men and women in our
society.

One of the most extreme expressions of this unequal relationship
is rape. Apart from the frequent real occurrence of violent assaults
on women, the fantasy of rape lurks in the background of very many
male/female sexual interactions. A survey by Hall and Nordby
suggested that an unknown male is the second most frequent figure
of threat in the dreams of the American population (with animals
coming first). But rape imagery can emerge in women's fantasies in
unexpected ways, as in the kind of 'rape fantasy' which some women
like to use for arousal while masturbating or love-making. Feminists
are often embarrassed that they can gain a pleasurable sexual
experience through fantasies involving punishment, torture, bondage
and rape. Women who enjoy this kind of fantasy are often ashamed,
and try to avoid indulging it. But the whole issue of alleged female
'masochism' is very complex, as Susanne Schad-Somers has pointed
out in *Sadomasochism*. We again have to look below the surface and
beyond the apparent significance of the fantasy to unearth
unconscious meanings which may be different from those our society
ascribes. The sexuality work pioneered in the USA in the wake of the
Masters and Johnson research, and described in Lonnie Barbach's *For
Yourself*, has offered some valuable insights to help our understanding
of such 'rape' fantasies. In Britain this work has been established by
Jenner Roth, who currently practises at Spectrum, a centre for
humanistic psychology, in London. In a sexuality group run along
these lines, the group leader is likely to take an approach which denies
altogether the existence of such a thing as a 'rape fantasy', telling
women something in this vein: 'Don't accept the interpretations and
labels that society places on your fantasies, but find out what they
mean for *you*. In a fantasy *you* can decide who is present, what they
look like, what they say and do. *You* decide exactly how they touch
you. You are completely in control. *Rape is nothing like this*. So what
is the fantasy about for you? Experiencing pleasure without guilt?
Being loved like crazy by someone, or being desired passionately by
several people at once? Being made love to in a variety of ways? Having
all your needs met? Receiving a lot of pleasure without having to lift

a finger? Rather than seeing the fantasy as "passive" you can see it as active and receptive. It is possible to explore how much sexual pleasure you can take in that fantasied state of receptivity, rather than when you are only concerned for the other person. Let yourself find out what the fantasy means to you, and don't buy labels like "rape fantasy".

Women writers have pointed to some of the issues which may underlie such a fantasy. Nancy Friday, in *My Secret Garden*, suggests that rape does for a woman's sexual fantasy what 'the first martini' does for her in reality, relieving her of responsibility and guilt: 'By putting herself in the hands of her fantasy assailant – by *making* him an assailant – she gets him to do what she wants him to do, while seeming to be forced to do what he wants.' In a society where a woman is expected to devote much energy to caring for the emotional and well-being of others, such fantasies allow attention and energy to be focused on her. Linking such fantasies with a carry-over from a woman's early relationship with her mother, Helle Thorning points out in *Heresies* that 'There is a feeling of omnipotence because she is having all of her needs met.' Thus, as Lynne Segal comments in an essay in *Sex and Love*, 'passivity and masochism in sex can, paradoxically, be demanding, self-centring and pleasurable'. Many women have stressed the element of guiltless pleasure, important in a society where we are brought up to believe that 'nice girls' do not feel lust. J. Lee Lehman, writing in *Heresies* about lesbian sexuality, stresses the importance of reclaiming lust, which 'as an expression of sexual desire can represent an affirmation of our collective right to unfettered, unguilty, undefined sexuality'.

In a Spectrum sexuality group, a woman with a masochistic fantasy would be encouraged to stop judging it, and to accept it. Fighting and denying a fantasy often feeds it more energy and increases its hold on us. Instead she would be encouraged to stay with it and let herself enjoy it as fully as possible, always aware that she is keeping it on the level of fantasy. This distinction is important. Quoting a study which shows that the service politicians most frequently demand from prostitutes is to be beaten, Lynne Segal stresses in *Sex and Love* that the problem with masochistic fantasy is not at all that it encourages submissiveness in real life, or reflects any desire for real pain, hurt or humiliation, 'but rather that, like any reliance on fantasy, it can make your sexual partner irrelevant, reducing sex to masturbation'. Symbolism is acting here as a barrier between the woman and the world, so that her sexual partner is not seen for her or himself. Again, it is important to decode the information packed into the symbol, so that it can become a channel to reveal the underlying issues and open up the possibility of change. As Lynne Segal puts it, we must 'seek to understand how sexual desire comes to express such a variety of other social needs: needs which are irrational, unconscious and not easily understood and changed'. The path to those irrational unconscious needs, and towards establishing a more realistic contact with the world, has to start from the elements and characters of the fantasies, which can be explored just like the dream symbols in the examples given in this chapter. As with dream symbols, we find that making an emotional and physical connection to the symbols can reveal a meaning very different from that which convention would attribute to them. Thus common and stereotyped symbols can become symbols of transformation – it is a question of recognising that we can work with our fantasies, rather than feeling trapped and shamed by them.

In this section I have deliberately chosen examples of dream work which show a palpable shift or transformation in the symbolism. This is not to imply that the process is easy: one may go through many dreams feeling stuck and trapped without the slightest sign of movement. Nor would I suggest that the method described here is the only valid way to work with dreams, whose richness allows for many different interpretations. My aim has been simply to show one way of looking into our dreams and fantasies for glimpses of alternatives to the dominant active/passive, male/female symbolism. All of us, whether women or men, need sometimes to be active and sometimes to be passive. We need to know the path between the two states, rather than being trapped in one or the other by male/female cultural stereotypes. For all of us there is a time to be outgoing and a time to be receptive, and it can be a long, slow process to learn to know our time.

Here are two exercises.

Drawing a Dream

Have a range of coloured crayons and a large sheet of paper ready.

Recall a recent or significant dream.

In a group, or with a partner, retell your dream in the present tense. Some people find that shutting their eyes while they do this helps them to focus on the dream.

At the end of the dream, open your eyes, take the crayons and draw your dream quickly, not worrying about whether you are creating a perfect art work. You can draw events and characters literally, or simply produce shapes and colours representing the feeling of the dream. Allow no more than three minutes for the drawing.

Then talk to the group or your partner about the picture and its symbols and colours. Start with the picture's most striking dream image and say what it means to you and what is important to you about it. Then move on to the rest.

When you have finished, your partner(s) may have some feedback, commenting on things they felt or noticed about the dream picture.

A Body Symbol

You can do this exercise alone, although it might help to have someone read you the instructions at first. The reading should be slow with long pauses. 'Cushion work' is easy when you get used to it, but at first you may feel self-conscious.

Sit comfortably with your knees and arms uncrossed. Your back and neck should be straight but relaxed. Take a few minutes to relax and breathe evenly.

Now let your attention go to an area of your body which you are particularly aware of or concerned about at the moment. Choose the first part that comes to mind. Take two to three minutes to imagine you are breathing into that area, and notice the sensations there.

Now see if a symbol for that area comes to mind. It could be a human, animal or plant symbol or an object or geometric shape. Take the first symbol that comes up, however unlikely.

Notice the details of the symbol such as colour, movement, shape, texture and anything else that strikes you.

Open your eyes and put two cushions on the floor. Choose one to be yourself and one to be the symbol.

Sit on the cushion representing the symbol. Shut your eyes and imagine you are that symbol. Now speak as the symbol and describe yourself, for example:

'I am a bridge, old but strong . . .'
'I am a shrivelled-up heart . . .'
'I am a hedgehog, very prickly . . .'
'I am a bare branch, no leaves at all . . .'

It might help to act out the symbol with your body. Say how you feel as the symbol.

Move to the other cushion. Now speak as yourself addressing that symbol/part of your body. Say how you feel about it, perhaps what worries you about it or what you want from it.

Change cushions and reply as the symbol. How does it respond to that worry or request?

And so on, letting a dialogue develop. Notice especially what the symbol tells about itself, as you may be able to learn from this. Before you finish, make sure the symbol states what it *needs*. Then, as yourself, see how you could give it that. How would it be possible? From where? From yourself? Or from other people or situations?

Afterwards it can help to write down or discuss with a partner what came up. If you really let yourself imagine the symbol speaking, it can spontaneously bring forward feelings and needs of which you had been unconscious. (For more ideas about developing personal symbols, see David Feinstein and Stanley Krippner's *Personal Mythology*.)

The Inner and the Outer

We turn now to the inner/outer divide. In two of the dreams discussed in the last section, the split between active and passive was paralleled by a split between 'inner' and 'outer'. In traditional Christian terminology this is expressed as the pure spirit trapped within the prison of the flesh, struggling to escape. This split between inner and outer may take specific forms: the outer self may be groomed endlessly to appear attractive to others, while the inner self feels worthless and inadequate; or the 'outer' works hard to be capable and hold her own in a man's world while the 'inner' feels delicate, shy and imaginative; the outer self is kept restrained and trim-looking while the inner self is feared as a potentially limitless and unbridled volcano; the outer body gains weight to provide protection and camouflage for an inner being terrified of invasion; the outer person keeps very busy while the inner feels empty; and so on. We saw in the earlier examples that Claire's dream symbolised her non-busy self as a hole or void, while Sarah visualised a paralysing cage. By becoming aware of the split between inner and outer, sometimes by accentuating and role-playing the two halves, women can move towards transforming the relationship between them; they can establish a contact and a dialogue. A division can become a dynamic. From being a trap, disguise, or defensive barrier, the outer can become the vehicle which the inner needs to express itself in order to reach out into the world.

If you are investigating this issue, the first step is to identify what the inner/outer split means for you. Recognising that the sense of the 'inner', private, life is often tied up with sexuality, Jenner Roth encourages sexuality group members to become aware of this split in their lives. In one exercise they look at the difference for them between 'What I say' and 'What I mean to say'. At another point they might be asked to spend a week noticing 'How do I get from the inside to the outside?', which could be in relation to any activity at all, in work, home or social life. In another exercise they are asked: 'How do you get inside? How do you find the pathway to get in there?', and are encouraged to look for physical experiences or activities which provide a route for them to enter their inner space.

An alternative way to look at this split is through the use of symbols. For example, you could use relaxation and breathing to create a receptive frame of mind in which you could allow symbols for your 'inner' and 'outer' self to come forward. Here is the written account of a woman who did such a meditation:

> . . . Perhaps the 'outer' me strongly disapproves of the 'inner' me, and the 'inner' me knows it and prefers to stay hidden.
>   . . . It suddenly came to me, that inside I feel like a war-blighted landscape, like a country devastated by war. Like the Lebanon. Trampled over by soldiers' boots, all my new green shoots burned or shrivelled . . ., my houses and cities razed to the ground. I cried and cried and it came to me that the bossy controlling organising 'outer' me is a compensation for this sense of inner devastation. As if each new shoot I put forth will be snatched from me, trampled . . .
>   So what my inner self needs, more than anything else, is for the invading soldiers to be kept out. Not for more soldiers to come and chase them away . . . but for NO SOLDIERS AT ALL. A fence, a moat, a BOUNDARY to keep them all out, so rebuilding can take place, so crops can be sown again. And my 'outer' me could help in that, instead of being bossy and turning her (or his?) back.

This woman might work with her experience in various ways: she could think of the ways in which her coping self could protect and nourish her inner self; she could draw or paint the inner devastation; she could do a visualisation of the green shoots growing on the waste land. She might also write a list of the times and places which allow her to feel her 'inner' self, and the situations and people which require a response from the 'outer' self, thus gaining a clearer sense of how the 'inner' and 'outer' selves emerge in patterns of daily living and how she might be able to create more situations and space for the 'inner'. She might use Gestalt techniques to act out a dialogue between the soldiers and the war-blighted landscape. This might provide insight about the role the 'soldiers' play in her personality: why does she 'need' them? what part of her do they represent? what is their history for her? and so on. She could also work with her body in various ways, for example using meditation or movement to explore sensations, memories and impulses in different parts of her body and thus build up a sense of the richness of the body's inner space.

The social pressures on women, whether to look attractive, to help and service others, or to achieve in a man's world, all tend to orientate us towards other people's needs and values while our own inner space can be experienced as very empty. It can be valuable for women to spend time consciously exploring the inner experience of their body, learning to take cues from their body rather than from external pressures and expectations.

That we see the 'inner' and 'outer' as split can be understood as part of our cultural heritage and a reflection of the repressive norms of behaviour in our society, rather than as a fact about 'human nature'. They could equally be visualised as points on a continuum, with energy continually spiralling in and out between the two, the inner feeding the outer and the outer feeding the inner. One way of developing such a view of the body is to focus attention on physical processes which are cyclical, operating through intake and output, through assimilation and elimination, build-up and discharge, or circulation. For example, our patterns of breathing in and out say a lot about the quality of our interaction with the world. The way we breathe may reflect our whole attitude to absorbing input from the outside, to assimilating it, and to expressing things, releasing, or eliminating waste: some people are afraid to breathe in deeply, or to hold the breath inside them, or to empty their chest fully on the exhale. Noticing patterns of breathing and identifying the most uncomfortable points in the cycle ('I hate the feeling that my lungs are full and bursting', 'I am scared of the space between breaths and so I can't let my chest fall fully on the exhalation') may highlight how a person relates to the 'inner' and the 'outer'. For example, an individual may habitually grab at experience rather than digesting it, or put on a brave front rather than allowing the full expression of feelings of grief or pain, or may fear to experience loss and emptiness, and so on. Karlfried Graf Von Dürckheim suggests in *Hara* that 'the fear which prevents the "letting-oneself-fall" into the exhalation' reflects 'a fundamental lack of trust in life'. Similarly, patterns of eating, assimilation and digestion of food may reveal something about a person's attitude to receiving nourishment from the world. At the end of this section I list some exercises to experiment with ways of learning from these physical models of movement between 'inner' and 'outer'.

A few days after writing the earlier piece about her 'inner' and 'outer' selves, the same woman heard about the assassination, by South African secret police, of a friend active in anti-apartheid work. In response to that event she wrote: 'It's as if the outer me is saying, "Don't mourn – organise! Get in there and help continue the struggle . . ."' At this point she might ask the questions: 'How do I get from the inner to the outer?' 'How can I both mourn and organise?' 'How can I use the energy released by mourning to activate me in the world?' 'Rather than seeing them as alternatives, how do I use my inner sensitivity and passion to inform my outer actions?' 'How can I bring the fruits of that huge inner area to harvest and out into the world?' It is easy to see how undermining it would be for her to deny herself the space to mourn, and how much more effective she would be if she acted with all the energy available to her, rather than just from an outer shell.

That we often feel split is undeniable. We can, however, understand that split neither as a human necessity, nor as an individual failing, but rather as a response to a socially specific situation. Under the pressures of twentieth-century capitalism that split has a useful function, enabling us to move through the world and to protect the 'inner' self even if it is at the expense of denying it. If we understand the social causes and the means whereby we became split, we have the possibility of reaching a different sense of ourselves, of adopting different patterns of behaviour, of healing the split. The 'outer' can express, rather than cover, the 'inner'. We all need both to engage and to recuperate. We all need contact with, and withdrawal from, the world, and we need to learn the means to move appropriately between the two states, rather than being trapped in one or lurching uncontrollably between the two. In the following pages I give some exercises for exploring those pathways.

Meditation, as an 'inner' experience, has often been seen as an escape from the world outside. Symbols, as the fruit of fantasy and imagination, have often been seen as irrelevant to the material world. We need to recognise how both meditation and symbols can be used for nourishment, as a channel to our inner resources. This can help us start to move towards a view and a life practice where the best of our sensitivity, creativity and power can be expressed in our involvement with the world around us.

Meditation to Prepare for Writing or Other Work

I find that if I can bear to allow myself the time to do this meditation before starting writing, or doing a piece of carpentry, I can work in a more enjoyable way, and often achieve more than if I throw myself into it in a manic, desperate, anxious frame of mind. I often find that by the end of the meditation I have surmounted a barrier to a particular piece of work, or can see the answer to a specific problem in it.

Sit comfortably with straight back and neck, preferably cross-legged on the ground or, if in a chair, with the soles of both feet on the ground. Arms and hands should be uncrossed.

Feel your weight. Relax. Feel your body being supported by the ground, and let your weight sink into it. Let your face relax. Empty your mind. Let it go blank.

There is nothing but you and a void.

Thoughts may crop up: ideas for your work; problems with it; concerns about people and events in your daily life. Don't try to banish such thoughts. Allow them in, look at them, turn them over in your mind as you might use your hands to explore the feeling of something, then let them go.

Return to the emptiness.

Allow this process to continue for ten minutes.

Now start to notice your breathing and imagine you are breathing in the emptiness. With each breath *ask* to receive the strength to carry your work through. Imagine each breath is filling you with energy, purpose and resolve. (Allow two minutes.)

Now give thanks for what you have achieved so far (however little you may feel it is). Give thanks for having survived to reach the brink of this piece of work.

Open your eyes and start work.

In this exercise, the 'asking' can be understood as a way of opening yourself to unconscious or temporarily inaccessible resources inside yourself. The 'thanks' may stick in your throat at first, but it is a way of being courteous to your creativity, and giving yourself some appreciation. I find I work better when on good terms with myself than when I feel churlish or self-punishing.

Breathing to Assimilate and Express

This is an exercise I learnt from Bob Moore of the Psykisk Center in Denmark. It is good for showing how breathing can be a metaphor for other activities: for how you take in, assimilate and express, in different areas of your life.

Throughout this exercise, breathing is not through the mouth but through the nose, and without stress.

Sit comfortably.

Place the middle two fingers of one hand on your solar plexus, at a point about one inch below where your ribs part.

Finding your own speed for the count, breathe in for the count of three, which will lift your solar plexus.

Hold your breath in for the count of three.

Breathe out for the count of five.

Do this for no more than five minutes each day.

If you draw anything into your body, whether it is an idea, an experience, or an understanding, you need to hold it in your body before you express it outwards again. The count of five is needed because it takes longer to express what you have taken in. Establishing a rhythm in your breathing like this can help to establish a rhythm in the move between 'inner' and 'outer' in other aspects and activities of your life.

Inner Body Landscape

This exercise can help you to appreciate the richness (both pleasurable and painful) of the inner landscape which is your body. Make sure that there will be time afterwards to talk about what it brought up for you. A partner should read for you, or one group member should read for the rest, at a slow pace and allowing plenty of long pauses:

Lie comfortably with your neck straight and arms and legs uncrossed. Shut your eyes, feel your weight on the floor, and breathe deeply and evenly for two or three minutes.

Now let your awareness go to your *feet*. Notice any sensations there. (Pause.) Notice any feelings or emotions in them. (Pause.)

Now let yourself be aware of the history of your feet throughout your life. Have they suffered any accidents? Do they have any memories of pain? (Pause.) Do they have any memories of pleasure? (Pause.) You may go right back to childhood.

Can you remember times you have been proud of them? (Pause.) Can you remember times you have been ashamed of them? (Pause.)

Now just let yourself think about the way your feet have been touched during your life . . . by yourself (pause) . . . by others (pause).

Now ask yourself what your feet do for you in your daily life? What role do they serve for you? (Pause.)

Now think about how you treat them. What do you do for them? (Pause.) What more could you do? (Pause.)

Think about what your feet need. (Pause.) How could you provide it for them? Or arrange for it to be provided?

Now let your awareness move on to the rest of your *legs*. Notice any sensations there. (Pause.) . . . (And so on, repeat as above for the feet.)

After *legs*, move on to *genitals*, then *pelvis* (including lower belly), then *trunk of body* (including front and back), then *arms*, and lastly *neck and head*.

This exercise can stir up painful feelings and memories about your body, and at the same time can give you a sense of the wealth of information and experience carried in that inner world.

Guided Fantasy: 'The Old Picture Book'

This guided fantasy is based on one referred to by Assagioli in *Psychosynthesis*.

A partner should read for you, or one group member should read for the rest, at a slow pace and allowing plenty of pauses:

Lie comfortably with arms and legs uncrossed and neck straight. Shut your eyes and breathe evenly to relax. (Pause.)

Now imagine you are wandering through a forest. It is wild, as if no one has been that way for a long time. The high trees arch above you, and bluebells carpet the forest floor. (Pause.)

Suddenly you catch sight of an old cottage set in the middle of the forest. What does it look like? (Pause.) You make your way towards it. When you reach it, you knock on the door and wait. There is no reply. You open the door and go in. Inside, the house is musty and dusty as if it has been abandoned. (Pause.)

You explore the house. What are the rooms like? (Pause.)

Now you notice a little door which leads down steps to the cellar. You go down. The cellar has an old earthen floor. Partly buried in the earth, and covered with dust, is an old book. You dig out the book. (Pause.)

The book has many pictures in it. You go through some of the pages in the book. What are the pictures of? (Long pause.)

Now open your eyes and slowly return to the room.

Talk about the pictures: what they were, and what they mean to you.

This is a fairly open-ended format which leaves people free to project on to the contents of the book and bring a wide range of unconscious material from their inner world out into the open.

Do not feel that you have to provide a rational explanation for all the images that come up as pictures in the book. Some of them may reflect painful or pleasurable memories which you have carried inside you since childhood, and simply experiencing them may be enough in itself. Assagioli suggests that through the psychological processes which happen during a visualisation or guided fantasy of this kind, there is a kind of 'symbolic catharsis' or release, parallel to the catharsis which is brought about by the recovery of repressed memories. The experience does not need to be analysed: Assagioli points out that many of our individual inner pains and problems have their roots in the earliest, pre-conscious years of childhood and can therefore be both expressed and healed on the non-verbal level of symbol.

Seeing Things in Black and White

One common way of symbolising the unknown 'inner' space is to describe it as 'dark'. Here we also confront our symbolic use of the colours black and white, which often expresses our sense of racial difference.

Our conventional symbolism, with its Christian concept of the 'forces of light' opposed to the 'forces of darkness', polarises the colour black into representing what is irrational, primitive, sinister, unconscious, physical, sexual, forbidden or evil, as in 'black magic'.

Recognising the significance of this kind of symbolism is crucial in tackling our society's racism which is manifest not only in discrimination over jobs and housing but also in people's patterns of thought and emotional reactions. Let us look briefly at how this symbolic set has been elaborated and justified in modern psychological theory, specifically in the work of C.G. Jung. When Jung formulated his theory of 'archetypes', which I discussed in Chapter 2, he counterpointed the 'persona' (the personality or mask we assume in social and public life) with the 'shadow' (those parts of ourselves which are unpleasant, and are banished from everyday life to the unconscious). The 'shadow' is pictured as black.

Here is Jung's account, in *Memories, Dreams, Reflections*, of one of his own dreams, in which the 'shadow' is expressed by the symbol of a dark-skinned man:

> I dreamt that I was in an Arab city . . . The casbah in the interior of the city was surrounded by a wide moat . . . Eager to see the citadel from the inside also, I stepped out on the bridge. When I was about half-way across it, a handsome, dark Arab of aristocratic, almost royal bearing came towards me from the gate . . . the resident prince of the citadel. When he came up to me, he attacked me and tried to knock me down. We wrestled.

In the struggle, both Jung and the Arab fell into the moat, where the Arab tried to drown Jung, and Jung in turn pushed the Arab's head under water to make him unconscious and incapable of fighting. Then the scene of the dream changed, and Jung found himself with the Arab in

> a large vaulted octagonal room in the centre of the citadel. The room was all white, very plain and beautiful. Along the light-coloured marble walls stood low divans, and before me on the floor lay an open book . . . I explained to him that now I had overcome him he must read the book . . . I placed my arm around his shoulders and forced him, with a sort of parental kindness and patience, to read the book.

Of this dream Jung comments that the Arab's dusky complexion marks him as a 'shadow' of his own self, representing the unconscious, emotional, primitive and vital elements of his personality which are suppressed in the predominantly 'rational' European civilisation to which Jung belongs. The attempted murder symbolises for him a violent assault by his unconscious psyche on this European identity. There are two ways we could understand this use of black/white symbolism. One is to do what Jung did: to conclude that the darker 'shadow' is a universal archetype expressing the less acceptable side of human beings. This involves assuming not only that humans necessarily have a polarised split between their inner and their outer selves, but also that darkness or blackness always and inevitably signifies unconsciousness, and that light or whiteness is intrinsically and *by its very nature* an apt symbol for consciousness. Thus Jung, after visiting an African community which celebrated the sunrise, commented in *Memories, Dreams, Reflections*:

. . . within the soul from its primordial beginnings there has been a desire for light and an irrepressible urge to rise out of the primal darkness . . . That is the pent-up feeling that can be detected in the eyes of primitives, and also in the eyes of animals . . . That sadness also reflects the mood of Africa . . . It is a maternal mystery, this primordial darkness. That is why the sun's birth in the morning strikes the natives as so overwhelmingly meaningful . . . In reality a darkness altogether different from natural night broods over the land. It is the psychic primal night which is the same to-day as it has been for countless millions of years. The longing for light is the longing for consciousness.

I have quoted this passage at length because it provides a clear example of how an unreflecting racism and patronising, Eurocentric notions about Africa combine with an elevation of the symbol of darkness as primitive and unconscious to the status of a universal principle.

There is another way to view this symbolism of 'persona' and 'shadow'. This is to suggest that in a society where the conditions of public life are often inhuman, an exaggerated split will develop between the outer and the inner person. Where a very limited 'rationality' is the only form of consciousness which is prized, other ways of thinking and feeling are relegated. Where only certain contained and 'packaged' expressions of sexuality are allowed, the unexpressed looms menacingly in the background. And in a society which contains oppressed groups, all these subordinated qualities will tend to be projected on to those groups. Jung's 'shadow' is not cast by the universal human psyche; rather its contours reflect the blind spots of western culture. In 'Jung: A Racist', Farhad Dalal has detailed how Jung explicitly equated the modern black with the prehistoric human; the modern black conscious with the white unconscious; and the modern black adult with the white child. Pointing to the guilt and fear underlying such projections, Dalal comments: 'His error was in assuming that because the black symbolised the primitive to himself, therefore they were primitive.' In *Made From This Earth*, Susan Griffin comments that ' "the woman" in pornography, like "the Jew" in anti-Semitism and "the black" in racism, is simply a lost part of the soul, that region of being the pornographic or the racist mind would forget and deny'. She goes on to point out that this pornographic and racist mind dominates our culture and that, through the ubiquitous influence of philosophy, literature, religious doctrine, art, film, advertisements and our commonest gestures and habits, it is a mentality in which we all participate.

Here are two examples of white women's dreams:

I am dancing in a café with many others. The music is traditional ballroom music. My partner is a black man, his skin very dark, his height and size about the same as mine. We are dancing closely melded together. There is a blissful harmony between us and I feel a kind of sensual ecstasy.

An upper class woman is leading a black man along the road by a noose which is fastened round his neck. He is some kind of slave and she has to control him in case he does unacceptable, bad, wild, sexual things.

These dreams could be understood as the meeting of the conscious personality with more unconscious, repressed qualities of sexuality, sensuality, intuitive rhythm, 'wildness' and physicality, again embodied in the symbol of the black man. However, rather than attributing any universal validity to such symbolism, one could see it as reflecting specific social realities: in a society where black people are denied access to social power, it is hardly surprising that a black person can be seen as a symbol of thwarted potential. In a society where black people are stereotyped (and feared) as less rational, more sexual, sensual and rhythmic than white people, then the dream and fantasy symbols which emerge in that society will reflect those stereotypes. As a white person I can write only about white racism, not about black people's experience, but some black writers have described how these stereotypes affect black people as well as whites. For example, in *Heresies* Sylvia Witts Vitale writes: 'Of course we all know that Black

people have no problems. Our men have big dicks and know how to
use them well. Our women are well endowed and hot in bed.' She
points out that black sexuality is surrounded by 'so many myths,
realities, half-truths, racist influences, capitalistic influences, classist
influences, and resistance' that need to be broken down and looked
at. Tracing some aspects of these stereotypes historically to conditions
of sexual abuse imposed by whites in the period of slavery, as well
as to white misunderstanding of African cultural norms of sexuality,
she concludes that:

> the oppressed seem to somehow take on the ideology of the
> oppressor. In the case of Black sexuality, Black people seem to have
> taken on some stereotypes created by the ignorance and racism
> of whites . . . when the Black male and the Black female go to
> bed, they are not alone. They take along with them all of the super-
> duper stereotypes of what it is supposed to be like with them . . .
> Black people, and Black women in particular, never had an
> opportunity to define ourselves because we've been so busy
> fighting so many racist myths.

Again, in *Black Macho and the Myth of the Superwoman*, Michele
Wallace pointed out the politically destructive effect of such myths.
She criticised the Black Power movement for its 'macho' image which,
in excluding black women and accepting white myths about blacks
as sexy, primitive and subhuman, masked the crucial economic issues
at stake: 'The white man's own nightmare could not be used to
conquer him.'

Breaking our existing cultural model of the black/white split is an
important part of the revolution of the unconscious. But as with other
restrictive symbols, we must face the question of how to do this.
Alongside a political struggle to change the ways in which sexism and
racism are institutionalised in our society, we need to make changes
in our personal lives, confronting the ideology and the symbols which
give shape to our perceptions. Working therapeutically with our
dreams and fantasies to re-own the projections in them is an important
part of this process. The woman quoted earlier, who dreamt about
the black man led on a noose, worked with it as follows:

> Choosing two cushions to represent the woman and the man, she
> starts by speaking as the upper-class woman. In this role she tells
> the man to keep in line and not be unruly. She is afraid that he

will leap around, break things, be sexual. Swapping roles to speak as the man, she at first replies resignedly with slumped shoulders: 'I have always had this noose around my neck', but as the dialogue develops this voice becomes angry and her figure straightens, 'Let go of me! I want to be free!' As this character she finally enacts breaking the noose, hits the other cushion with her fists and ends by throwing it to the other end of the room. She then rises, breathes deeply, and stretches out at full length, commenting on the sensations in her body.

After the dream work she talks about the black man as representing her sexual, physical side with which she is not always closely connected and which she experiences as 'other'. By using the dream work to *identify with those qualities in herself*, she is less likely to project them on to others, and less likely to fuel racist stereotypes which distort her vision of the society in which she lives.

Unlearning these stereotypes is obviously a very long personal struggle for each of us, but by becoming aware of the process of projection we become more likely to notice our habitual patterns and more able to work towards other ways of thinking.

Another area we need to examine is the process of perception itself. An important step towards demystifying our society's racist myths is to recognise that there do exist alternative ways of relating to the colour black itself. The rigid symbolic split dominant in the west limits our perception of darkness, which is far more than the absence of light.

In the early stages of learning meditation, it is common to do exercises in which you imagine white light being drawn through or over the body. At first impression this appears as yet another endorsement of the 'positive' qualities of whiteness as opposed to blackness. However, from questioning meditation teachers I respect, I have learnt that the main reason they do not use black in such initial exercises is precisely because of their awareness of our (socially created) negative associations with black. In the terms of physics, while white light reflects, black absorbs. While a white surface reflects all the colours of the spectrum together, and a green surface reflects everything except green, which it reflects into our eyes, a black surface absorbs everything. If we step outside our assumptions we can see the absurdity of making value judgments about any part of this process involving light and its reflection. The common symbolic use of black – to conceal our 'darkest' secrets and to project or carry our negativity – bears little relation to the blackness of the universe which carries its own validity, power and meaning like every manifestation of the natural world. We would laugh at the idea of labelling pine trees 'bad' and beech trees 'good'. Experienced meditators and teachers often use black as a positive symbol. They speak of it as a powerful colour, much less dense than white, valuable for achieving balance and relaxation. It is also recommended as a symbol for protection because of its powers of absorption.

I need hardly enter the argument that in any case 'black' people are not black, any more than 'white' people are white; even on this simple level the conventional symbolism is inaccurate. Racial discrimination against people of colour contributes to darkness being represented as a negative, primitive or potentially dangerous element: it is clearly untenable to suggest that a cosmic imperfection attaches to anything black. Again we are reminded of the relativity of our symbolic perceptions which have seemed so unquestionable.

Here are two exercises which may help you to experience darkness differently.

Sitting in Blackness

This exercise draws on the comforting quality of black, which meditation teachers emphasise. I heard of it from Isis Martins.

Sit in a completely dark room. Let your body be relaxed and your breathing calm.

Now imagine that you are letting blackness fill your body, through every pore and right into your bones.

Think of the blackness as a friend, and think of it as being able to absorb.

Sit in silence for ten minutes.

Dreaming the Darkness

This is an exercise to do before going to bed, which may affect the quality of your dreams. I was taught it by Bob Moore.

Just before going to sleep, sit in a comfortable position, close your eyes, and relax.

Now let your awareness move to your navel. Focus on your navel for a few seconds.

Now visualise blackness or darkness for a few seconds.

Now imagine a point six to eight inches above the top of your head, and let your awareness stay there for a few moments. Then let go of that contact and sit in silence for a few minutes.

Now go to sleep, and in the morning write down your dreams.

Focusing on certain points of the body, colours or symbols just before sleeping is a way of pointing the unconscious in a certain direction, and encouraging it to dream about particular issues. The three elements given in this exercise may encourage you to dream about themes of birth and death, which in dream terms can both symbolise transition. Dreaming about death can reflect the releasing of something you no longer need, like fear or blockages. Black is seen as an important colour if you are going through changes, moving from one state of consciousness to another, because black can absorb things which you cannot carry with you into the new state.

Day and Night, Conscious and Unconscious

One factor which feeds into our black/white symbolism is our ideology about consciousness and its relation to the unconscious. Two things happen here: one is that consciousness becomes associated with the faculty of sight and with light; the other is that consciousness is seen as sharply polarised from the unconscious.

When patriarchy became dominant in early Greece, the sun shifted from being linked symbolically with the belly to being linked with the eye. The sun god Helios, from his chariot high in the heavens, watched and reported on the actions of gods and humans. The sky god Zeus also had an important 'eye'. Our words to 'watch', 'observe', 'oversee' and 'keep an eye on' all carry the implication of separation from what is being watched, combined with a suggestion of superiority, control and judgment. Separation and control are necessary for manipulation, and it is significant that this faculty of sight has become emphasised in a society based on the manipulation of human and natural resources. The special relationship of twentieth-century capitalist society with the faculty of sight, epitomised in the visual media of film and television, is reflected in Jacques Lacan's concept of the 'Gaze', and is vividly described by Guy Debord in his pamphlet, *Society of the Spectacle*.

If consciousness is to do with control, the eye becomes a suitable symbol for it, and light is necessary for it to operate effectively. That which desires to evade control will come out at night; thus darkness and blackness become seen as potentially subversive. We project consciousness and morality predominantly on to our eyes; the other senses appear to us amorphous, undiscriminating, amoral. So an absence of light can appear to us to mean an absence of consciousness. This bears little relation to experienced reality, in which consciousness can be sustained in darkness: eyesight is the only sense which is impaired in the dark, while the other senses may be heightened to help us experience detail, texture and our own thought processes. It is our overestimation of the power of sight (to the neglect and improverishment of the other senses) that leads us to believe that the dark can offer us nothing but unconsciousness. The result has been a rigid dichotomy in which the unconscious becomes less and less familiar to consciousness. As Jane Roberts points out in *The Nature of Personal Reality*:

> The unknown seems to be threatening and degenerate. The colour black assumes stronger tendencies in its connection with evil . . . Self-annihilation seems to be a threat ever-present in the dream or sleep state. At the same time all of those flamboyant, creative, spontaneous, emotional surges that *emerge* normally from the unconscious become feared and projected outward, then, upon enemies, other races and creeds.

Jane Roberts points out that those who are most afraid of their own sensual natures will consider sexual behaviour depraved:

> They will ascribe it to primitive or evil or unconscious sources, and even attempt to censor their dreams in that regard. They will then project the greatest sexual license upon those groups they choose to represent their own repressed behaviour.

Women are among the groups who have to carry the burden of this projection, and are often attributed possession of the threatening powers of the unconscious.

Thus Jung devotes much of *Symbols of Transformation* to an interpretation of myths such as that of Herakles, doomed to struggle because of the enmity of Hera, as symbolic of the struggle of the sun hero against the night of unconsciousness: 'As a primal being the mother represents the unconscious'. As a psychotherapist Jung stresses the importance of achieving some integration between the conscious and unconscious minds. However, it is hard for a woman to feel encouraged by the role cast for the female in this drama, where the hero's 'great deed' really meant 'overcoming the mother and thus winning immortality'. For the paternal principle, the Logos, 'its first creative act of liberation is matricide'. Jung describes how the sun hero typically journeys by ship, fights a sea monster, is swallowed and struggles against being crushed to death. Often the monster is killed by the hero lighting a fire inside, 'in the very womb of death he secretly creates life, the rising sun'. His victory over the monster represents rebirth from the mother and the conquest of darkness and death: 'the rescue of the hero is at the same time a sunrise, the triumph of consciousness'.

In this struggle for 'deliverance from the mother', Jung does not question the sources of a symbolism whereby the male hero represents the sun and consciousness while the female represents death, darkness and the unconscious. The misogyny implicit in this casting of the female as primitive becomes explicit in comments such as 'it would be easier to keep one's eye on a boxful of spiders than on the females of a primal horde' (*Symbols of Transformation*). While Jung sees a myth such as that of Herakles as universal in significance, Greek history shows us that the myth emerged with the rise of patriarchy, and that many of the creatures Herakles has to fight in his labours (the lion, the birds), and indeed Hera herself, were symbols of the old woman-centred Cretan religion whose defeat by the male hero had a specific social significance. Myth can serve a political function. Jung's interest in this myth should, again, be seen against a specific historical background: that of our twentieth-century patriarchal society where the woman's socially restricted role, centred on the home, identifies her with a limited situation which the male child has to reject in order to take his place as a man in society at large.

To be reminded of the relative nature of such 'sun hero' symbolism, one has only to look to the earlier Aegean Bronze Age symbolism described in Chapter 7, in which the sun was actually identified with the female belly, a belly seen not as a trap or enemy of a male hero but as a source of life and power. Moreover, while the sun of patriarchy shines with the bright eye of midday consciousness, in early Crete the sun was most often shown low, i.e. rising or setting, and its night journey was an integrated part of its whole cycle.

We could perhaps take this as a starting point for a systematic deconstruction of the kind of sun symbolism taken for granted in our culture, epitomised in the writings of Jung. While the dominant patriarchal tradition emphasises the sharp contrast between sun and night, between daylight and darkness, conscious and unconscious, alternative spiritual traditions tend, like the Bronze Age Cretan religion, to focus on the movement between the two and on the phases of transition. Thus Mauss in *A General Theory of Magic* identifies sunset and sunrise as two of the times regarded as favourable for ritual in magical traditions; and the spiritual tradition described by Carlos Castaneda in his 'Don Juan' books ascribes much significance to twilight as the crack between two worlds. We can see that there is an element of choice at work in the notion of conflict between light and darkness, and in the emphasis on polarity rather than the movement between the two.

This symbolism can be deconstructed further. The identification of the sun setting under the earth with the mind sinking into unconsciousness depends on the notion of 'up' and 'down'. And yet in reality the sun does not sink: rather our earth turns laterally away from the sun. Nor is there a lower area in the body where the unconscious might be situated; there are only different states of awareness that humans move between. As Don Juan points out in Castaneda's *The Fire From Within*, to talk about the depths is a figure of speech: in fact there are no depths, there is only the handling of awareness. The Psychosynthesis method has tried to overcome this problem with the concept of a 'superconscious' as well as a 'subconscious', but unfortunately here the vertical symbolism is retained. More helpful is its adoption of the terms 'overt' and 'covert' to avoid tendentious light-dark symbolism.

If the unconscious is not lower, and is not darker, perhaps it is also not worse. In *The Nature of Personal Reality* Jane Roberts stresses that 'You must give up any ideas that you have as to the unsavoury nature of unconscious activity. You must learn to believe in the goodness of your being.' As part of the process of bridging the unnatural polarisation between conscious and unconscious, light and dark, her 'Seth' books present a strong case for changing our present pattern of sleeping up to eight hours in one block. Although difficult to combine with jobs and children, it is suggested that sleeping in smaller units of approximately four hours is not only a more healthy rhythm and one more appropriate to our organism, but is also a means of breaking down the artificial gap between conscious and unconscious and opening up to a fuller awareness of who we are as people. Jane Roberts points out that in our current beliefs consciousness is equated in a very limited way with our concept of intellectual behaviour, which we consider to be the peak of mental achievement, developing from the 'undifferentiated' perceptions of childhood, and returning to them again in old age. She suggests that a four-hourly wake/sleep pattern 'would acquaint you with the great creative and energetic portions of psychological behaviour – that are not undifferentiated at all, but simply distinct from your usual concepts of consciousness; and these operate throughout your life'.

The unconscious, then, is not misty and undirected, but vigorous and informative. Writers on dreams, such as Patricia Garfield and Jean Houston, have enumerated the many creative people who have drawn on their dreams not only for making works of art or literature but for solving mathematical, chemical and technical problems. Meditation teachers stress the difficulties created by letting the conscious take precedence over the unconscious and thus estranging ourselves from our sources of action. Jung emphasises that the power of decision is locked up in the unconscious. If we have thrown away the key, we may be puzzled by our own behaviour sometimes.

In classical antiquity, for example at the Greek temple of Asklepios, incubation, or sleeping in a sanctuary, was used as a way of opening oneself to receive wisdom or healing from the gods. A similar approach to sleep, aimed at gaining illumination from the wisdom of the unconscious, can be tried by lighting a candle (or simply sitting quietly) immediately before sleeping, and asking for help with a particular problem. It may help to repeat aloud, 'I want to know about x and I want to remember it in the morning.' Formulating your intention clearly and concentrating on it is important, as Patricia Garfield explains in *Creative Dreaming*.

Since we can reach the unconscious through a variety of means – drugs, dreams, meditation, psychotherapy – then it is perhaps not really unconscious but rather outside awareness. While different aspects of our being may be more 'overt' or 'covert' at different times, it seems that the polarisation between a bright acceptable 'persona' and a dark unconscious 'shadow' is highly suspect. It may be an accurate description of how people appear, or see themselves, or function, in our society; but we must hesitate before we accept it as an archetypal structure containing a basic truth about the nature of human beings. Jane Roberts' 'Seth' books recognise that we need some differentiation between dream and waking experience to enable us to operate within the narrower focus of daily life, but emphasise the damage caused by the dominant splits in our culture:

Many of your misconceptions about the nature of reality are directly related to the division you place between your sleeping and waking experience, your conscious and unconscious activity. Opposites seem to occur that do not exist in actuality. Myths, symbols and rationalizations all become necessary to explain the *seeming* divergences, the seeming contradictions between realities that appear to be so different. (*The Nature of Personal Reality*)

The book suggests that breaking down the barriers between conscious and unconscious would help to break down certain beliefs in part created by those barriers: 'If the unconscious is no longer feared, then the races that symbolized it are no longer to be feared either.'

What is described here is a two-way process. It is not a matter of trying to commandeer the unconscious, but of listening and learning from it. It is not simply a question of *using* the unconscious for the better living of daily life, but of expanding our idea of what 'living' is, so that it becomes, as Michael A. Daddio has put it, not a 16-hour experience but a 24-hour experience. If we question the splits that trap us, we can break the existing cultural mould and watch our world expand.

Book References

Page numbers relate to passages referred to or quoted, listed in most cases in the order in which they have been used. Where there are numerous references to the same text, or where the context may not be obvious, I have indicated the subject matter.

Assagioli, Robert, *Psychosynthesis: a Manual of Principles and Techniques*, Turnstone Books, London, 1975, pp. 180, 298, 288 (first publ. 1965).
—— 'Symbols of Transpersonal Experiences', Psychosynthesis Research Foundation, New York, 1969.
Barbach, Lonnie Garfield, *For Yourself: The Fulfilment of Female Sexuality*, Signet, NAL, New York, 1975.
Brown, Norman O., *Love's Body*, Random House, New York, 1966, pp. 260, 262.
Castaneda, Carlos, *The Fire From Within*, Black Swan, Transworld, London, Australia and New Zealand, 1985, p. 121.
Channon, Michael, *New Cinema of Latin America Part 2: the Long Road*, documentary film transmitted on Channel Four Television, 17 October 1983.
Chodorow, Nancy, *The Reproduction of Mothering: Psychoanalysis and the Sociology of Gender*, University of California Press, Berkeley, Los Angeles

and London, 1978, pp. 180–90 and *passim*.

Coward, Rosalind, *Female Desire*, Paladin/Granada, London, 1984, p. 15.

Daddio, Michael A., speaking at a Dream Seminar in London, September 1982. For information about Daddio's approach to dreams, contact Life Service Foundation, P.O. Box W, Huntington, NY 11743.

Dalal, Farhad, 'Jung: a Racist', *British Journal of Psychotherapy*, 4 (3) Spring 1988, pp. 263–79; I quote p. 272.

Debord, Guy, *Society of the Spectacle*, 'a Black and Red translation unauthorized', *Radical America*, 4 (5), and Black and Red, Box 9546, Detroit, MI 48202, 1970.

Ernst, Sheila and Lucy Goodison, *In Our Own Hands: a Book of Self-Help Therapy*, The Women's Press, London, 1981, pp. 151–60.

Feinstein, David and Stanley Krippner, *Personal Mythology: the Psychology of Your Evolving Self*, Unwin Paperbacks, London, Sydney, Wellington, 1989.

Ferrucci, Piero, *What We May Be: the Visions and Techniques of Psychosynthesis*, Turnstone Press, Wellingborough, Northants, 1982.

Freud, Sigmund, *Introductory Lectures on Psychoanalysis*, trans. J. Riviere, Allen and Unwin, London, 1922, p. 131 (also publ. Pelican Freud Library, Vol. I., trans. J. Strachey, Penguin, Harmondsworth, Middx, 1974).

Friday, Nancy, *My Secret Garden: Women's Sexual Fantasies*, Virago/Quartet Books, London, 1975; paperback edn 1976, p. 108–9. (first publ. Trident Press, New York, 1973).

Garfield, Patricia L., *Creative Dreaming*, Futura, London, 1976, pp. 37–58, 35–6.

Griffin, Susan, *Made From This Earth: Selections from Her Writing*, The Women's Press, London, 1982, p. 111.

Hall, Calvin S. and Vernon J. Nordby, *The Individual and His Dreams*, Signet Books, New York, 1972, pp. 19ff.

Harding, M. Esther, *Woman's Mysteries: Ancient and Modern*, Harper and Row, New York, 1976, p. 64 (first publ. C.G. Jung Foundation for Analytical Psychology, 1971).

Houston, Jean, in her Foreword to Kathleen Jenks, *Journey of a Dream Animal: a Human Search for Personal Identity*, Julian Press, New York, 1975, pp. xv–xvi.

Jung, C.G., *Symbols of Transformation*, trans. R.F.C. Hull, Routledge and Kegan Paul, London, 1956, pp. 211, 355, 251, 424, 442, 295, 347, 348 (all on struggle of sun-hero to overcome mother/monster/unconscious), 261 (women as spiders), 305 (power of decision in unconscious) (Vol. V of *Collected Works*).

—— *The Archetypes and the Collective Unconscious*, trans. R.F.C. Hull, Routledge and Kegan Paul, London, 1959, p. 96. (Vol. IX, Part I of *Collected Works*).

—— *Memories, Dreams, Reflections*, recorded and edited by Aniela Jaffe, trans.

R. and C. Winston, Collins, London, 1977, pp. 270–1, 298–9 (first publ. in UK by Collins and Routledge and Kegan Paul, 1963).

Lacan, Jacques, *The Language of the Self*, trans. and with notes and commentary by Anthony Ivilden, Johns Hopkins University Press, Baltimore and London, 1968.

Lao Tsu, *Tao Te Ching*, new trans. Gia-fu Feng and Jane English, Wildwood House, London, 1973.

Lehman, J. Lee, 'Lust is Just a Four-letter Word', *Heresies: A Feminist Publication on Art and Politics*, 3 (4/12), 1981 ('Sex' issue), publ, Heresies Collective Inc., P.O. Box 1306, Canal Street Station, New York, NY 10013, p. 81.

Lowen, Alexander, *The Betrayal of the Body*, Collier Macmillan, London and New York, 1969, p. 140.

Mauss, Marcell, *A General Theory of Magic*, trans. R. Brain, Routledge and Kegan Paul, London and Boston, 1972, p. 45 (first publ. Presses Universitaires de France, 1950).

Naranjo, Claudio and Robert E. Ornstein, *On the Psychology of Meditation*, Penguin, Harmondsworth, Middx, 1976 (first publ. Viking, New York, 1971).

Negt, Oskar and Alexander Kluge, *Öffentlichkeit und Erfahrung. Zur Organisationsanalyse von bürgerlicher und proletarischer Öffentlichkeit*, Suhrkamp, Frankfurt am Main, 1974, pp. 72–3. Quoted in Zipes, *Breaking the Magic Spell*, pp. 9–10.

Perls, Frederick S., *Gestalt Therapy Verbatim*, compiled and edited by John O. Stevens, Bantam, Toronto, New York and London, 1971, pp. 275, 61 (first publ. Real People Press, Lafayette, CA, 1969).

Roberts, Jane, *The Nature of Personal Reality*, A Seth Book, Prentice-Hall, NJ, 1974, pp. 309 (unknown/unconscious appear threatening), 310 (unconscious not unsavoury), 301–3 (on changing sleeping patterns), 308 (our limited view of consciousness), 452 (some differentiation needed), 306 (misconceptions from division between sleeping and waking), 304 (if unconscious no longer feared).

Schad-Somers, Susanne P., *Sadomasochism: Etiology and Treatment*, Human Sciences Press, New York, 1982.

Scully, Vincent, *The Earth, the Temple, and the Gods: Greek Sacred Architecture*, Yale University Press, New Haven and London, 1979, Preface to 1979 edition, p. ix (first publ. 1962).

Segal, Lynne, 'Sensual Uncertainty, or Why the Clitoris is Not Enough', in Sue Cartledge and Joanna Ryan (eds) *Sex and Love: New Thoughts on Old Contradictions*, The Women's Press, London, 1983, pp. 44, 43.

Silva, Jorge and Marta Rodríguez, *Nuestra Voz de Memoria, Terra, y Futuro*, film made in Colombia, 1981. See also 'Cine-Sociology and Social Change', in Julianne Burton (ed.) *Cinema and Social Change in Latin America: Conversations with Filmmakers*, University of Texas Press, Austin, 1986,

86

pp. 25–34.

Thorning, Helle, 'The Mother–Daughter Relationship and Sexual Ambivalence', *Heresies: A Feminist Publication on Art and Politics*, 3, (4/12), 1981, ('Sex' issue) publ. Heresies Collective Inc., P.O. Box 1306, Canal Street Station, New York, NY 10013, pp. 3–6.

Vitale, Sylvia Witts, 'A Herstorical Look at Some Aspects of Black Sexuality', *Heresies: A Feminist Publication on Art and Politics*, 3 (4/12), 1981 ('Sex' issue), pp. 63–5.

Von Dürckheim, Karlfried Graf, *Hara: the Vital Centre of Man*, trans. S.-M. von Kospoth, Allen and Unwin, London, Boston and Sydney, 1985, pp. 186 (quoting Okada Torajiro), 157 (first publ. Wilhelm Barth-Verlag, Munich, 1956).

Wallace, Michele, *Black Macho and the Myth of the Superwoman*, Dial Press, New York, 1978, p. 57 and *passim*.

Zipes, Jack, *Breaking the Magic Spell: Radical Theories of Folk and Fairy Tales*, Heinemann, London, 1979, p. 27.

4

DEMYSTIFYING THE OCCULT
Symbols of Alchemy, Tarot, Astrology and the Astral

There are more things in heaven and earth, Horatio,
Than are dreamt of in your philosophy.
(William Shakespeare, *Hamlet*, Act I sc. v.)

O nobly-born, whatever fearful and terrifying visions thou
mayst see, recognize them to be thine own thought-forms.
(*The Tibetan Book of the Dead*, ed. W.Y. Evans-Wentz)

At each turning point we have a chance either to make a new
myth for ourselves or to follow an old one.
(Stanley Keleman, *Living Your Dying*)

One of the most damaging myths we have inherited is that 'spirit' is
pure while 'matter' is impure; that 'up' is good, while the natural
world at our feet is inferior, base or evil. Life, and the sun high in
the sky, are 'male', while woman symbolises the nature and death
which our male-dominated society shuns. Again, this split reflects and
endorses the male/female stereotypes in our society.

This split has a specific history. Bronze Age Cretan religion seemed
to focus on what was 'on the ground', revering the plants, animals and
creatures which inhabited the physical terrain (see Chapter 7). The
subordination of women and the denial of the body, in early Greek
patriarchy, were paralleled by a growing emphasis on abstract, sky-
dwelling divinities. The philosophy of Plato crystallises the elevation
of the pure 'Idea' over the world of matter. As man became more
alienated from his own nature, so he became more alienated from the
world of nature in general. The centuries of the classical era witness
a gradual turning away from the natural world. It was a slow process.

In the early centuries AD Stoicism was a serious rival to Christianity, offering a sense of spirit in matter and a model of courage which could bridge 'the cleavage between reason and desire' (as Paul Tillich describes in *The Courage To Be*). But it was the dualistic traditions of Platonism which prevailed, via Neoplatonism and Christianity, to institutionalise a conflict between the reasonable and the sensual. God is high, noble, spiritual, pure and white, while the 'forces of darkness' below are base and material. But just as the physical is mis-recognised by being imagined as dark, so spirit is mis-recognised by being seen as all light. What is excluded is always jostling round the edges threatening to come in. Divorced from its body, the head becomes macabre. By its very emphasis on light (and hence its obsession with driving out darkness) the Church itself can take on a sinister aspect. No doubt the white light of holy inspiration shone fiercely in the eyes of the Spanish Inquisition torturers as they dedicated themselves to performing 'God's work' by punishing the flesh. By seeing nature as dark and dangerous, we can become blinded to the real sources of human violence and suffering. As Susan Griffin points out in *Made From This Earth*, we consider certain behaviours and events in our civilisation, such as rape or the Holocaust, as the result of something sinister in human nature which causes violence: 'We have blamed a decision made by human culture on our own natures, and thus on nature.' In fact, she suggests, the blame lies rather with those elements we regard as civilised: 'culture has opposed itself in violence to the natural, and takes revenge on nature'.

Although traditional religion has been eroded by science, our underlying symbolic splits have not changed substantially: we have instead a substitute formulation of pure white rationalism embattled against the forces of the 'irrational' or the 'animal' in human nature.

This is a loss. The denial of the physical world cuts us off from sources of regeneration in ourselves and in the world around us. In our post-Christian, post-scientific culture, we have little vocabulary with which to articulate the sense of communion we may experience on a walk through a forest, or the deep satisfaction we may derive from an exquisite back-rub. The deep divide between spirit and matter, between rational and irrational, leaves such experiences lost in a kind of limbo.

Polarity, or duality, is part of our cultural heritage and it has been fruitful as a way of perceiving the world, and of developing ideas. William Blake saw it as a force at work around him, and in 'The Marriage of Heaven and Hell' he cites the arguments for seeing it as a positive factor: 'Without Contraries is no progression. Attraction and Repulsion, Reason and Energy, Love and Hate, are necessary to Human existence.' Marx galvanised and revolutionised historical thought by suggesting that history unfolds through social forces interacting in a dialectical process: thesis, antithesis, synthesis. As a tool, the mode of duality is a useful one, particularly for the accurate description of the dynamics and development of our divided society and our divided selves.

It is, however, only one tool. Different societies have created different tools. Meditative techniques shaped by eastern traditions provide a possibility for us to approach the physical world in a less divided way. We can also turn to symbolic systems which have survived from earlier Mediterranean cultures, preserving elements of alternative Christian, and non-Christian, traditions; some of those traditions may be traced as far back as the ancient Greek society I described in Chapter 7. Though banished by Christianity, they have survived on its underbelly, often in forms distorted by centuries of repression, but still offering some kind of alternative to the dominant dualism. In the traditions of alchemy, astrology and the Tarot, for example, duality is not such a fundamental principle; we can turn to these disciplines in our process of forming new patterns of thought, fantasy and understanding.

These alternative symbolic systems are viewed very differently by different people, and this can affect how we work with them. Some followers of Jung and of Psychosynthesis, as well as some members of occult schools, would argue that the symbols of astrology, alchemy and the Tarot are already imprinted on our psyche as part of our collective unconscious. Some writers even affirm that they are the reflection of archetypes which have an independent prior existence; as such they need only to be unearthed and reactivated by our conscious minds in order to be recognised and used in our dream life. Another argument is that they have no prior existence but that we inherit them as part of our make-up along with other cultural baggage. Others argue only that our fantasy life is highly suggestible and the unconscious is extraordinarily sensitive in picking up symbols that are present in the conscious mind. By making ourselves familiar with these alternative symbols in our conscious life, we make them available for the unconscious mind to use in dreams and fantasies. This is my own approach. Liz Greene, in *Relating*, suggests that because we no longer believe in gods or dreams we have lost touch with one of the most valuable forms of contact with 'the ceaselessly changing and creative roots of our being'. She stresses that 'ultra-civilised as we are and so near self-strangulation by our own cleverness, our need is all the greater for vital symbolic alphabets'. I see such traditions as providing rich and varied symbolic alphabets which we can use.

I shall briefly discuss these alternative traditions and give relevant exercises.

The Alchemical Tradition

One such alphabet derives from alchemy, a tradition which presents an unorthodox view of the natural world. Whereas conventional Christianity sharply separates spirit and matter, the alchemical process works with the divine *in* matter.

Alchemy originally emerged in the second and third centuries BC, both in the Far East, especially China, and in the west, especially Alexandria, where the classical Greek and Egyptian worlds blended in a cultural melting-pot. While the eastern alchemical tradition survived more or less continuously, in the west it declined and from the fifth century AD was preserved within Arab culture, from which the Christian world relearnt it in about the twelfth century AD. Its heyday in Europe was from then until the seventeenth century, during which time it enjoyed a varied reputation, sometimes aligning itself with the Christian tradition, approved by kings and emperors, sometimes banned as an occult art.

The alchemical *opus*, or work, takes place on two levels. On one it is a series of chemical experiments aimed at producing the 'Philosophers' Stone', sometimes called the 'Tincture' or 'Elixir' which could turn base metal into gold. Simultaneously, it is a philosophical or religious search for spiritual 'gold'. The stages of the operation are variously listed as including Sublimation, Descension, Distillation, Calcination, Solution, Coagulation, Fixation, Ceration, Separation, Conjunction, Putrefaction, Cibation, Fermentation, Exaltation, and Multiplication. These are both physical processes and phases of psychic transformation: for example, *calcinatio* is literally burning by fire but is also compared to the 'furnace of affliction' through which Jesus had to pass, and which precedes the alchemist's spiritual death and regeneration. Alchemy thus provides a model for the integration of the practical and the spiritual: god is not separate from matter and flesh but embodied in it. In many cases alchemical texts use symbols which can be interpreted on both a laboratory and a personal level, and it is unclear how the two processes were combined, or how much the one was a metaphor for the other. We do know that the disciplines of chemistry and philosophy were not separate, and that physical processes were recognised as imbued with a metaphorical or philosophical significance. Currently, in the new science, these now separate disciplines are converging again (see Chapter 6), and several of the new psychotherapies stress how closely the physical, emotional and spiritual are melded in the make-up of human beings (see Chapter 5).

The alchemical *opus*, or process of transformation, conceives as its raw material (*prima materia*) matter which others would despise or discard, such as lead, excrement or earth. These substances are not denigrated as heavy, inferior or disgusting, but rather are seen as both very base and sublime at the same time. The alchemists saw the earth as a living organism in a constant state of change and growth: for them there was no such thing as 'dead matter'. Their task, then, was to work with the seeds of transformation contained within all matter, even starting in the gutter. As Cherry Gilchrist puts it in *Alchemy*:

Transformation does not come about by mixing or combining substances. It comes primarily through purifying and perfecting the original material. This is a declaration of faith, that the divine spark dwells in every single atom that exists, however corrupt and base it may appear to our eyes.

Transformation is thus something intrinsic, and the symbol used for this process of transformation in matter and consciousness is the Greek god of communication, Mercury, who is described in alchemical texts as both the highest and the lowest, the lightest and the heaviest, the sublime and the *terminus ani* (end of the anus). The alchemists' God is ambivalent, androgynous, and contains both light and darkness. In the process of transformation, death and decomposition are important elements. Unlike the modern notion of the 'objective' scientist, the alchemist was encouraged to be an active participant in his investigations on the path to knowledge. The ultimate goal is not to move away from earthly concerns, but rather to bring heaven and earth together.

Cherry Gilchrist points out that some eminent scientists, such as Robert Boyle and Sir Isaac Newton, were alchemists whose alchemical work influenced and assisted their contributions to the development of modern science. However, the successful discoveries made by alchemists in their search for the 'Stone' or 'Elixir' have been kept a secret from the uninitiated. We will see later how their theories resonate with ideas emerging from the new science and from modern practitioners of healing and esoteric anatomy. What interests me here is the symbolism used to describe the process. Jung revived modern interest in alchemy when he pointed out how its various stages parallel the stages of transformation often experienced by those undergoing analytical psychotherapy. In psychotherapy, as in alchemy, the starting point is often the 'negative': the individual's neurosis, depression, problems or difficulties, from which she moves into a process of change. Like the alchemist, the individual is aspiring to a higher consciousness or internal unity. Alchemy provides a rich source of symbolism which bridges the traditional split between spirit and matter, up and down, superior and inferior. Alchemical procedures do not develop primarily through interaction between two sides of a polarised duality. In fact, one of the main symbolic frameworks is fourfold, based on the notion of the four natural elements.

The Four Elements

The Greek philosopher Empedocles was already writing about the four elements in the fifth century BC, and they survived as significant factors within the alchemical tradition. The elements – earth, air, fire and water – are associated with four significant stages in the alchemist's work: *calcinatio* or healing/burning in a vessel called an alembic; *solutio* which is another way of breaking down the raw material by dissolution in liquid; *coagulatio* which is the reforming of the transformed material in solid shape; and *sublimatio* which is the crystallising out or manifestation of the spiritual essence of the transformed material. Translated into psychological or religious terms, these processes are not moral ones aimed at 'cleansing sin', rather they are aimed at teaching the individual to accept her/his own sin and ambivalence, and at enabling elements within the individual to become conscious. Without taking the four elements and the four stages too literally, we can draw on them as a resource offering symbols for sexuality and spirituality which are different from those of our dominant symbol system. Let's take them one by one.

Symbolism of fire has taken many forms – see Gaston Bachelard's classic *The Psychoanalysis of Fire*. In alchemical imagery, the fire of *calcinatio* can be a symbol of fever, rage, raw desire, yearning or lust and also of erotic longing for God. The process of *calcinatio* is always seen as sealed in a container: in the laboratory process it is a sealed vessel, the alembic, while in the process of psychoanalysis it could be seen as the confidential and structurally contained relationship between client and analyst. The material burns yet cannot escape, and the purification is effected through this contained burning. Liz Greene, lecturing on 'Living Alchemy', has compared this phase to staying in a difficult relationship or situation and working problems through, rather than leaving and running for relief which is comparable to 'breaking the alembic'. The burning, in traditional alchemical imagery, is linked to other symbols such as blood, the desert, lion, battle and sacrifice. What is particularly interesting for us here is that fire is not, as in Christian symbolism, primarily a symbol of lust, sin or hell. Rather it is a phase or mode of being which can relate *either* to sexual *or* to spiritual impulses. The quality of the energy and of the process is what is important, rather than the ostensible object to which that energy is directed.

Solutio is seen as a process of change which can precede, follow or replace the ordeal by fire. In this case the agent of change is water, and the energy or impulse, instead of burning, dissolves into emotion. Change comes through dissolution or merging. One image offered by alchemy is of the 'Old King' (representing rigidity, the old personality and old patterns) drowning. Other associated images are of bliss, waves, bondage, slavery and passivity. A psychological parallel lies in regressive emotional states and early childhood scenes of a 'primal' nature which offer in some way the opportunity to be reborn or to reform differently. 'Dissolve and coagulate' was one of the alchemists' maxims. What is interesting here is that this image of transformation by water has been linked by modern interpreters like Liz Greene with drug or alcohol experiences, with falling in love and with a religious or mystical sense of communion. In other words, the tradition again allows its image to be interpreted as an energy which may be either sexual or spiritual.

Here is a personal account from a woman who used ideas about the water element to deal with a sexual and emotional problem:

'I had recurrent cystitis, which I noticed often came on when I let myself feel open, intimate and vulnerable with a sexual partner. On those occasions I felt rather like a baby with very strong emotional needs. It was terrifying. During one severe cystitis attack I dreamt that I was on a steeply sloping beach known to me from my childhood, and my mother was sliding down and pulling me into the sea. I was swept away, far from the shore and rescue. Reading somewhere that the bladder was associated with the water 'element' and that in addition to its physical function it had a psychological function of keeping us from 'drowning in our emotions', I wondered if my cystitis complaint had psychological causes as well as physical ones. In addition to seeking medical help, I joined a co-counselling course and found that releasing emotions in the group really helped to ease the tension in my bladder. It was as if I had been afraid of being overwhelmed by my feelings and had been trying to hold them all in with my bladder. After the cystitis attack had passed, I also found it helpful to go swimming regularly. I focused on 'going with the flow' in my movements through the water (rather than counting how many lengths I had swum) and I found that after a while I could sometimes put my head under water, which previously I had been scared to do.

This account of a woman's process of change shows clear affinities with the alchemical process of *solutio* or transformation by dissolution in water. In his *Introductory Lectures* Freud suggested that birth was always represented by water in dreams; and esoteric traditions often link water to birth experience and the early relationship with the mother. In this woman's dream, there is a return to childhood and to the close, dissolving physical intimacy of the mother-daughter relationship, which the dreamer's adult self both wants and fears. Emotional control and emotional flow go together: if there is no control there can be no flow, but rather outbursts, floods, drying-up, desperate attempts to dam the tide when it is too late, and so on. Lacking any deep-seated confidence that she could regulate her powerful emotions – which probably dated back to childhood – this woman panicked when she had had strong feelings. Cystitis – an ailment which causes pain and difficulty in containing and releasing urine and can prevent love-making – may have been at least in part a reaction. The theme of water provided a key to tackling her ailment. In addition to the approaches she tried, this woman might also be helped by using appropriate symbols for visualisation. For example, the fear of water, reflecting a fear of being overwhelmed, could be addressed by imagining herself in a sailing boat in very shallow water and gradually increasing the depth daily.

After *calcinatio* and *solutio* there may occur in the alchemical process an interlude or hiatus known as *nigredo*, or blackness. Everything stops, seems to die, and disappears from sight. This could parallel the phases of depression which often occur when individuals experience changes either as a result of psychotherapy or in the transition from one phase of life to another. In the alchemical vocabulary, this stopping is seen as a necessary part of spiritual development. The phase of *nigredo* is associated with images of depression, burial, death, rotting or putrefaction. But whereas Christian symbolism contrasts the corruption of matter with the purity of God, the alchemical tradition asserts that 'this too is God'. I am reminded of the emphasis placed by the Psychosynthesis method on *using* what seems to be negative – embodied in the instructions to 'Bless the obstacle' and 'Turn the shit into manure'.

The next alchemical stage, *coagulatio*, involves the 'earthing' or grounding of the material in concrete form. The personality regroups; the changed entity now starts slowly to solidify in new form. Symbolic associations are with spiders, the spinning of fate, pregnancy, eating, traps, entombment. Issues linked with this phase concern limitations, separation, and the creative process which gives an experience material form.

The last stage, *sublimatio*, the manifestation of the spiritual essence from matter, could be read into this experience described by a man:

> I left my job and entered a phase of involvement with spiritual disciplines. I ate vegetarian food and did meditation regularly. I became involved in transpersonal psychology and did many guided fantasies on my own. The talisman that emerged for me during this period was a white bird. I used this symbol frequently in the fantasies. I felt I had moved on to an entirely new level. I afterwards went into a deep depression.

Here we see several common features of the phase of *sublimatio*, which is linked symbolically with elements like cold, bird, wind, wings, exorcism and mountain. Qualities of indifference, detachment and non-identification are associated with it. Whereas the stages of *calcinatio* and *solutio* may be induced by contact with a person, and *coagulatio* by the pressure of a situation, *sublimatio* is often entered, as in this case, through contact with teachings. Although *sublimatio* appears closer to the conventional Christian symbolism of achieving a spiritual goal at the end of the line, this way of understanding it is misleading. The freed spirit is seen by the alchemist as needing to remarry with matter; witness this individual's soaring 'high', followed by a slump into depression. Ascent is followed by descent as the qualities of the 'higher' levels are brought to the 'lower'. As Ralph Metzner puts it in *Maps of Consciousness*, in alchemy, 'The integration of levels of consciousness was seen . . . as the spirit becoming body and the body becoming spiritualized.' The stages of the alchemical process can be followed in any order or round and round, linking spirit always with matter and without any linear progression upwards to the kingdom of heaven. It refuses to fit in with conventional Christian symbolism.

In this brief account of some of the alchemical stages, I gave a specific example only for *solutio*-water, but any of these phases or elements can be approached using the techniques described in Chapter 3: acting out a dream element, meditating on a related symbol or holding a dialogue with the symbol.

Various attempts have been made to provide a chemical or physical basis for the symbolism of the 'four elements'. For example, Ralph Metzner has pointed out that 99 per cent of the atoms of proteins, which are the chief ingredient of living matter, are made up of the elements of carbon, oxygen, hydrogen and nitrogen, which could be seen as corresponding to the four elements. Cherry Gilchrist, in *Alchemy*, points out that 'All theories of the basic composition of matter are in time superseded, but each contains a certain understanding of the laws of nature, even if in an incomplete form.' The theory of the four elements could thus be seen as an inchoate antecedent of modern science. In a more symbolic vein, esoteric anatomy has correlated the four elements with different aspects of the physical body. The earth element has been linked to the base of the body, the legs, bones, muscles and cells. Water has been linked to the area of the belly, to emotional experience, to glandular systems and the conduction of energy as well as to the 70 per cent of liquid which makes up the body mass in blood, lymph, hormones and the fluid in cells. Fire has been linked to the perceptual aspect of our being, to the nervous system as well as to the solar plexus area and the process of digestion and purification of energy. Air has been linked to mental functions, to brain systems as well as to the breath and inspiration.

While partial attempts at scientific explanation for the 'four elements' are interesting, and the long history of these ideas may impress us, it is important to remember that there is nothing inevitable about any of these symbols. We can test them against our experience, use them when they are helpful, and abandon or transform them when they become a limitation.

Here are two relevant exercises on the four elements.

The Phoenix from the Flames

This is a meditation which explores the purifying and transforming qualities attributed to fire.

The phoenix is a fabulous bird connected with the worship of the sun in Ancient Egypt. At death it was believed to be consumed by, and then reborn from, fire. It is one of alchemy's symbols for transformation.

Sit (or lie) comfortably with back and neck straight but relaxed, arms and knees uncrossed. Close your eyes and breathe evenly for a few moments.

Now picture a fire, any kind of fire. Notice what it is like and where. Let yourself imagine its heat and burning power. (Pause.)

Now let yourself think of three things in your life which you no longer need; they may be qualities, activities or relationships. Choose the first three things which come to mind. (Pause.)

Now imagine putting those things on the fire. How do you feel about losing them? Watch them disappear. (Pause.)

Now inside the heart of the fire they are turning to something else, something or things you *do* need in your life. Having let go of them, something new can come into your life. That thing you *do* need is rising like a phoenix from the flames. What is it? (Pause.)

Imagine what it would be like to have that thing you *do* need in your life. (Pause.)

Slowly open your eyes and come back to the present.

To turn this meditation into a ritual, you could actually light a fire and, after taking some minutes to focus your attention, write on separate pieces of paper the names of the three things you would like to release from your life. Then, taking the pieces of paper one by one, read them aloud and place them on the fire. Diane Mariechild, in *Mother·Wit*, describes a similar ritual called 'Ritual to Release Fears or Negative Feelings.'

For the meditation (or ritual) to work, it is very important that you do not have a rejecting attitude towards the things which you are releasing. Rejection involves putting emotional energy into something and thus creates an attachment, which is the opposite of letting go. The only way to release anything or anybody is to 'kiss it goodbye'.

Following a Stream

This is a guided fantasy based on one in Assagioli's book *Psychosynthesis*; it provides a way to use water as a symbol to find out about yourself.

Sit or lie comfortably, with back and neck straight and arms and knees uncrossed. Shut your eyes. Relax. Breathe evenly for a few moments.

Imagine you are following the course of a stream.

Notice how wide, and how deep the stream is.

Are there any obstacles hindering the flow of the stream? What are they?

How turbulent or calm is the stream?

How clear or cloudy is it?

Carry on following the stream, and see what happens.

After five minutes, open your eyes and slowly return to the present.

Spend some time thinking, or talking with a friend, about how the different aspects of your stream might symbolise different aspects of your life.

(Assagioli suggests that the stream will reflect the individual's libido, as 'deep' or 'narrow'; that obstacles symbolise conflicts or problems of which the individual is unconsciously aware; that turbulence reflects disturbance over these conflicts; and clarity of water awareness. However, it is important that you should primarily make your own associations about what the symbols of the fantasy mean for you, and use others' ideas and interpretations only where they feel relevant.)

Trying Out the Tarot

The four suits of the Tarot deck (which correspond to the four suits of the playing cards in general use today) are linked with the same four elements of fire, water, earth and air. Interpretations vary, but in the symbol system of the Tarot, 'rods' or 'wands' ('clubs' as we know them) are the fire suit, linked with work and creativity; 'cups' ('hearts') are the water symbol, linked with love, pleasure, feeling, sensitivity and fertility; 'swords' ('spades') are the air suit, linked with stress, strife and intellect; 'coins', sometimes known as 'pentacles' or 'discs' ('diamonds') are the earth suit, symbolising money, stability or burdens.

This symbolism, which has been relegated to the area of the occult, sometimes seems to hold a certain resonace for us, even if we have no knowledge of the Tarot. Figures like the elusive Jack of Diamonds and the powerful Queen of Spades feature in songs and card games. In the actual Tarot deck, there are particular characteristics and significances attached to each number card of the four suits, as well as to the 'Major Arcana' figures which stand outside the suits. The 'Major Arcana' includes cards with names like 'The Empress', 'The Fool', 'Fortitude', 'The Sun', 'The Devil', 'The Lovers' and so on. They can be understood as symbols representing tools and methods of psychic transformation. When the Tarot is used, the dealer spreads a certain number of cards. Then, on the basis of the cards which happen to have been dealt, she tells the 'fortune' by relating their known meanings to issues in the life of the person concerned. Equally, you can deal the cards and make a reading for yourself.

The question again arises of where we should locate the origin of the 'Major Arcana' figures, and of the 'four elements' symbolism which occurs in both alchemy and the Tarot. The deep resonance which some people experience with these symbols has been taken as proof that they are in some way archetypal or innate in us. I would question this. One of the problems created by the modern western over-emphasis on 'rationality' is that its very denial of alternative spiritual traditions leaves people susceptible to being drawn towards a superstitious belief in the 'occult'. Again, it is important to look closely at the history of the various 'occult' systems, and their specific cultural application over a geographically limited area. Then we can appreciate that they do not have a universal validity which commands *belief*, but rather provide specific relevant symbols which we can *use*. It has been suggested, for example by Paul Huson in his book on Tarot, *The Devil's Picture Book*, that the cards of the Major Arcana indicate stages in a process of death and rebirth based on ancient Greek mystery religions. The cards' symbolism certainly seems to draw on Greek and Roman sources, as reflected in Gnostic traditions, but the exact line of inheritance is hard to trace. The cards' first appearance in Europe seems to have been around the fourteenth century, when they were in use both for games of chance and for divination. The court cards bear obvious parallels to the social structures of medieval feudalism, and early commentators linked the four suits with social classes (the wand representing the peasant or agriculture, the cup standing for the clergy, the sword for the warrior and money for commerce). The imagery of the Major Arcana seems to reflect a complex process of cross-fertilisation between different symbolic traditions over many hundreds of years, marrying symbols from late classical antiquity with those from the Christian tradition. As such these symbols are not mystically pre-ordained, but are part of our cultural heritage, absorbed unconsciously by us from an early age and corresponding closely with the other cultural forms and imagery through which we interpret our experience.

The process of fortune reading with the Tarot cards could thus be understood as follows. The richly evocative images on the dealt cards are the trigger for the reader's intuitive and perceptive powers to come into play to elucidate issues in the seeker's life. Jung, in *Symbols of Transformation*, has pointed out that we know far more than we realise about the present, and, if we can gain access to that knowledge, it provides pointers towards likely possibilities in the future. In so far as tomorrow is already contained in today, a better knowledge of the present facilitates some prognosis of the future. We have seen that dream and fantasy states can help give us access to this kind of unconscious knowledge, and that symbols can provide a useful channel for it to take shape. The cards, with their powerful history and associations, which resonate strongly with the unconscious of the reader, act as a bridge between the unconscious and conscious, and thus open up her ability to draw on the usually inaccessible wisdom of the unconscious. As such they are a tool which many feminists have found helpful. Marge Piercy has described using the Tarot often for herself, 'to meditate and try to understand my own life'. The riddle of how the cards work lies, as Juliet Sharman-Burke has pointed out, in the mind of the reader rather than in the cards themselves: 'The images act as mirrors which offer a reflection of unsuspected knowledge buried deep in the unconscious mind . . . Answers and knowledge arise out of the unconscious thought dream, fantasy and intuition, and the Tarot cards stimulate this intuition when sensitively read' (*The Complete Book of Tarot*). Magic there may be in the process, but the magic lies in the reader, not in the symbols themselves. Feminists have felt free to add to, or rediscover in, the Tarot cards symbols which reflect imagery of female power. Alternative symbolic traditions like the Tarot are there for us to embrace and draw on if we wish; however, we do not need to believe that these traditions, any more than the Christian ones, are beyond questioning, re-examining, and transforming.

Here is a basic exercise to try out the Tarot.

Tuning in to the Tarot

This is a preliminary approach to the Tarot symbols which is suggested by Ralph Metzner in *Maps of Consciousness*.

Simply look through the Tarot pack and pick out one card to which you have a strong positive or negative reaction.

Pin up that card at home, in a place where you will see it frequently during the day. At the end of a week, take it down and note the emotional reactions, associations or chains of thought it has triggered for you during that time. Notice too how your attitude towards the card has changed from your initial response.

You could try this with several of the cards in turn. Becoming very familiar with the cards is an essential prerequisite to using them to stimulate your intuition in a reading.

Sexing the Stars: Problems with the Sun and Moon in Tarot and Astrology

The symbolism of the sun and moon is a topic which will recur throughout this book.

In the Tarot, 'The Moon' is a female card. Writers in this field have connected the phases of the moon with the three phases of the 'Great Goddess'. The ancient goddesses Persephone, Artemis, Athena, Demeter, Hecate, Diana, Isis and Astarte have variously been linked with her changing phases. In the Tarot, the moon is linked with water and with qualities of fluctuation, inconstancy, deception, intuition and the occult. As Paul Huson points out, in traditions of practical witchcraft, moon magic has been associated with the use of mirrors, crystals and glass, which reflect the moon. A common allegation against witches was that they could 'draw down the moon' from the sky. The sun, on the other hand, has been linked to male gods such as Mithras, Helios and Apollo. Other common occult associations of the sun are with kingship, gold and fire, and with qualities like rebirth, success, joy and abundance. Occult rituals in past centuries may have included focusing the midday sun to kindle fire, and using fire for purification. Alchemy, as well as the Tarot, presents the sun as a masculine and the moon as a feminine symbol.

Consistent with these sun/moon associations, the fourfold symbolisms of fire, water, earth and air is generally divided in the symbolism of alchemy and the Tarot into a polarised grouping, where fire and air are masculine elements, while earth and water are female. Thus we are back to the same old duality: men are power, dynamism, regality and spirit while women are earthy and watery, linked with sexuality, material concerns, changeability and emotionality.

The symbolism of astrology also uses the fourfold classification of earth, air, fire and water, and all the signs of the zodiac are assigned to one of these four elements. Consistent with the ideas of Jung, humanistic astrology suggests that people belong primarily to one of these 'types': either 'fire-intuitive', 'air-thinking', 'water-feeling' or 'earth-sensation'. But again, we find that this four-way symbolism can get pushed into the duality mould. And again in astrology we find a masculine sun.

Jung has been very influential in embracing some of these alternative traditions such as alchemy and astrology, and giving them a modern psychological relevance and credibility. His identification of the sun and fire as masculine is frequent and explicit. Thus in *Symbols of Transformation* he writes: 'The visible father of the world is the sun, the heavenly fire, for which reason father, God, sun, and fire are mythologically synonymous . . . in worshipping the sun's strength we pay homage to the great generative force . . .' The sun and male principle are thus identified with the creative life force: 'the sun is the father-god from whom all living things draw life; he is the fructifier and creator, the source of energy for our world'. And again, 'The psychic life-force, the libido, symbolizes itself in the sun or personifies itself in figures of heroes with solar attributes'.

In contrast, the darkness from which the sun rises is seen as female. In Chapter 3 I mentioned Jung's concern with the 'fight of the sun-hero with the "whale dragon" who . . . is a symbol of the Terrible Mother, . . . the jaws of death'. The sun-hero's weapon is fire, because 'Fire-making is a pre-eminently conscious act and therefore "kills" the dark state of union with the mother'. Such symbolism is assigned primordial origins: 'The sun, rising triumphant, tears himself from the enveloping womb of the sea . . . This image is undoubtedly a primordial one'. With his assimilation of the sun to the father and the archetypal image of the 'animus', the moon to the mother and the 'anima', Jung has woven this symbolism into the fabric of his psychological theories about the make-up and development of human beings. Such symbolism has in turn been incorporated into the thinking of many modern psychotherapists.

In humanistic astrology such symbolism has important implications for the interpretations that astrologers are likely to make about the personalities and behaviour of women. In a natal horoscope the sun is seen as the self and the realisation of the self, the circle symbolising wholeness. As Liz Greene describes in *Relating*, it is seen as an active principle linked with will and consciousness. The female moon, on the other hand, is seen as the urge to unconsciousness, the secure womb, instinct, emotionality and merging of identity. It has important implications for women that the symbol of their self is seen as masculine. Liz Greene warns: 'In a woman's horoscope, therefore, the sun often suggests what she seeks from the masculine side of life, and from her men, in order to complete herself'. This symbolism defines identity as a male element and thus condemns a woman to finding herself through men and the 'male'. It reflects little advance from old-fashioned astrology, typified by Ingrid Lind's comment in *Astrology and Commonsense* that 'Leo is a positive, masculine sign and women Leos have to be careful not to be over-dominating'. It is hard to imagine the effect for women of finding the self and self-fulfilment embodied only in male symbols, such as the hero, and the possibility of wholeness denied except through a man.

So what is the basis for the symbolic sun/moon associations which have such far-reaching implications? Where is the evidence that a male sun is a 'primordial' symbol? Jung found his evidence in the similarity between the dreams and fantasies of disturbed twentieth-century psychotherapy patients and the religious symbolism of ancient and distant societies. In *Symbols of Transformation* he quotes patients' statements that 'God pierces the earth with his ray' and 'Jesus Christ has shown me his love by tapping at the window with a sunbeam'. In *The Archetypes and the Collective Unconscious* he also refers to a schizophrenic patient who asked him to look at the sun, saying, 'Surely you see the sun's penis – when I move my head to and fro it moves too, and that is where the wind comes from'. Later Jung came across the text of a Mithraic ritual which described a tube hanging down from the sun's disc, associated with the wind. He concluded that such archetypal images were innate, and his research produced other correspondences from patients unlikely to have assimilated such symbolism from a classical education.

This is where we need to draw a deep breath and look again to the early Aegean material discussed in Chapter 7. Astrology is a tradition with a history, a history which extends far beyond the first century

Fig 1   Fig 2   Fig 3

Our twentieth-century astrological symbols, Aries to Pisces (Figure 3) have reached us via the Egyptian zodiac symbols (Figure 2) from the Babylonians who developed astrology from the third and second millennia BC onwards. But notice the similarity to some of the most popular symbols of the Bronze Age Aegean in the second millennium BC (Figure 1). We know the people of the Aegean had some contact with the Babylonians, suggesting that the symbols were a common repertoire in the Mediterranean area at that time. But modern astrologers might be surprised to learn that in the Aegean many of those same symbols had a different, woman-orientated, meaning. So perhaps their value has been fluid, rather than fixed, over the intervening centuries?

AD when the Mithraic religion spread through the Roman Empire. Astrology began in the Near East, in the temples of Mesopotamia, from where it spread to Egypt. It is generally thought to have had no great influence on classical Greek life until late antiquity, but it is interesting that the Babylonian astrologers were charting out the zodiac constellations and assigning symbols to them during the third and second millennia BC; zodiac symbols may be identifiable on Babylonian cylinder seals from c.2000 BC onwards (see Frankfort's *Cylinder Seals*). This was contemporary with the early Cretans who, we know, had varying degrees of contact with the Near East during that period (see my book *Death, Women and the Sun*). In Chapter 7 I present evidence that these early Cretans practised sun worship, indicating an interest in the stars, and there is a correlation between the iconography used to depict the sun in the Near East and the Aegean during the period. It is also interesting that many of the predominant symbols in early Crete are identical with the zodiac symbols: the goat, the lion, the scorpion, the fishes, the scales, the bull. We can perhaps even find a (more tenuous) correspondence in Cretan pictures of the woman carrying a bough, twinned male figures and an emphasis on water-carrying (corresponding to Virgo, Gemini and Aquarius?). Figures 1-3 show some of these correspondences. With this number of overlaps, and the other evidence of cultural contact, we cannot assume that the symbolic correspondences are due to coincidence. All these symbols arose from the same pool of eastern Mediterranean cultures during the same period. It would be a surprise to many astrologers to know, as suggested in Chapter 7, that in the Aegean area in that period the sun was female. And what would they make of the evidence that the lion, traditionally associated in astrology with the fierce heat of the summer sun, was linked with the sun in Aegean symbolism of that period, and was itself also predominantly a female symbol? What Jung fails to notice is that his examples of male sun symbolism all come from the era of patriarchy. In the pre-patriarchal era neither lion nor sun were exclusively male symbols. We cannot therefore assume that a male sun shone at the foundations of astrology.

Nor has the underworld always been female. In Early Iron Age Greece the myth of Persephone tells of a female deity violently separated from her mother by Hades, the god of the underworld, who carries her below against her will. No sign here of a male hero trapped in the maw of the 'Terrible Mother'-night-underworld. Rather we have a heroine trapped in a male Hell. The stories of the male 'sun' hero which Jung stresses came later, along with the patriarchy whose values they reflect.

The mythological and archetypal underpinnings of Jung's sun/moon symbolism are thus seen to be shaky. What of the psychological underpinnings? Humanistic astrologers have given male/female, sun/moon symbolism a psychological ratification by linking it to Jung's ideas of the 'animus' and the 'anima'. Jung proposed that the 'animus' and 'anima' were archetypal principles representing the masculine and feminine principles within each individual. Thus each woman is seen as containing a 'male' side, and each man as possessing a 'female' side. This is an acceptable idea in itself until one learns that the 'animus' is primarily concerned with thinking and the 'anima' with feeling. The woman who has too much 'animus' is described as an unpleasant spectacle, dogmatic and competitive; while the man with too much 'anima' is described by Jung as 'touchy, irritable, moody, jealous, vain, and unadjusted' (*The Archetypes and the Collective Unconscious*). In other words, it is seen as grotesque and a psychological aberration for women to assume to any strong degree the qualities which society has decreed belong to men, and vice versa. Apart from being restrictive for heterosexual women and men, such thinking provides no recognition of the experience of lesbians and homosexuals whose relationships do not fit into conventional male/female patterns. These polarities of 'anima' and 'animus' can provide a rationalisation for the prejudice and homophobia that fears any behaviour or relationship outside the 'norms'.

Some Jungians stress that 'animus' and 'anima' relate not to male and female qualities but to male and female *principles* which are quite distinct from the actual sex of individuals; if they are so distinct, one wonders why a distinct and neutral terminology is not used.

Jung further suggests that these two principles reflect images of the father and mother respectively. In *Two Essays on Analytical Psychology* he postulates that 'An inherited collective image of woman exists in a man's unconscious with the help of which he apprehends the nature of woman'. Since the child's first experience is with his mother, Jung believed, as Frieda Fordham summarises it, that 'the image of his mother that occurs in each child is not an accurate picture of her, but is formed and coloured by the innate capacity to produce an image of woman'. Basic to such thinking is Jung's notion that such an image of woman is 'innate' rather than learned. Experience and documentation of the therapeutic process suggest it may be empirically true that we carry an internalised image of our parents which helps form our picture of what it is to be a woman or a man in our society. It has also been pointed out by feminist writers that because of the role women play in the family and in the economy we do, in a capitalist society, tend to be the carriers of feeling and emotionality for men, hence the 'feeling' anima. It also seems empirically true that the pressures of our society make it hard for women to take on 'male' characteristics, or for men to take on 'female' characteristics, with ease, confidence or grace. It is one thing to recognise these as empirically accurate comments about our psychological make-up and behaviour in this society; it is a different matter to suggest that these male and female stereotypes are innate and inevitable. It seems inordinately difficult for us to broaden our vision to imagine that qualities as fundamental as thinking and feeling, warmth and strength are human qualities, which are neither male nor female.

Anatomy has also been drawn in to lend support to male/female, sun/moon symbolism. The pale, watery, tidal moon is compared to the woman's nurturing womb full of flowing waters in which the baby swims. Again, I have stressed how relative our perceptions are. We will see, from the Cretan example, how a different world view can emphasise other qualities in the womb: its sun-like radiance, its powerful transforming and generative qualities, its ability to push life forcefully out into the world. Thus if a woman is more outer than inner, more active than passive, this does not make her less of a woman: it simply makes her that kind of woman. We have to deal here with a whole construct of symbolism which has been built up to reach metaphysical proportions. Thus, in Relating, Liz Greene asserts:

> Sun and moon are akin to the other paired symbols such as dark and light, spirit and matter, active and passive, mother and father, life and death, and every other pair of antitheses which constitute the great pillars sustaining the organism of life [my italics].

Why should the organism of life be sustained by paired columns of antitheses rather than by a triangle, a square, a pentagon, a hexagram, or a spiral? The notion that thinking is opposed to feeling is a product of our culture, with its restricted and distorted definition of 'rationalism' – which is itself often a disguised irrationality. Adrienne Rich has commented:

I experience no such division . . . between my female body and
my conscious thought . . . Woman-reading-Neumann, woman-
reading-Freud, woman-reading Engels or Lévi-Strauss, has to draw
on her own deep experience for strength and clarity in
discrimination, analysis, criticism.

(*Of Woman Born*)

The notion that the central realisation of the self is a matter of will
and consciousness, as opposed to the unconscious, reflects the values
of our society, which emphasises domination through will rather than
co-operation, and which has relegated so much else to
unconsciousness. As Adrienne Rich puts it, '. . . in the very act of
becoming more conscious of her situation in the world, a woman may
feel herself coming deeper than ever into touch with her unconscious
and with her body'. The very concepts of 'conscious' and
'unconscious', as well as the line between them, are revealed as social
constructs; just like our emphasis on the division between black and
white rather than on the blending and circling colours of the rainbow;
and just like our emphasis on the polarised opposition of life and
death, rather than on the elements of continuity which other societies
emphasise. In each case we choose to see opposition rather than
transition. We build our symbolic system with carefully selected items,
and the awesome elements of the universe are bent to fit. The sun
and moon may emit certain energies, but we cannot assume that they
bear any relation to our sense of sexual difference.

De-sexing the Stars:
Dealing with New Definitions

The questioning of this stereotyped sun/moon symbolism has
implications for the use and practice of astrology. Here is an example
based on one woman's horoscope reading:

In her natal chart, Sue has the Sun in the sign of Leo (the lion)
in a square aspect (i.e. in a jarring relationship or angle) towards
the Moon in the sign of Scorpio. In conventional astrological
terms, the sun/moon square represents a conflict between
conscious and unconscious, between head and heart, between
mind and feelings. The conflict is exacerbated by the specific
placings of the Sun and Moon: Scorpio, which has the moon in

it, is a sign of 'darkness' and the occult, while Leo, which has the
sun in it, is a strongly bright, optimistic, sunny sign, being the
Zodiac sign which is governed by the Sun itself. Scorpio is a 'fixed'
sign which would trap feelings rather than letting them flow; it
is also linked with sexuality.

A chart-reader tells Sue that this conflict between the Sun in
Leo and the Moon in Scorpio is analogous to the mythic conflict
between the Hero and the possessive, vengeful, dragon-like
Gorgon. Another chart-reader tells her that she will have trouble
in realising her potential, as Leo is a male sign and Leo women
always face this as a problem.

Here an inner conflict is apparently illuminated by astrological
symbolism and its mythic associations, in this case the male hero who
battles bravely against the power of the primitive female gorgon. But
once again we need to remember the history of these symbols. Like
alchemy and the Tarot, astrology has been shaped by centuries of
patriarchy. We cannot assume that the sun and the lion were originally
male symbols. This being so, our astrological interpretations take on
an entirely different face, for we no longer have a male hero linked
with the sun. Moreover, Chapter 7 shows us the prototype of the
hero/dragon struggle: the battle which the god Apollo, in association
with the Sun, fought against the old female snake goddess to gain
control of the oracle at Delphi. That symbolic struggle seems to be
about the triumph of the new patriarchal religion over the ancient
women's religion which centred in some places on the snake. The
snake had not been seen as sinister until patriarchy labelled it so: any
more than female sexuality was seen as threatening and destructive
before patriarchy attempted to control it, in order to guarantee the
stability of its own social structures. In early Crete, we have no gorgon
but a powerful, radiant, bare-breasted and sexual 'snake-goddess' or
'snake-priestess'. In Indian symbolism we find the snake as the symbol
of *kundalini*, the health-giving energy which rises from the base of the
spine up through the body. In *Energy and Character* David L. Smith
discusses the Ouroboros, the encircling 'World Serpent' which
devours its own tail, as a symbol of wholeness, which, in the child's
development, precedes maternal and paternal symbolism. With these
insights, prevailing astrological symbolism no longer seems to offer the
last word on this conflict in Sue's chart.

We might hypothesise that the process of symbol making happens
as follows. The sun and the moon are parts of the universe composed

of matter, gases, and energy, without sex. Of the two the sun shines more brightly and is the more powerful in its effect on day and night and on the seasons. In various societies it has been chosen as an image by means of which humans visualise their own power, entity or identity, the self. It is also often assigned to whichever sex is most powerful in a society. If men are more powerful, as in patriarchy, it is seen as male and attributed a penis; if women are more powerful, as perhaps in early Crete, it is seen as a woman and attributed a womb. Such assignment of sex to the sun will not have to be taught, but will occur spontaneously in individuals, reflecting their social experience. It seems that the sun will also often be predominantly connected with that part of the body whose functions are most prized. Thus for the early Cretans it was pictured as located in the woman's belly; it was closely linked with sex and regeneration. During the rise of patriarchy it gradually became male; reflecting a process whereby the head became the dominant part of the body, the sun was symbolically located in the head and was particularly associated with the prized faculty of the eye. The 'self' is now located in mind and consciousness rather than in the belly. Meanwhile, under patriarchy, women and sexuality are discredited – witness the Pandora myth described in Chapter 7 – and subject to increasing controls; they become, like all things repressed, a potential danger. Hey presto, we have our rational sun hero and our sinister female sexual gorgon. While these symbols may accurately reflect the form of inner conflict we are likely to experience empirically under patriarchy, somewhere behind them lurk other possibilities which could be drawn out: traces of a belly which takes the lead, a snake which symbolises energy and integration.

The hero/dragon myth can thus be understood as relevant only to specific conflicts present under patriarchy. The sun aspect of Sue's chart could be reinterpreted: one could say that she has a lot of power which she will express only with difficulty under patriarchy where women are not expected to shine brightly, and where the channels for expressing power in the world are through male-defined structures and by means of a narrow rationality, a narrow focusing of will from the head, and a repression into unconsciousness of many other important aspects of the whole person. In this sense we may agree that, empirically, the woman may find it difficult to express herself except through the 'male'. The lack of a *female* symbol for the life force can be seen as unsurprising in a society where the life force of women is damned up. However, we may also find this sad. Adrienne Rich has pointed out that although both Jung and Neumann have done much to bring into focus the role of the feminine in culture, they are 'primarily concerned with integrating the feminine into the masculine psyche'. Feminist astrologers have pointed out the dangers of calling the sun the 'masculine' principle or identifying it with the man in a woman's life. Lindsay River and Sally Gillespie, in *The Knot of Time: Astrology and Female Experience*, point out that:

> Through these interpretations astrologers have encouraged women to project their own strength, vitality, identity and direction on to men. This distortion negates the wholeness which is inherent in astrology, and highlights the necessity for each of us to connect with her own solar energy.

The Cretan symbolism offers us the possibility of posing the whole dilemma of Sue's chart in different terms. The sun, placed at the belly, could symbolise life force, *élan*, vitality and sexuality, and the moon symbolise the thought and reflectiveness which observes and assimilates that primary vitality. A prime solar force of energy and 'love-in-action' from the belly could thus coexist with a secondary force containing many of the elements traditionally attributed by astrology to a 'female' moon: a sense of history, reflection, contemplation, feeling-tones, and assimilation. In Sue's case, bearing in mind the 'square' or jarring aspect in her chart, we might end up with a conflict between a leading vital libidinal force in the belly (sun) and the more reflective, thoughtful, integrative powers of the moon. I propose this alternative interpretation only as an example: a new symbolic vocabulary can be articulated only as people change. The important point is to recognise that the symbolic system is open to change. The sun is the centre of the universe and is too important to be appropriated by only one sex. As a source of energy and a symbol of strength it should not be monopolised by men. We all grow, bask and work in its heat and light. As Lindsay River and Sally Gillespie put it in *The Knot of Time*: 'As we reach out to the sun we revitalise ourselves; we become centred, healthy and whole.'

Here are some relevant exercises.

Revitalising from the Sun

In Modern Greek, sunbathing is called *heliotherapeia*, which literally means 'sun therapy', suggestive of the beneficial effects of contact with the sun. In northern climates we get fewer opportunities for such contact, but can still use the sun as a symbol to get in touch with the qualities it represents for us. This exercise is a simple example.

Stand in a place you like, indoors or outdoors. It may help you to be facing towards the light.

Close your eyes. Check that your knees are slightly bent, not locked tight, and that your back and neck are relaxed but straight. Let your shoulders and face relax, and feel your weight sinking into the ground. Notice your breathing.

Now imagine that the sun is shining on to you. (You can imagine the sun at any height, intensity, or even location that you wish.) Imagine the sunshine filling you with warmth and vitality. through every pore. (Pause two minutes.)

Now let go of the image of the sun, and focus on your own body which is filled to the brim with sunshine. Imagine the warmth of the sun inside your body: your belly . . . your whole torso . . . limbs . . . right to your toes and fingertips. Stay with that feeling for a couple of minutes.

Now, still imagining the sun inside you, let some of that sunshine radiate out from your body all around. You might like to imagine it filling the room, or you might want to direct it towards a task in hand, or towards a person, for example someone you love or someone who has been giving you a hard time. Don't push it, just let it radiate. (Pause three minutes.)

Open your eyes.

I have found this exercise good when I am feeling tired and depleted, or when a situation or person is overwhelming me and I have lost a sense of my own power and positive energy to cope with problems. You can vary the timing.

The Myth of Persephone and Demeter: a Guided Fantasy

I have commented on Jung's preoccupation with the male child-hero's deliverance from the mother-monster-unconscious; he seems less interested in the female child's experience and her story. I give this myth as a guided fantasy because it focuses on the *daughter's* relationship with her mother.

Allow each episode to rest in your imagination for several minutes, and notice any associations, identifications, images, feelings, memories or thoughts which it brings up.

Sit or lie comfortably with arms and knees uncrossed. Breathe evenly for a few moments to relax.

It is a fine spring day by the seashore. In a meadow Persephone is playing with her girl friends and picking flowers.

Suddenly the earth yawns open and Hades, god of death, appears in his golden horse-drawn chariot. He seizes Persephone and carries her away to the underworld. Persephone cries out.

Her mother, the goddess Demeter, hears the cry. Throwing her cloak from her shoulders, she speeds like a wild bird over land and sea, searching for her child.

Finally she learns that Zeus had assigned Persephone to be Hades' wife. Demeter is so angry that she leaves the gatherings of the gods and disguises herself as a mortal, finding employment as a nurse to the son of Queen Metaneira. Famine and barrenness strike the land. No plant grows.

In her grief, the only person who cheered Demeter was Iambe, whose performance of obscene dance and jokes at Metaneira's palace made Demeter laugh.

Finally, the other gods protest to Zeus at the devastating effects of the famine on earth. He is persuaded to send the messenger of the gods, Hermes, to instruct Hades to release Persephone. Before she leaves, Hades persuades her to eat some pomegranate seeds; their magical effect is that she will be obliged to return to the underworld for a third of every year. To the joy of both mother and daughter, Persephone returns to the world where she can stay for eight months of each year. The earth blossoms.

Assagioli, founder of Psychosynthesis, advocated the use of myths as guided meditations, such as the story of the Holy Grail or Dante's *Divine Comedy* with its journey through hell, purgatory and heaven. Such myths are seen as a tool for liberating the mind and envisaging new possibilities. What seems important about the Persephone myth, of which I give here only a summary, is its focus on the relationship between two women. Female figures were often shown together in Greek Bronze Age art. We cannot tell the exact date of the original Demeter and Persephone myth, but this version (known as the *Homeric Hymn to Demeter*) was written down in the Archaic period, during the early period of patriarchy. If one were looking for archetypal myths along Jungian lines, one might find in this story not – as Jung did in *The Archetypes and the Collective Unconscious* – a 'bloodless maiden' whose over-identification with her mother constituted an 'invitation' to the man, but perhaps rather a 'primordial' statement about the rape and suppression of the female by the male. Personally I prefer to see the myth as a specific product of the experience of its time, from which we can draw out whatever issues may still be relevant to our time and experience, whether they are themes of reconciliation to male power (as Marylin Arthur suggests in 'Politics and Pomegranates'); loss and healing; Persephone as the sun; female identity and premature separation from the mother (discussed by Sheila Ernst in 'Can a Daughter be a Woman?'); expression of grief and the role of laughter; reactions to violence and abuse; or patterns of anger, depression and creativity.

The cult of Demeter and Persephone at their sanctuary of Eleusis near Athens (known as the Eleusinian Mysteries) provided one of the most important foci of religious life in Greece for over a thousand years. The Mysteries enjoyed a huge, devoted and loyal following – although Demeter was never officially granted equal status with the other Olympian gods. It seems a shame that in the selective plundering of Greek mythology their relationship has been devalued and their story eclipsed.

Circles of Growth: Creative Uses of Astrology

Although I am suggesting that we do not need to accept any astrological symbolism as beyond question, I still feel that there are many ways in which its imagery can be useful to us. While the language and concepts of psychology focus largely on neurosis, resistance, and patterns of development in childhood, astrology offers a far denser language concerning the *potential* of a human being. The symbolism of the planets, the signs of the zodiac, and the houses, offers a series of metaphors for different psychological functions and the relationship between them. It offers a structure for imaging many different qualities and areas of activity, which can be helpful to us in the process of change. One feminist, Frances, wrote in *Bread and Roses*:

> Through studying the ideas of astrological writers and the symbols used I can now understand myself in an expanding way, in a more comprehensive way, and I feel strengthened in my belief that I have potentialities for unfoldment in all spheres of my life; relating to people, music, work, travelling, etc.

While the horoscopes of tabloid newspapers seem to predict our path with a banal fatalism, humanistic astrology aims to serve as a road guide showing areas of tension, challenges to be met and problems to be solved on the journey to becoming a whole person. Astrology's images help us to broaden our ideas about sexuality and spirituality in particular. Astrology is based on the articulation of three different symbolic alphabets: the planets, the signs and the houses. In practical terms, the natal horoscope is a map of the sky at the moment of birth, and as such it aims to chart from which directions the various planets were beaming their different energies on to the individual at that uniquely impressionable moment: the energy of each planet being affected by its location on the sky or horizon (house) and by which constellations (zodiac sign) were behind it, influencing and altering its beam at that point in time.

There are a number of different ways of understanding the basis of astrology. Ralph Metzner in *Maps of Consciousness* has summed these up neatly as material or physical theories, (suggesting that there are forms of radiation and force fields that affect earth); the theory of 'planetary heredity' (postulating a synchronisation between cosmic and biological cycles); Jung's theory of 'synchronicity' (postulating a non-causal linkage between material and psychic processes); theories which see the relationship between cosmic and human factors as purely symbolic or metaphorical and ignore the causal question; and theories which focus on astrological factors primarily as an evolutionary map, 'a kind of script or scenario designed by the incarnating entity or soul as it chooses the time, place, and conditions of its life on earth'. Metzner discusses the evidence for a scientific basis to astrology, such as the research into the effect of sunspots and changes in blood albumen levels at different moon phases. What interests me more at this point is its use as a fund of symbols. The individual is complex; astrology gives a shape or pattern through which to understand ourselves. Like the Tarot, astrology can be understood simply as providing a framework for intuitive perception, to draw out and articulate our unconscious thoughts and knowledge about our lives.

As a system it is twelvefold (based on twelve zodiac signs and houses) and sevenfold (based on the sun, moon and five inner planets), or tenfold if you include the three outer planets: Uranus, Neptune and Pluto. The whole chart is drawn on to a circle which represents the heavens encircling the earth at the time of birth; the picture of the individual is mapped out as a circle. Here we are far away from the duality principle. We find that in this system sexuality is not seen as a focused, polarised, largely negative principle, but is actually spread around in the chart. Thus, sexuality as sex drive may be symbolized by the planet Mars (along with other kinds of drive); sexual affection may manifest through Venus (along with other kinds of affection and relating); the Scorpio sign is linked with secrecy, regeneration and transformation through union (which may take place through sex or through other processes). Similarly spiritual qualities and activities can be seen as manifesting in various parts of a person's chart. Thus Neptune is associated with transcendent feelings of connectedness, whether experienced through meditation, trance or dance; Pluto is linked with renewal of the spirit through what may be painful processes of confrontation amounting to miniature 'deaths'; the sign of Scorpio is associated with the occult and intense processes of healing, birth, death and transformation. The primary symbol is of one source of energy (the circle) which manifests in each individual through the various and complex patterns of the planet layout. The naming of the planets after Greek gods draws in a rich train of mythological stories and connections.

Let's look at some practical examples of how women can use these symbols in a process of self-understanding and change. In particular I want to point out the difference between being trapped in fixed, mystically ordained interpretations of the symbols, and understanding them in a historical, dynamic way. My first example concerns the planet Saturn (the Greek Kronos) who is seen as the 'Old King' and symbolises restriction and difficulty, as well as structure, impairing the sign he is placed in:

In her chart, Elaine has Saturn placed in the zodiac sign of Gemini which concerns thought and communication. In her dreams, she frequently sees a Gestapo officer who keeps telling her that she is incompetent and does everything wrong. She is helped by perceiving this man as a Saturn/Gemini figure. Using the Gestalt method to develop a dialogue with the figure, she finds that he gradually changes in quality and she is able to recognise in him some of the positive qualities traditionally associated with Saturn, such as discipline and making priorities. Losing the Gestapo uniform, he becomes instead a severe teacher, an inner voice which is difficult but helpful.

Harriet Bye has written in *Country Women* about using the Saturn image rather differently, to elucidate the process of 'psychological domination' which 'involves giving one's personal power and sense of self over to the power authorities and then accepting their hierarchical definition of who we are'. Connecting the 'destruction of self' to the Kronos/Saturn myth of the father who eats his children as soon as they are born in order to avoid the threat of a rival, she comments:

> As children (especially as girl children) we are taught to submit and not to battle with the Father, to give in to his authority, to identify with the conqueror, and to be afraid of dealing directly with experience. What this ultimately means is that the conqueror or Daddy winds up inside of us. The stronger ego dominates and the hostility that was first directed against Daddy gets turned around and directed towards ourselves. This is called internalized oppression.

Here two women use these symbols very creatively to illuminate and confront the issue of self-putdowns which so many of us experience. We should be clear, however, that these women are using the symbols and not the other way round. The Saturn image is not 'archetypal'. In Chapter 7 I trace the history of the time and place in which that myth was first recorded: the early so-called 'Geometric' period in Greece. The story of the separation of Heaven and Earth, of which the Kronos-Saturn myth is a part, seems to have served the function of explaining and justifying the hostility and exaggerated separation between the sexes in newly patriarchal, male-dominated Greece. Before that time, this story did not exist, because it was not necessary that it should – perhaps because fathers did not play such a dominant authority role and the issue of succession from father to son was not so crucial. Such issues were certainly not prominent in very early Crete, from the evidence of the surviving material remains. The Kronos-Saturn myth was created, and survived, because it rang true as a description of domestic and social tensions current at the time, and because Hesiod wrote it down, and because European interest in Greek culture has preserved many of Greece's early writings and traditions. It has also survived because it is a very good myth for illuminating certain features of patriarchal life. To say it is not more than that, and does not have a universal application, is not to denigrate this ancient and powerful legend but to pay tribute to the infinite range of possible symbolic stories and myths concordant with the enormous possible range of human experience.

Here is another example where a creative approach will be more useful than a strict adherence to traditional mythological meanings:

> In her chart Janet has the planet Mars conjunct (i.e. right next to and joined with) the planet Uranus in the sign of Gemini. Mars is linked, among other things, with the sex drive; Uranus symbolises an erratic movement; and Gemini has been likened to an airy butterfly which flits from flower to flower. This configuration is thus understood as giving her a tendency towards promiscuity. On the other hand, the planet Venus (symbolising relationships, affection) is placed in a very restricted and inhibited position in her chart. Her resulting conflict between promiscuity and strict fidelity is compard by her chart reader to the eternal conflict between Zeus the unfaithful husband and Hera the nagging wife: two extremes which can never agree but which somehow need each other. 'You will never escape from this conflict,' Janet is told.

Here a mythological situation is drawn in to elucidate a woman's internal conflict, and may well provide symbols which are relevant and helpful for her. However, it is worth remembering that the first Aegean deities were female figures who were not associated with any male deities. Hera's claim to great antiquity, generally recognised by historians, would place her among these original independent goddesses. There is no clear evidence for the god Zeus, or indeed any male god, before the closing centuries of the Bronze Age when Mycenaean influence prevailed in the Mediterranean. Zeus thus arrived late on Greek soil. The two deities were each separately the creation of a particular culture and time. Their conflict-ridden 'marriage', with Zeus assuming the dominant position, probably reflected the working out of political tensions between the peoples who created them, in which the patriarchal culture became dominant. The ongoing friction between Hera and Zeus holds sufficient truth as a reflection of life under patriarchy to have become a widely known myth. However, this interpretation of Hera is not the only one possible, any more than ongoing marital tension is the only option open to us in our daily lives.

Tuning in to the Zodiac Signs

It is a good idea to do this before having your horoscope read, so that you can actively bring your own understandings to the session.

Read a brief introduction to each of the zodiac signs.

Sit quietly and meditate on the signs. Notice which ones come to the fore in your mind, which ones you feel you have some affinity with or interest in.

Find pictures which express the quality of those chosen signs for you, whether literally or not (for example Leo could be a lion, or a playful picture, or a picture which suggests 'pride' to you).

Put those pictures somewhere where you will often see them. Let the images have an effect on you; notice your emotional reactions and mental associations. Which parts of you are like those symbols? How do the qualities of those signs manifest in your daily life?

When you feel thoroughly familiar with them, take the pictures down and make a collage, arranging them in a pattern which reflects how you feel those different parts of you fit together.

If and when you have your chart read by an astrologer, compare your collage with your chart.

Zodiac Animal Movement

This exercise, which I devised in collaboration with Barbara Mound, provides a different way of becoming familiar with the zodiac signs, through physical movement.

Lie flat on your back, relax and breathe evenly.

Now choose out of the following creatures one that interests you: ram, bull, crab, lion, scorpion, centaur, goat, fish. Pick the first one that your mind alights on, and stay with it.

Picture that creature. Notice how it moves. Notice its surroundings.

Now slowly get up, and keeping your eyes closed, start to move like that creature. Imagine yourself in its habitat. Get a feel of that creature in your body, and of its movements. You could open your eyes and explore how that creature reacts to the textures and objects in the room. Stay in character for at least three minutes.

Afterwards, notice how you felt about the creature. Is there a part of you which resembles that creature? How do you feel about that part of you?

Dream Characters, Fantasy Friends and Spirits

The hero, the gorgon, and the Greek gods have all been revealed as
creations of patriarchal tradition with a historical rather than a
universal application. This is a very unpopular thesis. Many of those
who are interested in dreams and occult traditions are dependent on
Jung's archetypes for their theoretical basis and are dismayed to learn
that those archetypes provide only a soggy foundation. Even many
feminists who would question the 'hero' myth like to think of an
archetypal Great Goddess lurking somewhere in the depths of history.
To represent Jung's thought accurately, one should make clear that
he saw the specific images of gods, suns, moons, lions and so on as
archetypal images rather than actual *archetypes*. The archetypes
themselves are theoretical entities which can be perceived only
through the symbols that clothe them. As Jung puts it in *The Archetypes
and the Collective Unconscious*:

> archetypes are not determined as regards their content, but only
> as regards their form . . . The archetype in itself is empty and
> purely formal . . . a possibility of representation.

Now either these archetypes are so empty of content as to be
meaningless, or they are being proposed as an innate structure around
which our patterns of thought, dream and fantasy will inevitably
crystallise. In which case we are left with the same Jungian thesis still
standing: that these archetypes are inevitably patterned in certain
forms. Jungians have suggested that all human experience –
regardless of race and time – can be related to symbols such as the
persona, the shadow, the animus, the anima, the wise old man, the
earth mother, and the self. However, in these chapters I have
systematically, pair by pair, shown this particular symbolic grid to be
socially created, reflecting a series of splits between conscious and
unconscious, male and female, white and black, thought and feeling,
which are peculiar to western society. Many have found Jung's
symbolic map helpful and enriching as a source of images. Some
feminists have stressed that the archetypes can be used as enabling
symbols, rather than restricting or limiting ones. However, those
committed to working with dream symbols often find that over time
they move towards a more diverse and individual symbolism. In
Creative Dreaming Patricia Garfield describes this process, telling how
on one occasion as a 17-year-old:

I did . . . see my own image of God in a dream. He was a great figure in the sky formed of pink- and blue-tinged clouds, . . . his body was muscular, he was bearded, and he wore a crown . . . Dreamers who have a clear conception of what to expect of a god or saint in a dream are likely to see their dream image distinctly. When religious figures appear in my dreams these days they are usually gods or, more often, goddesses of a uniquely idiosyncratic origin, rather than a stereotyped or archetypal image.

Such experience suggests that dream symbols are simply the material we have to hand with which to clothe the often elusive or ethereal qualities and insights offered by dreams. The less restricted our imagination, the wider our symbolic vocabulary, the greater the variety of clothing available. Jung himself uses the same metaphor when he suggests, in *Symbols of Transformation*, that the contents of the unconscious 'become visible indirectly to the conscious mind by stimulating the imaginative material at its disposal, clothing themselves in it like the dancers who clothe themselves in the skins of animals . . .'

The symbols that clothe our dream contents are thus variable and tell us more about the imaginative material available to the dreamer than about the actual nature of the dream contents. In this book I have expressed my differences with Jung, but I recognise that his work has been invaluable in attempting to chart and structure some of this imaginative material at our disposal in western society. He was the first to start to construct a syntax. If anything, he did not go far enough, for the possible symbolic vocabularies are far more varied and extensive than he envisaged, and many questions remain unanswered about the nature of the dream realities which those symbols attempt to express.

During the course of this and the previous chapter I have shown that there are many different levels on which dream and fantasy images can be understood. One important level is to understand them as carriers of information about our internal psychological world and our relationship to the external realities of daily life. In Chapter 3 I gave examples of women using Gestalt techniques to explore *dream* characters which reflect different aspects of their personality, conflicts, and their responses to the people and situations shaping their lives. Fantasy characters or friends imagined in *waking* life can be interpreted in the same way. For example, Frances Wickes, in *The Inner World of Childhood*, quotes a child's description of her imaginary companion:

Mrs Comphret lived on the cellar stairs. She was short and plump and comfortable, and she was always smiling. She wore a little black bonnet tied in a neat bow under her chin . . . She did not talk much but was just comfortable and smiling and slow and quiet. We liked to feel her there. I never went to school or anywhere without stopping to talk to Mrs Comphret.

In the case history of this child, the psychotherapist interprets Mrs Comphret as an imaginary figure who fulfilled a psychological need, embodying qualities of warmth, calm, slowness and quietness which were missing in the child's own mother. Mrs Comphret was understood as 'the personification of the things she had wanted in a mother and had not found'. In other cases a companion may be created to embody qualities lacking in the child's own personality, as when a slow child invents a 'friend' who is very clever and successful. As with all fantasies, these imaginary companions can either lead to dissociation and a splitting of the personality, or can be used to integrate latent qualities. It depends, as Frances Wickes points out, whether the fantasy is used as a compensation or as a resource to respond to the demands of living. In *Drawing Down the Moon* Margot Adler has described how empowering such fantasy figures were to her as a child:

I see them now as daydreams used in the struggle toward my own becoming. They were hardly idle, though, since they focused on stronger and healthier 'role models' than the images of women projected in the late 1950s. The fantasies enabled me to contact stronger parts of myself, to embolden my vision of myself.

The 'guided fantasies' I have mentioned, such as those used by Psychosynthesis, are a way of deliberately stimulating the waking mind to create such characters in order to gain understanding of gaps or problems, or to discover hidden possibilities in the personality. Rather as qualities unowned in the dreamer are projected on to characters and objects in a dream (and can be re-owned through Gestalt role-playing techniques), so in guided fantasy individuals are invited to project qualities on to objects and characters in an imaginary landscape or adventure. The symbols emerge spontaneously from the unconscious through the same process as in a dream, but in this case the process is deliberately activated by the structure of the exercise. Relaxing and shutting their eyes, individuals are led through the

fantasy ('You are walking up a hill . . . You meet . . . You see . . .').
Afterwards they are asked 'What was the hill like?' 'What was the wise
old woman like?' Through summoning up an image of a 'wise person'
or a 'guide' or 'guardian angel', the individual can gain access to parts
of herself which are not accessible or integrated in her daily
personality. The 'guide' can be understood as a projection of the
individual's own personality, symbolising latent qualities of strength
or wisdom within herself.

However, sometimes the process of 'Gestalting' and re-owning
dream or fantasy images as part of the personality can seem
reductionist, as if a dream symbol of a shimmering mountain turns
out to signify 'only my father' or 'a joyful part of my personality which
I repress'. Experience of working in depth with dream symbols shows
that in fact no dream symbol can simply be translated as meaning
something else. We cannot wrench meaning from a dream: it may shed
layer after layer of meaning like an onion and still retain a numinous
quality. As James Hillman points out in *The Dream and the Underworld*,
'the dream belongs to the underworld, but ever since Freud,
interpretation of the dream has meant translation into the
upperworld'. Although dreams can teach us a great deal about waking
life, they are not reducible to its terms. It has been suggested that in
some dream states, we are involved in physical activity which happens
at energy wavelengths too subtle for us to grasp. Thus in *The Nature
of Personal Reality*, Jane Roberts suggests that:

There are as yet undiscovered, bizarre changes in the brain during
certain dream states, an acceleration that quite literally *propels* the
consciousness out of its usual space-time continuum . . . The
dream world exists in terms of energy also, of course, but simply
at ranges that are not physically obvious . . .

On this level of experience, Jane Roberts suggests, there are no
symbols or images:

Images as you *think* of them are based upon your own neurological
structure, and your interpretation of these . . . Perception without
images seems impossible in that context. Yet in some dream
situations you enter a state of awareness quite divorced from that
kind of sense data. Images as such are not involved, though later
they may be manufactured unconsciously for the sake of
translation.

She suggests that often our remembered dream experiences are already translations, without which the dreams would make no sense to us at all. Personally I would not see dreams simply as a 'sensible' and rational way of identifying and solving problems; that would be to reduce their power and meaning. I do not feel qualified to dismiss the idea that in dream states people experience changes in consciousness, and contact energies or forces which exist beyond the individual and outside our space-time framework, energies which need to be clothed in images of our own creation in order for us to apprehend them.

The only way to investigate such states is empirically, based on experience. Many people can recall some experience of telepathy or prognostication through dreams, whether dreaming something about a friend which later turns out to have happened to that friend, or glimpsing an event which eventually seems to come true in their own life. Some record a contact which does not seem to be with the living. Here is an example of one of Jung's dreams for which he found a psychological explanation unsatisfactory. It was about his wife, who had recently died:

> I suddenly awoke one night and knew that I had been with her in the south of France, in Provence, and had spent an entire day with her. She was engaged on studies of the Grail there. That seemed significant to me, for she had died before completing her work on this subject. Interpretation on the subjective level – that my anima had not yet finished with the work she had to do – yielding nothing of interest . . . for me.
> (*Memories, Dreams, Refections*)

Here Jung apparently thinks in terms not of a psychological projection from himself but of a visitation by what he might term the 'soul' of his wife. Other writers use a different terminology, referring to psychic 'entities', 'forces' or 'energies'. If, as in sleeping or trance states, a part of our consciousness can move on to a dimension or vibrational rate not normally familiar to it, the suggestion is that we may interact with entities existing on that vibrational rate whom we cannot normally apprehend. The question still remains as to how our symbolising faculties are at work in shaping what we apprehend. Take, for example, this unusual experience undergone by three women whom I know:

Lesley, Mary and Gabrielle lived in neighbouring houses as part of the same collective housing complex. Lesley had mentioned that she did not like her room but had never stated why.

One night Lesley was away and Mary had occasion to sleep in her room. She had an unpleasant dream which made her half-wake with the feeling that a big heavy man was lying too close to her in bed. At first thinking it was Ray, an ex-lover who in illness had often felt too hot and heavy in bed, she then recalled she had gone to bed alone. Fearing an intruder, she woke fully in terror and put the light on. She found herself alone. The feeling of fear stayed with her for a long time, but she thought it would be tactless to mention the experience to Lesley.

She did, however, mention it to Gabrielle, who said that she too had once stayed in Lesley's room, after a row with her boyfriend, and had had a terrifying experience. In the middle of the night she had the impression of a tall man leaning over her, whom at first she imagined to be her boyfriend. She was paralysed with fear and could not scream. She also did not mention the experience to Lesley.

Some time later, in a conversation about ghosts, Lesley told Mary that since living in that room she had experienced the same dream recurrently: that someone big and heavy was in bed with her. She felt that he didn't want sex but was sucking the warmth out of her. On the last occasion she saw him crawling across the room to her, and half-waking she thought 'Oh, I'll let him into bed', which she did, and went back to sleep. She did not have the dream again.

Here explanations based on coincidence or projection would be stretched. Some suggestibility and some fear communicated from one woman to the other might account for each one having a bad dream in the same room. However the similarities in the three experiences, which were reported independently of each other, suggest some kind of psychic entity associated with, and present in, the room. It would appear to be attracted to, and to need something from, women. But does this mean we might literally conclude that a big man actually lived or died in the room? Not necessarily. In our society any woman's symbol for a terrifying creature might take the shape of the large figure of a male intruder. That terror, combined with the women's vulnerability and their experience of giving succour to men in relationships, might leave – as it were – a kind of hollowed-out psychic mould open for a troubled or needy entity or energy to pour itself into and inhabit. The shape of the heavy impinging man would thus have been their own creation. We are so illiterate in the vocabulary of such experiences that we cannot assume we can readily translate them into our own language of understanding.

In western society such experiences are most likely to be reported from the dream state, but – again – this does not mean we can assume we are justified in dismissing accounts of similar experiences from other cultures where they are reported to have happened in the waking state. Anthropologists have sometimes used psychological explanations to dismiss possession rituals or ceremonies in non-European religions as the result of hysteria, delusion, or some form of compensatory hallucination. We should perhaps hesitate before defining the experience of other peoples, whose perceptive faculties may be considerably less restricted than our own. Although contemporary Christianity allows for the occasional vision or exorcism, it is generally rare in our society for such experiences of contact with 'spirits' to be treated as anything other than the product of mental illness, ignorance or gullibility.

Without entering the complex discussion about whether ghosts and spirits have an independent existence outside our imagination, I am concerned here with examining the symbols through which people apprehend them. If such things exist, how are they filtered and defined by the limitations of our symbolic framework? While sceptics tend to see all spirit forms as symbols of psychological projection, believers tend to think that we can make statements about the intrinsic nature such entities might have on the basis of the forms in which they appear to us. I would question both attitudes.

Emmanuel Swedenborg, the eighteenth-century mystic and man of letters, described a hierarchy of spirits with which he communed and which he believed to interact with human life. He is firmly placed within western Christian culture, with its strong symbolic structure of angels and devils, and his experiences have been filtered through Christian symbolism, but he does imply that the distinction between 'inner' and 'outer' is not as clear-cut as people might wish to make it. According to him the spirits attached to a person have a disposition similar to that person's. Enthusiastic spirits are with the enthusiastic. The attachment or contact can apparently happen only because of some resonance between the inner and the outer. In normal people Swedenborg believed that spirits attach to unconscious levels of the mind so that they flow into feelings or thought like unconscious impulses without the person being aware of them. Spiritual teachers stress that you can only attract what you are, what you have in your own nature; if you recognise and deal with your own 'negative' side, you are less likely to attract 'negative' energies from outside yourself. Bruce MacManaway in *Healing* comments that in states of deep relaxation or heightened awareness it is quite common to see and talk to 'imaginary' people, who can be considered either as 'a personalized form of one aspect of the subconscious' or as 'real "people" who have every human attribute except a physical body' and are around ready to help us. Perhaps these alternatives are not incompatible, and such experiences result from a combination of the two.

The same topic of the active role we play in attracting and apprehending phemonena of the 'spirit' world recurs in the Castaneda books. The continuing debate about the veracity of these famous books does not detract from their richness as a source of symbolism of the spiritual. In one incident during his spiritual apprenticeship, described in *The Second Ring of Power*, Castaneda has a frightening encounter with four entities or 'allies' which he perceives as taking the shape of a man with a bald head, a feline, a coyote and a large rectangular shape. He is surprised later that evening when his companion in the encounter tells him that she perceived them completely differently, and explains that the allies in fact have no form but rather are like a presence, a wind, or a glow. In their encounter her experience of one of these 'allies' was as a blackness that wanted to get inside her body. The others she experienced simply as colours, but with a glow so strong that they made the path look as if it were daytime. She explains to Castaneda that an ally is only a presence, a helper that is nothing and yet is as real as a living person. Castaneda is disturbed by this explanation, as he had thought that the 'allies' had a consensual form, a substance which everyone could perceive equally. At another point in his apprenticeship, described in *The Fire From Within*, his tendency to see psychic energies as taking certain physical forms is attributed by his teacher Don Juan to people's almost unavoidable desire, or necessity, to render the incomprehensible in terms of what is most familiar to them. Again it is a question of recognising how strongly our internal symbolic set may be filtering and determining our apprehensions of psychic energy.

Robert Ogilvie Crombie, a psychic associated with the founding of the spiritual community of Findhorn in Scotland, has written an account of meeting, and conversing with, a vision of the god Pan in a public park in Edinburgh. He does not conclude from this experience that the god Pan is an entity with an independent existence. Rather, his interactions with the world of visions, of which this is one, make him believe that shapes like Pan are clothing that our culture has made available for the formless entities or energies to assume. Perhaps the same is true of visions of the Virgin Mary. He points out that in our myths, legends and fairy tales, humans have created a vast gallery of what we refer to as 'supernatural' beings:

> To what extent these beings were the product of man's own creative imagination or the result of inspiration from an outside source is difficult to determine. Suffice it to say that there exists a vast reservoir of 'thought forms' produced by the existence and persistence of these tales.
> (*The Magic of Findhorn*)

These forms have been preserved both by traditional oral means and in print, and are often thought and talked about: 'Thus, an elemental entity wishing to assume a body can "put on" any of these thought forms and then appear personified as that particular being – Greek or Norse god, elf, gnome, faun, fairy, and so on.'

This view of these symbols as human-created shapes, through which psychic energy is mediated, is a far cry from Jung's theory of pre-formed archetypal structures. In *The Magic of Findhorn* Crombie testifies that the entities he meets can take on a wide range of forms: the elementals with which he communicated apparently 'varied from place to place, an infinite variety of beings whose color, form and shape changed with the terrain and the seasons'.

From other cultures we hear the same term of 'thought-forms' used to describe similar experiences. Tibetan yoga disciplines apparently state that images and visions met in dreams or after death are created by the person experiencing them, and that such images can be changed or transformed if a person has the necessary awareness (see Evans-Wentz's *The Tibetan Book of the Dead*). A thorough recent appraisal of this whole issue can be found in Hilary Evans' *Gods: Spirits: Cosmic Guardians*.

Changes of awareness are the topic of my next section. First, I give an exercise to experiment with meeting a character from your unconscious. I will not give an exercise to contact a 'spirit guide'. Such exercises are given in several books (for example, in Jean Porter's *Psychic Development*, and Amy Wallace and Bill Henkin's *The Psychic Healing Book*). Personally I feel wary of devoting too much time and interest to inviting such experiences: it is easy to glamorise them and to forget that their symbolic forms are our own creation. Most of us already have enough on our hands in learning to deal with the living.

Waiting for a Figure to Emerge from a Cave

This is based on an exercise in Assagioli's *Psychosynthesis*. It provides a structure to help you imagine, and encounter, a figure from your unconscious. One person should read slowly for their partner or a group:

Sit or lie comfortably with arms and knees uncrossed. Let your back and neck be straight. Shut your eyes and relax. Notice your breathing. (Two minutes pause.)

Now imagine that it is twilight and you are in a wooded area in front of the mouth of a cave. Picture the scene. (Two minutes pause.)

There is a sound from inside the cave and you have the feeling that someone or something is going to come out of it. You hide yourself behind the thick trunk of a nearby tree, and wait. (Short pause.)

The twilight is thickening. You hear another sound, and then a figure comes out of the cave. Who or what is it? How do you feel? (Two minutes pause.)

Is there any meeting or exchange between you and the figure? What happens? (Pause.)

When the encounter is over, open your eyes and write or tell what happened.

Assagioli comments that in most cases 'a real or mythological-like figure or figures appear, either a parent, friend, a dragon-killer, a goddess, a giant; also all kinds of animals, more or less aggressive in nature. Such forms are usually symbolized projections of suppressed or undeveloped areas of the subject's personality.' Think, write or talk about what part of you the figure may have represented, and how you might be able to allow that part of you to express more in daily life in positive ways.

The Dream Body

Many spiritual disciplines stress that it is possible to change the level of awareness which we take into our dreams. 'Lucid dreaming' involves taking enough consciousness into a dream to be able to make a decision *in the dream* to move towards a frightening dream image, change the ending of a dream, or develop a relationship with 'dream friends', characters or creatures, who give advice and provide help in threatening dream situations. In *Creative Dreaming*, Patricia Garfield describes practices which have been attributed to the Senoi in Malaysia, and gives advice about how to develop the faculty of lucid dreaming in yourself. It is a faculty which offers the dreamer a different relationship to her dream, and makes available new resources for dealing with frightening dream experiences. Writing in *Country Women* magazine, Sharon Hansen describes how reading about the Senoi inspired her to try the technique out for herself during a nightmare. In the dream she had just stopped her car at night by a bridge and had got out of the car when she saw walking towards her a full-sized tyrannosaurus rex with its fangs bared:

> I turned to run away but I remembered reading about facing your fears in dreams and decided to try it. I walked towards the monster and the closer I got the smaller it became until, as I got right up to it, it had shrunken down to a toy cloth alligator lying on the street. This dream and others in a similar vein help me to deal in waking life with the difficult task of facing my fears and encountering, rather than avoiding, them.

In such accounts of unusual awareness, whereby the dreamer takes charge, we find several familiar themes. One is the recognition that our dream symbols are of our own making and that we have the power over them, to confront them or change them if we will. Another is the possibility of achieving a continuity between our 'conscious' and 'unconscious' states which the dominant culture refuses to recognise as possible. Yet another is the evidence that both of these activities contribute enormously to the power and range of resources which we can use to deal with our daily lives.

In the early stages of Castaneda's apprenticeship, Don Juan teaches him to start to bring this kind of increased awareness into his dream by taking the initial step of looking for his hands in the dream. I personally have found that whenever I have gathered enough awareness in a dream to look at my hands, the resulting jolt to my consciousness has caused an uncomfortable spasm in my stomach which has then woken me. Clearly the change in consciousness is closely linked with changes in the body. The terms in which these experiences are described by those who undergo them enlarge our understanding of the relationship between mind and body and make ever less sense of the socially described 'split'.

This is especially true of the experience in which consciousness is thought to leave the body altogether, during sleep or unconsciousness, and to travel. Typically such an experience involves the sleeper feeling that they are slipping out of the physical body, often with particular sensations, then thinking they are awake and finding themselves looking at their sleeping body on the bed. Similar experiences are recounted by people who have survived a near fatal accident or operation. Raymond Moody in *Reflections on Life After Life* cites the following account of a middle-aged man who had a cardiac arrest in hospital and clinically died:

> I remember everything perfectly vividly . . . Suddenly I felt numb. Sounds began sounding a little distant . . . All this time I was perfectly conscious of everything that was going on . . . I saw the nurse come into the room and dial the telephone, and the doctors, nurses and attendants came in. As things began to fade there was . . . a rushing sound, like a stream rushing through a gorge. And I rose up and I was a few feet up looking down on my body. There I was, with people working on me.

In a sleep situation, some individuals have learned to control such movements in and out of the body. Colin Wilson in *Mysteries* quotes Frederick Van Eeden's account of dreaming he was lying on his stomach looking through a window when it struck him that he was actually in bed lying on his back:

> And then I resolved to wake up slowly and carefully and observe how my sensation of lying on my chest would change into the sensation of lying on my back. And so I did, slowly and deliberately, and the transition – which I have since undergone many times – is most wonderful. It is like the feeling of slipping from one body into another, and there is distinctly the *double* recollection of the two bodies . . . It is so indubitable that it leads almost unavoidably to the conception of a *dream body*.

In the Castaneda books this process is called *dreaming* and the part of the being which leaves the body in this way is sometimes termed the 'dream double'. As part of his training Castaneda learns to control his movements and travel in this state. In *The Eagle's Gift* he gives an account of learning to leave his flat by means of what some schools might call 'astral travelling' with the 'astral body'. One notices the physicality, albeit of an unusual kind, which is involved in the experience as he describes how he woke up and jumped out of bed only to be confronted by himself still sleeping in bed. He watched himself asleep and had the self-control to remember that he was *dreaming*. Remembering Don Juan's instructions not to examine his sleeping body but to leave the room, he suddenly found himself, without knowing how, outside his room. The hall and staircase, in real life quite commonplace, seemed monumental to him and he could not conceive how to cover such vast distances. After vacillating, he found that something made him move. It was not a walk, though, and he could not feel his steps. Suddenly he found he was holding on to the railings; he could see his hands and forearms but could not feel them. He experienced himself as holding on by the force of something that had nothing to do with his musculature as he knew it. Again, when faced with walking down the stairs he did not know how to do it, but with a supreme effort managed to bounce down the steps rather like a clumsy ball. He describes needing an incredible degree of attention to reach the ground floor and simultaneously to maintain the bounds of his vision, in order to prevent it from disintegrating into the fleeting images of an ordinary dream. Eventually he learns how to reach a coffee shop which he has been used to visiting in the early hours; he sees the usual night waitress and a row of customers at the counter. Only one of them seems to sense Castaneda's entrance, and turns round to stare at him. The story has a humorous postscript. A few days later Castaneda goes to the same coffee shop, awake, at the same early hour of the morning, and finds the same man there. The man takes one look at him and seems to recognise him. He looks horrified and runs away without giving Castaneda a chance to talk to him. Perhaps the man thought he had seen a ghost? Personal accounts of experiments with this faculty of moving have been given by Oliver Fox in *Astral Projection* and Robert Monroe in *Journeys out of the Body*. Fox's fascinating record includes attempting to meet friends in a similar state.

What concerns me here is not the veracity of these experiences, but the symbolic framework used. Recurrently, in these esoteric traditions, we find mention of a *body* which is akin to, but in some way other than, the physical body. Fox and Monroe describe sensations such as smell, touch and something resembling a sexual experience. As Jane Roberts points out in *The Nature of a Personal Reality*, even in a normal dream experience consciousness ignores space-time relationships to a large degree, and yet it is still firmly based upon the body's corporeal mechanism. Dreams then are physically experienced. You perceive yourself running, talking, eating, in quite physical activities – except that they are not performed by the body that lies on the bed.

What then do we know about this 'dream body'? What is its relationship to the normal physical body? How have such experiences been understood, and theoretically grounded, in these traditions outside the Christian church? These are questions I will tackle in the next chapter. Here I want only to point out that we are again dealing with a world view which does not divide 'mind' or 'spirit' from 'body', but sees spiritual activity as another (to us unfamiliar) dimension of bodily activity.

Here is a relevant exercise.

Contacting Another Person in the Sleep State

Those who teach that telepathy is a means of passing information between sleeping people also suggest that it can facilitate other kinds of communication during the sleep state, such as unconsciously working towards resolving problems and conflicts.

To start exploring this possibility on a small scale, I will give here an exercise which I believe derives from the traditional medicine workers of Hawaii, the Kahunas (described by M.F. Long in *The Secret Science Behind Miracles*). Since I was taught it, I have found it very useful. It comes with the caution that it must be used very responsibly.

If you have a problem with a close friend or lover, find a time to talk to them while they are asleep. S/he may be asleep in the bed next to you, or separate from you; at this level of communication, distance is not thought to be material.

Speak to your friend, telling *how you feel* and *what you would like*. Do not be blaming, guilt-tripping, reproachful, accusatory or hostile. Remember that if such communication can get through in the sleep state, s/he is very vulnerable and lacks the defences s/he may use for protection during waking hours. By the same token, s/he may be able to take in information which s/he resists hearing when awake. Speak in simple sentences phrased without too many negatives ('I would like it if you did . . .' rather than

'I wish you wouldn't . . .'). Keep very scrupulously to giving information about your feelings ('I would like it if you spent more time with me'; 'I am unhappy about what happened today') and remember that though you can speak about what you would like or need, it may not be possible or appropriate for your friend to respond to your need. To exert pressure in this situation, or intrude in areas which are not your business, would be a violation.

The Last Divide: Dreaming of Life and Death

We turn lastly to the polarity between life and death. The funeral practices of the early Cretans suggest a belief in some form of rebirth linked to the rising sun (see Chapter 7). Archaeological evidence indicates a circular world view which associated the regeneration of the dead with the yearly regeneration of vegetative life. These early Cretans were not afraid to handle, and live with, the bones of the dead: death apparently lacked the horror it carries for us. With the advent of patriarchy, the social divide between male and female created a split between mind and body, culture and nature, which destroyed the symbiosis with the natural environment on which such a circular regenerative world view depended. In the Archaic period legislation restricted mourning rituals, and fear of pollution from the dead increased.

In the poems of Homer, the abode of the dead is a cold and fearful place of no return, a dead end. That fear of death has stayed with us over the centuries of patriarchy in the west, spreading a chill which mystery religions and alternative spiritual traditions have never been able completely to dispel. Although offering resurrection at a price, Christianity's fear of the body has inexorably drawn in its train a fear of mortality. The black-cloaked, skull-faced reaper of medieval pictures still stalks our imaginations, and twentieth-century science has done little to appease our fears. The mechanistic model of medicine presents the human body as a highly complex piece of apparatus which eventually, like all machines, breaks down and simply stops. The awareness of one's own mortality is hopeless, intolerable; death remains one of the great unmentionable topics in the west, and despite the many cultural shifts in the intervening centuries, the split between life and death is as stark today as in the pages of Homer. And, as Barbara Macdonald painfully describes in *Look Me in the Eye*, it is still women on to whom a male society projects its fear of ageing and death.

In the meantime, other cultures outside the west, and the experience of individuals within western society, continue to offer different perceptions of death. These often reflect the notion of some form of continuity between a number of human lifetimes, as in reincarnation. Many people recollect noticing at some time in their life a sensation of *déjà vu*. In *Memories, Dreams, Reflections*, Jung describes such an experience during his childhood, which convinced him that he was recalling a previous life. He describes how, while living in Klein-Hüningen, he one day saw driving past his house an ancient green carriage from the Black Forest, an antique which looked as if it had come straight from the eighteenth century:

> When I saw it, I felt with great excitement: 'That's it! Sure enough, that comes from *my* times.' It was as though I had recognised it because it was the same type as the one I had driven in myself . . . I cannot describe what was happening in me or what it was that affected me so strongly: a longing, a nostalgia, or a recognition that kept saying 'Yes, that's how it was! Yes, that's how it was!' . . .

Jung describes a clear image of another part of himself who was an old man in a wig and buckled shoes driving such a carriage.

What interests me here again is not so much the 'scientific' basis of such experiences, but the symbols that have been used to picture this process of reincarnation. In Buddhism the image of the wheel is used to symbolise the continuing cycle of death and rebirth. In the Castaneda books a different spiritual tradition represents the human being, not as a soul/body duality, but as a cluster which is joined during life and separates again after death. In *Tales of Power* Don Juan explains to Castaneda that the *nagual* is the unspeakable in which all the possible feelings and beings and selves float like barges, peaceful and unaltered forever. Then the glue of life binds some of them together and a being is created; but as soon as the force of life leaves the body all those single awarenesses disintegrate and go back again to where they came from, the *nagual*.

Again, various symbols have been put forward for the space between lives, the after or 'inter' world beyond our normal consciousness. Jung, unconscious during a near-fatal illness, had a vision in which:

> It seemed to me that I was high up in space . . . Far below my feet lay Ceylon, and in the distance ahead of me the subcontinent

of India . . . I knew that I was on the point of departing from
the earth.
(*Memories, Dreams, Reflections*)

In space he finds a huge block of dark stone which had been hollowed
out into a temple inside. At the entrance sits a Hindu in lotus position.
As he approaches this stone he has a feeling of the 'whole
phantasmagoria of earthly existence' being sloughed away but a strong
sense of his identity and history remaining, and 'I had the certainty
that I was about to enter an illuminated room and would meet there
all those people to whom I belong in reality. There I would at last
understand – this too was a certainty – what historical nexus I or my
life fitted into.' At this point the vision is interrupted; Jung describes
how the image of his doctor pulls him back, eventually, to normal life.
Jane Roberts in *The Nature of the Psyche* uses a metaphor which
compares human life to a television drama being shown on your
channel, and points out that before and after showing it doesn't go
anywhere but simply '*is*' until reactivated to be re-shown: 'In the same
way, you are alive whether or not you are playing on an earth
"program". You *are*, whether you are in time or out of it.' How real
is the TV drama? In some of this symbolism, human life becomes a
performance or masquerade enacted within the framework of a
greater reality. In *Memories, Dreams, Reflections*, Jung describes a dream
in which, on a walking trip, he enters a wayside chapel to find no
Christian accoutrements but:

> . . . on the floor in front of the altar, facing me, sat a yogi – in
> lotus posture, in deep meditation. When I looked at him more
> closely, I realised that he had my face. I started in profound fright,
> and awake with the thought: 'Aha, so he is the one who is
> meditating me. He has a dream, and I am it.' I knew that when
> he awakened, I would no longer be.

The unorthodox strand of Rosicrucian Christianity has symbolised
death as an awakening after a dream, and each lifetime as a day in
a cosmic school where we learn to battle against ignorance. In a
similar vein, Jane Roberts in *The Nature of the Psyche* attributes to life
the transitory nature of a stage play, and, comparing an individual life
to one of many roles which the same actor can play, gently mocks
our western fear of death:

You say: 'I must maintain my individuality after death,' as if after the play the actor playing Hamlet stayed in that role, refused to study other parts or go on in his career, and said: 'I am Hamlet, forever bound to follow the dilemmas and the challenges of my way. I insist upon maintaining my individuality.'

Such symbolism as I have given here provides an alternative to the stark polarity of death as the diametrical opposite of life. According to such symbolism, death remains an end, but perhaps not a completely final one. It takes its place against a wider background of continuing life, even without individual survival. It becomes a certainty that we can look in the face rather than shy away from. It becomes a teacher whose poignant lessons can be contemplated rather than banished. Don Juan teaches Castaneda to regard death as an adviser who puts feelings of self-importance, anxiety, petty annoyance and self-pity into perspective. In *Journey to Ixtlan* he points out to Castaneda that death is our eternal companion, and asks how anyone can feel so important when we know that death is stalking us. He tells Castaneda that the thing to do when he is impatient is to turn to his left and ask advice from his death. He suggests that an immense amount of pettiness is dropped if one catches a glimpse of it, for death is the only wise adviser that we have.

Modern humanistic psychotherapies have also stressed the importance of integrating the awareness of death into the experience of living. They suggest that only a willingness to face the unknown can free us to live with the immediacy and vibrancy which makes a full life. Laura Perls, a founder of Gestalt therapy, has said in *Gestalt Therapy Now* that in her experience real creativity is inextricably linked with awareness of mortality:

The sharper this awareness, the greater the urge to bring forth something new, to participate in the infinitely continuing creativeness in nature. This is what makes out of sex, love; out of the herd, society; out of wheat and fruit, bread and wine; and out of sound, music. This is what makes life liveable . . .

In his book *Living Your Dying*, Stanley Keleman connects death with all the endings or 'little deaths' which we experience throughout life, and suggests that by denying death and loss, and making no space for mourning and grief, we impoverish our lives and rob ourselves of the chance to engage fully with the present. He points out that in our society, 'The myth is that death is an enemy to be overcome, . . . and that it is intrinsically evil'; he suggests that by replacing our social images of death with our experience we have the chance to create a new vision of our lives: 'At each turning point we have a chance either to make a new myth for ourselves or to follow an old one.'

In this book I am suggesting that the same is true not only of the split between life and death, but also of the split between masculine and feminine, black and white, active and passive, sun and moon, conscious and unconscious. In our society we are surrounded by old myths which perpetuate these splits. We can follow these old myths, or we can question them, look more clearly into our own experience, and create a new vision. The choice is ours.

We have a choice, too, about how we view one of the biggest splits of all, which is the subject of the next chapter: the split between mind – or soul – and body.

Book References

Page numbers relate to passages referred to or quoted, listed in most cases in the order in which they have been used. Where there are numerous references to the same text, or where the context may not be obvious, I have indicated the subject matter.

Adler, Margot, *Drawing Down the Moon: Witches, Druids, Goddess-worshippers and Pagans in America Today*, Beacon Press, Boston, 1986, p. 16 (first publ. Viking Press, New York, 1979).

Arica teachings of Oscar Ichazo: see, recently, references in Gabrielle Roth with John Loudon, *Maps to Ecstasy: Teachings of an Urban Shaman*, New World Library, San Rafael, CA, 1989; also in John C. Lilly, *The Centre of the Cyclone*, Paladin, 1973 and John C. Lilly and Antonietta Lilly, *The Diadic Cyclone*, Paladin, 1978.

Arthur, Marylin, 'Politics and Pomegranates: an Interpretation of the Homeric Hymn to Demeter', *Arethusa*, 10 (1) Spring 1977, pp. 7-47.

Assagioli, Robert, *Psychosynthesis: a Manual of Principles and Techniques*, Turnstone Books, London, 1975, pp. 295, 298 (first publ. 1965).

Bachelard, Gaston, *The Psychoanalysis of Fire*, trans. A.C.M. Moss, Beacon Press, Boston, USA, 1964 (first publ. Librairie Gallimard, 1938).

Blake, William, 'The Marriage of Heaven and Hell' (c.1793) in J. Bronowski (ed.) *William Blake: a Selection of Poems and Letters*, Penguin, Harmondsworth, Middx, 1958, p. 94.

Bye, Harriet, 'Of Cabbages and Kings', *Country Women*, 24, April 1977

('Personal Power' issue), publ. Country Women, Box 51, Albion, CA, p. 11.

Castaneda, Carlos, *The Eagle's Gift*, Pocket Books, New York, 1982, pp. 50-53.

—— *The Fire From Within*, Black Swan, Transworld, London, Australia and New Zealand, 1985, pp. 286-7, 293.

—— *Journey to Ixtlan: the Lessons of Don Juan*, Penguin, Harmondsworth, Middx, 1974, pp. 50-51.

—— *The Second Ring of Power*, Hodder and Stoughton, London, Sydney, Auckland and Toronto, 1977, pp. 151-2.

—— *Tales of Power*, Penguin, Harmondsworth, Middx, 1976, p. 263.

Crombie, Robert Ogilvie, ('Roc') writing for the original Findhorn Garden pamphlet, cited in Paul Hawken, *The Magic of Findhorn*, Souvenir Press, London, 1975, pp. 143, 156.

Cumont, F., *Astrology and Religion among the Greeks and Romans*, G.P. Putnam's Sons, New York and London, 1912.

Ernst, Sheila, 'Can a Daughter be a Woman? Women's Identity and Psychological Separation', in Sheila Ernst and Marie Maguire (eds) *Living with the Sphinx*, The Women's Press, London, 1987, pp. 68-116.

Evans, Hilary, *Gods: Spirits: Cosmic Guardians: A Comparative Study of the Encounter Experience*, The Aquarian Press, Wellingborough, Northants, 1987.

Evans-Wentz, W.Y. (comp. and ed.), *The Tibetan Book of the Dead*, trans. Lama Kazi Dawa-Samdup, Oxford University Press, 1980, p. 147 (first publ. 1927).

Fordham, Frieda, *An Introduction to Jung's Psychology*, Penguin, Harmondsworth, Middx, 1972, p. 53.

Fox, Oliver, *Astral Projection: a Record of Research*, Rider and Co., London, 1939.

Frances, 'Astrology', *Bread and Roses*, Summer 1975, publ. The Bread and Roses Collective, 29, Glossop Street, Leeds 6, pp. 6-7.

Frankfort, H., *Cylinder Seals*, Macmillan, London, 1939, pp. 156 ff.

Freud, Sigmund, *Introductory Lectures on Psychoanalysis*, trans. J. Riviere, Allen and Unwin, London, 1922, p. 138 (also publ. Pelican Freud Library, Vol. 1, trans. J. Strachey, Penguin, Harmondsworth, Middx, 1974).

Garfield, Patricia L., *Creative Dreaming*, Futura, London, 1976, pp. 33-4, 80 ff.

Gilchrist, Cherry, *Alchemy the Great Work: a History and Evaluation of the Western Hermetic Tradition*, Aquarian Press, Wellingborough, Northants, 1984, pp. 109 (alchemy and Christianity), 106 (symbols at both laboratory and personal level), 68 (transformation through purifying), 69 (Mercury as highest and lowest), 126 ff (Newton and Boyle), 30 (theories about composition of matter).

Goodison, Lucy, *Death, Women and the Sun: Symbolism of Regeneration in Early Aegean Religion*, Institute of Classical Studies, London, 1989.

Greene, Liz, 'Living Alchemy', seminar paper, given in London, 14 June 1981. To my knowledge it is unpublished, but see Liz Greene, 'Alchemical Symbolism in the Horoscope', in Liz Greene and Howard Sasportas,

Dynamics of the Unconscious, Arkana/Penguin, Harmondsworth, Middx, 1989, pp. 225-360.

—— *Relating: an Astrological Guide to Living with Others on a Small Planet*, Coventure, London, 1977, pp. 235 (vital symbolic alphabets), 33-4 (sun and moon), 170 ('libido').

Griffin, Susan, *Made From This Earth: Selections from Her Writing*, The Women's Press, London, 1982, p. III.

Hansen, Sharon, 'Lucid Dreaming', *Country Women*, 24, April 1977 ('Personal Power' issue), publ. Country Women, Box 51, Albion, CA 85410, p. 16.

Hillman, James, *The Dream and the Underworld*, Harper and Row, New York, 1979, p. 91.

Homeric Hymns, see Chapter 7 Book References.

Huson, Paul, *The Devil's Picture Book. The Compleat Guide to Tarot Cards: Their Origins and Their Usage*, Sphere Books, London, 1972, p. 234.

Jung, C.G., *The Archetypes and the Collective Unconscious*, trans. R.F.C. Hull, Routledge and Kegan Paul, London, 1959, pp. 50-2 (sun's penis and Mithraic ritual), 70 (man with too much 'anima'), 88-90 ('bloodless maiden'), 79-80 (crystal formation) (Vol. IX, Part I of *Collected Works*).

—— *Memories, Dreams, Reflections*, recorded and edited by Aniela Jaffé, trans. R. and C. Winston, Collins, London, 1977, pp. 430-1 (dream about wife), 50-1 (ancient green carriage), 320-3 (vision of earth), 355 (dream about wayside chapel) (first publ. in UK by Collins and Routledge and Kegan Paul, London, 1963).

—— *Symbols of Transformation*, trans. R.F.C. Hull, Routledge and Kegan Paul, London, 1956, pp. 50-1 n. 18 (threads of future in present), 89, 121, 202, 251, 211, 355 (all on sun linked with fire, father, hero and consciousness), 412 (God's 'ray' and Christ's 'sunbeam'), 430 (using imaginative material like clothing) (Vol. V of *Collected Works*).

—— *Two Essays on Analytical Psychology*, trans. R.F.C. Hull, Routledge and Kegan Paul, London, 1953, p. 188 (Vol. VII of *Collected Works*).

Keleman, Stanley, *Living Your Dying*, Random House/Bookworks, New York and Berkeley, CA, 1974, pp. 3, 15, 5, 71 (all on changing attitudes to death).

Lind, Ingrid, *Astrology and Commonsense*, Hodder and Stoughton, London, 1962, p. 65.

Long, Max Freedom, *The Secret Science Behind Miracles*, DeVorss, Marina de Rey, CA, 1986 (first publ. 1948).

Macdonald, Barbara, with Cynthia Rich, *Look Me in the Eye: Old Women, Aging and Ageism*, The Women's Press, London, 1984 (first publ. Spinsters, Ink, San Francisco, 1984).

MacManaway, Bruce, with Johanna Turcan, *Healing: the Energy that Can Restore Health*, Thorsons, Wellingborough, Northants, 1983, p. 79.

Mariechild, Diane, *Mother Wit: a Feminist Guide to Psychic Development*,

Crossing Press, Trumansburg, NY, 1981, p. 148.

Metzner, Ralph, *Maps of Consciousness*, Collier Books/Macmillan, New York and London, 1971, pp. 90 (on alchemy), 87-9 (suggested chemical basis for four elements), 78ff (on using Tarot), 108ff (theories about the basis of astrology).

Monroe, Robert A., *Journeys Out of the Body*, Souvenir Press, London, 1986 (first publ. Doubleday, Garden City, NY, 1985).

Moody, Raymond A., *Reflections on Life after Life*, Bantam Books, Toronto, New York, London, Sydney and Auckland, 1977, p. 15.

Ouseley, S.G.J., *Colour Meditations: with Guide to Colour-Healing*, L.N. Fowler, Romford, Essex, 1976, pp. 27-8, 32, 47 (first publ. 1949).

Perls, Laura, 'One Gestalt Therapist's Approach', in Joen Fagan and Irma Lee Shepherd (eds) *Gestalt Therapy Now: Theory, Techniques, Applications*, Harper and Row, New York, Hagerstown, San Francisco and London, 1971, p. 129.

Piercy, Marge, on the Tarot, cited in Karen Lindsey, 'Feminist Spirituality', *Spare Rib*, 62 (Sept. 1977), publ. Spare Rib, 27 Clerkenwell Close, London EC1, pp. 38–41.

Porter, Jean, *Psychic Development*, Random House, New York and California, 1974, pp. 12ff.

Rich, Adrienne, *Of Woman Born: Motherhood as Experience and Institution*, Virago, London, 1977, p. 95n (first publ. W.W. Norton, USA, 1976).

River, Lindsay and Sally Gillespie, *The Knot of Time: Astrology and Female Experience*, The Women's Press, London, 1987, pp. 74–5.

Roberts, Jane, *The Nature of Personal Reality*, a Seth Book, Prentice-Hall, NJ, 1974, pp. 439, 452, 455.

—— *The Nature of the Psyche: Its Human Expression*, a Seth Book, Prentice-Hall, NJ, 1979, pp. 13, 162.

Rosicrucian Christianity, see, for example, Max Heindel, *Rosicrucian Christianity Lecture No. 6: Life and Activity in Heaven*, The Rosicrucian Fellowship, Oceanside, CA, undated. See also, more generally, Christopher McIntosh, *The Rosicrucians: The History, Mythology and Rituals of an Occult Order*, Crucible/Thorsons, Wellingborough, Northants, 1987.

Sharman-Burke, Juliet, *The Complete Book of Tarot*, Pan Books, London, Sydney and Auckland, 1985, p. 17.

Smith, David L., 'Archetypal Foundations of Grounding', *Energy and Character: the Journals of Bioenergetic Research*, 11 (2) May 1980, Abbotsbury Publications, pp. 48-60.

Swedenborg, see G. Trobridge, *Swedenborg: Life and Teaching*, The Swedenborg Society, 20/21 Bloomsbury Way, London WC1, 1974 (revised version of *Life of Swedenborg*, first publ. 1907).

Tillich, P., *The Courage To Be*, Collins, London, 1962, pp. 20ff; I quote p. 15.

Wallace, Amy and Bill Henkin, *The Psychic Healing Book*, Turnstone Press,

Wellingborough, Northants, 1981, pp. 194ff (First publ. Delacorte Press, New York, 1978).

Wickes, Frances G., *The Inner World of Childhood: a Study in Analytical Psychology*, Coventure, London, 1977, pp. 156, 158, and 156-194 *passim*.

Wilson, Colin, *Mysteries*, Grafton Books/Collins, London, Toronto, Sydney and Auckland, 1979, p. 372 (quoting Frederik Van Eeden, 'A Study of Dreams', 1913).

5

THE LUMINOUS BODY

All bibles or sacred codes have been the causes of the following Errors:
  1. That Man has two real existing principles: Viz: a Body & a Soul.
  2. That Energy, call'd Evil, is alone from the body; & that Reason, call'd Good, is alone from the Soul.
  3. That God will torment Man in Eternity for following his Energies.
  But the following contraries to these are True:
  1. Man has no Body distinct from his Soul; for that call'd Body is a portion of Soul discern'd by the five Senses, the chief inlets of Soul in this age.
  2. Energy is the only life, and is from the Body; and Reason is the bound or outward circumference of Energy.
  3. Energy is Eternal Delight.
(William Blake, 'The Marriage of Heaven and Hell')

Blake's assertions that 'Man has no Body distinct from his Soul', that the 'Body is a portion of Soul discern'd by the five Senses' and that 'Energy is the only life, and is from the Body' are as revolutionary today as when he etched them 200 years ago. Whatever other changes the twentieth century has brought, we are still dominated by the centuries-old Christian credo that the body is separate from the soul and is at best flawed, at worst evil. Advanced capitalism has only reinforced the basic ethic that the body is an object, and not a particularly pleasant one; at best it may be a *useful* object, if its labour can be exploited for profit or its appearance can be exploited to promote a product, a media personality, a political image. The sexual pleasure it gives is seen as a potential threat to society's moral values. Seductive, saleable, suspect, it remains far from being recognised as a 'portion of Soul'.

How have we been taught to think of it as suspect or evil? What are the symbols and images used? One basic symbol, which can be traced back to Plato and the Greek tradition, represents the body as a dark container imprisoning the divine light of the soul. It is also morally weak: in Christian language sins are 'of the flesh'. The body torments the soul with sexual desires whose fulfilment is forbidden. Its separate parts, when they are not evil, are sinister, frightening or disgusting. From clanking skeletons to the recent spate of 'body horror' films, the physical provides meat for our most frightening fantasies as well as our rudest terms of abuse. In our conscious lives, we find many ways of denying our connection with it: we slim to disguise our body's shape, we use make-up to cover our skin, deodorants to disguise our smell. The body tends to be disregarded and forgotten, except when exercise, cosmetic or medical attention is needed to 'fix the machine' and keep it looking good and running smoothly. Severe 'health and fitness' programmes can become another form of tyranny to make it perform or conform to certain ideals.

But what is denied has a habit of dogging us. This very attitude turns our physicality into a powerful spectre which haunts us perpetually. A Catholic cathedral dedicated to the purity of the spirit is filled with images of flesh mortified: the straining muscles of crucified bodies, bleeding hands pierced with nails, the embalmed corpses of medieval saints. The soul has no texture, while there is an obsession with the physical in every form except that of the living, whole, happy human body. Modern advertising's spectacle of disembodied parts (legs without bodies, torsoes without heads) also dismembers our sense of the whole human body, and its emphasis on 'glamorous' images makes us feel there is something unacceptable about ordinary body shapes and functions. The result of banishing and objectifying the body is that its elements can take on a grotesque and often menacing life of their own. Skin colour assumes a magical power to determine whether or not a person is 'socially acceptable'. The penis becomes fetishised as a symbol of power which distorts and impairs its bodily function and its sensitivity in giving and receiving pleasure. By denying the body we give it power over us, because we always walk in fear of it.

Of course, this is not the only possible attitude to the body. Blake was not entirely accurate in suggesting that 'all bibles or sacred codes' deny the body. Our physical being does not have to be symbolised as an assemblage of dislocated horrors, and there are a number of spiritual traditions from the east and west which have survived to offer us a very different view of our physicality. In this chapter I am going to propose a framework for experiencing and understanding our bodies which draws on several of these traditions, and which thus opens up the possibility not only of adopting a different attitude to the body, but also of beginning to live differently with it in practice. It is a framework which I have found very useful.

I am not proposing this framework as any kind of final truth about the body, but rather as a coherent alternative to our society's prevailing image of the body. It is an alternative which offers a completely different symbolic view of spirituality and its relationship to body functions. Ultimately every model we have for understanding matter is a symbol. Even 'scientific' hypotheses are couched in man-made symbolic frameworks which must be open to question and revision: witness the continuing debate about whether we can most accurately symbolise light as waves or particles. Again it is a question of moving away from symbols which trap and restrict us towards those which enable us to ask new questions and articulate, in turn, new symbols which reflect more closely the phenomena of our experience. I suggest that the symbolic view of these alternative traditions is enabling in just such a way, and I see them as a fruitful basis for developing closer understandings about the body and its processes.

Several of these alternative traditions are ancient and derive from the east, but their ideas have in some cases been developed by schools of twentieth-century physotherapy; there are also some parallels in spiritual teachings from the Americas. What concerns us here in all these teachings is the central idea that 'spiritual' energy is not separate from the body but immanent throughout it. This energy is thought to express through the body in different ways at different points on a number of different frequencies, including sex. 'Spiritual' energy, or 'fine' energy (as it is sometimes called), is thought to run through the body along certain paths; and also to radiate out from the body into a wide energy field or 'aura' surrounding the body. This 'aura' is believed to comprise several layers and to contain fibres or threads which can connect us to other people and things; it also contains a series of vortices or whirlpools (sometimes called 'chakras') which draw 'fine' energy into and out of the body.

This model of the body appears in a parallel form in a number of different teachings. The structure which these traditions propose for energy movement in the body corresponds closely to that which Wilhelm Reich arrived at from a very different starting point in his psychotherapeutic work. He suggested that 'vegetative' or 'orgone' energy moves along the body and that any blocking of such energy by tension in various parts of the body can result in physical illness or neurosis. The tension can, he believed, be related to the holding in of emotional expression, often as the result of childhood trauma or suppression. Reich worked to unlock such blockages by assisting physical and emotional release, aiming in this way to restore the flow of energy throughout the body and return the individual to a healthy state.

The 5000-year-old Chinese discipline of acupuncture similarly proposes a series of meridians which lead energy up and down the body: the dramatic effects sometimes achieved by acupuncture could be understood as the result of pressure applied at certain points on the meridians, affecting the circulation of energy. Experiments have recorded a greater electrical charge between known acupuncture points than between other points on the body. Yogic traditions speak of an aura (see, for example, Mishra's *Fundamentals of Yoga*), and the ancient Indian system of the 'chakras' locates seven vortices of energy at different points along the body, by means of which energy is drawn in for distribution through the body, or discharged from it. These points are actually places at which 21 different acupuncture meridians cross, and the chakra system dovetails neatly with the system of acupuncture.

The spiritual teachings expounded by Carlos Castaneda in his famous and controversial 'Don Juan' books present a highly compatible picture of an energy field around the body, which is described as a luminous egg containing fibres. This would suggest that such ideas are not unknown in the Americas.

Recent decades in the west have seen some interest in 'Kirlian' photography, named after the work of the Ukranians, Valentina and Semyon Kirlian, and described in the Snellgroves' book, *The Unseen Self*. Recording, on photosensitive material, electrically induced corona discharges from the skin, the method has produced many photographs of an irregular radiation from the skin surface. While perhaps merely reflecting radiation of heat and moisture, such photographs have also been taken to reveal an inner layer of the energy field around the body.

In this century many of these understandings have been brought together into a system of 'subtle anatomy' known as radionics (see David Tansley's *Radionics and the Subtle Anatomy of Man*). The understandings are incorporated, in varying degrees, by those teaching psychic and healing skills in the west today. I will draw on all of these sources in outlining this alternative view of the body.

The model of 'fine energy' within and around the body offers itself as a unitive concept. Not only does it unite body and soul, sexuality and spirituality, but it also provides a means for us to interpret many otherwise fragmented, disconcerting and apparently mystical phenomena in our lives, which may have emerged in meditation, drug states, dreams or as flashes of intuition. For example, meditation (during which some researchers – such as Durand Kiefer – have recorded changes in brain waves) could be understood as a means of tuning in to a greater awareness of the quality of 'fine energy' in and around the body; perhaps some people reach a similar experience doing yoga or T'ai Chi. Kirlian photography suggests that the aura changes in relation to the mood and state of mind of the individual; such changes are perhaps reflected in expressions about picking up 'good vibes' or 'bad vibes' from someone. Esoteric or 'subtle' anatomy also suggests that in certain states (sleep, under the influence of psychedelic drugs), the energy field expands. This could be understood as a factor contributing to the feeling of intense communion, sometimes amounting to virtual identification, which individuals on LSD sometimes feel towards people, animals, or plants. Experiments carried out with Kirlian photography also suggest that the energy field has a certain autonomy from the physical body. The radiation around the leaf held its shape consistently even after part of the leaf had been broken away. The comparison has been made with people who claim to feel pain in a limb even after its amputation, perhaps reflecting some awareness of the limb's surviving energy field. In certain conditions, part of the energy body is thought to leave the physical body altogether and to move away. This is the 'astral body' and in esoteric traditions the process has been termed 'astral travelling'. The physical body is left inert and a Kirlian photograph of it at this time will apparently show no radiation. We are thus provided with a coherent and non-mystical anatomical framework to understand the type of experiences mentioned in Chapter 4, as when people report the sensation of having actually travelled in their sleep, or describe watching their own body from above during a hospital operation.

Many people have on occasion experienced an 'intuitive flash' when meeting or looking at another person; we might understand this as a process of unconsciously picking up energy emitted by the person. Similarly many of us have had some experience of what seemed to be a telepathic communication: dreaming or suddenly 'knowing' that a friend or relative is ill or in trouble. Rather than being disconcerted by this as a 'mystical' experience, we could understand it as a transmission of energy from one person to another, rather like a radio transmission. Interested in the possible military uses of this faculty, the Russians have conducted a series of 'psi' experiments and have found that the energy transmitted in telepathy most closely follows the behaviour and patterns of electromagnetic energy, and yet is different in certain key aspects (see Sheila Ostrander and Lynn Schroeder's book, *Psi: Psychic Discoveries behind the Iron Curtain*). In the next chapter I will touch on the relationship between theories of the 'energy body' and the findings of the new physics. Here I am primarily concerned with suggesting the possible relevance of such theories as a framework for understanding the phenomena of our bodies differently, reducing the fear which surrounds them and providing a theoretical model for certain experiences which mystify us. The model of esoteric or 'subtle' anatomy not only renders certain 'occult' experiences less frightening; it also transforms our whole sense of the body from one of dead weight to one of vibrant landscape, from a prison to something nearer a temple. It is hard to feel the same repugnance for physicality, waste products and illness if we can accept that every inch of our being is infused with delicate and dynamic patterns of fine energy.

Throughout this book I have presented evidence for the influence of society in the construction of symbols. Of course, society does not account for everything: there *is* a real world out there for us to apprehend, and we *do* have a certain apparatus for perception which may predispose us towards certain interpretations. However, we have also deeply absorbed certain social biases which incline us to prefer certain interpretations of reality; this applies as much to our perceptions of the body as to our dreams and fantasies. As Mary Douglas puts it in *Natural Symbols*, 'The social body constrains the way the physical body is perceived. The physical experience of the body, always modified by the social categories through which it is known, sustains a particular view of society'. Thus we could see the mind/body split as a reflection of our society. In a society where power is centred at the top and is effectively denied to the mass of people, we have a view of the body which overvalues the head and downgrades the rest of the body. Its lower parts are especially devalued. Whether a woman's legs are banished underneath a nun's habit or used in advertising to sell cars, they are denied and objectified; an example of the way in which capitalist and patriarchal oppression is rooted in the very quick of our flesh. It is hard to appreciate the deeply debilitating effect this mind/body split has upon our self-respect and our ability to use our full power to act in the world. If we believe that no unequivocal good can come from the body, it becomes extremely hard for us to take our experienced needs and desires seriously or to act on the basis of them. This in turn diminishes our political potency. Hence, to work with a model in which spirituality is immanent in, and expressed through, the body is a way in which we can make some return to a concept of wholeness, and take the revolutionary step of refusing to see ourselves as split.

As I have stressed throughout, it is not possible for us simply to decide voluntaristically to throw out old symbols, such as the mind/ body split, and adopt new ones. It requires, rather, a slow process of investigating alternative symbols, and trying them out for size, a process which needs to walk hand-in-hand with a deconstruction of the old ones, and thrives on new experiences which require new symbols to articulate them. So, as I embark on a fuller investigation of ideas about the 'energy body', I shall include exercises in which we can try these ideas out practically and see how they might enlarge and extend our experience.

All serious researchers into the nature of the human energy field arc at pains to stress that they are not 'cranks'; such is the stigma attached to straying outside our social norms of thought. For myself, I see the questioning of received opinion and the testing of assumptions as a central part of any intelligent enquiry into the nature of reality, and an important expression of the urge for a better society. It is not the nature of the *object* of enquiry, but rather the *method* of enquiry, which makes knowledge scientific. In response to the discoveries of the new physics, scientist Fritjof Capra has proposed calling

> any approach to understanding reality scientific that satisfies two criteria: first it must be based on systematic observation, and second it must involve the process of model-making, . . . of interconnecting the observed data in a . . . logically coherent way into a conceptual model which will always be limited and approximate (that recognition is very important).

Bob Moore of the Psykisk Centre in Denmark, on whose work much of this chapter draws, teaches self-development through various kinds of energy work. He has been involved in such a process of observation of the human energy field and model-making for many years. While all phenomena of the natural world remain breathtaking and ultimately incomprehensible, including those which science has attempted to chart such as light and gravity, I remain reassured by Bob Moore's teaching that 'there is nothing mystical in the psychic'.

So how is the 'energy body' believed to work? What kind of alternative does it offer to the mind/body split, and how can it help us to pay attention to sensations or experiences we overlook, and so to value the body differently? I will start with the energy whirlpools described by clairvoyants and spiritual teachers in many different cultures and different parts of the globe: the chakras.

The Chakras

Almost all sources which describe the aura report a series of vortices of energy located in it corresponding to different activities in our lives, like grounding, relationships and self-expression. These are most commonly described in the terminology of the Indian chakra system. Although accounts from different sources vary considerably, and there is not even agreement about the number of chakras, seven are commonly described, placed at points along the body. Here I will mostly follow the version I was taught by Anne Parks and Bob Moore. Each chakra is understood as drawing a certain quality of fine energy into the body for processing, and discharging unwanted energy from it. We have the root chakra at the base of the spine, the 'centre' chakra or hara at the belly; the solar plexus chakra; the heart chakra; the throat chakra; the pineal or 'third eye' on the brow; and the crown chakra at the top of the head. Thus the chakra map, whether or not you take it literally (anatomically), stands as a metaphor for the make-up of the human being. The map is outlined clearly by David Tansley, as well as by C.W. Leadbeater in his rather archaic classic, *The Chakras*. Here I will mention some of the interesting connections that have been made between the different chakras and aspects of our daily lives.

The 'root' chakra is located on the back of the body near the base of the spine where the hips divide, just above the coccyx at the third sacral vertebra (difficult to pinpoint as they merge together here). The energy moves down and back away from the body rather like a tail. This chakra brings in 'earth' energy and is linked to our legs and feet, genitals and anus. It is from here that the very powerful *kundalini* energy, sometimes symbolised as a coiled sleeping serpent or as the goddess Shakti, can rise up the spine through the other chakras with dramatic (and sometimes disastrous) effects on the individual; see the personal account of such an experience in Gopi Krishna's *Kundalini: the Evolutionary Energy in Man*. In terms of life issues, this chakra relates to the material and physical base of our being and issues such as work, food, shelter, security, the will-to-be. It is concerned with your root situation and what you are doing every day: do you like your job? how are you using yourself? what happiness or unhappiness do you obtain in the things you are doing? If you have no joy in basic daily activities it is hard for the rest of you to function. The energy of this chakra is at the slowest rate of vibration and relates to elimination and grounding. If you have insufficient connection with this 'grounding' energy, you may feel unstable and insecure, while at the other extreme you may feel heavy, bogged down, and stuck in a rut. As Diane Mariechild points out in *Mother Wit*, the balanced functioning of this chakra is crucial to your ability to survive and make changes.

The second, or 'centre', chakra is located in the belly, about two inches below the navel (if you place one finger in the navel, then three fingers'-breadth down is where it is strongest). A similar point has been given various names in different systems: *hara* in Japanese Zen, *kath* in Sufi schools. At the back the chakra radiates from a point slightly higher on the spine, just above the waist at the third lumbar vertebra. This 'centre' chakra is linked to the belly and pelvic area, and to the functions of the bladder, the colon, the small intestine and the reproductive system. The energy of this chakra is described as relating to vitality, instinctual movement and drives, generation, and sexuality in its broader sense of *expression* through sexual contact. It is connected to strength, physical power, rhythm and letting go (which does not imply raw outbursts of feeling but rather a strong sense of emotional attunement and control). Japanese tradition stresses that the *hara* is not only a sustaining and renewing but also an *ordering* power, which is the key to flow in all activities whether carrying, climbing, cycling, gardening, dancing, writing, typing, speaking or singing (see, for example, Von Dürckheim's book, *Hara*). I will discuss this important chakra more fully later.

The third chakra is generally located at the solar plexus, about a hand's width above the navel, just below where the ribcage divides; again it is slightly higher at the back. It is connected with the functions of the stomach, gall bladder, diaphragm and nervous system. The energy with which it deals relates to raw and strong emotions such as fear and anger, and its function is connected to intake and assimilation: just as this area digests food, so it also transmutes feelings, and the change from an emotional to a non-emotional state happens through the solar plexus. If you face or 'digest' your fears, for example, they become less debilitating and free you to love; similarly, working through jealous or possessive feelings can loosen their hold. This is the area of personal history and is activated in the operation of personal power and strong personal attachments to others. If it is unbalanced it can affect the quality of relationships, leading to conditional affection and 'love with strings' which seeks to control others: 'I'll love you if you love me'. If balanced, this chakra plays an important role in our ability to understand and to help others, for example through counselling or therapy.

The fourth, or 'heart', chakra is not located at the physical heart but in the centre, just above the breasts; at the back it is, again, slightly higher. It is linked with the functions of the heart and the circulatory system. It is concerned with feelings of a less attached kind, such as dispassionate love, compassion and the impulse to serve humanity. While solar plexus love can cling sentimentally, heart love usually expresses itself less invasively and can respect boundaries and give another space. A balanced activity in this chakra enables you to see emotional connections with others in a clearer, less involved way.

The fifth, or 'throat', chakra is located at the dimple at the bottom of the neck in front, and at the groove at the top of the neck behind. It relates to the functions of throat, mouth, voice, lungs, arms and hands and is linked with discrimination, creativity and self-expression. When this chakra is impaired there may be difficulties in communication, as when 'words get stuck in the throat'.

The sixth, or 'brow', chakra is placed on the forehead just above where the brows come together; it extends inside the skull to a point which can be located by placing one fingertip at the top, back point of each ear and imagining a line running from each to meet at a central point inside the head. This chakra is commonly linked to the pineal gland and to the functions of intellect and intuition. Sometimes called the 'third eye', it is also associated with psychic abilities such as clairvoyance.

The seventh, or 'crown', chakra, which is located very slightly forward from the crown of the head, reflects changes in the other chakras and relates to issues of overall development and attunement with energy forces inside and outside the body. This chakra can be opened through meditation and can balance the process of intake and expression of energy of the whole organism. It is perhaps symbolised by the flame shown over the head of Buddha, and the halo in Christian art.

There are also secondary chakras in the hands and feet which I am not discussing here; dozens of minor chakras, for example on the tip of the nose, are also sometimes mentioned.

This chakra system is based on the seven main chakras of Indian yoga, and in the west they are sometimes called by their Sanskrit names. There are also correspondences between the chakras and the spheres on the Tree of Life in the Cabbalistic system (see Will Parfitt's *The Living Qabalah*). The chakras are said to vibrate at increasingly high speeds as we move up the body; they are sometimes symbolised as lotus flowers, the number of petals reflecting the frequency of vibration from four at the root to nearly a thousand petals at the crown. The chakras have also been linked with musical notes from 'C' up, and music has been specially composed to harmonise with meditation on each chakra. They have also been associated with the colours of the rainbow from red at the root chakra to violet on the crown.

The flow of energy through each chakra is said to reflect the degree of openness or blockedness which an individual has in each of these areas of her life. The circulation of a chakra may be faint, or overactive, or impaired by blocks, with varying results in daily life: for example, an over-open solar plexus may make you vulnerable to picking up other people's feelings and confusing them with your own. Esoteric disciplines such as radionics or spiritual healing aim to balance the activity of each of the chakras so that the energy flows evenly up and down between them, instead of a person being 'all in her head' or 'stuck in her gut emotions' or 'unable to express herself'. Each chakra is seen as a doorway: it clears energy out from the body if there is too much which needs releasing; and it brings energy in if the body is low on that kind of energy, if it is unbalanced or particularly vulnerable. The suggestion is that the chakras are connected via *nadis* or subtle energy channels to endocrine glands, some of which are neuro-secretory in nature, which transmute the energy and feed it into the bloodstream (see also Leadbeater's suggested connections between the chakras and the nervous system). As with any other area of a human being, various factors may damage or impair their functioning, as David Tansley explains in his book on radionics:

Chakras can be damaged by traumatic accidents, and especially by sudden, dramatic, emotional shocks. Nagging fears or anxiety can, through constant wearing activity, disturb the functional balance. Chakras are frequently found to be blocked, either at the point where energy enters, or at the point where it exits to flow into the etheric body. If a blockage occurs at the entrance, the energy flowing in is frequently driven back to its point of origin on the astral or mental planes. This brings about psychological problems and endocrine dysfunction.

With practice, the chakras can be sensed with the hands; clairvoyants see them, and can also perceive blockages. Some body-orientated psychotherapists, such as John Pierrakos, have attempted to correlate chakra malfunction with various types of psychological disturbance.

When two people come together in a close relationship, the pattern of activity of one person's chakras connects with their partner's, and they may link more strongly through some chakras than others. This could be seen as parallel to the comments people may make that their relationship is 'primarily sexual' or 'we have a strong spiritual bond' or 'I have powerful gut feelings for her', 'we relate best through exchanging ideas', 'I love her as a friend but I don't feel sexual towards her', 'she makes me feel steady, secure and grounded' or 'I feel strongly attached and I can't let go of her'. Psychics seeing the two people together can sometimes perceive the connections between them and tell which are stronger and which need to be strengthened in order to create a more balanced relationship on all the different levels of being. The painful process of separating from a relationship involves cutting these 'cords' between two people. (Below I give an exercise which may help this process.)

The chakras are described as bell-like formations with the open end towards the outside of the body, connected to the body through a stem. On a newborn baby they appear limp. On an adult, when undeveloped they are seen as a small dull circle or flat saucer one or two inches across. When developed or 'awakened' they get deeper and the centre develops. The word 'chakra' means wheel, and when shown diagrammatically they are seen to develop from a four-spoked wheel (or crossed circle) pattern when moving slowly, to a whirling motion resembling a swastika shape. They are described as having the luminosity of butterfly wings and, as Pierrakos puts it poetically in *Energy and Character*, when developed they 'are seen as blazing whirlpools, much increased in size to about 4 or 5 inches and resemble miniature suns'. The movement of the chakras is spiral, and I am reminded of the recurring spirals, four-spoked wheels, suns, swastikas and circular symbolism in early Aegean art.

The chakra model is relevant to this book because it does not suggest a duality, either in the relationship it describes between spirit and matter, or in the model it proposes of the human being. Spirit and matter are not separate elements; rather there is a continuous spiralling movement of expansion and contraction between them, and they are seen merely as different vibrations of energy. The model offered of the body is a seven-part system in which 'fine' energy is drawn in at points all along the body, and is involved in many different planes of the body's activity, from grounding and housing, sexuality, relationships, through to intuition and meditation. Development in one area is of limited value without a balanced development over all aspects of living: proficiency in meditation, for example, is of limited value if there is emotional suppression or insufficient grounding. The functions of each chakra can be seen both on a physical and a psychic level: thus the solar plexus is concerned with digesting experience as well as food (as in the expression, 'I can't stomach it'), and the throat chakra is concerned with 'inspiration' as well as with the intake of air into the lungs. The whole system can be used metaphorically as a symbolic map of the various functions and activities of the human being.

The best way to start to investigate the chakras for yourself is simply to relax, send your awareness to the site of each chakra in turn, and notice what you experience. You may draw a blank, or you may come up with images or thoughts which increase your self-understanding. Here is an example of a woman using meditation to tune into her chakras in this way:

In the group we were given time to lie down, relax and breathe fully. Then we were guided to bring our awareness to the location of each chakra in turn. In each case we were asked to be aware of physical sensations, memories, and of any images or music which came up. Below I list the images which came to me, followed by comments which I made later about how I could relate the images to issues in my life.

Root Chakra: Image of a person being tortured by being put on a sharp edge with weights on the feet, i.e. being sliced in half. I also thought of the resistance song 'We shall not be moved' and of the anthem of the anti-apartheid African National Congress 'Nkosi Sikelel' i-Afrika' (God bless Africa'). I can connect the torture image to my deep sense of being split in half between 'male' survival abilities and my 'female' qualities. 'Nkosi Sikelel' i-Afrika' is a very gentle and beautiful song and I was moved by it coming up in that way: it was like a healing for the tortured splitting of the 'impalement' image, just as the people of South Africa set their 'People's Charter' with its broad socialist anti-racist vision in opposition to the divisive bigotry of apartheid – love to heal violence. My politics as an important base for me in the world.

Hara or Centre Chakra: Image of empty marsh flats. No sense of any history here. I have the sense of not having lived much in this part of my body.

Solar Plexus: Seems like the bit in the middle that gets overlooked. (Like me in my family.)

Heart Chakra: I have an image of a spear in it. I am scared to pull it out, because that would be when I would die. Feels like a block in my compassion, and a certain 'maleness' of which I seem to have a lot.

Throat Chakra: Symbol of a radio microphone with a broken leg-stand. I have a voice and I am articulate, but the connection is broken, it needs connecting down so that I can speak from all of me and from a deeper sense of self, not just from the top half of my body.

Third Eye: Image of a lighthouse beam which is too bright and it drives people away. It changes to a candle but this is too weak to light the surrounding darkness. My mind needs to shine bright but not drive people away. It would be better if I could connect to people more through the lower chakras and not so much through talking and ideas.

Crown Chakra: Blank. Nothing there. Then an image of my mother pulling my hair into plaits, which made me want short hair like I have now. I later read that hair, like the spire of a church, is seen as a vertical connection with 'God' through which the spiritual force may descend. But can't make much sense of this one.

This woman might work on balancing her chakras with massage connecting her top and bottom halves and feeding the 'bit in the middle', or on linking her two sides. She might try some 'Natural Dance' classes to strengthen her connection with her *hara* chakra, or she might take time daily to breathe into the belly area. Work on the chakras can also be done by meditation, visualisation, exercises, or by making conscious changes in lifestyle: for example, leaving or starting a job, making changes in relationships, housing, diet, or clothes. Here are some relevant exercises.

Contacting Your Own Chakras

This is the first step towards exploring the chakras. Remember, the exact chakra positions are given earlier in this section.

Sit or lie comfortably with arms and knees uncrossed. Relax for a few minutes, just noticing your breathing.

Now send your awareness to your root chakra. If you are uncertain whether you are making contact with it, it can help to place your fingers on the point.

Notice any sensations, symbols, thoughts or associations which arise.

Continue for ten minutes.

Afterwards write down or tell a friend what came up. If a symbol came up, you could draw it and explore it.

This exercise can be repeated for each of the other chakras.

Chakra Colours

This is a good exercise to move on to from the last. Alternatively, if you drew a blank when simply contacting the chakras, you may find that the colours help stimulate your unconscious.

Repeat the previous exercise, but when you contact the root chakra, imagine the colour red there.

Again, stay with an awareness of the chakra and the colour for ten minutes, and notice what came up.

The colours for the other chakras are: *hara*, orange; solar plexus, yellow; heart, green; throat, blue; brow, indigo; crown, violet.

Chakra Dreaming

Some people do not take easily to meditative and visualisation exercises. In this case you may find it more fruitful to approach your chakras through your dreams.

Choose one of the three lower chakras: root, *hara* or solar plexus.

Just before going to sleep at night, imagine placing the relevant colour (i.e. red, orange or yellow respectively) on that chakra point for 30 seconds.

In the morning, try to recall your dreams. They may include material relevant to the functioning of that chakra.

You may notice throughout this chapter an emphasis on the lower part of the body, which reflects the way I have been taught esoteric anatomy. Despite our society's tendency to visualise the spiritual as a quest to reach 'upwards', my experience has been of a more integrated view of the body, in which much of the work is done on the lower chakras.

Chakras for Expression, Control, and Balance

This exercise was taught to me by Bob Moore.

Although all the chakras are connected by energy flowing up and down the spine, some of them have a special relationship with others and can be usefully linked in meditation.

One such link is the circulation between the root and throat chakras, which relates to expression. I understand this connection as follows: the throat chakra is concerned with expression, but if you do not know where you are coming from it is very hard to have anything authentic to express; so a firm sense of grounding via the root is essential for the throat chakra to operate properly. Discomfort in your root situation, for example a job you dislike, inhibits expression and can even affect the quality of your voice.

Sit upright in a comfortable, untwisted position. Relax. Close your eyes.

Send your awareness to the root chakra. (Pause a few moments.) Then send your awareness to the throat chakra. (Pause again.) It does not matter how you imagine making the movement between them as long as there is a circulation between the two points, with a pause each time. Do not use any colours. You may find it helps you to place your fingers on the two points. Continue imagining a circulation between the two points, at a steady speed which suits you, for ten minutes.

The second circulation is between the *hara* and brow chakras, and relates to emotional control or harmony between thought and gut reactions. The *hara* can be the site of emotional turmoil, or it can be a source of calm strength: it partly depends on its connection with the brow chakra. The head and belly need to work together, not be at war. The emotional control that comes from a good relationship with the *hara* is very different from emotional holding or suppression. That is where this circulation can help. Repeat the exercise as with the root and throat chakras, but this time moving from the *hara* chakra to the brow chakra.

The third circulation is between the solar plexus and the crown chakra, and relates to balance. The solar plexus has been described as the graveyard of many people's ambitions for change, as it is the place where we hold on to fears and rejections which may date back to earliest infancy. Although the crown chakra is not really a chakra that we can work to develop (it mainly responds to the development of the other chakras), in this exercise it can help to bring some balance to the circulation of energy between it and the solar plexus. Repeat the exercise as with the root and throat chakras, but this time moving from the solar plexus to the crown.

When the focus is on a circulation of energy, as in this exercise, you are not particularly looking for symbols, and in fact they may distract your attention. So if symbols come up, just notice them, let them go, and return to the circulation.

The Energy Field

Feeling drained or depressed, suffering a heart attack, having poor circulation, going through a nervous breakdown, surviving a separation or having a baby, are all experiences which have correspondences in the aura. A closer look at the anatomy of the energy field offers a different approach to understanding changes in our health, mood and relationships, an approach which drastically challenges the prevalent mind/body split.

Subtle anatomy offers, for example, a new way of understanding experiences of intimacy, of connection with others, and of communion. Esoteric traditions stress that our energy field connects us with the world around. 'Fine' energy is described not only as running through the physical body but also as occupying an area around it. The space around our body is also part of us. A clairvoyant investigated by neuropsychiatrist Shafica Karagulla reported detecting 'a "vital or energy body or field" which substands the dense physical body, interpenetrating it like a sparkling web of light beams' (*Breakthrough to Creativity*). These light beams can appear as strands which extend beyond the body: in *The Second Ring of Power* Castaneda is told that a complete person looks like a luminous egg made out of fibres which look like taut strings. The fibres apparently connect us to other people (for example, as channels linking two people who have a close relationship) and may also connect us to objects and features of the natural world. As John Pierrakos has put it in *Energy and Character*: 'The waves of energy move through the space from you to everyone and everything around you.' In *Journey to Ixtlan* Castaneda describes the first time he sees these lines of energy, which he actually perceives as an extraordinary profusion of fluorescent white lines crisscrossing everything around him. The lines were constant and were superimposed on or were coming through everything in his surroundings. They were visible and steady even if he looked away from the sun. A friend of mine brought such perceptions home to me by reporting a similar experience after receiving a massage: 'I was lying on the table and she had been working on me for quite a while. I opened my eyes and saw strands of silver thread criss-crossing the room. I closed my eyes. I opened my eyes again, and the threads were still there.' David Tansley, in his book on radionics, stresses that 'subtle' energy connects us to the world around us:

man has a body of highly attenuated matter, which he derives from the energy field in the earth, and which links him with all life . . . Man is a series of high frequency energy systems which integrate him into the universal scheme of things.

We are familiar with the notion of the spiritual experience as a revelation of interconnectedness; Alexander Lowen, for example, in *Bioenergetics* describes the soul as the 'sense . . . of being part of a larger or universal order'. While we are accustomed to associating that sense with whatever divinity our society sustains, descriptions of the energy field provide a framework to ground that experience in human anatomy. The implication is not that in certain states of religious emotion we *imagine* ourselves connected; it is that for the sustenance of our life we actually *are* connected, by forces which we can sometimes experience and can gradually chart.

The dichotomous mind/body split is further challenged by esoteric anatomy's identification within the energy field of a number of different layers, the outermost of which reaches several feet from the solid body; its outer circumference perhaps corresponds to the outer limit of the 'luminous egg' of the Castaneda books, while Pierrakos describes it as a 'cloudy, pulsating envelope'. Tantric yoga also mentions the notion that human beings have several 'bodies' which are described as a series of 'sheaths' (see Govinda, *The Foundations of Tibetan Mysticism*). These layers or subtle bodies have been named as the 'etheric', the 'astral', the 'mental' and the 'soul' (or 'quality') aura; each is thought to relate to a particular aspect of our functioning. The 'etheric' body runs through the physical body and closely around it, extending a few inches away from the skin; its job is to vitalise the solid body. The seven chakras are placed within it. Beyond it, the 'astral' body is ovoid in shape and extends up to one, two or three feet away from the solid body; this layer relates to the individual's emotional state and feelings such as fear, courage, happiness and depression. Unresolved and conflicting emotions or strong temper throw the astral body into turmoil and make its sparkling colours turn harsh or muddy; such conflicts can filter into the etheric and solid bodies and affect them badly, causing tiredness or even illness. Known in Rosicrucian tradition as the 'desire' body, this is the source of those selfish urges often blamed on 'the flesh'. It is also activated in trance and drug states and is the site of visions: whether the angels of mystical religious experiences or, at the other extreme, demons and the hallucinated monsters of a bad LSD trip. This is the body which can leave the solid body in near-death experiences or 'astral travel' as described in Chapter 4; esoteric anatomy thus provides a non-mystical framework within which to place such experiences. The next layer, the 'mental' area of the aura, is seen by clairvoyants as a cloud of rapidly moving particles which reveal thought patterns, whether reflecting bigoted repetitive thoughts, mental chatter, clarity, intellect or understanding. The layer furthest out is the 'quality', 'soul' or intuitional level which may extend three to four feet – or with some unusual people much further – from the physical body. This layer carries qualities and potential that we were born with; clearing blockages in the inner layers helps these qualities to reach the solid body and express in our lives.

While these parts of the energy field are given separate names and may in certain situations have some autonomy from the solid body, teachers stress that they are not separate but an integral part of the whole activity of our physical make-up. Instead of notions of spiritual energy being 'trapped' in the solid body or 'attached' to it in some arbitrary way, we have rather the metaphor of the physical body as the tip of an iceberg: the only visible part of a far larger structure of which it is an intrinsic part. It is a reflection or condensation of those qualities present in the energy field. Instead of imagining an alienated soul on the inside trying to get *out*, we have a closely connected continuum of subtle energies trying to get *in*, to express *through*. The physical form that most of us see is the embodiment of the fine energy movements unique to each person; it is indeed, in Blake's words, 'a portion of Soul discern'd by the five Senses, the chief inlets of Soul in this age'. Recently the findings of the new physics have questioned our traditional distinction between 'energy' and 'matter', thus endorsing spiritual teachings which insist that the soul/body division is an illusion and that the human being is a continuum of energies ranging from the subtlest to the densest, from the outer limits of a luminous egg several feet wide to its crystallisation at the centre of the egg in flesh and bones. In Japanese tradition, according to Sato

Tsuji, the body is 'a concrete revelation of the Dharma'. So far from being a worthless box, a trap or a machine, this solid body is a condensation of those fine energies and is the only means through which they can be expressed.

Thus the relationship between the solid body and the energy field is intricate and organic. In *Radionics*, David Tansley stresses that the fields 'have an anatomy and physiology of their own'. The etheric body contains certain prevailing streams of energy each of which performs a specific task in linking etheric and physical energy. Subtle anatomy offers new ways to understand the causes of illness. There are descriptions of blocks in the field just as may happen in the solid body; these phenomena in the energy field may reflect traumatic events in the individual's early history. Psychics can sometimes detect in the aura traces of such past events, like scars, or signs betraying a current situation of conflict or suppression. Illness can also be detected in the energy field before it manifests in the solid body. A change of colour in the field may reflect the malfunction of a specific internal organ such as the kidney. Different speeds or rates of vibration can be found within the field: if someone is ill, a slow vibration will be noticed from that part of the body. Mental illness is also reflected: for example, a characteristic bulge in the back of the aura has been noted with some schizophrenics. In 'The Case of the Broken Heart' John Pierrakos links heart disease with the denial of emotional expression and with a corresponding blockage in the aura in front of the chest in some patients.

Altered states of consciousness are also associated with changes in the energy field. The aura is also sometimes described as having holes in it: one explanation offered for the abilities of mediums is that they have passages through which they can admit certain types of energy from outside themselves; like leaky boats, this also makes them more vulnerable. In Castaneda's *The Second Ring of Power* we find the idea that bearing children leaves a hole in the aura at the belly. Under the effect of certain drugs, the aura may expand far and not properly return; excess of alcohol or drugs can have a destructive effect by unravelling much-needed protective layers, as David Tansley explains in *The Raiment of Light*.

The subtle body is also affected by age, environmental factors and human contact. The energy field, like the solid body, moves through certain phases during life, and it has been suggested that it changes on a seven-year cycle. In *The Raiment of Light* David Tansley describes how X-rays can burn the aura and leave it brittle, while telephone wiring, electrical circuits and television radiation in the home can upset its polarity, creating imbalances which leave us vulnerable to anxiety or illness. Dr Jean Munro has recently spoken publicly about her work at London hospitals treating patients suffering from 'electromagnetic pollution' caused by things like overhead power lines and computers. The aura apparently has the ability to contract into, and expand away from, the surface of the solid body: for example, pleasant sounds may prompt it to withdraw, while it may extend to push away sounds that are found unpleasant. Two auras can overlap and in this situation certain exchanges of energy may take place between the two individuals. These may be beneficial; for example an old person may derive vitality from the excess energy radiated by a healthy younger person during a conversation, or a patient from a therapist, without any loss to the giver. However, Leadbeater distinguishes between those who receive in this way and those who tap others' energy before it has been processed, to supplement a deficiency in themselves. This resonates with various familiar experiences, as when a depressed person leaves you feeling 'drained', or, if two people are living together, often one feels tired and the other 'high' and then vice versa. Bob Moore suggests that if a person is functioning at an intense emotional level, or is intellectually powerful, they may need to supplement their field and will be able to draw that energy from others. In *The Raiment of Light*, David Tansley uses the word 'sappers' to describe those who are expert in syphoning off others' energy, often using intense eye contact, emotive subjects or personal comments to obtain an empathy or resonance with you, or chattering to distract your attention, and then unconsciously using their solar plexus and astral body to plug into your weak spot, usually your solar plexus. Clairvoyants describe tentacle-like streamers of energy which are put out by the individual to do the 'sapping'. There are various exercises to protect and clean your aura from this kind of experience; I give some at the end of this section. However, spiritual teachers stress that we are vulnerable only where we are ourselves blocked, suppressed or unresolved, and the best long-term strategy is to clean up our own act and reach a balance within ourselves. They stress that ultimately the answer is not to try to shut people out; our best protection is our own clear, disinterested, positive energy.

Esoteric anatomy thus provides a non-dualistic framework within which to place 'mystical' experiences, illness, thought, feeling, vitality and human relationships. It also illuminates the process of perception. In *The Fire From Within* Castaneda describes a model for perception as explained to him by Don Juan. Speaking of 'emanations' (which are like 'filaments of light', and are sources of energy) *outside* the human cocoon, and 'emanations' *inside* the cocoon, Don Juan suggests that perception takes place where the two are aligned. Humans use only a very small proportion of their available emanations to align in this way, and their point of contact with the outside rays (or 'emanations at large') is called the 'assemblage point'. The particular alignment that we perceive as the world is understood as the product of the specific spot where our assemblage point is located on our cocoon. In infants this point is very mobile within the range available to humans, and their socialisation involves them gradually learning to keep the assemblage point steady at an acceptable position so that their perceptions tally with those of other members of their society. The assemblage point moves involuntarily during sleep, which accounts for our different state of perception and awareness in dreams, as we can align ourselves with emanations at large which are beyond the narrow waveband we are attuned to in daily life. The same can happen randomly as a result of drug-taking or a 'catalytic act': a small shift leads to fantasies, a bigger shift to 'hallucinations'. The anthropologist Mauss lists numerous magical procedures and ceremonies in different societies (such as fasting, special clothing, prayers, ritual dances, music, fumigation and drug-taking) all aimed at inducing special states in the participants; Don Juan states that all the many complex techniques and bizarre devices of sorcery have ultimately only one value, which is to break the fixation of the assemblage point and make it move. However, the assemblage point can also be moved voluntarily as the result of new habits. While Don Juan recognises the role of rituals, he prefers to bypass them in order to teach the moving of the assemblage point directly through discipline and new patterns of behaviour.

In *The Fire From Within*, Don Juan suggests that the assemblage point makes us perceive in terms of clusters of emanations which receive emphasis together, such as the solid human body, while another part of our being, the luminous cocoon, does not receive emphasis and is relegated to oblivion because the assemblage point makes us disregard certain emanations. The process of clairvoyance or, in Don Juan's terms, *seeing*, happens through the alignment of emanations that are not ordinarily used; this is the means through which information about the aura is gained. Perceptions obtained this way, like those of dreams, to some extent need translating in order to be grasped by the everyday mind and put into words. Some clairvoyants speak in terms of colour, density or intensity of vibration. Some sensitives use touch, smell or hearing to detect qualities and movements in the energy body. Some, when 'reading' the aura, pick up images: Bob Moore has stressed the importance of symbols in capturing the elusive quality of very fast-moving energy. In order to communicate what they have perceived, all sensitives have to push it through the mesh of their everyday thought-patterns and vocabulary, and some retain a strong emphasis on dualities such as 'higher' and 'lower', male and female. My aim here is not to assess the validity of such descriptions, but merely to take descriptions of the human energy field as a series of sincere accounts of human experience, and to point out the potential in them for departure from our prevailing split view of the body.

This description of the energy field may leave the sceptic feeling disconcerted or dismissive – which is hardly surprising, since the view of the human being I have presented conflicts strongly with the accepted notions of our society. Our eyes have been trained to see what we have been taught to expect. Unlearning is difficult. I like to remember that between Aristarchus of Samos in the third century BC and Copernicus in the Renaissance, all those who said the sun was the centre of the universe were regarded as crazy. At the least we can keep an open mind.

Golden Cocoon Protection Exercise

This is a meditation to protect you from being affected in a negative way by the energy of others. Sara Thomas passed it to me.

Sit or stand comfortably with back straight, arms relaxed and knees uncrossed. Shut your eyes. Feel your weight on the furniture or ground.

Breathe gently into your belly for a few breaths.

Now each time you inhale imagine golden light coming into your belly until it is filled with light. Then imagine the light beginning to spread throughout your whole body, travelling down your legs to your feet, then up your trunk to your arms and hands, and into your neck and head, until you are filled with light.

Now let the golden light begin to expand outwards all around your body. Let it move out all around you for at least a foot or two until you are surrounded by an egg-shaped cocoon of golden light, like a giant bubble.

Imagine that you are a source which can send positive energy *out* from the bubble into the world. But unwanted interference from outside cannot penetrate *into* your cocoon.

Sit with the cocoon for at least three minutes. Now release your contact with the image, but it will remain there as a protection for you.

You can do this exercise in the morning and imagine that the cocoon will stay around you all day.

This exercise is helpful for getting used to the idea that your aura extends into the space around you.

Gold is a good colour for protection. Notice also the emphasis on sending out positive energy from the bubble: other people's energy hooks on to your own conflicts and unresolved negative feelings, so trying to shut them out in a fearful or hostile way does not give you effective protection.

Further protection exercises are described in Phyllis Krystal's book, *Cutting the Ties that Bind*.

The Vortex: Cleaning Your Energy Field

This can help to clean off any unwanted energy you have picked up from people or situations around you.

Relax your body and stand with your back straight, feet parallel and knees slightly bent. Shut your eyes.

Imagine a point above the top of your head. The centre line of the vortex runs straight down through the centre of your body to a point below your feet.

Send your awareness to the point above your head and from there imagine a line moving very slowly spiralling downwards round your body. On its way down it picks up unneeded physical, emotional and mental debris which is cluttering your aura. The vortex widens around the centre of your body, and narrows again towards your feet.

It ends up at the point below your feet, taking all that debris down to drain into the energy of the earth, which will disintegrate it and recycle it.

After the first vortex has come down, you may feel another one coming down after it.

Again, this exercise helps you to visualise that you extend beyond the solid body into an egg-shaped aura around it. The spiral is seen as an important principle in the movement of subtle energy around the body. Further exercises for learning to sense the aura are mentioned by David Tansley in *The Raiment of Light*.

'Cutting the Cords': Ritual to Separate from Someone

I was taught this exercise by Anne Parks.

Clairvoyants describe seeing the energy lines or 'cords' connecting people who are emotionally involved with each other. If these are from past relationships they may be a hindrance and problem to you. This exercise may help you to 'cut the cords' linking you to a friend or lover from whom you have parted.

Light a candle and sit comfortably in a quiet room.

Shut your eyes, feel your weight on the ground, and breathe calmly for a few minutes.

With eyes open or shut, imagine the person you need to separate from. Picture the person a few feet in front of you. Recreate them in detail.

Be aware how you feel towards the person. Be aware what ties you to them (for example pain, need, lust, jealousy, dependency, resentment or anger).

Now imagine there are cords running from your solar plexus on your midriff to the person. Pick up an imaginary pair of scissors and cut the cords. Continue until they are all cut.

Now the cords are gone, imagine your solar plexus chakra whole and filled with sunshine.

Wish that person to achieve as much happiness and understanding as is possible in their lifetime.

Teachers stress that energy is affected by thought. The key to the success of this exercise lies in a genuine *intention* to separate, which needs to be reinforced by your practical behaviour (for example resolving emotional conflicts and creating enough distance between you).

Holding on to past attachments can be destructive, preventing both of you from recovering and making a fresh start. Cutting the cords symbolically can help to free you. The good wishes at the end are very important: if you part in anger, the anger holds you both together. Forgiveness gives you freedom.

I have focused here on the solar plexus because that is where we most often hold damaging attachments. For example, love itself, connecting through the heart, does not bind in the same way. For more about 'cords', see Diane Mariechild's *Mother Wit*. See also Phyllis Krystal's *Cutting the Ties that Bind*.

Animals, Plants and Places

In urban western society we tend to use pet animals as substitutes
for people, while undomesticated animals may feature in our dreams
to symbolise the disowned 'animal' part of our nature. Apart from the
appreciation of some gardeners' 'green fingers', there is little
recognition of any relationship between people and plants: they are
simply there to entertain and feed us. And the earth itself, seen as
quite separate from 'man', is treated as a passive object whose
resources are fair game for human society to exploit to the utmost
in its pursuit of 'progress'.

In contrast, esoteric anatomy tells us that every living animal and
plant, as well as stones, wood, metal and the earth itself, have a
complex energy field comparable to our own. So far from being
suitable objects for our projections, fantasies, appropriation and
exploitation, they are living beings involved in an intricate energic
interaction with our own energy fields.

Thus plants apparently emit energy which is very beneficial to
humans; Leadbeater suggests that trees' process of energy assimilation
is similar to ours, so that the excess energy they radiate is precisely
suitable for the cells of the human body. This notion recalls for me
the early Cretan scenes of people reverentially touching plants, and
resonates with several other spiritual traditions, for example the story
that Buddha attained enlightenment under the bodhi tree, while the
Nordic god Odin hung on the ash tree to obtain the secret knowledge
of the runes (see Davidson, *Gods and Myths of Northern Europe*). The
qualities or essence of a particular plant's energy have sometimes been
symbolised as a character or personality; one thinks of Castaneda's
vision, on a mescalin trip, of the peyote plant's guardian spirit
'Mescalito', described by him in *The Teachings of Don Juan* as having
enormous eyes, a head pointed like a strawberry, and green skin dotted
with innumerable warts very like the surface of the peyote cactus. The
garden of the Findhorn Community in Scotland yielded astounding
returns, which the gardeners attributed to positive radiations from the
community members, and to direct communication with the essences
or *devas* of the plants concerned (see *The Findhorn Garden*).

The prehistoric Cretan rituals of dressing up as birds and other
creatures seem to reflect respect and the desire to absorb their
qualities. It is interesting that two of the most important animals in
Bronze Age Aegean religion, the goat and the horse, have both been
associated with the devil, while the snake and the dog were already

by the Greek classical period linked in a negative way with the underworld (cf. the sinister snake-goddesses the Erinyes, and Cerberus the hound guarding the gates of hell). Unorthodox and suspect, too, in later Greek times, were the magical ceremonies of the goddess Hecate, who was associated with the dog, although the dog retained some acceptance as the companion of the healing god Asklepios. Medieval traditions of witches' animal 'familiars' were condemned by the Christian church. In a hierarchical religion centred on an abstract male sky god there is little space for emphasis on the importance of spiritual attunement to animal and plant life. There are ways of redressing the balance, for example by learning to sense the energy field and healing properties of plants and animals. There is an interesting exercise about attunement with plants, and a ritual with a stone, in Diane Mariechild's *Mother Wit*.

In *The Raiment of Light* David Tansley stresses that the earth itself 'is a living being whose aura we live within, and could not survive without'; he expresses concern at the increasing pollution of its electromagnetic field through radiation from TV and radio stations, military installations (radar), and other sources. The suggestion has been made that some parts of the earth's aura are more beneficial than others: as David Tansley describes, beaches have a lifting atmosphere, perhaps because sand can store energy and the sea carries a high energy charge, while forests are 'reservoirs of the life-force' and mountains have a sparkling atmosphere. In contrast, some areas are electromagnetically polluted, and in others 'Terrifying events loaded with negative astral energies will imprint themselves into the physical fabric or space in the immediate area.' One thinks of the atmosphere of concentration camp sites. On an infinitely smaller scale, the 'ghost' of the 'dark stranger' described in Chapter 4 could be attributed to a similar energy trace from a past event in the room. While some of these imprints result from human actions, and city dwellers are said to be strongly affected by the ripples of human violence and suffering around them, some areas of the earth's surface have a specific energy of their own which can affect us: thus in *The Fire From Within* Castaneda learns that some seers suggest that the Sonoran Desert has a particular confluence of emanations which shifts the assemblage point and makes people belligerent. In the same book, Don Juan teaches Castaneda that the earth itself is a living being with a 'luminous cocoon'. One of the first tasks he sets (described in *The Teachings of Don Juan*) is for Castaneda to find the spot in his yard where the energy will be most beneficial for him, and in *Journey to*

Ixtlan he stresses that an important part of Castaneda's process of accumulating 'personal power' is for him to find, and frequent, places which will restore and build his energy. Similarly, all parts of the earth's landscape, such as rocks and stones, have a specific energy field with a particular effect upon the human aura, from the frightening 'power' stone described in Castaneda's *The Eagle's Gift* to the many gems and semi-precious stones whose alleged healing effects David Tansley lists in *The Raiment of Light*. Shafica Karagulla discusses the differing energy fields of different types of gem, and the strong energy charge accumulated by objects with an emotional or religious history. I am reminded again of early Cretan religious customs – especially the carrying of carved sealstones and talismanic gems, the emphasis on *baetyls* (sacred boulders) and the choice of rocks and caves as sites for cult – while the notion of the earth having its own aura resonates with the ideas about planetary energies expressed in the traditions of astrology. The implications of the teachings of esoteric anatomy are again, here, a healing of splits and a transformation of our relationship to the natural world around us: from appropriation and abuse to respect, from contempt to connectedness.

Tapping into a Tree

This can help to restore you if you are feeling depleted.

Find a large tree that you can lean against.

Stand against it with your body straight and as much as possible of the back of your body touching the tree-trunk.

Shut your eyes and be aware of both yourself and the tree having your base in the ground. Breathe calmly for a few minutes.

Imagine that strength and energy is coming into your body from the tree at every point where it touches. Stay with the contact for 5–10 minutes.

If you wish, silently thank the tree before you leave.

Old and mature trees are powerful batteries and can be a great source of calm and consolation in a difficult world. Oak, spruce, pine and eucalyptus trees are said to be particularly beneficial (In *Tales of Power*, Castanada describes an experience with eucalyptus.) Even from holding a leaf in your hand you may be able to feel energy moving up your arm.

The Belly and Menstruation

I will now investigate what this alternative approach to the body might mean for our understanding of some aspects of our physicality, starting with the belly and menstruation.

Every symbolic view of the body contains a notion of where the body has its prime source: what directs it, what activates it, what is the prime mover or driving force. In western culture this is the head. The head leads and the rest of the body follows, whether willingly or reluctantly. The head decides, it guides the rest of the body, it 'knows best'. 'Use your head', we are told. It is the 'headquarters' which provides initiative and direction. The most our belly is thought to provide is a 'gut reaction' which is little valued. An upheaval is required to imagine a world in which the hindquarters are a prime mover.

As we saw earlier in this chapter, the Indian chakra map understands the second chakra at the belly as being related to vitality, instinctual movement, sexuality, generation and emotional flow. This chakra relates to the elimination of waste and also to gestation: it is described by some teachers as a cauldron, granary or storehouse of energy which has been stored in the body since birth. It is understood as the site of our power and our centre of gravity spiritually and emotionally. Different chakras are compared to different levels of evolution, and this centre chakra is matched with the organisation of insect life, in particular with the qualities of instinctive movement and synchronicity. Each chakra is traditionally associated with a colour: this one is linked with orange, and is pictured radiating energy like the sun.

What seems striking here are the parallels with the early Aegean material of Chapter 7: from the emphasis on the belly; to its association with the sun; to the comparison of the belly with a granary or vessel; to the association with synchronicity and insect life (recalling the recurrence as symbols in early Cretan art of insects like bees whose organisation has a highly synchronous and collective nature).

In contrast, our culture attaches no such significance or value to the belly, and the head is locked in a perpetual struggle to suppress or cut off its powerful impulses and messages. It is easy to imagine how its functions are impaired by our denial of the lower body and our drowning of its signals with endless mental chatter. Ron Kurtz and Hector Prestera, in *The Body Reveals*, suggest that the 'Hanged Man' of the Tarot cards, who is not hanged by the neck but hangs upside down with a halo about his head, is a statement that enlightenment requires the dominance of the belly over the head.

Japanese traditions again stress the importance of this area of the body, termed the *hara*. In his book on the *hara*, Von Dürckheim points out that western ideas of beauty reject the belly and prefer a flat abdomen, which involves tensing the chest and drawing up the muscles, shifting the centre of gravity upwards and producing instability. In contrast Japanese traditions see the *hara* or belly as the hidden 'treasure of life' based on 'the vitalizing bond with the solid earth'. It is not only seen as the most important and strongest part of the body, but also the most sensitive. Like a receiving set and a transmitter rolled into one, it can both perceive *and* act; action that is done 'with the belly' signifies an action that comes from the whole person.

Don Juan, in the Castaneda books, also stresses the belly as a source of action. He uses the term 'will'. This is not the Victorian notion of 'will-power' which represses and denies impulses in the self and imposes itself over others: Don Juan (in, for example, *A Separate Reality*) criticises denial which, he says, is the worst kind of indulgence and warps the will. True will, he states, has no connection with thoughts or wishes. It is what makes you succeed when your thoughts tell you that you are defeated, but it is nothing to do with having 'character' or a strong disposition. It is an impetus which is very clear and powerful and which directs our acts. It is a link between individuals and the perceived world. And, strange perhaps to us, this power is described as *coming out by the navel*. Don Juan tells Castaneda that human beings have a gap in them, like the soft spot on a child's head which closes with age, except that this gap opens as a person develops their will. Through this gap near the navel the will shoots out like an arrow, a force that comes from within and attaches itself to the world outside. It is interesting that a system of spiritual teachings so geographically distant from Indian and Japanese traditions places a similar emphasis on this point as the site of a central life force concerned with perception of the world and movement towards it.

The concept of 'will' as expressed in the Castaneda books bears similarities to that presented by Roberto Assagioli in his handbook, *Psychosynthesis*. This method links the notion of will with 'willingness', 'good will' and 'free will', stressing its importance as a moving force towards self-expression and self-realisation rather than towards tyranny over the self or others.

As one of the organs associated with this energy centre in the belly, the womb is an extremely important source of power for women. I will deal here not with the momentous experience of giving birth but with the womb's more regular monthly function of menstruation.

Since our teens we have been taught to be ashamed of menstruation. In *The Wise Wound*, Penelope Shuttle and Peter Redgrove describe the many taboos, negative attitudes and forms of suppression which make menstruation a painful secret for most women. There is little social recognition or understanding of the accompanying physiological changes (such as in pain sensitivity, temperature, sense of smell, weight and blood calcium), nor of the mood changes induced by pre-menstrual tension. In *Female Cycles*, Paula Weideger suggests that such symptoms are exacerbated by social pressures which make women ashamed of their experience during this part of their cycle.

In contrast, some esoteric teachings suggest that the changes brought about by this physical cycle also include an increase of psychic power. In *The Second Ring of Power*, fellow apprentice la Gorda tells Castaneda that she had learnt certain feats of sorcery during her menstrual periods. She states that at that time she becomes a 'little crazy' and more daring, and that Don Juan had shown her that during that time a crack opens up in front of women: two days before her period a woman can open that crack and step through it into another world. Women are believed to be 'better sorcerers' than men because they always have this crack in front of them, whereas a man has to make it.

According to this symbolic view, menstruation is not something we should deny and hide, a physical function totally divorced from our higher being, but is a source of spiritual power. The physical process is itself imbued with psychic energy.

Whether menstruating or not, the womb is, according to the Don Juan teachings, a seat of power and a starting point for psychic activities. In the last chapter, I referred to accounts of travelling with the 'dream body'. Don Juan teaches Castaneda that this process, which he calls *dreaming* (and which may correspond to what others call 'astral travelling'), is directed and motivated by the belly. He states that the energy used for moving in *dreaming* stems from the area an inch or two below the belly button, and is none other than the *will*. In a woman both the attention and the energy needed for *dreaming* originate from the womb which is her centre. La Gorda tells Castaneda in *The Eagle's Gift* that in order to start *dreaming* or to stop it all she has to do is place her attention on her womb. Having learned to feel

the inside of it, she only has to see the reddish glow for an instant
and then she is off.

Even from these brief remarks it is clear that we could start to
explore a different symbolism for the womb and menstruation. We
can move away from the implicit idea that menstruation is abnormal,
undesirable and debilitating. We can move away, none too soon, from
the ancient biblical pronunciation of the menstruating woman as
unclean. We can move towards a different relationship with the belly
and the womb, which recognises them as a seat of power. It is hard
to know exactly how, as twentieth-century women in western culture,
we may do this. We can learn from, but we cannot simply adopt,
traditions that have evolved in other societies. I can only point to some
ideas and activities that have emerged in the women's movement,
threads that can be followed to see where they lead.

One area we can look at is the current language and images used
for menstruation, from 'the curse' to 'jam rags'. We can explore these
terms and their effects on us. We can also investigate alternatives: does
one of the few potentially positive symbols, 'flowers', date as far back
as the Greek myth of Persephone, who gathers flowers before she is
raped by Hades? What other images are suggested by our personal
and collective experience of menstruation? What happens if we use
different words for the process? What happens if we talk about it more,
in different ways, breaking the ban of silence?

Another area is how we treat our bodies: everyday actions like
walking reveal how we relate to the belly's functions and how we
locate it in the body as a whole. In workshops at the Women's Therapy
Centre in London, we sometimes do an exercise where we ask people
to walk with their heads leading ('Walk from the head') and then to
switch to walking with the belly leading ('Walk from the belly'). The
difference between the two walks is very noticeable. Most of us run
our lives with the attitude that 'mind controls matter': this involves
straining with the head to keep control and make things how we want
them. The head and the upper half of the body do a lot of extra work,
struggling and 'trying', while the power of the lower body is unused.
And yet structurally the lower body is in the ideal position to support
and move us; trying to walk with the shoulders is highly inefficient.
Cold feet, poor circulation in the legs, back or shoulder ache may be
the physical symptoms resulting from this upside-down way of living.
There are ways of redressing the balance physically. Learning new body
habits is an important part of approaching the world differently. T'ai
Chi and other eastern self-defence disciplines can help to lower the

body's centre of gravity and locate the greater physical power that comes upwards through the body from the belly. Movement, breathing and body awareness exercises can teach us to listen to the sensations of the body and allow impulses and decisions to come from the inside, and particularly from the belly, to inform our actions in the world. Meditative exercises can help to still the mental chatter which interferes with those messages from the body.

Some women have moved into the area of ritual, sometimes adapting rituals believed to have been used in earlier societies where women were more powerful, sometimes creating their own. An example is the summer solstice ritual created by Barbry MyOwn and Hallie Mountainwing and described by Carol P. Christ in *Heresies*. In this ritual the women simulated a birth canal through which they 'birthed' each other into their circle. They then placed their hands on each other's bellies and chanted together to raise the power of the group. Finally, as Carol Christ recounts:

they marked each other's faces with rich dark menstrual blood saying, 'This is the blood that promises renewal. This is the blood that promises sustenance. This is the blood that promises life.' From hidden dirty secret to symbol of the life power of the Goddess, women's blood has come full circle. The degree to which this ritual seems indelicate or shocking indicates how far modern culture is from perceiving the sacrality of the female body.

We also have much to learn from simply watching more closely our own experience of the womb's functions such as menstruation. The kind of awareness la Gorda has of her womb is not accessible to us without the devotion of much time and attention to noticing the subtle events and changes taking place in the body. Women have challenged the widespread taboo on sex during menstruation, suggesting that some actually experience heightened desire at that time; they have also kept records of their dreams, noting the changes in patterns of dreaming during menstruation (as described, for example, in *The Wise Wound*). I have also found it interesting to observe how menstruation corresponds to cycles of expression and creativity. Here is one woman's experience:

I was building up to writing a poem. I could feel it brewing inside me and I experienced tension and discomfort. My urge to write battled with my panic about putting pen to paper. I got into a

languid and irritable mood which I recognised as similar to PMT:
a feeling of waiting for something. Ideas accumulated but I was
terrified to start. Finally I sat down and started writing. I had an
enormous sense of relief, the words really poured out.
Simultaneously my period started a week early. It was as if my
creative and physical cycles were in harmony, but I wasn't sure
which was following which.

Esoteric anatomy teaches us that menstruation is a cycle of clearance,
physical, emotional and etheric: a 'beginning again'. With greater
consciousness, it is possible to imagine that we could use the cycle
constructively to help us make such clearances as are necessary in
different aspects of our lives.

Whether the approach is through language, body awareness, dreams
or ritual, if we see each area of the body as infused with psychic energy,
then all its functions – including, and perhaps especially,
menstruation – can be explored and drawn on for spiritual power.
Spiritual energy is not something divorced from the body, which
happens in churches, synagogues and mosques in response to a God,
but is immanent in and moves with physical processes.

Hara Breathing

This is a simple exercise to help you become more aware of your
belly. I learnt it from Bob Moore.

Sit or lie comfortably with your eyes open or shut, and relax.

Bring your thoughts to the *hara* area and keep them there while
you continue to breathe in and out with a normal rhythm through
nose or mouth. (Five minutes.)

As you end the exercise, imagine breathing your thoughts out
on the last exhalation.

This breathing will not only help to energise your pelvis, but may
help with any health problems in the bottom area of the body (for
example, with ovaries, uterus or prostate).

Night Water Triangle

This is based on Bob Moore's work. It may encourage illuminating
and relevant dreams.

Immediately before sleeping, place a glass of water three-
quarters full by your bedside (the container must be transparent).

Relax for a few moments, then follow these three steps:
Visualise a triangle (upright).

Do two minutes of the *hara* breathing described in the previous exercise.

Look into the water from the top for a few minutes. Repeat several times. Remember if you see anything in it.

In the morning, write down any dreams you had and if possible talk about them with a friend. In particular, look at the atmosphere of the dream.

Thought affects energy, so visualising symbols creates an impact on your aura. The triangle is an important symbol often associated with balance, energy distribution, and creative thought patterns. It may bring forward past situations which you can look at in a new way. The breathing can help to increase your awareness. The *hara* has traditionally been associated with the element of water, which is a good conductor and as such has a strong attraction for many people (including those who fear it). The water can serve as a crystal or reflector of images. Further images may be reflected in your dreams afterwards.

The Language of Sex

I believe Nietzsche wrote that Christianity gave Eros poison to drink, but instead of dying Eros turned into vice. I suggest that the process began in the west some centuries earlier, and that in Greece Eros had been in poor health since the Iron Age, when issues of patriarchal power required the control of women, turning woman into an enemy in a man's house and his sexual feelings into an enemy in his body. The notion that 'reason' is alien to sexuality, inherited through Platonic and Christian ideas, has been perpetuated by philosophers like Descartes in the seventeenth century, and for us the body remains the passive field on which issues of social power are enacted. In 'Reason, Desire and Male Sexuality', Victor Seidler has suggested that in our culture the measure of 'male identity' is the ability of his 'reason' to master his body and desire. As the object of male power, women's pleasure has also been sacrificed. Margaret Jackson, in *The Cultural Construction of Sexuality*, charts how twentieth-century sexology has viewed female sexual instincts: she suggests that the notion that these need to be 'wooed' and 'awakened' has not in fact been liberating, but has rather been an attempt to eroticise women's passivity and oppression. It has taken a leap of imagination for the women's movement to assert the opposite: that there is power *in* body pleasure.

As an alternative to the division between 'body' and 'mind', in recent years we have seen the emergence of the term 'bodymind'. There has even been a book of that name, written by Ken Dychtwald. This term implies the understanding that the millions of cells in the body are not passive subjects of an autocratic brain, but each have their own tiny minds and play a semi-autonomous role in keeping the body alive. When an individual dies, the cell structures take time to die because they each have their own cycle of activity. Each cell holds a blueprint for the entire human being, and can also retain much other information. The involuntary thought activity of the cells continues throughout life. The cells can also hold memories. Thus painful memories may be held in a certain part of the body and may be released when that part is touched in a certain way, with a release of the associated emotion which was locked into the cells when that memory was originally stored. This process is one of the basic tenets of Reichian and bioenergetic therapy, which work to release tension from the body tissue. The term 'bodymind' implies the understanding that cells all over the body can remember, think and know.

This approach requires us to revise our symbolic view of the body, from a monarchy to something nearer collectivism, with a lot of power at the grass roots. Each part of the body has stored different experiences, is geared towards a different function, and has different things to teach us. According to this view the genitals, like every other body part, are permeated with fine or 'soul' energy and carry their own part of our mind. They deal with, and can teach us about, a number of different issues, if only we can be prepared to lift the curfew imposed on them and hear what they have to say.

It has been suggested by the Arica training that one of the issues the genitals can teach us about is orientation. Other things, apart from sex (such as art, music, ideas), can turn us on. What do we move towards? What away from? The issue is the flowing of life from us towards something, and the flowing of something towards us. The genitals deal not only with sexual attraction, but can also be related symbolically to issues of attraction in a wider sense. The vagina, and the penis, can also be associated with drive and the ability to get things done. The themes associated with the genitals are thus concerned with movement towards and away from the world.

Another theme which has been associated with the sexual organs is release. The stages of the sexual experience which have been recognised in the west in recent years are excitation, followed by the build-up of a charge or tension, then release or discharge, followed by relaxation or resolution. Though generally modelled on heterosexual intercourse, these stages are applicable whether the sexual experience is hetero- or homosexual, whether with another or alone in masturbation. All work in this area has been strongly influenced by the detailed research of Masters and Johnson in the USA, but the idea of charge and discharge was first stressed by Wilhelm Reich in *The Function of the Orgasm*.

Reich believed that the ability to achieve a full release of sexual energy through a feeling orgasm was the sign of a healthy individual. He was not referring to a purely physical discharge divorced from the totality of the person, but to an orgasm which involved their whole response system and their ability to make contact with another. For him sexual energy had an almost sublime status. He felt that the inner life of the individual centred on sexuality and that orgasm was the process which most effectively relieved tension and anxiety. The movement of the whole body in involuntary contractions reflects the discharge of unwanted energy from the energy flow which runs throughout the whole body, bringing health and balance to the organism.

Esoteric anatomy, while not attributing the same centrality to sexuality, likewise emphasises that a full sexual experience can send energy moving up and down the body and enable a release from the whole body. It stresses the involvement of not only the lower body chakras but other energy centres, especially the heart chakra. In her book *The Esoteric Philosophy of Love and Marriage*, Dion Fortune describes how, during sexual activity, the subtle energy forces are involved throughout the body on all seven 'planes' (which are analogous to the seven chakras):

Esoteric science declares that [sex] has mental and spiritual aspects in addition to those under which it is usually recognised; and that upon each plane it expresses itself differently, functioning according to the laws of that plane . . . Moreover, it is on the subtler planes that the sex forces originate and are controlled.

She comments that sex in its sevenfold scope is of greater significance to the esotericist than to most people, 'to whom it is a temptation rather than a source of energy'.

This process of energic release within the body has been symbolically compared to death or dying. Death is seen as a release or freedom, and in sex the energy release, accompanied by the surrender of 'ego' consciousness to orgasm, is seen as a parallel process in miniature, a 'little death' bringing release, transformation and regeneration. As with menstruation, there may be a correlation between cycles of sexual release and cycles of expression and creativity in other areas of life.

Esoteric anatomy recognises, however, that the movement or release of energy during love-making involves not one but two bodies: the two energy fields blend closely and if there is a sympathetic response they become encased in one auric shell, allowing a powerful exchange of energy between the two people. Some teachers even suggest that each takes on a little of the other and is never quite the same again; an idea which would promote wariness in considering sexual partners. In *The Fire From Within* Don Juan tells Castaneda that during sex there is a profound agitation of the emanations in the cocoon, culminating in a fusion of a piece from the glow of each. Implying that sex can be depleting, he recommends that sexual energy be controlled and used with great care – not as a matter of morality, but in order to save and rechannel energy. It has been suggested that a long build-up of excitement is needed to draw the necessary energy into the aura. Some teachers suggest that the exchange of energy in a sexual encounter is triggered not by orgasm itself but by sympathetic proximity or intimacy. Some individuals in spiritual training prefer to obtain their sexual release through masturbation, where the aura is not impinged upon by another.

One idea which is frequently put forward is that in this energy movement between two people during sex, the most important factor is the exchange which takes place between the two poles of 'male-positive' and 'female-negative'. As Dion Fortune puts it:

> for any form of creation two forces are necessary, one of which shall be actual and one inertly potential . . . positive and negative, male and female – the positive or male-force being the stimulator, and the negative or female force, by means of latent energy, performing the actual work of creation under the influence of the male or stimulator . . .

We are on tricky ground here: such symbolic language reflects certain values and norms of a male-dominated society, particularly the norm of heterosexuality as 'natural' sexual behaviour, and the attribution of passive qualities to the female. The symbolic ideas of 'male-positive' and 'female-negative' are then used in turn to provide some kind of mystical endorsement for those norms. This use of the terms 'positive' and 'negative' draws on an analogy with electricity: we need to be aware that such language is not value-free, and that the very terms of 'positive' and 'negative' are social creations bearing little relation to the actual movement of electricity, let alone providing a sanction for stereotyped roles of behaviour. I discuss this point more fully in Chapter 6. Some esoteric teachers however move beyond the limitations of this terminology and stress that as we all contain both 'female' and 'male' energy, a comparable exchange can take place when partners are of the same sex. It is also said that while the female energy pattern is to take in at the genital area, it puts out from the chest area, and that the male pattern is the exact reverse, so that even with heterosexual sexuality the male is no more active or positive than the female, but rather there is a reciprocal exchange of energy between the two partners.

In traditions which see sex as a source of spiritual power, heterosexual union remains the norm. Thus the modern witchcraft 'Wicca' manifesto quoted by Margot Adler in *Dancing Down the Moon*, states, 'We value Sex as pleasure, as the symbol and embodiment of life, and as one of the sources of energies used in magical practice and religious worship.' As Margot Adler explains, a woman who, through ritual, has incarnated the Goddess and a man who has incarnated the God can have a physical union that is divine.

The significance of the fusion of male and female is an important concept in Tantra, most clearly summarised in Philip Rawson's *Tantra*. Tantric yoga is a discipline which originated in the third or fourth century AD, and has both a Hindu and a Buddhist tradition. While much of Buddhist religious thought has emphasised voidness or *sunyata*, Tantra emphasises *vajra*, the thunderbolt or creative energy. It is believed that spirit is reached through the senses; thus the tradition features body practices and, in what seems to be the original, i.e. 'left-handed', Tantra, the sexual practice of *maithuna*. In Tantra the emphasis is not on reaching orgasm; in fact orgasm may not be encouraged. In one rite, *stri-puja*, there is apparently a long period of preparation with the two partners sleeping progressively closer together, outside then within the same bed, clothed and then unclothed, before making love. The emphasis is on sexual intercourse as the expression of a spiritual bond, with a significant flow of psychic energy between the partners. Through it, the *kundalini* energy may be raised up the spine to heighten spiritual activity in centres throughout the whole body. Interestingly, as Francis King describes in his book on Tantra, in the Hindu tradition this rising dynamic force is seen as female (the goddess Shakti) while what gives it form is the male god (Shiva); in the Buddhist tradition the roles are reversed and the passive form is female.

Against the background of the Christian denigration of sex, it is salutary to learn about disciplines which recognise a strong spiritual element in sexuality. It is inspiring to come across maxims such as, 'While being caressed, . . . enter the caressing as everlasting life' (quoted by Paul Reps in *Zen Flesh, Zen Bones*). However, as women we still have a lot to learn about the nature of this spiritual element for us. It will not help us to adopt ready-made formulae or to wrap around sex a new kind of mysticism derived from our (often imperfect) understanding of other cultural traditions. We do not need to adopt unquestioningly their emphasis on male/female polarity and heterosexuality which is reflected in many modern books on Tantra (like Nik Douglas and Penny Slinger's *Sexual Secrets*). In 'Against Yin and Yang and Androgyny' John Rowan has queried the identification of 'yin' and 'yang' with 'female' and 'male', which he suggests was a later addition. The recent western redefinition of female sexuality which recognised the importance of the clitoris (first stressed by Ann Koedt in *The Myth of the Vaginal Orgasm*) and the role of the G-spot (see the book by Alice Kahn Ladas and others) does in any case lead us away from a mechanistic, polarised 'ball-and-socket' view of sex. In 'Variety Is the Spice of Life', Muriel Dimen points out that some societies define more than two genders (for example, the Navajo allow three) and suggests that adult humans may be 'polymorphic'. There are many all-women covens in modern American Wiccan traditions. Audre Lorde makes me recall the bare-breasted ladies of Cretan religion when she recommends a celebration of the erotic as 'an assertion of the life-force of women, of that creative energy empowered'. We can adapt existing spiritual/sexual traditions, and can create our own rituals to help us cope with actual situations of sexual tension or trauma in our lives (for example Diane Mariechild's 'Ritual to Stop Harassment' and Z. Budapest's spell in *The Holy Book of Women's Mysteries* to regain psychic balance after rape). We do not need fresh mystiques: our first priority is to unwrap the mystiques which already cloak sexuality in our culture, generally as a result of ignorance.

One such mystique is that sexuality is about our deepest sense of self. Richard Sennett and Michel Foucault argue that it is precisely the enforced repression and privatisation of sexuality, in the context of the isolation experienced by twentieth-century individuals, which has given it an artificial role as a kind of secret barometer of our 'true selves'. Writing in the *London Review of Books*, they point out that sex is as basic as eating or sleeping, but is treated in modern society as something more:

> It is the medium through which people seek to define their personalities, their tastes. Above all, sexuality is the means by which people seek to be conscious of themselves . . .
> The idea of having an identity composed of one's sexuality puts a tremendous burden on one's erotic feelings . . .

Pointing out that what is feared or ambiguous often becomes urgent to a person, Foucault and Sennett suggest that it is the very uncertainties and problems surrounding sexuality which make us magnify its importance and its role in defining ourselves; the result is that it 'has become charged with tasks of self-definition and self-knowledge it can't and shouldn't perform'. The authors comment that the 'privilege' accorded to desire is a Christian heritage which we are far from ready to cope with. What is most secret becomes the deepest sense of self. The individual alone with her sexuality in masturbation faces a legacy of acute fear, and the first modern researchers on sexuality believed that they were opening up 'a terrifying Pandora's box of unrestrained lust, perversion and destructiveness in looking at the sexual desires of people alone without the civilizing restraints of society . . . A person alone with his or her sexuality appeared to be a person alone with a very dangerous force.'

Pandora's box was originally a jar, and in Chapter 7 I describe the historical process whereby sexuality was hived off and sealed away in patriarchal Greece, when the symbol of Pandora's jar first emerged as the container for forces the very denial of which made them appear dangerous and threatening. Similarly Foucault and Sennett try to understand the fears expressed during the late Enlightenment and Victorian eras about the individual's sexuality, not as blind prejudices or as aberrations of scientific enquiry, but rather as the result of culturally inherited symbolic patterns of thought: 'These fears expressed ideas about the relation between mind and body, speech and desire, of which the Victorian doctors were themselves unaware.'

It is this relation between mind and body which I am involved in questioning. Its manifestation as the breach between speech and desire, between the spoken and the unspoken, which Foucault and Sennett describe, is recognised and explicitly challenged in the sexuality workshops which have sprung up in the wake of Masters and Johnson's research. These groups, pioneered in Britain by Jenner Roth, start from the experience of a woman alone with her sexuality and slowly peel away the wraps of fear and ignorance which surround that experience. The groups involve an intense programme of homework: long baths, self-examination, physical exercises, learning physiological information, exploring sexual history, body smells, parents' attitude to sex, masturbation without orgasm, masturbation with orgasm. Always there is sharing in the group, where women report back on their homework, bridging desire and speech, giving that solitary individual experience a voice in the world – What did you feel? When? In which part of your body? And which other part? Phrases like 'that mysterious glow' and 'I don't know how it happened' are not encouraged. Participants are asked: 'How did you do it?' 'What turned you on?' 'What didn't?' In an article describing the 'Sexuality Group' Jenner Roth writes:

> The mystery, the feeling that all the information about us belonged to someone else disappeared and allowed us to know and discover ourselves and our sexual uniqueness more clearly . . . This moves us away from the idea that we can be turned on and off by others as passively and casually as a light switch or that we are dependent on other people for our sexuality.

The focus is on making one's sexual experience accessible and on taking responsibility for it. There is also emphasis on making links between your sexuality and the rest of your life: if you rush orgasm, what else do you rush in your life? If you push your body in sex, how else do you push yourself? If you find it hard to say 'no' in sex, how hard do you find it to say 'no' in the rest of your life? This helps sex to become less separate and shows how it is just another area of living in which many of our familiar patterns and behaviours appear.

Such an approach is important given our cultural legacy in which sexuality has been denied. From its being the most forbidden and secret subject, there is a danger of us over-reacting by exalting it as the most sacred subject. We need to be wary of placing an emphasis on sexuality which is as distorted as the Christian church's denial of it; to exalt and to deny are only different sides of the same coin. Sexuality can carry spiritual energy, but then so can each area of our body; the point of reinstating it is not to fetishise its importance. Some – especially women and gay men – have found it necessary, in the social arena, to speak out from their sexual identity against the particular forms of oppression which they incur, as Seidler points out; this is, however, different from allowing our sexual parts to define the whole, determining our total individual sense of identity. Jenner Roth refers to sex as one door among many. In 'Sexuality Group' she takes the analogy that we are each like a house with many windows and doors, and comments that:

> Putting one of these doors or windows – called sexuality – in good working order doesn't change what is inside or outside the house . . .

In the sexuality groups, participants are encouraged to gain access to the full range of their sexual feelings, from the need for a period of celibacy to the desire for a bit of 'good dirty sex'; from the need for affection which need not be confused with sex at all, through to the yearning for a deep spiritual union with another being through making love.

This approach is in keeping with writings in the women's movement about de-fetishising sexuality. Feminists have been moving away from penetration as the be-all and end-all of the sexual act; away from orgasm as the 'big bang' to make it all worth while; away from purely genital sex towards an all-body experience of caressing and closeness; moving towards a consciousness where we can be aware of ourselves as sexual beings 24 hours a day, naked or clothed, in bed or on the bus. This does not mean becoming obsessed with sex, rather the opposite. It means that the sexual dimension of our experience is available to us more of the time: it is thus much more on a par with other parts of the personality. This approach means placing sexuality, not in a box, in a Pandora's jar, or on a pedestal, but on a continuum of pleasurable physical experiences.

My interest here has not been to offer a new symbolic orthodoxy about sexuality to replace the old. My concern is, as ever, with alternatives: sex as orientation, sex as release, sex as death, sex as transformation, sex as exchange of energy, sex as spiritual union, sex as continuum. Perhaps all these ideas offer us more than the old symbolic view of, say, sex as evil or sex as conquest, but some of these symbolic ideas also present difficulties. Sex as death draws on the old dichotomy between conscious and unconscious which I discussed in the last chapter; it also places a centrality on orgasm questioned by both feminists and esotericists. Sex as release can be misused to construct a 'hydraulic' view of sexuality, problematic for women (as pointed out by Lucy Bland in *Sex and Love*). Sex as a meeting of the opposite poles of 'male' and 'female' needs revising to include gay and lesbian relationships. Sex as spiritual union can lead to a new kind of fetishisation. These are merely ideas from other spiritual traditions which are as man-made as Christian ideas about sex; they are ideas which we can try out as we develop the symbols which correspond most closely to our experience and illuminate it most fully. Only we can do that for ourselves.

To embark successfully on any of these projects we need first to unload from sex all the excess baggage that has been heaped upon it, not only by the punitive moralism of the Christian tradition, but also by the male-created so-called 'permissive' society. This, by making eroticism a commodity, has increased feelings of frustration and allowed the transformation of our sexual desire into the need to consume. Such excess baggage can numb the body and cut us off from the physical sensations which inform us about what sexuality could be for each of us. If we perceive sex less as an identity and more as a language, it is a language which we have been forbidden to speak, or allowed to speak only with certain words dictated by others: we know only the crudest of its vocabulary and grammar, as Jane Rule has pointed out. As a physical conversation, it can be guarded or open, intimate, assertive, serious or playful. For many of us the first step may be to learn slowly to listen to the genitals for what they have to teach us, and to disentangle all the inappropriate expectations and feelings which have been imposed on them, whether these are issues of fear, vulnerability, self-hatred or identity. Gradually we may find that we can learn to use the psychic dimension of sexual power for ourselves – to release what? to surrender what? to transform in which ways? to exchange what? Here I am putting forward a new symbolic view of sex as an event which involves the 'fine' energy of the body in a powerful cycle of build-up and clearance and which can be used as a vehicle for spiritual expression; articulating how we may want to do this is a long process, which has hardly started.

Backs in Harmony

This is an exercise from Bob Moore. It is simple but very useful to do with your sexual partner, to help bring you into harmony and encourage a beneficial exchange of energy between you.

(a) On a carpet or cushions, sit back to back with your spines touching down their whole length for 10 minutes. Notice changes in your body sensations. It is best done naked; if you are clothed, wear natural fibres (cotton, wool) as synthetic fibres have their own energy field which interferes with the energy moving between you. If you are different heights, your chakras will unfortunately not be level with your partner's. Notice the quality of the contact you feel with your partner in this position.

(b) Repeat, but this time let yourselves fall into the same rhythm of breathing. This can give the exercise more impact. A partner who is in better contact with her/his own rhythm can help the other.

(c) Repeat back to back as before, but this time hold hands palm to palm. We use our hands to sense and project energy, and there is a particular energy contact point in the middle of the palm. This way of doing the exercise helps to move energy and vitality from one to the other.

(d) Repeat, but this time hold one of your partner's hands and move the other to an area of your body which is causing a problem for you. Decide jointly with your partner which hand to release, then decide independently which area you will put your free hand on. For example, you may choose to put it on:

– the *hara* chakra for problems in achieving sexual satisfaction or emotional control, or if you are angry, jealous or envious.
– the solar plexus chakra if you suffer fear (for example, of your partner, or of the dark).
– the heart chakra if you suffer from depression or sadness, or if you feel sorry for your partner or yourself.
– the throat chakra for problems of suppression (for example, if you want to say things to your partner and cannot).

When you put your hand on a spot, you will eventually get a reaction. After the exercise, talk to your partner about it; clearance comes through expression.

Each chakra has its opposite positive qualities: thus in the *hara*, anger can become calmness; in the solar plexus, fear can become love; in the heart, sorrow can become joy; and in the throat, suppression can become release. The negative qualities are like covers holding energy in, and so resemble obstacles which need clearing; but the positive qualities emerge through a process of expression, and so you cannot have too much of them.

The Power of Dance

In western society, dancing seems more at home in a discotheque than in church. It is hard for us to imagine dance as a spiritual act. And yet, like the other physical processes and activities I have mentioned, dance too can take on a numinous quality and be imbued with psychic energy.

Since its early days under the Roman Empire, the political institution of the Christian church has held a hostile attitude to dance, linked with its denial of the body. But other historic religious traditions – of Africa, India and the Americas, as well as Europe – are rich with examples of the use of dance: for the worship of a deity; for communication with spirits; to allow possession by deities symbolising natural forces; to celebrate or encourage the transformation of the seasons and the movements of the heavenly bodies; or for the magical promotion of success in war, agriculture or healing.

Dance was a central part of Aegean Bronze Age religious rituals (see Chapter 7). Its association with plants and animals suggests that its purpose was honouring, and perhaps inviting possession by, nature spirits or deities, while dances to the sun were perhaps intended to harness the sun's power and encourage it on its path. The regeneration of vegetation and the reappearance of the sun were apparently linked to a belief in some form of birth for the human dead; dance seems to have been a means of attuning to, and facilitating, that process. Lillian B. Lawler, in *The Dance in Ancient Greece*, gives evidence of continuing traditions of circular dance and funerary dance in later, classical, Greece.

Circular forms used as a means of attuning the dancers to the heavenly bodies also seem to figure prominently in traditions of Sufi dancing. As Jill Purce puts it in *The Mystic Spiral*, 'By dancing and emulating . . . the whirling of the planets or the dance of atoms, man actively incorporates the creative vibrations and ordering movements of the cosmos. His body becomes the universe, his movements its movements . . .' Sufi dervishes whirl round and round, maintaining a still point in their centre. It is interesting that teachers of esoteric anatomy state that circular and spiral forms are also significant in the movement of 'fine' energy around the body, for example in the chakras.

Circular dance is also important in modern revivals of witchcraft traditions. 'Raising a cone of power' is done by chanting or dancing, or both, or running round the circle in order to intensify the combined wills of the group, as Margot Adler explains in *Drawing Down the Moon*. The 'cone of power' is then focused and directed towards, for example, healing or some other objective. Teachers of esoteric anatomy suggest that the energy of the individual can be strongly affected, and very much raised, simply by holding hands with others in a circle.

Within the Jewish religion the Hassidic tradition is one which placed a greater value on the life of the body in spiritual activity than mainstream Judaism. It has preserved accounts of dance being used as a channel for spiritual power. Thus Martin Buber in *Tales of the Hassidim* records a story from eighteenth-century Poland about a *zaddick* (holy man) who, when near death, announced that it was the time to dance and performed a dance in which 'every step was a holy meaning'. Here again dance is used to mark or assist a time of change or transformation. Dance could apparently also be used to focus and direct psychic power to achieve certain aims, such as in the story of the 'Dance of Healing': Rabbi Moshe Leib heard news that his friend, the Rabbi of Berditchev, had fallen ill, and on the sabbath he repeated his friend's name many times and prayed for his recovery. He then:

. . . put on new shoes made of morocco leather, laced them up tight and danced. A zaddick who was present said: 'Power flowed forth from his dancing. Every step was a powerful mystery. An unfamiliar light suffused the house, and everyone watching saw the heavenly hosts join in his dance.'

In our culture we have heard of traditions of dance being used to build up energy, impetus and confidence in times of crisis, as before a battle in 'war dances'. In 1984 such dances were still being performed by Mozambiquan FRELIMO troops before and after battles against the South African-backed MNR guerillas. What is perhaps quite new to us is the idea that dance could be used, not only as a preparation, but in itself, to direct energy and achieve specific results. The Castaneda books refer to dancing as a psychic tool not only for achieving specific objectives but also for gaining knowledge. Don Juan refers to dancing as a psychic ability which parallels his own ability of *'seeing'* (perhaps equivalent to clairvoyance). In *A Separate Reality* Don Juan tells Castaneda about Sacateca, a 'man of knowledge' whose predilection is dancing and who 'dances and knows', by dancing 'with all that he has.' Castaneda's bewilderment at this notion is increased by a visit to Sacateca. When he ignores Sacateca's indications that he is unwelcome, Sacateca uses a dance to send him on his way: Castaneda experiences a strange apprehension and his thoughts become dissociated. Quite automatically, he turns around and leaves. When Don Juan hears this he roars with laughter and explains that Sacateca had *seen* Castaneda and then danced and stopped him with his 'will'. The dance was a vehicle for his psychic power, successfully directed towards making Castaneda leave.

These examples of the use of dance in spiritual activity may leave us bemused. Not only are they alien to the mainstream of Christian spiritual practices, but even as a secular activity dance itself is completely missing from many people's lives in our culture. Ballet performance denies the real body to create the illusion of the perfect body: elegant, ethereal and weightless, while most dance of the 'keep-fit' or 'aerobic' variety emphasises work on the muscles rather than the whole body (i.e. the skeleton, posture, weight, gravity, nerves, breath, internal organs). Women tend to regard dance as a means of keeping slim and attractive rather than a means of highlighting our physical strength, awareness and pleasure (see Judith Hanna's *Dance, Sex and Gender*). We are familiar with dance as a way to unwind and clear tension, and recently the 'Release' school of dance has taught methods of using dance, with awareness of breathing, to allow expression and release of energy. This remains far from the use of dance to build and direct energy as in some of my earlier examples. I have seen some very creative and socially relevant dance performance work, such as Jacky Lansley's use of the medium to deconstruct sexual stereotypes, and Christopher Bruce's 'Ghost Dances' which indicts fascist persecution in South America; performance, however, remains different from dance in which people participate. Some women have found it empowering to reclaim 'belly dancing' traditions (see Wendy Buonaventura's *Belly Dancing*). There has been a revival of interest in pagan 'sacred circle' dance, and some feminists have been fertile in inventing their own dance rituals. Some teachers have also been specific about the need for the involvement of the inner self in dancing. Thus Helen Poynor, in her article, 'To Live is to Dance', writes that

Dance . . . is more than just a physical activity. It is essentially an expressive medium and as such demands the participation of the inner self. If I move but am 'absent' from my movement, thinking about something else, not committed to it, I will not be dancing . . . If I repeat the same movement, however simple, with my whole consciousness involved in the motion, allowing it to spring from or touch my deeper self, then I begin to dance.

Such involvement of the whole consciousness in dance is evidently part of those practices described earlier, but we are nowhere near being able to understand the apparent use of 'fine' energy in such subtle, specific and directed ways as those examples suggest. Although not strictly dance, T'ai Chi and the *mudras* of Tantric yoga offer body gestures, positions and movements which are believed to encourage the flow of spiritual energy through the body. However, the possibility that more than a tiny minority of people in our culture might use dance creatively – to participate in the movements of the natural world around us, to celebrate or re-enact times of change and transformation either in the seasons or in people's lives, to prepare for or conclude stressful action, to gain intuitive or psychic knowledge, or to direct energy to achieve a healing effect – this possibility remains very remote in our body-despising culture. It remains a possibility we can cherish.

Pouring the Pelvic Bowl

This is a 'contact/release' exercise which I learnt from Linda Hartley. It is good for developing awareness in your torso and can develop into a dance with a partner.

Do this exercise after relaxation, a shake-out, or some basic movement. Allow several minutes for each phase.

Imagine your pelvis is a bowl of water and experiment with tipping it in as many different ways as possible.

Now do the same with your shoulders.

Now combine the two, tipping both pelvis and shoulders in various ways.

If you are dancing with a partner, approach her/him and experiment with tipping the water from pelvis and shoulders into her/him in various ways.

Let the movements develop into a dance.

The pelvis and the shoulders are thought to be energically connected, so that relaxing the one helps the other.

Mudras: *A Posture for Power*
_____

I was taught this by Anne Parks.

Mudras are meditative postures which are part of Tantric
knowledge. Although they do not involve movement I include one
here because they are based on the idea that adopting certain
precise body positions has a specific effect on the alignment and
movement of body energy, as, for example, releasing unwanted
energy, bringing clarity, or improving contact with the ground.
When you try this one out, follow the instructions very carefully.
Stay in the posture for five to ten minutes at first.

For action. Relax your body. Sit cross-legged on the ground with
your left hand resting on your left knee, palm upwards with the
tip of the thumb and the tip of the first finger touching and the
other fingers straight. Your right hand is pointing down to the
ground in the middle of your knees. This *mudra* has been linked
with a mantra about love and caring, and the position symbolises
bringing love or spirit through action into the world, the right
hand directing energy downwards into the earth and matter. It is
said to counteract 'ego' patterns of indolence or self-absorption,
such as when someone is too lazy to take their essential energy
seriously, or to cultivate it and use it in action.

Familiarity with the *mudras* may inspire you to develop your own
postures, or movements, which have a particular meaning and
effect for you.

Work with the Senses

Blake described the body as a portion of soul discerned by the five
senses, the 'chief inlets of Soul in this age'. Valuing the information
and experiences conveyed by the senses is an important part of several
non-Christian spiritual traditions. Witches interviewed by Margot
Adler in *Dreaming Down the Moon* stress their affinity with the earth,
and one defines a witch as someone 'who can become excited over
the feel of a pebble or the croak of a frog'. Tantric knowledge
understands the five senses as the medium through which we can
contact psychic energy: as well as *maithuna* or sexual union which
I mentioned earlier, it offers a series of other practices based on the
senses. In Castaneda's *The Fire From Within* Don Juan suggests that
our senses have the potential to detect everything surrounding us, for

we have tapped only a very small portion of ourselves. Traditionally, western culture is suspicious of the senses. And yet every time someone dons perfume or takes a fragrant bath they are acknowledging the power of smell to relax or attract, and phrases like 'I smell a rat' are suggestive of a power colloquially acknowledged but perhaps not often consciously realised. Aromatherapy is a form of treatment based on using specific, appropriate smells to achieve a healing effect.

Our favoured sense is sight, and we are perhaps used to the idea that the eyes can communicate intuitive knowledge and personal power in human relationships: 'His eyes riveted me to the spot'; 'As soon as I saw her I just knew'; 'It was love at first sight'; 'I was mesmerized'. We are less familiar with the idea that they can transmit knowledge and power in a spiritual context, and yet clairvoyance and the ability to 'see' the aura are perhaps faculties which have atrophied in us; yogic teachings describe procedures to awaken the 'third eye'. We are familiar with the idea that a good painting can communicate a sense of well-being and deep satisfaction; it is not a big step to the Tantric practice of *yantras*, which includes the visual meditation of a ritual diagram or mandala. The mandala (like the labyrinth) is said to represent a map of the individual's process towards unification. Again, we are familiar with the idea that colour affects mood, as when we describe colours as 'calming', 'cold', 'relaxing', 'hectic', 'warm' or 'claustrophobic'; but we are not familiar with the idea that colours can be used consciously and positively to heal people. Esoteric disciplines teach a variety of techniques for 'colour healing', ranging from the wearing of an appropriate colour, lighting with a coloured light bulb, visualising colour, imagining you are breathing a colour in, to sending it to a part of your body which is unhealthy, or imagining sending it to another person. 'Colour healing' is a developed method which classifies the effect of various colours, for example as 'activating', 'pacifying', 'expressive' or 'penetrating'. Various shades are also recommended to heal particular bodily functions (see the writings of Theo Gimbel, David Tansley and S.G.J. Ouseley). However, each colour also has an individual meaning for each of us, reflecting our own life story, and will affect other people differently. It is important not to become trapped in systematising and, especially at first, it is vital to develop your own sensitivity and intuition about which colours help you, before using them to heal others.

Esoteric anatomy suggests that all the senses can be used, not only for perceiving 'fine' energy, but also for channelling it to achieve a healing effect. As sight is our favoured faculty, it is important to develop the other senses to balance it. We can relieve our eyes by learning both to listen and to use sound in a new way. We are used to appreciating that sound can change people's state of mind (as with 'mood music'), and can bring people involved in spiritual activities into harmony (as with Christianity's Gregorian chants and hymn singing). It is also possible to use sound outside institutional contexts like the church, to work with spiritual or 'fine' energy. Such practices are based on the idea that sound affects matter, that it is an organising principle which can move matter just as a magnet can rearrange iron filings into alignment with it.

The Tantric tradition includes work with 'mantras', sacred syllables and phrases which are repeated to evoke a certain state of consciousness and to make connections with, and clean, the *nadis* or force lines running up and down the body. Certain sounds, such as 'Om', have been used for centuries and are thought to carry an accumulated charge of psychic power. The repetition of a mantra affects the vibrations of the body, clearing 'thought chatter' so that it becomes possible to tune in to the body's internal sound; the mantra may release tension, unleashing pain clenched in the body, perhaps since childhood, or it may act as a scaffolding of tranquillity around problems and imbalances. The vibration affects every cell of the body along with the bricks and mortar where chanting is done, leaving an atmosphere permeating the building. In eastern martial arts traditions, fighters often make a sound before striking, on the principle that sound releases energy; similarly feminist self-defence teachers emphasise the importance of using the voice to enhance and amplify physical strength in the case of an attack. Singing can unknot the debilitating effects of fear. Often the simple act of voicing a problem, as in psychotherapy, can provide release and relief. Chanting or humming together is a powerful way of raising and harmonising the energy of a group. Sound pollution, like traffic noise, can be damaging, just as a whining or insincere voice can 'grate on the nerves', whereas a well-pitched voice can be used to create a healing effect. Teachers of esoteric anatomy suggest that suppression in an individual is reflected in their voice: in a healthy person the voice should move up and down the body and can be tuned to different pitches appropriate for communicating with different people. Thus psychic healers may use sound in the healing process, and individuals can use improvised sounds, or 'toning' as it is called, to release tension from the body as a method of self-healing. In some spiritual teachings we also find the idea that certain instruments resonate with, and have a health-giving effect on, certain parts of the human being: for example, the flute on the spine and certain types of bell to clear blockages in the aura.

From Christianity we are familiar with the idea that we move towards God into the light; these esoteric disciplines suggest that we move into the light *and the sound*. The idea of the 'music of the spheres' first appears in the west associated with the Greek philosopher Pythagoras, but esoteric teachers have incorporated it: as a city has a hum, so does a countryside and so does a planet, while the hum of planets together makes the music of the spheres. They draw on eastern ideas that sound created form and held the universe together. Such ideas are partly familiar from the Judaeo-Christian belief that 'In the beginning was the Word'.

What concerns us here, however, is simply the idea that light and sound have been understood as different vibrations on which we can receive and transmit 'fine' or spiritual energy. I will devote a separate section to the sense with which I have most experience of working: touch.

Groaning and Toning

The tone of our voice affects us and all around us. Making sounds can improve that tone and can have a healing effect by moving body energy.

(a) Stand with your eyes shut, back and head straight, feet parallel and shoulder-width apart, knees slightly bent. Relax and imagine light filling your body.

Start groaning softly on the exhale and then let the groan rise. Focus on letting your voice express your body feelings instead of being controlled by your mind. Let the sound go. Start low, rise and keep the high note. Repeat and continue for ten minutes.

When you have got used to this exercise, you will be able to do it lying flat on your back in bed or driving in a car. It is a good way to draw yourself together and focus your energy at the start of each day. The emphasis on expression can help to unknot depression. You may be able to develop your own variations, for example by inventing your own chant, or throwing your voice out like a child throwing a ball, or using sounds like 'ho! ho! ho! ho!'

(b) This is a way of using sound to focus on one part of your body which has a problem.

Choose a sound to work with. A simple vowel sound like 'ah' or 'eh' or 'i' can be a good way to start, or you could use 'om' or 'hu'.

Stand as before, close eyes, relax and breathe calmly for a few minutes.

Now send your awareness to a part of your body which needs attention (it may be stiff, sore, numb or tingling). Imagine you are breathing into that part, and on the exhale push the sound out of that part to clean it.

You need to bring all your energy out with the sound (which doesn't necessarily mean the sound will be loud), otherwise it is just singing. The clarity of the sound is important.

You can experiment with different sounds to see which works best for you.

For more information, see Laurel Keyes' *Toning: The Creative Power of the Voice*.

The Mantra 'Om'

'Om' is a sound that has been used for centuries and is believed to be particularly effective for getting in touch with your inner silence.

Take up a relaxed, untwisted position. This could be standing in the position described in the previous exercise, sitting cross-legged on the floor, or seated on a chair with arms and legs uncrossed. Close your eyes and relax.

The sound 'Om' (sometimes spelt 'Aum') starts at the back of the mouth with the 'a', passes through the centre of the mouth with 'u' and ends up on the lips with 'm'. Each stage is slow and resonant, and the whole sound may take 15 seconds or longer before you can take a deep breath and repeat it.

Colour Meditation with Gold, Pink and Blue

This a Bob Moore exercise which I have found very calming and healing. It involves three meditations which are repeated in order.

(a) Sit in a comfortable position with knees uncrossed. Close your eyes and relax.

Imagine a gold colour. Place it at a point about six to eight inches above your head and imagine it falling down around your body through your aura, like water from a shower nozzle, until it reaches your feet.

Now choose one of the following words: PROTECTION or ATTRACTION. Bring your awareness to the word you have chosen and try to get some understanding of its place in your life. For example: what does protection mean to you? What do you need protection from? Why is protection necessary? Or: what sort of attraction do you create? What do you attract? Who are you attracted to? The meditation may bring up a past experience, such as a past attraction: how did it work out or not? What were the problems? (We can attract experiences and situations as well as people.) Allow whatever comes up to evolve and look at the issues it raises for you. (Twenty minutes.)

Now visualise white light at your feet and draw it up round your body through your aura, like an eggshell, until it reaches the point above your head where you started.

(b) Next day, repeat the exercise, but this time the colour is rose pink and the words to choose between are GIVING or SHARING. These may bring up different issues, for example: what do I give to others? What part of myself do I give from? Often when giving we expect something in return, so look at what receiving means. Giving and receiving are a relationship. Many people can give but have difficulty receiving. If receiving, what area do you receive in? In contrast, sharing involves allowing oneself to be equal with another in a sharing of mutual benefit without looking for any return. Sharing involves compassion and is a communication or communion between people based on the value of what is shared, not restricted by the idea of exchange.

(c) Next day, repeat the exercise, but this time the colour is pale blue and the words to choose between are FORGIVENESS or FREEDOM. Forgiveness raises important issues, as letting go of hurts, grudges or guilt creates a clearance of debris from the past so that we can move forward. This includes forgiving yourself. Freedom is not just doing what you *want* but involves discipline in order to allow your *needs* to operate.

Each of these three colours relate to different levels in yourself and different layers in the energy field: gold is an etheric colour linked to protection and attraction; rose pink is related to the astral level and to giving and compassion; pale blue is associated with your mental state and with calmness and peace.

Always do the meditation in this order, with one colour following the other, and always using the same words with each colour. However, it is entirely up to you which one of the two

possible words you choose each time: you may alternate or stick
with one for weeks, if, for example, you have a particular problem
with forgiveness.

The effect of the meditation is cumulative, and is revealed as
you repeat it over time.

Map of Body Tastes and Smells

This is based on exercises used by Jenner Roth in her sexuality
groups. It is good for developing your sensitivity to taste and smell,
and getting to know your own body better.

Be naked in a warm comfortable private room where you will
not be disturbed. Have some paper and coloured pens or pencils
handy.

Close your eyes and spend ten minutes exploring how each part
of your body smells and tastes.

Open your eyes and draw a picture of your body based on your
impressions of how it tastes and smells. It does not have to be a
literal picture. Work quickly, but be careful to use the colours that
feel right for each part.

You might like to write down, or share with a close friend,
anything you learnt about your body from the exercise.

Intuitive Massage and Healing

The transmission of psychic energy through touch can happen not
only in sex, as I mentioned earlier, but also in massage. The massage
which functions in this way is called 'intuitive' or 'psychic' massage.
It has much in common with bioenergetic massage, based on the work
of Reich, which is founded on an understanding that painful memories
and repression are held in our bodies as muscle blocks which can be
released through massage of tense areas. Bioenergetic massage uses
a detailed and technical approach to release those blocks and improve
the flow of 'vegetative' or 'orgone' energy through the body. In intuitive
massage, however, technique is secondary to an awareness of what is
happening in the overall movement of 'fine' energy through the
person's body. This means that the masseur will focus primarily on
using her hands to sense energy movement and blocks in the person's
body, and on using her hands in whatever way is appropriate to
channel positive energy into the person's body to assist the circulation

and release the blocks. In practice this means that the body is approached with ritual and a reverence which predispose both the giver and the receiver of the massage to be open to fine energy. The masseur will start with a meditation to clear her own channels and allow energy to pass through her body and her hands; she will then spend some time tuning in to the energy of the person to be massaged. In *In Our Own Hands*, Sheila Ernst and I give a brief practical description of how to set about doing an intuitive massage, including certain basic ground rules like always using a warm, safe room, and avoiding vulnerable sexual parts of the body. There are excellent books describing detailed strokes for a full-body massage (for example, George Downing's *The Massage Book* and Sara Thomas in Lucinda Lydell's *The Book of Massage*); as confidence in intuition grows, it becomes easy to develop, and improvise on, technical strokes.

The ability to tune in to another individual, as with the other ways of working with fine energy which I have described, depends not on a special gift but on a basic human sensitivity which most people can develop. In Chapter 3, I suggested that we can question our culture's split between 'conscious' and 'unconscious'; similarly the process of sensing energy flow in our own bodies and those of others has nothing mystical about it, but rather consists of bringing to consciousness experiences which previously existed outside our awareness. In intuitive massage, the body is recognised as a delicate instrument with complex patterns of tension and response. It is not forced or pummelled. While some massage methods work effectively by using strong pressure on muscle tissue from the outside, intuitive massage is understood as working by channelling energy into the subtle anatomy of the body, which will enable it to heal itself from the inside out, shedding muscle blocks and tensions. There is a simile for this process in the story of the wager between the North Wind and the Sun about which could more quickly make a traveller on the road below shed his cloak: the harder the North Wind blew to snatch the cloak off, the tighter the traveller wrapped it round himself; but when the Sun shone warm the traveller soon discarded it of his own accord. Similarly the idea is to communicate to the person massaged the positive energy which will give her the feeling of strength, balance and confidence that will enable her to drop tensions and defensive patterns of her own accord in her own time.

The person massaging will notice that different parts of the body feel different, not only in terms of tightness or looseness of muscles, roughness or smoothness of skin, or temperature (hot head, cold buttocks): she will also feel that different parts give off certain messages, such as a solar plexus that almost jumps to the touch and feels angry, a pounding heart, a scalp that feels 'buzzy' and anxious, delicate nervous belly, hands that feel lonely, overloaded shoulders, neglected feet. These are the ways that she may interpret the variations in the 'fine' energy contact she experiences at different parts of the body. She becomes aware how these different parts need to be touched: intuitively she follows where her hands are 'called' and may find her hands drawing out tension here, invigorating there, giving loving reassurance in another place, in a way that bypasses the everyday 'thinking' mind. It is a question of her being sensitive to, and responding to, the messages received from the other's body.

The receiver may use various symbols to describe her experience of the energy movement in her body: 'It feels like a warm electrical current running down my legs', 'It feels like a fire in my belly', 'Your hands on my legs feel like giant vacuum cleaners picking up stuff'. A face massage may feel 'as if you were sweeping clouds out of the sky'. The person massaging may also visualise certain symbols, such as the sun, the moon, water, or a colour, which may come to her mind intuitively to depict the quality of the energy it is appropriate for her to communicate. Symbols are often used to depict the character of an energy movement, sensed in oneself or another, which may be difficult to describe in words. Since health depends on a movement, rather than a trapping, of energy, helpful symbols are those which allow a process to change to start or continue. Thus a masseur might visualise a triangle to bring in the quality of balance to energy movement, while the symbol of the circle can assist continuity, circulation and flow. The symbol of the cross may be used to reflect the relationship between horizontal and vertical movements of energy – independently of any Christian associations – and polarity takes its place as one principle of energy movement among many.

Studies have been made to measure the physiological effects of healing (see, for example, Bruce MacManaway's summary in *Healing*), and the successful use of 'therapeutic touch' by nurses in New York hospitals (described in Dolores Krieger's book) has started to ease the acceptance of massage into mainstream medicine. However, healers are still investigating its possibilities empirically, and are far from reaching agreement on the nature of the forces at work. My own first experiences with this kind of massage were extremely disconcerting. How was it that while giving a massage my hands were urgently and inexplicably drawn to touch an elbow which the other person afterwards told me had been aching all week? It did not fit with my world view. In my earlier description of the process of intuitive massage, I have several times used the word 'channelling'. But channelling what? From where? Different schools and beliefs use different language to describe the source of the energy which they believe feeds the energy field and is channelled to the receiver in massage and healing.

Some practitioners, like 'faith healers', see themselves as opening to the power of 'God' which flows through their hands and into the person being touched. They associate the process with 'doing good', attributing to it a divine morality along the lines of human morality: God is guiding the hands and helping the person to health. Many of the existing books about body energy are written in these terms. Others see the language of 'channelling' simply as a symbol for gaining access to the knowledge of the unconscious mind. The careful preparation, meditation and visualisation of a clear channel are seen as the means of enabling us to bypass the ego and our personal emotions, obsessions and daily concerns, in order to contact our intuitive understanding about what kind of touch the other person's body needs. This view is based on the idea that we know much more than we realise about what others feel and need, and presupposes that what happens during a massage is basically an exchange of energy between two people: that if the masseur stays aligned and focused on channelling positive energy then she will give only good things and will not run the risk of picking up unwanted energy from the other.

Others symbolise the forces involved as 'cosmic' energies in the sense that Reich understood them: energies which have an objective external presence in the atmosphere and the universe around us, and which are always available to whoever chooses to be aware of and open to them. In eastern beliefs such energy is sometimes called *prana* energy. Some esoteric teachers suggest that the energy derives ultimately from the sun: along with the light and heat we are aware of receiving, other more subtle energies are also radiated to us, of which we are less aware. This last suggestion reminds me of the recurrence of the sun in early Cretan art and its positioning on the source of new life, the belly; I am also reminded of the suggestion in the Castaneda books (for example, in *The Second Ring of Power*) that the human being, that luminous energy field with a solid body at its centre, is in origin a 'piece of the sun'. In this view, the human being receives energy not only directly from the sun but also sun energy as processed by the earth and by animal and plant life (for example through food). The body splays *prana* energy into different frequencies as a prism splays light into different colours, for use in the various body functions. Recent researches into the nature of this energy in the body (such as that of Dr Julian Kenyon at the Centre for the Study of Complementary Medicine in Southampton), most favour the model of some form of electro-magnetic energy. Energy flow, if distorted or blocked in illness, can be restimulated by acupuncture needles or, in healing, by suitably charged hands. Whatever source is visualised for these subtle energies in the atmosphere, they are thought to channel through healing hands, not thanks to the will of God but according to certain more objective principles: energy, like water, finds its own level. Bob Moore stresses that there is nothing magical in the process of healing: all these energies work within laws, whether we know about and understand these laws or not. If the person receiving massage is low in a certain kind of energy which abounds in the atmosphere, and if a channel is open to her through the masseur, then the energy will be transmitted through to rectify the balance as inevitably as a bolt of lightning conducts electricity from sky to earth, or the positrons and neutrons exchange in the smallest electrical spark. Strength will move to fill weakness, warmth to heat a cold part. Excess or unwanted energy will be drained off according to the same principle, and is generally thought of as being channelled into the earth for recycling, rather like the 'earthing' in an electrical circuit. I have come to feel that in the working of such laws the 'divine' is no more – and no less – present than in the workings of gravity, light, heat and the seed that grows into a plant.

Thus the role of the masseur or healer is simply to receive, concentrate and transmit streams of energy. The work is not approached with a pious attitude or even a conscious intention to 'help' the other person; emotional involvement, the desire to 'fix' things or 'make them better' can interfere with the process. One cannot alter another's life without their permission. Respect is reflected in the careful process of clearing your own resistances and attuning to the person receiving, in order to clear a channel; the energy will do the rest. Each person can only receive the input for which they are ready; Ouseley has described true healing as a 'partnership'. A healing massage does not involve effort, nor attitudes of rejection or approval. The work lies in aligning oneself and co-operating with the forces of the universe: the love that operates is not the opposite of hate but is neutral, like the sunshine.

Blind Walk

This is a preliminary exercise to develop your sensitivity in touch. You need a partner to do it with.

One of you closes her eyes, and the other takes her on a walk around the room, introducing her hands to a variety of different objects and textures. Allow at least five minutes.

Exchange roles.

Preparation for Meditation and Self-Massage

This is an exercise devised by Patti Howe and myself. It is good for developing the relaxation and receptivity you need to give a massage.

Sit in a comfortable position with knees apart. Feel your weight on the ground. Shut your eyes. Breathe calmly for a few minutes. Notice sensations in your body. (Two minutes.)

Now imagine you are in a quiet beautiful place where you feel happy and peaceful (it might be a beach, meadow or mountain). Imagine the sun is shining up above you. (Two minutes.)

Now, as you breathe in, imagine you are breathing the sunlight in through the top of your head and down into your belly and your hands. Imagine the sun's rays streaming into your torso and arms. (Two minutes.)

Now focus your awareness on your hands. Imagine them full of the light and warmth of the sun. Notice any sensations in them, perhaps tingling. (Two minutes.)

Now use your hands to explore your face. Try out different ways of touching it, with different parts of your hand (thumb, fingers, palm), with different pressures and with different movements (long strokes, circles, tapping, holding). (Two minutes.)

Now be aware of what your face needs. How do your cheeks and eyes like to be touched? Which other parts need attention, perhaps to calm them or to tone them up? Try some strokes out. (Two minutes.)

This exercise can also be extended to exploring your feet with your hands, feeling the bones and muscles, hard and soft places; and also touching your hands with your feet, to see how different those sensations are.

With practice, you will be able to do the first part of the exercise, with the sun flowing into your hands, in about two minutes altogether and this can be a very valuable routine to do just before giving a massage.

N.B. After giving a massage, it is a good idea to wash your hands and wrists in cold water, and/or place your hands palm down on the floor to clear from them any unwanted energy you may have picked up.

Some Healing Strokes

I learnt these from Bob Moore.

These are strokes which are simple but touch on important body energy patterns, and, unlike many massage strokes which need to be done on a naked horizontal body, they can be done on a clothed person, lying, seated or standing. Clothing should preferably be natural fibres (cotton, wool) as synthetic fibres have their own energy field which interferes with the touch. N.B.: Exact chakra positions are given earlier in this chapter.

(a) *Legs and Root.* Here the person receiving should lie flat on the ground on their front. Place one hand on their root chakra at the back. With the other hand, starting from the big toe of their right foot, run your fingers *up* the back of their *right* leg to their pelvis and *down* the left leg to the toe. Repeat for several minutes. The direction of the stroke is important because it follows body energy streams.

(b) *Sacrum and Crown.* This is good to do after (a). Place one hand on the person's sacrum, and the other on the top of their head on the crown chakra. Let the hands rest for several minutes. This helps to increase the energy flow up and down the spine.

(c) *Belly and Spine.* This may be easiest with both of you seated; an upright chair or stool is best. It has a stronger effect directly on the skin, but the receiver can be clothed. Place one hand on her *hara* chakra and keep it there. Place the middle two fingers of the other hand in the hollow at the base of the skull at the back, and slowly and gently draw them down the spine to a position below the root chakra; then draw them right away. In this way you will be drawing out excess energy. Repeat for at least five minutes.

(d) *Forehead and Spine.* This can be a continuation of (c). Place the palm of one hand over the pineal chakra on the forehead and keep it there throughout. Place the middle two fingers of the other hand on the spine below the root chakra and slowly draw them up the spine to the hollow in the base of the skull, then draw your hand right away from the body. Repeat for at least five minutes. Excess and unusable energy will stick to your fingers like a magnet and by drawing it right away at the end of each stroke you may help to clear blockages in the spine.

(e) *Chakra holding.* It can be beneficial to hold the front and the back of someone's chakras simultaneously. With the throat chakra, heart chakra, solar plexus and *hara* chakras, place one hand on the front position and with the middle two fingers of the other hand rotate anticlockwise (up to their right, down to their left) on its back position. With the root chakra you can place one hand flat on the root chakra area at the back, and the other hand on the area between navel and genitals at the front. Hold the back hand steady and rotate the front hand anticlockwise (up on their left, down on their right) for a few minutes. Then keep the front hand steady on the belly and rotate the back hand in ever-widening circles anticlockwise (up on their right, down on their left) until you are including the whole torso; then make the circles gradually smaller again until you finish by holding both hands still as you did at the start. (The direction of the circular movement is important because it follows energy streams.)

(f) *Diagonals across the back.* Place one hand on the left shoulder, the other on the right shoulder. Slowly draw your hands down diagonally across the back so that each hand ends up at the opposite hip. Your hands will cross in the middle of the back. (A problem with the left shoulder will affect the *right* lower body.)

(g) *Head massage.* The receiver should be sitting. Stand behind her and work with the centre two fingers, using both hands symmetrically. Start on the centre forehead, draw your hands round close over the top of the ears to the hollow in the base of the skull at the back, where you draw your hands off. Repeat for three minutes. Now start just above the ear on each side, move your fingers down the back of the ear, the sides of the neck, along and off the shoulders on each side. Repeat for three minutes. The touch should be very light. This can be very relaxing and good for headaches.

Preparing to do Healing

Take this very slowly at first.

Stand with back and neck straight, feet parallel and shoulder-width apart, knees slightly bent. Close your eyes and imagine you are breathing out any tension or preoccupations.

Be aware of the ground underneath your feet, feel it supporting you. Imagine that strength from the ground is rising up your legs into your belly and torso. Feel a continuous flow of energy rising into your body.

Now be aware of the light falling all around your body. Imagine your body is soaking in energy from this light. Feel a continuous flow of energy pouring into your body from above and all around.

Imagine your whole body filled with energy from below, above and all around: every little bit of your body from top to toe and to the tips of your fingers.

Now imagine that the energy can flow down your arms and out through your hands. Imagine it extending outwards from your palms and fingertips.

Now you are ready to place your hands on the person you wish to heal.

After preparing like this, you might want to use some of the set strokes described above, or you might want to improvise. With practice you will learn to do a preparation like this in a few moments. Remember to wash your hands afterwards.

Intuitive Healing

Healing can be done following set strokes, as described earlier, or intuitively. For the latter, you need first to devote time to developing your sensitivity to the energy of others; here are two exercises which might help you to do this.

(a) Sit facing your partner, close your eyes and relax. Imagine you are gradually expanding your aura to include your partner. Now scan her or his body in your mind's eye. How are you aware of it? Do any symbols come up for you, such as a picture? Colour(s)? Gesture? Sound? Song? Is there a part of your partner's body which attracts your attention? (Always take the first idea that comes to you.) After a few minutes, withdraw your aura, become aware of yourself again, disconnect from your partner and imagine a glass sheet dropping between you. Talking to your partner afterwards can help you find out if any of your perceptions were accurate or helpful.

(b) Since the energy field is also a physical part of the person, it is possible to learn to sense it with your hands. Do one of the preparation exercises given above, and then experiment with moving around feeling your partner's aura. Move your hand towards and away from the solid body to see if you can detect different densities or texture. Try different areas around the body. Becoming anxious will hinder you. Stay relaxed, keep an open mind, and notice everything you experience. Sensations and symbols may come to you subliminally at first. Afterwards talk to your partner about what you experienced.

After repeated practice, you may feel ready to try intuitive healing. Always do a preparatory meditation first so that you are receptive. Work slowly. You may wish to work on the aura or the solid body. Stick to the latter at first, often allowing your hands to rest still. Holding two points encourages a movement of energy between them. It is not wise to assume that you know what another needs: simply allow your hand(s) to go where they are drawn, and then ask that your partner receives what she or he needs. In this way your conscious mind will not interfere, and you will allow the energy to move as appropriate.

Journey through a Body Landscape: a Personal Account of Massage

To give an example of the process of intuitive massage, and to show the kinds of symbol that can come up and be worked with, I will cite the case history of a woman whom I massaged over several years. I am changing her name and several other details. Her story is severe, and the account is dense to read, like a rich meal. She is in some ways a remarkable woman. She has a particular flair for this sort of work, which is not equally accessible to all, and I hope her story will provide ideas and inspiration for others. Having suffered a particularly difficult and traumatic early life, she faced many problems. Some of these problems were unique, while others will be easy for women to identify with. She proved herself extraordinarily ingenious and persistent in dealing with them.

Peggy, as I will call her, came from a Jewish family who, like many immigrant families, had made great efforts to blend into their surroundings and become anglicised. As refugees from Hitler's Germany, the family had moved around the world and had come to England when she was ten years old. She had been the victim of sexual abuse as a child. During the period of receiving massage, she was also involved in long-term ongoing analytic therapy. There is not space for her full story to be told here. I will draw out only a very few threads from a complex process of therapy and massage, but even this may suffice to show how deeply touch can reach and affect a person. I am not suggesting that the many changes Peggy achieved were the result of massage only: these changes resulted largely from her own efforts and from her long-term therapy. What I am concerned to show is how touch, far from being 'purely physical', can connect to a person's emotional and psychic experience and contribute to a process of healing. Throughout this book I have argued that our society's prevailing stereotyped symbols of the body are not universal and preordained, and this account shows how creative, varied, rich and sensitive personal body symbols can be. In this woman's case, I will show specifically how they relate to both family and social experiences of aggression towards women, to the denial of the body, racial persecution and migration. And I will show how such symbols can change.

When Peggy first came for massage, she described her body as 'in pieces': she experienced some parts as too numb to feel anything and others as too excruciatingly tender to bear being touched. She had chronic back trouble. She suffered from asthma, breathed shallowly, and was unusually troubled by her reaction to body smells like sweat. Living alone, she found it hard to cook adequately for herself. She was also anxious about penetration.

Each time she came to see me, we spent some time discussing how her body was feeling from day to day, how it was responding to issues raised in her analytic therapy, and how she experienced it in the various physical exercises and meditations which she had started to do; this determined what kind of massage seemed appropriate. During the massage she talked about the sensations and symbols which the touch brought up for her, and how they related to her life.

Some lines she wrote give a vivid description of how she felt about her body at this early stage:

mynoseisshut
myeyesareshut
mylegsareattachedtomyheadtheywillnotmove
myfeetfelloofftheendofthebed
&
theyaresittingonthefloortogetherlookingat   me

they are smiling
they always do
they are always d anc i ng

                          & l aaaaaaaaaaaaaaaaaaau ghing haaaaahaaaaa ha ah ah aaaaaa.

but they   always do it without   me.

I mentioned in Chapter 3 how patterns of breathing can reflect fears, beliefs and associations in other areas of life. To help her become more aware of her body during the massage sessions, one of the first things I did was encourage her to breathe more deeply. She found this hard, as many people do. She said she felt she was breathing air 'better left to other people' and that breathing in provoked fear because 'it's too full inside'. More specific associations with the act of inhaling took some time to emerge. Her father had died of a lung infection and it was during an asthma attack that she first made the connection: 'Breathing is linked with a fear of dying'.

How far her father's death had had an impact on other body functions became clear when we talked about her relationship with food. She described her recurrent difficulty in providing food for herself and eating as she needed. During a massage of the front of her body she remarked that she felt nauseous and then went on to mention her father's death. An image of death came up again during her massage on the same day, with the remark 'Eating turns into shit'. During another massage, she experienced an image of putrefaction simultaneously with a picture of the old woman who came into the house to cook for the family after her father died. She also wrote, in a poem, about time 'gobbling':

'there isn't a day of the week you gobble up time like the pillarstuds of camps concentration poles of wirenetting prisoners stranding timeless naked no boundaries between when and now and tomorrow. Time is death alive.'

It seemed that part of the reason she found it hard to feed herself was that, for her, nourishing the body meant acknowledging unpleasant aspects of physicality, linked with time and mortality, as in her association of 'sickness' with her father's death. The absorption of air and food, two vital life-supporting activities, were for her associated with 'taking in' death.

The fact that it was not only her father's death but also the deaths of millions of Jews in Hitler's Germany which were involved in this chain of association became even clearer when we discussed her sense of smell. Peggy had a very keen sense of smell and spoke one day about how she felt repulsed by the body smell and physical contact of some women in the dance class she had joined. In the same session she talked about her parents having given her a non-Jewish first name, as if to deny her Jewishness. She said she felt for the Jews who died in the concentration camps, but sometimes seeing Jewish old ladies in shops she experienced a flash of hostile feeling: 'Hitler didn't do a good enough job.' She seemed to be expressing anti-Semitic feelings which she had sensed in her parents in their denial of their own Jewishness and hers. 'Sometimes I feel the urge to flaunt my Jewishness in the family,' she told me, and volunteered that there was a link with her problems in accepting body smell, because for her body smell was 'the smell of death'. The hatred expressed by Nazism had eaten its way into Peggy's senses so that the smell of a living body, because that body was Jewish, had become for her the stench of death. Thus wide-scale racial persecution has its echo in the individual's relationship to her body. Massage, as a positive, pleasurable experience for her body in all its living richness, was evidently a good way to confront those negative feelings about her physicality. During her massage that day, her eyes streaming with tears from hayfever, Peggy announced: 'I realise I don't want my relations and the other victims of the camps to have died alone without someone to carry on their memory. I can carry it on.' Pleasurable experience in her body made her more able to accept, rather than deny, her bond with other Jews.

Another way in which the issue of smell came up was that Peggy regularly bathed just before coming to a massage session, as she could not imagine that I wanted to touch a 'smelly body'. I often explained to her that I enjoyed body smells like sweat. When, after many months of sessions, she arrived stating with a touch of humour, 'Today I've brought you a smelly unwashed body,' it seemed an important act of bravery and self-acceptance.

Peggy's relationship with her father, and her feelings about being Jewish, affected not only her patterns of breathing and eating and her sense of smell, but also her attitude to her sexuality. When she first came for massage she had a history of aggressive feelings towards her genitals. In the course of the massage, which at all times specifically avoided sexual areas, she found it very difficult at first to bring her awareness into the lower half of her body, to be aware of sensations there and feel that it belonged to her. She often experienced a blockage at her solar plexus. During one early massage, to help her bring her awareness down, I accompanied long strokes down her body with the suggestion that she visualise breathing in through the top of her head and out down through her legs and feet; she commented that the breath became 'dirty and broken up' when it reached her pelvis. She described how during her teens her father had made her feel that her body and her new-fledged sexuality were disgusting: 'You smell – here's an Amplex', was one of his recurring remarks which had particularly stuck in her mind. After some time she reported an interesting dream: she was pushing an old jalopy with her sister and brother, heading for the Midlands. When they got there they found a tangle of road blocks in which the workmen were musicians. In the dream she decided she could not get through and should go south instead. When asked what associations the dream brought up for her, she talked about having shared an interest in music with her father. She linked the 'road blocks' at the 'Midlands' at which the workmen were musicians (linked with her father?) with blocks in her body at her solar plexus (the 'midriff' or midlands of her body), and felt that the suggestion to go 'south' meant going lower in her body to deal with the issues that had got locked into sexuality for her. She talked about how she felt she carried the burden of her father's negative feelings about his physicality and sexuality, tied up, through her Jewishness, with fears of smell and death. It was helpful for her to air these issues and to see how stubbornly the negative feelings had been implanted in various parts of her body. The massage helped her to associate her lower body with a pleasurable, rather than an uncomfortable, experience. At first she expressed surprise that I could bear to touch her pelvis. Over time she described gaining more distance on the feelings her father had projected on to her body, and gradually started to enjoy the massage more. During massage she became aware of her lower back, which had previously been numb, as 'dense with feelings'. After some time she reported having had, the previous day, a pleasurable experience of masturbation in which she had the sensation that the sexual parts of her body 'were being allowed to speak for the first time and start a dialogue with each other'. She recounted that it was as if 'so much had been put on them which didn't belong to them' and it was starting to be 'decoded, peeled off and unravelled'.

Her feelings about her body had also been affected in a specific way by the migration of her family. She often described her distress at being uprooted from everything she knew to come to England at the age of ten. She also described how before the move, her parents bought an incinerator to burn their papers and other material they did not want to bring, and the children had to feed this incinerator. This experience had disturbed her: 'Why did they burn all that furniture? It wasn't in such bad taste as my mother made out . . .' She described it as 'a holocaust', a choice of word which suggested that what was being burnt was not just papers and 'bad taste' furniture, but an identity as Jews which her parents wanted to leave behind. Echoes of this experience of moving recurred in her present daily life. She found it very difficult to travel anywhere and hard to take even the minimum of luggage with her. It was revealing that, during one massage after this discussion, the same image recurred when she referred to her pelvis as plump and distasteful because it carried 'excess baggage'. Again, her sexuality seemed to be linked to her Jewishness as something undesirable which should be denied and 'left behind'; the effect on her daily life was as palpable as her inability to travel with luggage. Much of the massage of her pelvis was aimed simply at helping her accept it as a part of her body. This, together with other therapy work she was doing on the issue of sexuality, had an effect not only on her attitude to her body but also in related areas of her life: after some time she reported not only going to stay for a week with a friend in the country, but also taking her duvet and pillow with her. The 'baggage' was apparently beginning to be accepted.

Her sense of violation at the eradication of her Jewishness and the destruction of her life before the move compounded her experience of a different kind of violation: sexual abuse by her brother as a young child. Her parents' favouritism towards this brother, and other aspects of the family dynamics, are too complex to discuss here. As an adult she was still very prone to feeling violated by other people's demands or contact with her. This came up in a variety of forms in her daily life. In a sexual situation she found that her desire disappeared when the slightest pressure was exerted or even when strong enthusiasm was displayed by the person with her. She refused to be massaged on a certain pink sheet of mine which, though washed, had previously been used by someone else; that contact with another person, she said, invaded her, deadlocked her and paralysed her. (It was a great gift, and strength, of hers that she always managed to see the funny side of such phobias as this about the sheet.) In a training situation she felt very resistant to her teacher, as if information was being 'forced' on her. Another primary experience of invasion and violation involved the enemas which her mother forced her to have when she was very young. After watching a TV programme which showed young girls being circumcised, Peggy became very distressed: 'That young girl who has been held down and prized apart, how can she ever put the world together again? How can she believe it is a safe place for her? It is a kind of murder. Her trust is murdered.' She seemed to be speaking not only about the film but about her own experience. She described vividly how the screams of the young girl in the TV programme rang in her ears and resonated with what she remembered as her own 'silent screams' as she was herself 'held down and prized apart' for enemas as a young child. One result seemed to be that she found it hard to let anything into her body. I remember suggesting in one meditative body exercise that she imagine allowing light or energy to enter her body, to which with characteristic candour she retorted, 'I'm not having that coming in here!' It was a slow process by which she reported teaching herself to 'carry' or 'hold' the long-tried and trusted affection of her analytic therapist inside her, to fortify her in time of difficulty: at the outset even that could not be internalised without her experiencing a fear of invasion. The massage made some contribution towards teaching her to allow contact without fear of violation. Her body, which I often experienced as delicate or jumpy to the touch, seemed to call for slow strokes and a steady, reassuring quality of contact. She once described a massage on the front of her body as feeling like a 'blanket over troubled frothy waves'. Sometimes it was enough simply to use my hands to hold her, resting them on head and shoulders, or shoulders and back. Sometimes water seemed a suitably calming symbol to bear in mind while I was massaging her. On one occasion when I mentally used that symbol – though I said nothing – she commented that a long stroke down her back felt like a 'long slow wave,' suggesting that the quality of the energy I was sending, clothed in the symbol of water, could be accurately sensed by her.

Another important part of the process involved reversing the fear of invasion by helping her to recognise and articulate impulses and needs which came from inside her *out* into the world: so that the starting point was her own body rather than the initiative of another towards her. Telling me what kind of massage she wanted gave her valuable practice in this. Sometimes she would keep her clothes on throughout the massage, remarking, 'My skin doesn't want to be touched.' At other times she became vociferous about exactly where and how she wanted to be touched: 'Not there', 'Further over'. After some time she began to ask for deeper muscle work, commenting that she was dealing better with physical penetration and was able to start to learn more about what was 'inside' because her skin had become a 'better boundary'. Learning to ask for what she wanted in massage was rather like the process of learning to move from inner to outer (which I discussed in Chapter 3), or bridging the gap between desire and speech, as discussed earlier in this chapter.

Learning to make this move from inner to outer through her *voice* seemed especially important for Peggy, because her family history of violation in the area of her genitals had affected her feelings about, and her use of, her throat and mouth: the fear of invasion connected to a corresponding fear of expression. When she described her difficulties with expression I was reminded of esoteric anatomy's suggestion that there is a special link between genitals and mouth in the patterns of movement of 'fine' energy through the body. On one occasion, for example, she described how a difficult phone conversation with her mother during the week had rendered her speechless, 'as if I had no tongue or there were a big block in my throat'. The tension then moved down her body so that her stomach tightened and she felt sick, and then her legs cramped 'as they must have done when my mother gave me enemas'. In situations of stress such as this she described experiencing an intense fear of letting anything into or out of her body. She herself was aware of a link with sexuality: 'No wonder my father stopped me opening my mouth, telling me I had bad breath,' she said; 'it was because of what I might say, secrets about the level of repressed violence in the family'. Those secrets included her experience of abuse by her brother, of which she had never spoken. During one face massage she described the sensation of fearing to expose the bottom half of her face in case people might see into her mouth: she described it as a fear of invasion and volunteered that it felt connected to her vagina. She described a whole pattern of behaviour reflecting this mouth-vagina connection: on occasions when she felt angry she often entered a state of speechlessness; instead of expressing her anger outwards she would become numb and would turn the anger against herself, masturbating over-vigorously and sometimes hurting herself. This reflects a common pattern amongst women, who may react to feelings of powerlessness by turning anger against themselves not only through self-injury but in a number of other ways such as self-hatred, depression, pulling their hair, becoming accident-prone, or staying in a relationship with a violent man.

Dealing with this issue in the sessions called for throat massages to help release the tension there. However, one of the most useful ideas for finding a way out of the deadlock of her speechlessness arose with Peggy herself when she did a chakra meditation, like the ones described earlier in this chapter. Telling me about it afterwards, she described how, when trying to contact her throat chakra, she had experienced the image of a bridge. I asked her what the bridge meant to her. 'I don't have words to come from that place,' she replied (referring to the state of anger or pain she would be experiencing inside when she became speechless), 'I can't tell everything that I am feeling; I need something halfway.' It emerged from discussion that in practical terms something halfway, which broke the silence but did not tell everything, a bridge between herself and the world, might simply be to use a phrase like 'I feel awful' or 'Something awful's happened'. Between all and nothing, she could make a first step. She found that even this minimal communication, shared with a friend, could help to ease her sense of isolation, paralysis and craziness. This example shows how useful people's individual symbols can be: her image of the 'bridge', which came up in a body meditation, helped us to work out a way in which she could reach out from that place of numbness and pent-up aggression and get help before she turned it against herself in painful masturbation. Instead of being locked into a panic-stricken fear of anything coming in or out, which triggered a kind of private re-enactment of her childhood genital violation, she could start learning to reach out into the world outside for help. She less frequently turned her anger against herself, and was able to ask for support from women in the self-help group she had joined, and from a widening circle of friends.

Also connected with the issue of violation was the relationship between her right and left sides which often came up during massage and which seemed to reflect in an uncanny way her relationship with her brother. It is a common idea, not only in esoteric anatomy but also in many body-orientated therapies, that the right side of the body is the active, aggressive side and the left side of the body is passive and internal; in our culture these are predictably described as 'male' and 'female' sides of the body respectively. During one massage Peggy reported that her left side felt big and flowing, while her right felt tight and gnarled like a wrought-iron gate. It was always her right hand which had been the aggressor, masturbating fiercely or occasionally tearing the skin on her left lower arm in previous years – just as it had been her brother who had been the aggressor towards her in childhood. On several occasions during massage she reported other sharp differences between the two sides, and sometimes protested that one side was not receiving exactly the same massage as the other, using fierce tones reminiscent of sibling rivalry: 'My left foot feels left out.' She told me that her right side sometimes went numb when she was angry, and while her right side was being massaged, she often became aware of a 'persecutor voice', an internal voice which continually criticised her and her actions as worthless and inauthentic: 'You've wasted your life', 'It's all your fault', 'You're not really ill, you're just indulging'. This persecutor, which blamed her and always placed the worst interpretations on her behaviour, was part of an internal dialogue which continued alone at home as well as during the sessions. In contrast, massage on her left side made her aware of her desires, a small but growing sense of wanting touch and physical joy and comfort for herself. I asked her if there was any reply she could make to silence the persecuting voice, and eventually she found the short phrase: 'I want you to help me': again the expression of her needs emerged as a healthy starting point, to counter feelings of persecution. She wrote the phrase on a piece of card and hung it on her wall to remind herself. On one occasion I cited to her Lowen's opinion that the main characteristic of a neurotic person is a pleasure deficiency and that such a person has no sense of self because there are no feelings of pleasure to give a basis for what they want. I often asked her what gave her pleasure in her life. Massage was only one of a number of activities (self-massage with cream, baths, swimming, dancing) which she used over time to build up a history of pleasurable experiences in her body. Eventually she stated that the 'persecutor', though still present, was no longer able to drown out her sense of her own desires.

On one occasion, when the persecuting voice had been particularly strong, I suggested that she concentrate on her left side during the massage; she then started talking about needing to separate from her brother with whom she was so close in age that they had been referred to as 'the twins'. It was as if the right side represented a sadistic persecuting element which her brother had acted out as a child and which she had internalised and carried with her in her body, reflected in the 'gnarled' sensations in her right side, in her use of that hand as the aggressor in self-injury, and in the persecuting voice which came from that side. She thus carried her history in her body, and it was hard for her to separate herself from her past without disowning a part of her body. During the same massage she spoke about separating emotionally from her dead father, and described the distress she had felt recently at selling some possessions of his. I suggested that it was not a question of cutting off from, or denying, her relationship with her father and brother, any more than she could disown her right side. Both her right and left sides were needed and had something to contribute, but some kind of balance and harmony was required between the aggressive right side and the more vulnerable, pleasure-seeking left side. During the massage on this day she asked to have both sides of her body touched at once, which she said enabled her to keep a sense that they were both parts of the same whole.

On another occasion soon afterwards she reported that circular movements on her back made her feel like a 'snake with one body'. This is another example of how massage both brought to the surface, and helped to heal, problems knotted within the body. It is also an example of how working with conventional splits, between right and left and between 'male' and 'female', can lead to an integration which transcends those divisions: in this case it was important for Peggy to own her own active and aggressive feelings and learn to express them in a regulated way, rather than her previous pattern of denying them and then being overtaken by them in a violent outburst of aggression against herself, mimicking her brother's behaviour. The point was not to deny she had ever had a brother, but rather to re-own her right side and re-own her own anger and aggression, thus pushing him out of her body and lessening his hold over her. This process took a long time and involved a lot of work with those limbs which body therapies describe as built for relating to others through reaching and aggressing: the arms. This involved slowly improving the flow of energy down her arms into her hands, learning how to express aggression in safe ways and to reach out for positive contact with another person. The self-destructive energy in her shoulders and arms, symbolised at one point as a 'hornets' nest', turned gradually into 'honey-making bees' as stagnant energy lost its 'poisonous' qualities in becoming part of an overall lively circulation. Arms are for relating, and Peggy also felt much strengthened by the relationships she developed within her women's group: 'Being with women who had lived through all sorts of experiences, who could talk openly about things like sexuality, both laughing and with reverence, it gave me a context, a place to be in the world, rather than feeling crazy.'

The connection, or lack of it, between her hands and her body also appeared in an unusual way as a metaphor for the connection between herself and the human race in history. At one session she described a distressing experience. She reported how, when she was standing in the middle of London's Holloway Road one winter day, the thought flickered across her mind that people in concentration camps were naked in such weather. The thought, she said, came from nowhere: it was 'like the twitch of a hand severed from a body' because 'what connection have I with them, or with the young girl screaming as they circumcise her? It was just like seeing a finger twitch in the road.' Peggy's symbol for the suffering of those other human beings was the twitch of a hand severed from the body to which it belonged; the rest of the body, she said, was paralysed and 'the finger had no past or future'. Developing a better flow of energy down Peggy's arms, establishing the connection between hand and body, seemed part of helping her build a better connection to the world as a whole, not only to her friends but to the collective experiences of humanity.

In this it seemed important to guide Peggy to a stronger awareness of her own centre of gravity and of her current physical well-being. This could provide a solid base from which to respond to the wrongs of the world, so that she did not have to cut off from them or feel paralysed by such disembodied visions of atrocity. Jane Roberts' 'Seth' books point out that if you become *overwhelmed* by unsafe signals from secondary experience – for example, human suffering elsewhere or in the past – then you undermine your strength and ability to act in the present, 'you speak and act from a position not your own, and deny the world whatever benefits your own present version of reality might allow you to give' (*The Nature of the Psyche*). Massage generally helped Peggy to be aware of her senses and their pleasure in the present moment, but work on her belly seemed particularly important to ground her in the present and help her respond appropriately to the pain both in her own past and in the world as a whole – rather than responding with symbols and actions of disconnected violence (self-injury, the finger twitching). I often massaged her belly, using symbols of warming and filling what she sometimes described as a 'hole' there. I also worked on connecting her belly with her hands through long strokes moving from her belly up her trunk and then down her arms, as well as by simply keeping one hand still on her belly and another on her hand, to encourage the circulation between them. She enjoyed massage on her fingers which, she said, could stop her 'contracting with anger into my torso and getting paralysed'. As her sense of pleasure came more into evidence, so did her sense of fun and her sense of humour, which had always made our sessions lively and unpredictable.

The process of establishing a flow of energy down her arms was helped by her returning to a long-standing artistic talent, and developing her drawing and painting on large canvases, as well as increasing her self-expression in many other ways. From being a 'stick' her arm became a 'juicy sausage'. It was, however, a slow process with many setbacks. On one occasion she reported having taken the unusual step of allowing herself to express pent-up anger to a friend by shouting at her; she said that afterwards her arms felt very good with tingling all down them, and in the next massage she reported experiencing more energy moving through her shoulders. In this situation it seemed a creative step for her to have released some of her aggression in a relatively non-destructive way, and the result seemed to be an increased energy flow in her arms. This, again, had positive effects. Some days later she experienced feelings of wanting contact with another human being which emerged at a very extreme, almost desperate level: 'I don't want to continue living my life in this isolation.' I pointed out that although they felt extreme to her, articulating such feelings was new and valuable, apparently reflecting a greater ability to 'reach out' metaphorically with the increased flow of energy in her arms.

However, on this particular occasion, the impulse to reach out in a new way was followed, as often happens, by a reversal: a few days later she rang up to report: 'I feel cut off and numb. I want to attack my arms with a knife because then at least something would come out of them – blood.'

One way of understanding this reversal was that it was precisely the increased flow of energy through her arms which made her need to cut off from them: like most changes in our body patterns, this increased flow may at some level have seemed threatening to the organism, disrupting its precarious balance. I suggested to Peggy that increased flow through the arms might need increased grounding through the legs to anchor it and create a new balance; without this, the change might feel unsafe and might produce the impulse to cut off. If the upper half of the body is for relating, the lower half is for support, and there is a need for the latter to match the former otherwise we become top-heavy and unbalanced. Peggy often commented that massage on her feet made her feel 'less crazy'.

In fact, work on her legs was a mainstay and crucial part of the massage process. In times of stress she often made comments that 'everything is happening above my waist' and that 'I am calm in my legs if only I could get down there'. But what made it so hard for her to 'get down there'? This took some time to uncover. She often remarked that she tended to forget she had legs between her body and the ground, commenting that it was hard for her to feel they belonged, or to connect with them as hers, 'as if the thread is missing'.

'What would the thread put you in touch with if it was there?'

'Our home before we came to England.'

'What makes it difficult or frightening to connect with the thread?'

'It was barbed wire once.'

The move to England, painfully associated with the Fascist persecution which had made her family travel the world, had made her connection with her childhood roots spiky and untouchable: her connection with the ground was broken, and her legs felt as if they were missing. She went on to tell me that she had just started some embroidered smocking, undertaken with the thought of connecting herself to that earlier home, of providing 'the thread'. I was impressed once again by her ingenuity in combining her practical skills (here needlework) with her personal insight and symbols to work creatively at problems. I was also reminded of reading about cultures where weaving was a practical task with psychic meaning, perhaps not unlike the numinous quality which seemed to be imparted to simple tasks like watering plants in the early Cretan culture. While American Indians produced 'magical' fabrics, Peggy was using sewing to regain the 'thread' of continuity in her life.

During one massage she remarked that the soles of her feet felt raw, like a placenta that had been separated from the mother, and the same issue around her legs and her disconnection from her roots perhaps lay behind her frequent experience of waking in the morning feeling adrift or 'at sea', as during the boat journey to England. Another way in which she was 'legless' was in the problems she experienced in moving around the country or leaving it for a holiday, 'because if I travel that means there are Nazis'. She also discussed the recurrence of Nazi imagery in her life, such as her fondness for a pair of high black boots which she owned. It was as if the lack of real roots (which had been torn away as the result of persecution) was covered up by her assuming the trappings of the very persecutor responsible for the loss: the foot which feels as raw as a torn placenta assumes protection in the form of the jackboot. On one occasion she asked to be massaged on her body while keeping shoes on her feet, and I was half-way through the massage before she felt safe enough to take them off.

The feeling of rawness she described and her symbol of the placenta reminded me of a Chilean woman's description of her plane departure from her homeland into exile: 'the second painful moment was after taking off, when I saw the mountains for the last time. I felt as if my umbilical cord had been severed and the uterine contact with my country had disappeared.' Quoting this account in *Mental Health and Exile*, Liliana Muñoz draws a parallel between exile and bereavement: in this account, as with Peggy's symbols, the loss of the childhood home is clearly associated with separation from the mother. In Peggy's case, it seemed that the uprooting effect of the migration served to exacerbate problems about grounding which had already existed because of her early relationship with her mother. This relationship had been difficult. On one occasion she remarked that as a child she did not have the experience of being physically held, which could have given her a sense of herself and the world. The way she put it was: 'My mother did not give me the *ground* to start from' (my italics), and without an early basis of trust in the physical world she felt she had to 'create the world anew each minute'. Part of the work to be done on her legs was to help her connect with the fact that the ground was solid and supporting beneath her feet and at this point in her life the physical world was in fact a safe place for her to be. She wrote in a poem that 'I cannot locate my days nor the land I walked my feet upon', and on one occasion she said she did not want to take off her socks because 'I'd pour out – I need to be contained.' Massage techniques such as holding the soles of her feet were useful for giving her a sense of containment, for healing the rawness she felt there, and for teaching that she could feel something warm and steady beneath her feet.

Over the long term her sensation in, and connection with, her legs increased consistently. Once while her feet were being massaged she described feeling like a tuning fork on which a vibration moved from her feet right up to her head, connecting through her whole body: an expressive image which seemed to be using musical tone as an analogy for the energy movement she was experiencing through her body. She often remarked that massage on her feet put 'the soul back in the body', and she became more aware of her feet in daily life. 'I'm much happier when I listen to my feet,' she remarked once, 'they have the answers.' From feeling isolated in the world, dislocated in a limbo of time overshadowed by visions of past atrocities, and despondent about her 'failure' to 'do' anything with her life, she gradually became aware of the possibilities of the present and of a desire to belong to a wider community and have a more grounded sense of her place in a public world.

This progress in 'grounding' the body was part of an overall slow transformation. When Peggy first came for massage she often said that her body felt 'in pieces' and needed to be 'put back together' again. As I have described, over time she became more articulate about where the divisions between the 'pieces' were: between left and right, between arms and trunk, between upper and lower arms, between legs and the rest, and so on. We identified how different aspects of her history had been embedded in those different parts: her brother in her right side, her father in her stomach and sexuality, the Holocaust in her sense of smell, the migration in her 'missing' legs, and so on in a pattern far more complex than I have been able to do justice to here. With this greater awareness, and with her physical sensations becoming more coherent, she gradually began to experience her body as a whole, and to reclaim it as hers, reducing the hold those painful and oppressive experiences had on her. Though she would often remark during massage, 'It's as if I'm not in my body to be touched', her detailed requests for particular limbs and areas to be touched or avoided reflected a growing clarity about what her body wanted, needed and enjoyed. This progress was reflected in changes in her life. She reported an improvement in her sexual experience. Her back trouble disappeared and she noticed a gradual change in the quality of her movement at her dance class. Although very many problems remained to be solved, she began to take her place in the world in a new way. She built closer personal relationships and gained a sense of belonging to a wider community. She developed a new line of work. Paralysing depression and self-injury became things of the past.

This transformation process, which had a number of causes, focused partly on the symbol of landscape. This symbol was with her from the earliest sessions: during one early foot massage she remarked that her right foot felt like 'a garden with potted plants and bees buzzing' while her left foot suggested to her the image of a mountain view with tundra and a very blue sky, 'a bit cold but very exhilarating'. Her sense of her body as a place where she could find joy and stillness radiated from the base of her body. On one occasion she mentioned envying a woman friend her positive memories of childhood and mourned her own lack of 'innocence'; the only way she could recapture that innocence, she said, was through walking in landscapes of nature. Over time she became able to travel to stay with a friend in the countryside where she could take long walks; at times of stress in city life she found she could recall that countryside to give her a sense of calm. In *Problems in Materialism and Culture* Raymond Williams has remarked that 'Men come to project on to nature their own unacknowledged activities and consequences . . . Into a green and quiet nature we project, I do not doubt, much of our own deepest feeling, our senses of growth and perspective and beauty'. Similarly nature seemed to symbolise for Peggy her own sense of calm and perspective. Gradually, however, she reported a growing ability to recognise that there was a peaceful landscape not only outside her, but also *inside her*: she began to recognise that calm as her own. Moving from a situation where she felt that everything powerful was aimed threateningly against her, she gradually reached a state where there was power in a quiet place inside her which could reach in a positive way out into the world. Life is rarely easy to lead, especially in our society, but she gave the impression of slowly finding a peace within herself which could almost be described as spiritual. Contrary to conventional views of spirituality, this quality had started at her feet. I am hesitant ever to use the term 'cure', but this hard-won reclaiming of her inner landscape was accompanied by many concrete changes in her everyday living, all reflecting a growing ability to engage with human life: to stand up for herself and to move towards others.

In this account, there are many problems, issues and discoveries which I have not even mentioned. Many of the changes I have described here were the result of Peggy's ongoing analytic therapy and I certainly would not suggest that they were the results of massage alone. What I do want to point out is how emotional and psychic experiences are rooted in the physical, and how they reverberate in the body. I have also been interested to show the kind of symbols which can arise from that physical embodiment of psychic process. This woman's symbols included conventional symbolism of right and left, common imagery drawn from Nazism, symbols deriving from women's roles (threads, textiles), as well as a wealth of images of insects, water, weather, luggage and landscape which were mixed in a complex pattern all her own; these symbols, and the relationship between them, changed over time as she changed. The symbols show how deeply we have internalised and carried our oppressors in our bodies, and how they can damage and immobilise us unless we confront their influence over that inner space. The symbols which came up also show how the seeds of innovation and health are always there waiting to flower within the breathtaking terrain of our physicality.

Conclusion

As an alternative to the mind/body, spirituality/sexuality split, I have in this chapter presented a different view of the body. I have shown how the notion of a body imbued with 'fine' energy could affect our attitudes and behaviour towards body functions like menstruation and sexuality. I have shown how it can be used through massage as part of a process of personal change and healing. I am not putting forward a new gospel or a new set of 'universal' symbols, but rather a working hypothesis: I am suggesting that this alternative model is worth trying out and working with to see what can be learnt if we allow it as a possibility.

It is a big step from seeing the body as an inferior or evil container for the soul to seeing it as a portion or condensation of the soul. It is a step which has implications for day-to-day living and political struggle. The body is the place where in the last instance all the cruelties of oppression are carried out. Peggy's account shows what a powerful and traumatic imprint racial and sexual oppression can leave on the body, even without extremes of imprisonment, starvation or torture. The model of 'fine' energy offers us a subtle approach for reclaiming the body from the pervasive and paralysing effects of such common experiences of race, class and sexual oppression. But the solid body not only receives experiences − it can also fight back. Appreciating the full dimensions of the luminous body suggests ways in which we can tap greater resources of its power to bring into interaction with the world; it suggests that when we engage with our physicality in a material struggle we can put our soul into it.

Book References

The page numbers relate to passages referred to or quoted, listed in most cases in the order in which they have been used. Where there are numerous references to the same text, or where the context may not be obvious, I have indicated the subject matter.

Adler, Margot, *Drawing Down the Moon: Witches, Druids, Goddess-worshippers and Pagans in America Today*, Beacon Press, Boston, 1986, pp. 102 (on sex), 109 (on 'cone of power'), 419 (on witches' affinity with natural world) (first publ. Viking Press, New York, 1979).

Arica: see Chapter 4 Book References.

Assagioli, Roberto, *Psychosynthesis*, Turnstone Books, London, 1975; Penguin, New York, 1976.

Blake, William, 'The Marriage of Heaven and Hell' (etched c. 1793), in *William Blake: a Selection of Poems and Letters*, edited with an introduction by J. Bronowski, Penguin, Harmondsworth, Middx, 1958, p. 94.

Bland, Lucy, 'Purity, Motherhood, Pleasure or Threat? Definitions of Female Sexuality 1900−1970s', in Sue Cartledge and Joanna Ryan (eds.) *Sex and Love*, The Women's Press, London, 1983, pp. 8−29; I refer to p. 9.

Buber, Martin, *Tales of the Hassidim: the Later Masters*, Schocken Books,

New York, 1948. pp. 91, 98–99, 90.

Budapest, Z., *The Holy Book of Women's Mysteries Part I*, Susan B. Anthony, Coven No. 1, Member of C.O.G., P.O. Box 42121, Los Angeles, CA, 1979, pp. 122ff, 74–5.

Buonaventura, Wendy, *Belly Dancing: The Serpent and the Sphinx*, Virago, London, 1983.

Capra, Fritjof, speaking in a radio interview broadcast, *Minding the Earth*, produced by The Strong Center, Berkeley, CA, Spring 1981.

Castaneda, Carlos, *The Eagle's Gift*, Pocket Books, New York, 1982, pp. 10–14, 136.

—— *The Fire From Within*, Black Swan, Transworld, London, Australia and New Zealand, 1985, pp. 63, 126–7, 140, 151, 200, 213, 153–4, 187, 137–8, 142, 71–2 (all on the energy field and the assemblage point), 166 (on Sonoran desert), 222 (earth as living being), 75–6 (on sexuality), 52 (on the senses).

—— *Journey to Ixtlan: the Lessons of Don Juan*, Penguin, Harmondsworth, Middx, 1974, pp. 267 (on the 'lines of the world'), 160–170 and 121–6 (on 'places of power').

—— *The Second Ring of Power*, Hodder and Stoughton, London, Sydney, Auckland and Toronto, 1978, pp. 119–20 (the energy field), 161–2 (menstruation), 137 (the sun).

—— *A Separate Reality*, Penguin, Harmondsworth, Middx. 1973. pp. 153–5 (on the will), 16–17 and 19–20 (on dancing).

—— *Tales of Power*, Penguin, Harmondsworth, Middx, 1976, p. 177.

—— *The Teachings of Don Juan: a Yaqui Way of Knowledge*, Penguin, Harmondsworth, Middx, 1987, pp. 100, 30–36 (first publ. University of California Press, 1968).

Christ, Carol P., 'Why Women Need the Goddess', *Heresies: a Feminist Publication on Art and Politics*, Spring 1978 ('The Great Goddess' issue), publ. Heresies Collective Inc., P.O. Box 1306, Canal Street Station, New York, NY 10013, p. 11.

Davidson, H.R. Ellis, *Gods and Myths of Northern Europe*, Penguin, Harmondsworth, Middx, 1964, pp. 143ff.

Dimen, Muriel, 'Variety is the Spice of Life', *Heresies: a Feminist Publication on Art and Politics*, 3 (4/12) 1981 ('Sex' issue) publ. Heresies Collective Inc., P.O. Box 1306, Canal Street Station, New York, NY 10013, pp. 66–7.

Douglas, Mary, *Natural Symbols*, Penguin, Harmondsworth, Middx, 1978, p. 93 (first publ. Barrie and Rockliff, London, 1970).

Douglas, Nik and Penny Slinger, *Sexual Secrets: the Alchemy of Ecstacy*, Arrow, London, 1982 (first publ. Hutchinson, London, 1979).

Downing, George, *The Massage Book*, Penguin, Harmondsworth, Middx, 1974.

Dychtwald, Ken, *Bodymind*, Wildwood House, London, 1978.

Ernst, Sheila and Lucy Goodison, *In Our Own Hands: a Book of Self-Help*

Therapy, The Women's Press, London, 1981, pp. 134–6.

The Findhorn Community, *The Findhorn Garden*, Intro. by Sir George Trevelyan, Turnstone Books/Wildwood House, London, 1975.

Fortune, Dion, *The Esoteric Philosophy of Love and Marriage*, Aquarian Press, Wellingborough, Northants, 1974, pp. 28, 95, 29 (first publ. Rider, London, 1924).

Gimbel, Theo, *Healing Through Colour*, C.W. Daniel, Saffron Walden, Essex, 1980.

Govinda, Lāma Anagarika, *The Foundations of Tibetan Mysticism*, E.P. Dutton, New York; Rider, London, 1960, p. 148.

Hanna, Judith Lynne, *Dance, Sex and gender: Signs of Identity, Dominance, Defiance, and Desire*, University of Chicago Press, Chicago and London, 1988.

Heindel, Max, *Rosicrucian Christianity Lecture No. 4: Sleep, Dreams, Trance, Hypnotism, Mediumship*, The Rosicrucian Fellowship, Oceanside, CA, undated, p. 1.

Jackson, Margaret, ' "Facts of Life" or the Eroticization of Women's Oppression? Sexology and the Social Construction of Heterosexuality', in Pat Caplan (ed.) *The Cultural Construction of Sexuality*, Tavistock, London and New York, 1987, pp. 52–81.

Karagulla, S., *Breakthrough to Creativity*, De Vorss, Santa Monica, CA, 1967, pp. 124, 147ff, 242.

Kenyon, Dr Julian, 'The Dove Project', Centre for the Study of Complementary Medicine, 51 Bedford Place, Southampton, Hants. See also Julian Kenyon, *21st Century Medicine*, Thorsons, Wellingborough, Northants, 1985.

Keyes, Laurel Elizabeth, *Toning: The Creative Power of the Voice*, De Vorss, Marina del Rey, CA, 1987 (first publ. 1973).

Kiefer, Duran, 'EEG Alpha Feedback and Subjective States of Consciousness', in John White (ed.) *Frontiers of Consciousness*, Avon, New York, 1974.

King, Francis, *Tantra for Westeners: a Practical Guide to the Way of Action*, Aquarian Press, Wellingborough, Northants, 1986, pp. 94, 30–1.

Koedt, Ann, *The Myth of the Vaginal Orgasm*, New England Free Press, Boston, MA, 1970.

Krieger, Dolores, *The Therapeutic Touch*, Prentice-Hall, NJ, 1979.

Krishna, Gopi, *Kundalini: the Evolutionary Energy in Man*, with an intro. by Frederic Spiegelberg and a psychological commentary by James Hillman, Shambala, Berkeley, CA, 1971.

Krystal, Phyllis, *Cutting the Ties that Bind: How to Achieve Liberation from False Security and Freedom from Negative Conditioning*, Turnstone Press, Wellingborough, Northants, 1982, pp. 156ff, 94.

Kurtz, Ron and Hector Prestera, *The Body Reveals*, Harper and Row/ Quicksilver Books, New York, San Francisco and London, 1976, p. 68.

Ladas, Alice Kahn, Beverly Whipple and John D. Perry, *The G Spot*, Corgi Books/Transworld, London, 1983.

Lawler, Lillian B., *The Dance in Ancient Greece*, Wesleyan University Press, Middletown, CT, 1978 (first publ. 1964).

Leadbeater, C.W., *The Chakras*, Theosophical Publishing House, Wheaton, ILL, Madras, and London, 1985 (first publ. 1927).

Lorde, Audre, 'The Erotic as Power', *Chrysalis*, 1979, quoted by Harmony Hammond in 'A Sense of Touch' *Heresies: a Feminist Publication on Art and Politics*, 3 (4/12) 1981 ('Sex' issue) publ. Heresies Collective Inc., P.O. Box 1306, Canal Street Station, New York, NY 10013, p. 44.

Lowen, Alexander, *The Betrayal of the Body*, Collier Macmillan, London and New York, 1969, pp. 31–2.

—— *Bioenergetics*, Coventure, London, 1976, p. 67.

Lydell, Lucinda, with Sara Thomas, Carola Beresford Cooke and Anthony Porter, *The Book of Massage*, Ebury Press, London, 1984.

MacManaway, Bruce, with Johanna Turcan, *Healing: the Energy that Can Restore Health*, Thorsons, Wellingborough, Northants, 1983, pp. 39, 36.

Mariechild, Diane, *Mother Wit: a Feminist Guide to Psychic Development*, Crossing Press, Trumansburg, NY, 1981, pp. 42 (root chakra), 45–6 ('cords' between people), 48–9 (plant meditation), 146–7 (stone ritual), 149 (ritual to stop harassment).

Miller, Roberta Delong, *Psychic Massage*, Harper and Row, New York, 1975.

Mishra, Rammurti S., *Fundamentals of Yoga*, Julian Press, New York, 1959, pp. 188ff and *passim*.

Muñoz, Liliana, 'Exile as bereavement: Socio-psychological Manifestations of Chilean Exiles in Great Britain', in *Mental Health and Exile: Papers arising from a Seminar on Mental Health and Latin American Exiles*, World University Service, 20 Compton Terrace, London N1, 1981, pp. 6–9; I quote p. 8.

Munro, Dr Jean, interviewed by Cynthia Kee in 'The Waves We All Live In', *The Observer*, 8 March 1987, p. 51.

MyOwn, Barbry, 'Ursa Maior: Menstrual Moon Celebration', in Anna Kent Rush, *Moon, Moon*, Moon Books and Random House, Berkeley and New York, 1976, pp. 374–87.

Ostrander, Sheila and Lynn Schroeder, *Psi: Psychic Discoveries behind the Iron Curtain*, Abacus Sphere Books, London, 1973.

Ouseley, S.G.J., *Colour Meditations With Guide to Colour-Healing*, L.N. Fowler, Romford, Essex, 1976, pp. 64–9, 86–7 (first publ. 1949).

Parfitt, Will, *The Living Qabalah*, Element Books, Shaftesbury, Dorset, 1988.

Pierrakos, John C., 'The Case of the Broken Heart', in David Boadella (ed.) *In The Wake of Reich*, Coventure, London, 1976, pp. 400–22.

—— At the head of The Core Group of the Institute for the New Age of Man,

'Life Functions of the Energy Centres of Man Part I', *Energy and Character*, Vol. 7(1), January 1976, pp. 54–67; I quote pp. 54–5.

Poynor, Helen, 'To Live is to Dance', *Human Potential Resources*, March-May 1982, p. 13, now *Human Potential Magazine*, 3 Netherby Road, London SE23 3AL.

Purce, Jill, *The Mystic Spiral*, Avon and Thames and Hudson, London, 1974, p. 30.

Rawson, Philip, *Tantra: the Indian Cult of Ecstasy*, Thames and Hudson, London, 1973.

Reich, Wilhelm, *Character Analysis*, trans. V.R. Carfagno, Touchstone/ Simon and Schuster, New York, 1972 (first publ. 1933). See also David Boadella, *Wilhelm Reich: The Evolution of his Work*, Arkana, London, Boston and Henley, 1985 (first publ. 1973) and developments of Reich's work described in Alexander Lowen, *Bioenergetics*, Coventure, London, Penguin, Harmondsworth, Middx. and New York, 1976, and David Boadella (ed.) *In the Wake of Reich*, Coventure, London, 1976.

—— *The Function of the Orgasm*, trans. T.P. Wolfe, Panther, London, 1968 (first publ. as *Die Funktion des Orgasmus*, 1927).

Reps, Paul (ed.) *Zen Flesh, Zen Bones*, Penguin, Harmondsworth, Middx. 1987, p. 157 No. 41 (first publ. Charles E. Tuttle, 1957).

Roberts, Jane, *The Nature of the Psyche: Its Human Expression*, A Seth Book, Prentice-Hall, NJ, 1979.

Rosicrucian beliefs: see Heindel.

Roth, Jenner, 'Sexuality Group', *Human Potential Resources*, Sept.-Nov. 1981, now *Human Potential Magazine*, 3 Netherby Road, London SE23 3AL.

Rowan, John, 'Against Yin and Yang and Androgyny', *Self and Society*, 9 (4) July-Aug. 1981, pp. 192–5.

Rule, Jane, 'Homophobia and Romantic Love', in *Outlander: Stories and Essays*, Naiad Press, P.O. Box 10543, Tallahassee, FL 32302, 1981.

Seidler, Victor Jeleniewski, 'Reason, Desire, and Male Sexuality', in Pat Caplan (ed.) *The Cultural Construction of Sexuality*, Tavistock, London and New York, 1987, pp. 82–112; see pp. 92–3 and *passim*.

—— *Rediscovering Masculinity: Reason, Language and Sexuality*, Routledge, London, 1989.

Sennett, Richard, in Michel Foucault and Richard Sennett, 'Sexuality and Solitude', *London Review of Books*, 21 May-3 June 1981, pp. 3–7.

Shuttle, Penelope and Peter Redgrove, *The Wise Wound: Menstruation and Everywoman*, Paladin, London, 1986 (first publ. Gollancz, London, 1978).

Snellgrove, Brian and Marita, *The Unseen Self*, Kirlian Aura Diagnosis, 56 Carshalton Park Road, Carshalton, Surrey, 1979.

Tansley, David V., *Radionics and the Subtle Anatomy of Man*, Health Science Press, 1972, (republ. C.W. Daniel, Saffron Walden, Essex), pp. 28, 7–8.

—— *The Raiment of Light: a Study of the Human Aura*, Arkana/Routledge and Kegan Paul, London and New York, 1984, pp. 157–8 (effects on aura of drugs), 160, 183 (both on effects on aura of x-ray, TV, etc.), 153–5, 162 (both on 'sappers' and protection), 190 (earth's aura), 27 (beaches and forests), 113 (imprint of terrifying events), 16–17 (aura affected by city life and violence), 174ff (gems).

Tsuji, Sato, 'Sato Tsuji: The Teaching of the Human Body', in Von Dürckheim, *Hara*, Allen and Unwin, London, Boston and Sudney, 1985, pp. 190–201 (I quote p. 190).

Von Dürckheim, Karlfried Graf, *Hara: the Vital Centre of Man*, trans. S.-M. von Kospoth, Allen and Unwin, London, Boston and Sydney, 1985, pp. 100 (*hara* as ordering power), 97 (*hara* key to flow in activities), 67 (western rejection of belly), 196 (shifting gravity upwards), 65 (*hara* as treasure), 68 (bond with earth), 192 (*hara* strongest and most sensitive), 56 (receiver and transmitter), 53 (action done 'with the belly') (first publ. Wilhelm Barth-Verlag, Munich, 1956).

Weideger, Paula, *Female Cycles*, The Women's Press, London, 1978, pp. 44–6 (first publ. Knopf, New York, 1976).

Williams, Raymond, *Problems in Materialism and Culture*, Verso/New Left Books, London, 1980, p. 81.

6

EVERYDAY MAGIC
Spirituality, Politics and Daily Life

What is now proved was once only imagin'd.

Eternity is in love with the productions of time.
(William Blake, 'The Marriage of Heaven and Hell')

Throughout this book I have challenged the splits that run through
our thinking and imagining: the splits between male and female, soul
and body, day and night, white and black. But the manifestation of
the spirit/matter split which is perhaps hardest to bridge is the deeply
entrenched division between spirituality and politics. In the west,
individuals involved in either activity are usually scornful of the other.
As the journal *Country Women* described it, 'To "political" women,
"spiritual" means institutions and philosophies which have immobil-
ized practical changes . . . To "spiritual" women, "political" means
institutions and philosophies which deny the unity of people and have
channeled women's creativity into destroying and fighting each other.'
Rationalism seems to combat faith, practical action seems
incompatible with the acceptance and surrender associated with the
spiritual life. As a political activist in the 1970s who embarked on
training in meditation and healing, I have seen those conflicts resonate
in my life and friendships.

For me those divided strands are like threads which need twining
together to make a lifeline strong enough to haul us out of the maze
of late capitalism. The fabric of contemporary life in the west depends
on the divisions I have described, and they are personally and
politically debilitating for all of us. I will describe the geography of
the gulf between spirituality and politics and some of the ways it can
be and has been bridged. In approaching this difficult terrain I will
use accounts of events, conversations, dilemmas, debates and

situations which I have experienced or heard about: I will discuss the questions raised by the 'new physics' and the 'new age' Aquarian spirituality, as well as by daily life experiences of illness and death, demonstrations, street violence, peaceful protest and 'prayer'. I shall be pointing always towards ways of recognising and using spirituality in daily life – especially in a life involved in political action for social change.

One implication of bridging the divide between spirit and matter is that we need first to re-examine the discipline which has had the strongest claim to describe and define the laws of matter, and which has provided the basis and justification for twentieth-century rationalism: science. We need to question the categories that science has offered us for charting the workings of the natural world. In part, this process has already started from within the ranks of scientists themselves, with the birth of the 'new physics'.

New Views from the Laboratory

In the last decade Fritjof Capra and another writer, Gary Zukav, have become well known for popularising recent discoveries in physics and showing how they challenge some of the basic assumptions of conventional science. One such assumption is the distinction between energy and matter. Quantum physics has undermined this assumption with the idea that at the most minute level of scrutiny of the material world, what we are actually dealing with can ultimately be seen as energy vibrating at different frequencies, some of which make that energy appear to us as solid matter. The terms 'mass' and 'energy' are actually interchangeable. What this means for us is that our notions of separateness are challenged: the distinction between a person and the air around, or between one person and another, so apparently self-evident to us, can be seen from this perspective as a culturally based and inadequate description of what is in fact a series of energy movements. These revelations bring to mind parallels with eastern spiritual ideas. In *The Dancing Wu Li Masters: an Overview of the New Physics*, Gary Zukav summarises the implications of Einstein's theory of relativity, dealing with planetary movements:

There is no such thing as 'gravity' – gravity is the equivalent of acceleration, which is motion. There is no such thing as 'matter' – matter is a curvature of the space-time continuum. There is not even such a thing as 'energy' – energy equals mass and mass is space-time curvature . . .

In other words, there is nothing but space-time and motion, and they, in effect, are the same thing. These findings cast a new light on certain religious practices such as the apparent worship of stones by the early Cretans (see Chapter 7). We tend to think of a stone as an inert object but, as Zukav points out, in describing matter Taoist and Buddhist philosophies speak repeatedly 'of dancing energy and transient, impermanent forms. This is strikingly similar to the picture of physical reality emerging from high-energy particle physics.' Far from being dead matter, the stone is revealed as a mass of vibrant energy.

Our prevailing western view of humanity as a collection of isolated individuals also has to yield ground to those spiritual traditions which emphasise the interconnectedness of all life. This shift is significant, because the traditional scientific model had been projected outwards to dominate our view of human behaviour and social organisation. From the scientific discoveries of Isaac Newton and the rationalism of Descartes we have inherited a mechanistic world view of separate objects, and mind separate from matter, which is inappropriate not only for atomic phenomena but also for social phenomena, as Capra pointed out in a radio interview:

In our psychology, medicine, economics, health care, politics and so on, we are trying to apply these same Cartesian concepts to describe a world which is fundamentally inter-related, in which phenomena have biological aspects, psychological aspects, social aspects, and all these are interrelated, and the Cartesian world view does not provide us with the kind of ecological perspective which is needed to describe this world.

The model of a world which is fundamentally interrelated has clear political implications and summons up the possibility of more unified and collective forms of social organisation.

It follows that another theoretical model which is up for questioning is that of centralisation as a necessary principle of organisation. Our view of the body is of an organism ruled by the central authority of the head, whose instructions are passed down to organs, tissues and cells in a pyramid of power. Again, however, recent scientific work suggests that this symbolic view is not one which is endorsed by close observation of the functioning of the human body. For the purpose of argument I will take the example of the eye. According to prevailing understandings of the body, the eye has been regarded as a simple receiver which transmits visual messages to the brain for the brain to process and make a response. However, as Ralph Metzner points out in *Maps of Consciousness*, it now appears that in addition to the afferent fibres carrying electrical code impulses from the peripheral sense receptors to the brain, there are efferent fibres from the brain to the periphery which screen, select and filter unnecessary data. Electron microscope research into the structure of the retina at the back of the eye (which receives the imprint of visual images) apparently makes the retina look rather like a piece of peripheral brain, and justifies regarding it as an extension of the brain on the end of the optic nerve.

Another researcher, K.H. Pribram, reported in *American Psychologist* that a series of studies 'demonstrated corticofugal [away-from-the-brain] influence as far peripherally as the cochlear nucleus and optic tract'. This instance suggests that the brain may not be such a centralised all-powerful force, but may be decentralised throughout the tissues of the body which make their own active and intelligent contribution to assimilating external data. The extension of the analogy of the eye to other body tissues would imply a 'bodymind' in which every cell is to some extent sentient, rather like the models of the body proposed by the alternative psychological and spiritual theories discussed in Chapter 5.

The question of which model of the body we favour might seem to be of little importance on the larger scale, but it is these ostensibly 'objective' scientific models developed on the small scale that have been used to justify wider forms of social organisation. Thus the vision of a hierarchically organised body, or a hierarchically organised natural world, is used to convince us that hierarchy is a natural law and that hierarchy in the church, in government, in the organisation of work and of the family, is a necessary and unavoidable fact. Capra argued, in the same radio interview, that the levels or strata of organisation in nature are in fact very different from human hierarchies, as they have levels in a stratified order but no hierarchy of power: 'In a human hierarchy, power flows from the top to the bottom; information flows up but power flows down predominantly. In a natural multileveled system there's an interaction between all levels, each level interacting with its total environment.' The recent dramatic development of the 'chaos' theory – based on studies of issues like weather prediction and fluctuations in wildlife populations – has highlighted how nature operates as a series of interlinked systems in which, as James Gleick puts it, 'a butterfly stirring the air today in Peking can transform storm systems next month in New York' (*Chaos*). What emerges is that scientific models could serve equally well to validate an interdependent and collective society as an authoritarian society.

The relativity and interchangeability of these different world views leads us to question one of the most tenacious assumptions of science: the notion of objectivity. What has been presented to us as '*the* truth' becomes exposed as simply being '*a* truth': a statement about the world as seen from a particular standpoint, which, in the social context, can be propagated by a dominant person or social group – government or media – to suggest that it is the only possible view. The German physicist Werner Heisenberg found that in order to describe atomic particles, using quantum mechanics, you can accurately record *either* their position *or* their momentum, but not both simultaneously: if attempted simultaneously, as the one measurement increases in accuracy, the other increases in uncertainty (Heisenberg's 'uncertainty principle'). The very act of recording the one aspect means that the measurement of the other is rendered uncertain – increasingly uncertain as the original measurement becomes more accurate. Things present a very different face depending on the position and method used to perceive them, and on the conceptual frameworks they are fitted into. Often the very act of perception interferes with and alters the object – like entering a dark room where people are kissing, and turning the light on. The old Newtonian physics remains valid within its limits, in the large-scale world where apples drop from trees at predictable speeds; though even here gravity, the force of one body acting on another at a distance, can be recorded but not explained and was described by Newton himself as 'so great an absurdity'. The 'chaos' theory has recently highlighted the role of the random and the unpredictable in everyday systems – like traffic, machinery and the weather – and how a small factor can have huge consequences. In the subatomic realm Newtonian physics is completely inadequate to describe the invisible universe which forms the fabric of everything around us. Apart from Heisenberg's uncertainties and the interference caused by measurement, the *tools* used affect what we are *able* to see: thus one experiment will show that light is wave-like in form, while another will show it to be composed of particles. Both 'wave' and 'particle' are symbols used to give a partial description of reality. The way we observe reality determines what we see. As one physicist, John

Wheeler, has put it:

> 'Participator' is the incontrovertible new concept given by
> quantum mechanics. It strikes down the term 'observer' of
> classical theory, the man who stands safely behind the thick glass
> wall and watches what goes on without taking part. It can't be
> done, quantum mechanics says.

Where the observer's method and conceptual framework so clearly
affect what is observed, it becomes impossible to maintain the myth
that science is value-free. All the more dangerous for us to construct
models of human behaviour on the basis of that myth.

A clear example of the powerful influence of scientific terminology
on perception can be found in the widespread use of the terms
'positive' and 'negative', which Benjamin Franklin gave to the two kinds
of electrical charge. Now basic school physics tells us that every atom
consists of a central nucleus containing 'positively' charged particles
called protons, around which are distributed a number of 'negatively'
charged electrons. The electrons balance the protons, and in its
normal state the atom is electrically neutral with as many electrons
outside the nucleus as there are protons in it. However, some atoms
can temporarily hold more than the normal number of electrons; so
if you rub, say, glass and silk together, the glass gives up some electrons
to the silk (recognisable to us as 'static electricity'). Thus when we
say now that the silk has a 'negative' charge, we mean that it has *more*
than its normal number of electrons; while the glass has a 'positive'
charge which actually means it has a *deficiency* of so-called negative
charge. The particles that are dynamic, that move, that gather in excess
or whose absence leaves a gap are actually the negative electrons. The
positive/negative nomenclature and symbolism, chosen by Franklin,
is revealed as inconsistent and inappropriate even for electrical
particles. It is on his apparently 'objective' scientific terminology that
a mythology has been constructed which divides people into dynamic,
active, positively charged males and passive, magnetic, receptive,
negatively charged females, each expected to behave appropriately.
There is nothing 'positive' or 'negative' about either side of the
electrical exchange, and the two kinds of charge could equally well
have been called 'green' and 'red'. They hardly provide a convincing
prescriptive model for human behaviour.

Instead of that reassuring myth of objectivity we have to recognise
that scientific models are, as Einstein put it in *The Evolution of Physics*,

'free creations of the human mind'. We, as human beings, are a part of nature studying nature, and the best that scientists can provide is a set of tentative descriptions, influenced by socially based concepts, and offering little more than a metaphor for reality.

These developments cast a new light on the highly prized tool of 'objective analysis', rationalism. Its area of operation is revealed as only one field in the landscape of knowledge. I pointed out in Chapter 2 the role played by intuition and imagination in scientific discoveries of the past; as John Dewey put it, 'Every great advance in science has issued from a new audacity of imagination'. The new physics has also shown that some of the most recent discoveries of subatomic science reflect ideas that have been part of traditions of intuitive and spiritual wisdom over centuries in different parts of the world: in Blake's words, 'What is now proved was once only imagin'd.'

In the centuries of 'rationalism', these faculties of intuitive perception have been undervalued, relegated to the background, and their contribution overlooked, to our loss. We need to redress the balance, not at the expense of our intellectual development but by reuniting the intellect with intuition. Rationality is not enough; we need to reclaim the audacity of imagination. This does not imply giving up the attempt to know and understand. It implies extending the area of what we are trying to know, extending the means we use to know by, and approaching the whole project with greater humility. As part of his spiritual apprenticeship described in *The Eagle's Gift*, Castaneda is taught, as precepts, firstly, that everything that surrounds us is an unfathomable mystery, secondly, that we must try to unravel these mysteries, but without ever hoping to accomplish this, and thirdly, that a warrior takes his rightful place among mysteries and regards himself as one too. Instead of believing that the only valid methods of obtaining knowledge about the world are limited to certain areas, certain kinds of evidence, and certain tools of enquiry, all of which are centred on quantification and conventional scientific experiment, we can recognise that mysteries need new tools to apprehend them. Paul Riesman argued in the *New York Times Book Review* that we can expand our vision of what is scientific:

It is not the object we are trying to know that makes knowledge scientific, nor is it the kind of knowledge we have about it (e.g. intuitive, quantifiable, dream, etc.) but rather the fact that *the person knowing has done the best he could to show others exactly how he came by that knowledge.* [My italics]

In other words, we could be investigating astral travel, and apprehending it via a completely different medium from that of analytic quantification, and could still regard our work as 'scientific'. Fritjof Capra has urged a broadening of the framework of science to include an approach to understanding reality which can deal with values and subjective experience. As long as the two key elements of *systematic observation* and *model-making* are involved, he has said that he sees no problem in part of the scientific data resting on subjective experience: 'as a twentieth-century physicist that doesn't bother me, because since Heisenberg we know that science is subjective anyway'.

The new physics has drastically eroded the underpinnings of that bastion of rationality and materialism, science. The recent discoveries have revealed the limitations of traditional science as the basis of a satisfactory and comprehensive world view. What of that other great materialist and rationalist tradition, which has pushed for economic changes to cure the ills of humankind? Years of division and defeat in the west have eroded the credibility of the movement for socialism and have shown the limitations of the traditional Left's claim to provide its own comprehensive and satisfactory world view.

The Parts the Traditional Left Doesn't Reach

The symbolic splits I have been describing in this book help to sustain a series of splits in our society: between rich and poor; between classes; between 'brain' workers and manual workers; between the social roles of men and women; between the work available to black and white people. Tragically, the movement for social change itself suffers from the same divisions. It is radically split from religion. Socialism in the west gives little space to spirituality. The movement which offers an overall challenge to western capitalism, including specific critiques of sexism, racism, class and work structures, has remained divided from certain crucial areas of human experience. The traditional Left has little vocabulary with which to talk about illness, birth and death, animal life and the natural world, the stars and the universe. However, Marx himself described religion not only as 'the opium of the people' but also, in the same passage, as 'the heart of a heartless world, the soul of soulless conditions' (*On Religion*). He also believed that alienated labour 'alienates nature from man' and spoke hopefully of the 'union of man with nature, the veritable resurrection of nature' (*Early Writings*). In fact, the stripping of the sacred from political and economic life is not a 'natural' or inevitable but an historical phenomenon, accelerated in Europe by the scientific advances and social dislocations of the Industrial Revolution. Since this secularisation of society, those with a desire or vision to make the world a better place have spoken either about wages and housing or about sin and salvation: either about material issues or about spiritual values, rarely both. As a result the socialist tradition, skirting whole areas of human experience (the psychological, the spiritual) and denying our human connection with the natural world, has become arid and visionless. Without that sense of relationship, it has been easy for the Left to slip into a mode of guilt-inducing self-righteousness and dogma. As Trevor Blackwell and Jeremy Seabrook put it in *The Politics of Hope:* 'Socialism's determined and wilful reducing to rubble of all other worlds save that to be constructed in its own secular hereafter, has banished the spirit which gave it birth.'

While the Left lectures on economics, the areas of emotional and spiritual experience have been prey to appropriation by the Right. As Reich pointed out in *The Mass Psychology of Fascism*, leaders like Hitler have been able to manipulate feelings of fear and hatred which the Left had not addressed itself to transforming. Recently the revival of fundamentalist religion, especially in the United States, has shown the frightening success of anti-humanist 'church' organisations in exploiting people's need for spiritual values, and in co-opting that need to swell a powerful reactionary force in society. At the same time, adherents to 'new age' spiritual schools have multiplied. If socialism has suffered from the lack of spirituality, spirituality – including 'new age' spirituality – has also suffered from the lack of socialism. While fundamentalist religions are often overtly reactionary, the 'new age' or 'Aquarian' spiritual movement presents a more progressive face which can be deceptive.

Towards the Age of Aquarius?

At the London Festival for Mind, Body and Spirit, I was standing between a stall about flying saucers and a woman practising palmistry, when we were called to silence to join in a mass meditation. A personality well known in healing circles asked us to shut our eyes and imagine moving through a peaceful and beautiful forest. In reality, we were hot, we were crowded, we were loaded with shopping, we did not know one another. We were asked to hold hands, which was pleasant enough but embarrassing. We were asked to imagine a beautiful pool. Some people fidgeted. Then we were asked to imagine peace in the world. 'What about Thatcher?' a woman near me muttered. Most people seemed relieved when it was over.

This meditation seemed to typify much of what I have experienced as the best and the worst of the 'new age' phenomenon: its optimism, its good intentions, its willingness to try something different – and at the other end its market-place mentality, its credulity, its wilful political blindness and its failure to recognise the emotional and physical reality of people's experience.

What is often termed the 'new age' movement includes a number of spiritual disciplines and techniques: some of these have emerged from European non-Christian religious traditions, some are imported from eastern religious practices, some have been invented by enterprising North Americans. Thus under the same heading I might include a number of different disciplines which have recently started to enjoy a greater popularity in the west, such as the Tarot, astrology, psychometry, meditation, teaching about past lives, yoga, colour healing, laying on of hands, dowsing, Bach flower remedies, and so on. I am not writing about these techniques in themselves, but about the way they have been taken up by what could loosely be described as a movement. There are many strands within the movement, but broadly speaking it offers a view of the world apparently less rigid than either religion or science: a view where the role of spirit is recognised without the dogmatic framework of traditional religions, and where the fruits of science such as Kirlian photography and electronic music are integrated with belief in the importance of ley lines and reincarnation. As we turn from conventional religion and science, it might seem that this movement could offer us new guidelines for living that can bridge the great divides patriarchy and capitalism have created. But can it?

There are many sincere and dedicated people involved in these alternative spiritual disciplines. There are wise and gifted healers whose results impress the most sceptical. I have no intention whatever of criticising these people. However, there are certain tendencies within other parts of this movement which merit critical scrutiny. As I hope to point out in this section, there are certain ideas running through some of the 'new age' activities which undermine their credibility for people with a social consciousness.

Perhaps the biggest single problem is the way these disciplines and techniques lend themselves to be used, and in some cases quite blatantly *are* used, to endorse and facilitate the functioning of the competitive, hierarchical and divided status quo. Thus in the very presentation of these disciplines, there is sometimes a suggestion that they will help people to succeed under capitalism. The notion that relaxation or meditation helps you to 'get ahead' summons up images of businessmen sitting in a lotus position in order to prepare themselves to perform their best at board meetings. Recent years in the west have seen a huge growth in the membership of the Nichiren-Sho-shu Buddhist sect, whose practice includes long periods of chanting for things you want in your life. Kirlian aura photography is said to reveal hidden abilities which may be 'useful in your career'. The recognition that each person has enormous latent power is sometimes used to inflate the same selfish ambitions that capitalism has always encouraged into an ego-orientated vision of 'unlimited potential'. This often goes hand in hand with a very familiar competitiveness and élitism. Some disciplines operate with an explicit hierarchy of consciousness in which certain people are defined as more spiritually developed or 'evolved' than others; this feeds into the creation of new élites with 'special' spiritual knowledge and skills. Sometimes such values and judgments are unstated, but implicit. For people who are committed to breaking down hierarchies, enfranchising people and building collective power, it is disconcerting to find that most of the disciplines have gurus or other exalted leaders, rather than teachers. It is also disconcerting that in many cases the leadership patterns tend to perpetuate class, sex and race inequalities. Apart from eastern masters who have gained a following in the west, and a few exalted 'primitives', the 'masters' within the 'new age' movement are generally white, male and middle class.

Existing relations between the sexes may be endorsed or even glorified by the addition of spiritual overtones. In a book review in the journal *Link Up*, Shauna refers to 'the search for the new feminine in this present age and the separating and rebalancing of masculine and feminine energies', reflecting a commonplace of 'new age' thinking which places heterosexual preoccupations at the core of the spiritual enterprise. Many different schools repeat the familiar stereotype of 'male energy' as active and 'positive', while 'female energy' is 'negative', passive and closer to nature. I pointed out earlier how the positive/negative model is not even appropriate as a description of electricity, the prototype from which the metaphor is derived; in some of these disciplines it is elevated to the status of a polarity of cosmic forces with the inevitable condoning of stereotypes of sexist behaviour. Eastern ideas, such as that of 'yin' and 'yang', can be co-opted to endorse the same stereotypes.

Another idea which presents difficulties for the politically aware concerns a rather deterministic notion of trust. Over the years, at various 'new age' groups and courses, I have heard the belief expressed that the universe is perfect and that everything occurs exactly as needed for its future evolution. Things are 'meant' to happen. The implication is that we should face the inequalities and atrocities of the world with a placid attitude of trust that all such happenings are for the best. A spiritual or trusting frame of mind is set against active involvement in social affairs and the concept of struggle. A related idea which occurs intermittently concerns choice. It is believed that people create their own reality from their own thought forms, and should take responsibility for what happens to them. The implication in this case might seem to be that the oppressed should be left to stew in their own juice as they have on some level 'chosen' their situation. These two issues, which have such serious implications for the project of combining a spiritual with a politically active life, will be discussed in greater depth later. Another significant element is a strong tendency towards consumerism. Celebrating intuition at the expense of rigorous thought, and therefore lacking a coherent theory, the 'new age' movement sometimes seems to offer no more than a series of unconnected and competing fads. Spirituality, or health, or higher consciousness, can be presented as attributes which we can acquire if we buy the right pyramid or pendulum or training, or pay for the right hands to be laid on us. What is lacking is the understanding that under capitalism, as Blackwell and Seabrook have put it, 'Every liberatory impulse, whether it be religious or socialist, must be captured and transformed into what the system can sell.' Without a serious questioning of the consumer ethic, psychic interests and phenomena can start to appear as a parade of gimmicks offering goodies to the individual purchaser. In this disconnected form, it is easy to feel disgust at their apparent irrelevance in the light of poverty, pollution, unemployment, wars and other pressing issues in western culture.

A further consequence of the divorce of intellect from intuition is the apparently undiscriminating credulity which is sometimes found in the new spiritual disciplines, and which has provided a very easy target for the sceptical to parody. Abandoning old ideas of 'objectivity' has apparently meant swinging the other way and opening the door to admit every single occult practice and practitioner without question. It is as if the secularisation of our society has left us so inexperienced in matters of the soul that we are spiritually illiterate, and lack the means to distinguish the wise and genuine from the charlatans and fools. Beneath the scientific trappings and apparatus that are a feature of many of these practices, one need only scratch the surface to see that there is often little that is remotely scientific in the best sense of empirical investigation aimed at establishing models and connections. Sometimes scientific equipment seems to be used mainly to mystify and impress. Both Riesman and Capra, in their suggestions for a new definition of science which I quoted earlier, refer to the need to use experience as the basis of systematic observation and model-making. In contrast the 'new age' spirituality seems to betray a deep-seated reluctance to examine experience or organise it into a coherent system. For example, there seems to be little interest in relating the phenomenon of 'talking plants' to psychometry in a way that could demystify both; little interest in investigating what actually happens in a process of meditation or healing, no attempt to move beyond the 'oohs' and 'aahs' in order to understand how the effects are reached. My own questioning – not to say argumentative – attitude was satisfied by finding a teacher whose slow and meticulous work with the body and its energy fields is concerned with constructing models of energy movement on the basis of the detailed observation of experience, both his own and his students'. Questions are welcomed, hypotheses revised. The work involves practice and discipline. There are equally stringent training programmes for healing techniques such as acupuncture, cranial osteopathy and the Alexander method. But many of the currently thriving alternative spiritual schools offer no such stringent apprenticeship: trial and error, empiricism, the open-minded questioning of experience, are replaced, as in traditional religion, by blind faith and dogma. The guru or spiritual teacher is 'right'. The new 'truths' of the Aquarian age, whether these concern healing, male/female energy, reincarnation or telepathy, are not open to question. Innovatory ideas, such as the idea of a female sun which I discuss in this book, are not even considered or entertained; to propose them is to lay oneself open to being treated rather as a heretic or deviant used to be treated by conventional religion.

The failure to evaluate experience can lead to a disregard for the factors of time and space which locate our experience in the physical dimension in which we are living: there can be a denial of history. Thus we sometimes find an unquestioning deference to, and embracing of, 'ancient rituals' without any consideration of which ancients performed the rituals, where, when, in what context and with what significance. It is fine to invent our own rituals, but we cannot inaccurately co-opt the past to lend them extra glamour or authority. Feminist spiritual activities are not entirely free of this ahistorical mysticism. For example, celebrations of 'ancient rituals of the Goddess' are attributed a timeless power, though they are usually the product of a specific time and a specific culture. It is not possible to trace an unbroken tradition even from medieval witchcraft; modern Wicca seems to be its own creation, as Margot Adler explains in *Drawing Down the Moon*. Similarly, spiritual disciplines and practices from the east need to be adapted for use in the west. We cannot simply adopt practices from other cultures as we might buy a tourist trophy to hang on the wall. It is a kind of cultural imperialism to believe that we can simply appropriate the spiritual activities and experiences of people of other cultures and historical ages. This kind of indiscriminate religiosity reflects a belief that there exist 'universal' truths which claim priority over the truths suggested by the specifics of lived experience. The influence of religions like Buddhism has perhaps also lent power, within parts of the 'new age' movement, to the notion that certain prescribed spiritual truths exist beyond and outside the specificities of material existence, and in some way override it.

Underlying these elements within the 'new age' spirituality is a common failure to connect the 'spiritual' to the physical and material fabric of daily life. By omitting to address political, economic, social and emotional factors, such 'new age' practitioners maintain the existing gap between spirit and matter. In a movement which talks a lot about 'acceptance', there are many instances of what can only be described as denial. By remaining oblivious to prevailing social conditions, it fails to reach any critique of them and thus unwittingly condones them and allows them to mediate apprehensions of the spiritual. In many cases the inevitable result is the exploitation of spiritual power for personal and corporate gain; the creation of a new élite of professionals and entrepreneurs who look set to control the new paths to healing and spirituality as firmly as doctors and priests have controlled the old; the disenfranchisement of people who enter those paths; and the development of a whole new era of consumerism which sells back to us what is already ours, a series of faculties and potentials which exist in everyone. What some in the new movement ignore is the fact that physical and spiritual health cannot be bought but must be lived, and are inseparable from the social conditions which are the context for that living. By failing in many cases to address material factors, these disciplines land us fairly and squarely back in the blind faith of conventional religion. For all the scientific trappings of the 'new age' spirituality, it is in many cases merely dispensing traditional religious values in 'new age' bottles more appropriate to the conditions of twentieth-century laissez-faire capitalism.

Moving Heaven and Earth — Towards a New Spirituality

Where do we go from here? Many socially aware people who have some slight interest in, or openness to, spirituality, look no further. Recognising the often sexist, reactionary and consumerist manifestations of spirituality in parts of the 'new age' movement, they are deterred and dismiss that whole area of experience. This is a loss. The record and tape business may be rife with commercial, sexist, and often outright reactionary values; but music can also be performed sincerely, self-recorded, improvised, sung as an expression of revolutionary ardour, whistled on building sites, chanted round the fire at a women's peace camp, hummed to get a baby to sleep. Like music, spirituality is a human faculty. Instead of dismissing this whole dimension of human experirence, we can ask how it belongs in the movement for a better world.

In this book I present the concept of an 'immanent spirituality', apparently practised in prehistoric Crete and strongly echoed in esoteric anatomy's description of 'fine energy' permeating everything physical. If the divine is immanent in matter, rather than separate from it, then spirituality will be concerned with the here and now rather than the hereafter. The paragraphs that follow will look at the various other consequences, problems, pleasures and possibilities of an immanent spirituality. If the divine is not 'up' but 'in' everything, then spirituality cannot be hierarchical, it cannot elevate one sex or race or class. It depends on interconnection. Such values can inform daily life and political activity in whatever work people are involved and in whatever arena of political activity people find themselves placed.

Feet on the Ground

Feminist self-defence disciplines teach women techniques to use when walking in the street alone at night. These include breathing well, moving

*calmly, feeling strong, keeping alert to anything moving in your peripheral
vision, letting your mind clear so that you are free to respond quickly to
possible danger, knowing how fast you can run and how most effectively
to counter an attack. With your feet firmly on the ground, and radiating
confidence, you may discourage attackers. With clarity, knowledge and
purpose, you will be able to give of your best in protecting yourself from
harm if you are attacked. Walking down the street is one of the most
everyday activities; and these practical instructions are remarkably close to
meditative techniques, a simple example of 'everyday magic'.*

One of the most tenacious ideas of the Christian religion, which has
survived into the 'new age' spirituality, is that there is something 'up
there' which is more important than what is 'down here'. The
implication of an immanent spirituality is that there is nothing 'up
there'. My massage teacher Anne Parks used to tell us that 'spirituality
only expresses': it does not exist separate from the manifest
expressions of it. What matters is what is 'down here'. This is not
'materialism' as reflected in the consumeristic and mechanistic
attitudes of our culture. This is a materialism which suggests that
nothing is more important than the living flesh and substance of the
world we live in. Permeated by subtle energy fields, it is the material
through which we express our spirituality, and if anything is divine,
it is. As Blake put it in 'The Marriage of Heaven and Hell', 'everything
that lives is Holy'. Such a view presents physicality, not as something
to be abused and exploited, but as a manifestation of the divine which
should be treated with respect. In Chapter 5, I discussed some of the
repercussions of such an attitude on our bodily activities and the way
we relate to, say, dance, sex, or menstruation. It can also affect how
we walk down the street. Spirituality is not separate from such
intimate and mundane activities, but works through them. As Von
Dürckheim comments in *Hara*, every action which is repeated often
– whether walking, running, speaking or writing – 'conceals the
possibility of inner perfection'. Meditative techniques can be useful
when children are being infuriating, when worry keeps you awake at
night, or when the car won't start. Spirituality is not divorced from
activities like washing or making a cup of tea; it expresses through
them, for, as Jane Roberts puts it in *The Nature of the Psyche*, '. . . in
each simple gesture, and in the most necessary of physical acts, there
is the great magical unknowing *elegance* in which you reside . . .'
   Such an approach suggests a different starting point for political
activity: precisely in the mundane activities which take up so much

of our life. By virtue of the stereotyped roles traditionally thrust on them, women often have a closer relationship than men with such mundane physical activities and tasks of servicing and maintenance. This has affected the issues which women have raised politically, as they demand changes in the fabric of street, home and family life around issues such as nurseries, housework, domestic violence, sexual relations, pornography, street safety, health and the control of education as well as in larger issues of law and the means of production (see Sheila Rowbotham's *The Past is Before Us*). If women's work in the home is geared towards the reproduction of labour power, their work outside the home, such as cleaning and servicing, often entails reproducing and maintaining certain physical elements for their own sake, with no ulterior motive of extracting a product or profit from them. A swept office, a fed child, a clean hospital patient: the project is often precisely the sustenance of the physical in its own right and for its own sake, rather than its exploitation for other purposes.

There is also the related issue of specificity. While patriarchal thought tends to swing towards the abstract, the ideal, the 'norm' or the 'average', women's involvement with the minutiae of the reproduction of life has tended to give them an eye for detail, for the specific, the particular. It can also root them in a stronger sense of locality. This attitude to the specific, written large, can inform a whole political perspective; as Rosemary Ruether writes in *Womanspirit Rising*, 'The new humanity is not the will to power of a monolithic empire, obliterating all other identities before the one identity of the master race, but a polylinguistic appreciativeness that can redeem local space, time and identity.' In terms of political activity this implies respect for the autonomous struggles of different groups based around race or sexual orientation, and for anti-imperialist and anti-racist struggles to affirm the language and culture of oppressed ethnic minority groups and 'Third World' countries. It has ramifications in, say, education, in the struggle against the imposition of normative standards which children compete to reach.

It is a typical reflection of our value system that it is not usual to think of practical perspectives and activities as bearing any relation to spirituality. And yet spiritual teachings often emphasise the importance of grappling with the realities of everyday life. In the Castaneda books, an important part of Castaneda's sorcery apprenticeship is learning the art of '*stalking*', a series of instructions about creating greater room for manoeuvre, effectiveness and power in the realm of daily situations and interaction with people. A description of them can be found in *The Eagle's Gift* and *The Power of Silence*. The rules, which are embodied in a series of detailed and fascinating anecdotes, teach strategies such as choosing your own battleground, discarding what is unnecessary, simplicity and concentration in every battle as if for one's life, relaxation, tactical retreat and so on, and develop qualities such as patience and improvisation. Such skills and qualities are relevant for engaging in an effective and creative way with any personal or political struggle. We start wherever we are, in the specific time and location of our material setting. This is the grist of the spiritual life, whose expression is through the quality of the way we engage with our daily activities whether working, shopping, cleaning, looking after children or walking down the street.

Equality and Empowering the Self

A major consequence of the idea of an immanent spirituality is that the notion of 'superior beings' comes severely into question. If every physical thing, people, plants and creatures, are manifestations of the divine, what use do we have for concepts and deities that loom over us? What use do we have for organisers of institutionalised religion who claim to have superior knowledge of, and privileged access to, the divine? What use do we have for hierarchies of priests? The idea is a great equaliser. Possibilities become open for the organisation of religion or spirituality on a more communal grass-roots basis. There was an apparent lack of hierarchical organisation in early Cretan religion, as well as a lack of separate or grandiose buildings for religious activities; the emphasis seems to have been placed on aspects of the natural world such as plant life. Some modern parallel can be found in the Quakers' concern with the natural world, and with the non-hierarchical style of their meetings, where each person can speak as and when they wish and there is no priest to direct proceedings or to stand between them and their God. Such traditions will help the individual feel on a direct line to the divine. A spirituality whose activity centres on a tree rather than a cathedral allows a freer access to the participants to establish their own connection with what they experience as a source of strength, without it being diverted through an authority structure. It also allows greater equality among the participants.

The early Cretans' concern with plants is echoed in some modern esoteric traditions. In Chapter 5, I described how one can approach trees as batteries of stored energy, and how leaning against them and letting the energy flow through your body can help you to feel relaxed and regenerated. The full psychic implications of such contact with a tree are spelt out in *The Eagle's Gift*, when Castaneda and another apprentice are repeatedly suspended in a harness from the highest branches of a tall tree, with the instruction that they should pay attention to the awareness of the tree and the 'signals' it would give them as its guests. As Castaneda describes the experience, while they were suspended they experienced a flood of physical sensations, rather like mild charges of electrical impulses. Castaneda is told that while mobile creatures draw their awareness from the surface of the earth, the awareness of a tree draws nourishment from the earth's depths, so there is no sense of strife in a tree. The deeply peaceful sensation drawn by Castaneda from the contact with the tree is not unlike that which people have described from communion with God. It is also not unlike the solace that nature-lovers can intuitively draw from trees. Here is an experience remembered by a friend of mine:

> The cedar tree, very big and very dark, must have been a contemporary of the centuries' old Provençal church it stood next to at the top of a hill above the village where I was staying. It had watched over so much history: so many births and deaths, joinings and partings. The idea was soothing and made me feel connected to something bigger than me – important since every area of my life was falling apart at the time and I dreaded returning home. The last morning I stood under the great protecting spread of the cedar, it 'taught' me a song and a dance which I took back with me, and it helped me through.

If peace and regeneration can be obtained from an unmediated contact with sources of energy in the natural world, as described here and in Chapter 5, does this mean that we have no use for teachers or priests? Many people interested in spirituality are involved with a teacher at some point. While many question the all-powerful Godhead of Christian religion, many also find within the Christian religion elements they can use; while others have turned to new symbols of superhuman power, such as the Goddess or Jung's archetypes. Are there ways of using such structures without becoming disempowered?

The problem of learning from spiritual teachers without losing your own integrity and autonomy is well described by Joyce Collin-Smith in *Call No Man Master: Fifty years of spiritual adventures, in praise of teachers but wary of gurus.* The question always reminds me of psychotherapist Jenner Roth's reply to someone in one of her groups who confessed to putting her on a pedestal: 'That's fine. It can be helpful to admire people. But remember that if you come closer to me, you'll find that I fart.' Jenner's joke captures a serious point: teachers can educate us, guide us, inspire us; but it is another matter when we forget that they are human too, and that ultimately we are the only ones who can live our own lives.

The issue of looking to *super*human figures of divine power raises different questions, which are graphically explored in the anthology *Womanspirit Rising.* Many women have pointed out that the symbols at the core of Christianity mirror and legitimise patriarchal power, the oppression of women, and a violent and intolerant history. At the same time, Christianity is for many women a pre-existing tradition and, on the principle of starting from where they are, it is the place from which they can start. Some women have drawn out of Christian tradition elements which they found self-actualising and which they could use: Eve as an initiator; Christ as a man of the people; his female disciples, including prostitutes, as followers who did not betray him; the bi-sexed deity described in Gnostic Christianity; the possibilities Christianity offered for independent lives for women through the monastic institutions; models of powerful women through sainthood; and so on. Some Jewish women have similarly been able to find within the Jewish tradition elements that can embody the new truths which women are articulating. We find, for example, a new Passover service which includes the herstory of Jewish women from the time of the Pharaohs to twentieth-century resistance fighters. This appropriation of elements from existing living traditions suggests that we can incorporate inherited materials in building our own pathway to the spiritual.

Others, basing themselves on the many prehistoric female figurines from Europe and the Middle East, have opted to adopt a monotheistic Goddess who is an alternative and counterpart to Christianity's male God. With the uncovering of the part played by women in early technological advances, the Goddess is reclaimed as inventor and as warrior. Some find these pre-patriarchal images of women empowering, and suggest that whether or not they are historically accurate, they perform the important role of expanding our sense of female and religious possibilities. My own difference with this approach hinges on this point: in early Crete I found no single Goddess, but rather a completely different and apparently non-hierarchical sense of the spiritual; I wondered whether the Goddess can legitimately be resurrected into the twentieth century, and feel that we should think carefully about whether we want to replace a monotheistic God with a monotheistic Goddess rather than moving towards a radical restructuring of our ideas. We are entitled to invent our own religion; however, if we do, we should be clear that its authority does not rest on history or tradition, or indeed anything larger than ourselves, our own invention, faith, and sense of possibility.

There are similarly conflicting attitudes concerning the use of Jung's archetypes as superstructures which could provide a female spiritual identity for us to look up to. Many women have chosen to adopt them for their celebration of 'feminine' qualities such as intuition and emotional awareness. In this vision, woman no longer represents evil and temptation but is the source of life, nourishment and intuitive wisdom. However, while the 'Goddess' image can subsume some traditionally male roles such as those of the inventor, counsellor and warrior, this identification with exclusively 'feminine' qualities can be seen as reinforcing limiting stereotypes about men and women, and maintaining the duality of two ultimate principles. Moreover, as Elisabeth Fiorenza points out in *Womanspirit Rising*, 'Both the fear and demonization of women and the mythic exaltation and praise of feminine qualities presuppose the myth of the magic life power of the female.'

Though I do not personally find myself working within any of these traditions which offer images of superhuman power, I can appreciate the reasons why others may find such a process helpful. What seems crucial to bear in mind, however, is that the process is essentially one of working with symbols. The Goddess is first and foremost a symbol, as is the divine Christ of the Christian religion. Such symbols become restrictive only when we relinquish our ability to question our choice and move on. There may come a time when they will need to be adapted, even abandoned. As symbols they must, I feel, remain secondary and subordinate to lived experience, and they need to be open to change in accordance with that experience. As Jane Roberts points out in *The Nature of the Psyche*, there is a difference between a story told to a child about woods, and a real child in a real forest. Both the story and the forest are 'real', 'But . . . the child entering the real woods becomes involved in its life cycle, treads upon leaves that fell yesterday, rests beneath trees far older than his or her memory,

and looks up at night to see a moon that will soon disappear . . .'
She points out that 'If you mistake the symbols for the reality, . . .
you will program your experience, and you will insist that each forest
look like the pictures in your book.' We do not want to insist that
real women look like the pictures in Jung's book. We need to be able
continuously to change our symbols to articulate our experience more
accurately; reflecting, for example, qualities of female power which
we may develop that are not simply the counterpart of traditional male
qualities. No symbol, not even the Goddess, has any authority or
existence separate from our formulation of her as a personification of
what we sense as the divine. Ultimately the power does not rest with
any imagined godhead but with our individual and collective selves.

Since the religions we know, even popularised versions of eastern
religions, locate authority in God, priest or guru, it requires a
revolution of thought to imagine this consequence of an immanent
spirituality. It also requires a revolution of thought to redefine what
we mean by 'individualism'. There is a tendency among socialists to
regard individualism as a reactionary force – a belief that capitalism
encourages people to be individuals, whereas socialism or commun-
ism requires people to be more uniform as they 'buckle under' to the
collective project. A little thought suggests that the opposite might
be true: that uniformity of belief and behaviour belongs to capitalism,
which – while paying lip service to the notion of personal freedom
– ubiquitously pressurises us to conform to certain stereotyped roles
as women and as men, as workers, as competitors, and as consumers,
and seeks to absorb all other social systems into its own likeness.
Challenging capitalism involves questioning the mould into which it
attempts to cast all human aspiration and desire.

One of the recognitions that emerges from even a slight involvement
with spiritual techniques and disciplines, like those described in
Chapters 3, 4 and 5, is a sense of how different one person is from
another. For each, therefore, different forms and styles of spiritual
activity will be appropriate, and different pathways to the divine.
Margot Adler, in *Drawing Down the Moon*, advocates a 'radical
polytheism'. Citing Breasted's comment in *The Conquest of Civilization*
that monotheism is 'simply *imperialism in religion*', she points out that
fundamentalists of whatever country are at war with 'the diversity of
life and ideas', and encourages us to 'be comfortable in chaos and
complexity'. Respecting the diversity of persons, like respecting the
diversity of races and cultures, can only strengthen and enrich a
society or a movement. Individuality is thus not a threat to the

collective enterprise, but a gift. As Fred Steward pointed out in *Marxism Today*, the ecology movement has recently opened up the possibility of combining 'the collective and the individual, common purpose and personal choice, in a new way'. Marx himself saw the development of individuals as important, and described the process of human emancipation as one of individualisation: as he writes in *Pre-Capitalist Economic Formations*, 'Man is only individualised [*vereinzelt sich*] through the process of history.' He looks towards a social system which could reflect 'the universality of needs, capacities, enjoyments, productive powers, etc., of individuals, . . . the absolute elaboration of [man's] creative dispositions . . . i.e. the evolution of all human powers as such, unmeasured by any *previously established* yardstick . . .' The evolution of all human powers and the development of human individuality is thus not a distraction, but an objective of political emancipation. The more individuality we can command, the better equipped we are to contribute to that emancipation.

One way of gaining a surer contact with that individuality and with the sources of power in the self is through stillness. In Chapter 3, I described how strengthening and nourishing it can be simply to sit in meditation; and how such meditation can contribute to practical work. In my own experience I have found that if I sit quietly for ten minutes before writing a pamphlet I can gain access to a part of myself that functions with much greater clarity and economy. Other common activities can give an opening to similar experiences, although the people doing them might never think of describing them as 'spiritual'. Fishing, with its slow rhythm, long periods of waiting and closeness to nature might be experienced as similar to meditation. Catching fish is 'often just a bonus', as one enthusiast explained in a television programme. Even people who deny individualism and spirituality may in their own lives find nourishment in solitary walking, gardening, or listening to music: all activities which can impart an experience of peace, communion and well-being that in previous centuries might have been described as religious. For us they are secular activities, but remain ways in which we can take time and space to contact the sources of life within ourselves.

In my own most evangelical phase of political activity, I used to dismiss all religion as a 'con' and a delusion. Thus I arrogantly denied the experience of millions of people over the centuries. It took me some years to realise that despite the reactionary and violent history of institutionalised religion, and specifically the Christian church, what underlies organised religion is the real spiritual experience of the people. One of the reasons for the tenacity of such organised religions is that – often using fear to maintain their hold – they feed off and claim monopoly over people's spirituality. Rather than throwing out the baby with the bathwater, people can reclaim that spirituality as their own. Whether the sense of self is developed through the choice of Christian or other symbolic structures, or through secular activities which allow the individual space and time in their own company, it is clear that self-denial and self-hatred help no one. We need to value our own experience before we can understand another's, and before we can begin to use our unique individual creativity and strength for the benefit of all. This involves using not part of our experience but all of it.

'Nothing That Is Of Us Can Be Alien To Our Theology'

One veteran of various 'new age' movements, Lawrence Hooper, has stated in an interview: '. . . I know lots of TM (Transcendental Meditation) people, Muktenanda and Zen people, who are very proficient in meditation skills, but they're virtual imbeciles as human beings. They literally can't live outside a monastery or an ashram. And this to me isn't spiritual life, because to me, I finally realized, spirituality is essentially integrity.

'That means you are always taking all of you into account . . . I noticed the healers and ministers involved with spiritual growth I personally felt were spiritual weren't at all interested in exploiting the capacity of the human nervous system to have abstract experiences. They were more interested in how capable they were of being at home with all life.'
(San Francisco Sunday Examiner and Chronicle, 3 August 1980)

In the group where I first received massage training, I found that many areas of human life were excluded or denied. Emotions were sometimes seen as interfering with meditation; we were encouraged to 'rise above' them. Issues of élitism, rejection, competitiveness and sexual attraction between group members were rarely acknowledged or addressed. The raising of issues of social injustice was not welcome. Our teacher stated that in her experience political people were usually motivated from 'the head' or from anger rather than from the whole person. The spiritual, emotional and political were presented as conflicting and incompatible. I felt caught between a number of different partial views of the world, each denying the other's validity. The consensus view within the group allowed no dialogue, and there was no vocabulary for reconciling these partial views.

Being 'at home with all life' involves a commitment to acknowledging every aspect of our humanness and grappling with whatever inhibits it. The separation of these different aspects of human experience – spirituality, emotion and politics – is essentially a result of stereotyped patterns of thinking. The bridges are there if we let ourselves see them.

One example can be found in the chakra system described in Chapter 5. Understood by esoteric anatomy as the seven vortices which bring fine energy in and out of the body in relation to different areas of life and personality, these chakras can each be related to political activity. The 'whole' person of esoteric anatomy can be seen as the 'whole' person involved in a socially conscious way with the world around. Thus, briefly, the root chakra, as the area concerned with one's material situation, can be related to struggles around welfare benefits, hospitals, housing, wage claims, campaigns for the environment and against water and food pollution, and other actions aimed towards fulfilling our most fundamental physical and material needs. The second chakra at the belly, linked with sexuality and instinctive movement, would be involved in struggles for autonomy and self-determination in the area of sexuality. The third chakra at the solar plexus could be related, among other things, to fear of authority and repressive state apparatus, and anger at the powers that exploit and control; it can also help to make debilitating emotions manageable and usable. The heart chakra could be seen as playing a large part in the mutual support and solidarity that are important in any social movement, and is the source of compassion without which socialism is only dogma. The throat chakra is traditionally linked to self-expression and can be related to the way people 'find their voice' when they recognise what is unjust in their situation and respond actively to change it. The sixth chakra or 'third eye' would seem to be involved both in mentally understanding social and political processes, gauging effective tactics and so on, and in making the intuitive leaps of perception and intuition that suggest what is likely, what is important, what may happen. The spiritual aspect of the crown chakra can be related to the visionary sense that we have a common bond with all life on this planet and can move together towards some kind of flowering.

In this way the factor so often reified as 'spirituality' can be understood as a quality of fine energy present in all life's activities, including the usually divorced world of socialist politics. Again, with the area of the emotions and psychological problems, the bridges are apparent if we look. The emotions, personal thoughts and anxieties which 'interfere' with meditation are precisely those which require attention; thus meditation makes you aware of things unresolved and undone, and motivates you to deal with them in ordinary life. The areas of emotions and personality are recognised as important in several spiritual disciplines. The Castaneda books describe a spiritual training which involves an enormous amount of work on what we might call the 'personality': Don Juan uses the word *tonal* and teaches not how to abandon it in the spiritual enterprise but rather how to order it, sweep it and keep it clean; only then can the warrior survive encounters with the limitless, or *nagual*. For Castaneda the process of cleaning involves his working hard to give up unnecessary characteristics like self-importance and self-indulgence, in order to develop a strong and fluid *tonal*. In *The Eagle's Gift*, he describes a technique called 'recapitulation' which involves spending several years recollecting one's life down to the most insignificant detail; in its use of concentration and the breath to foster and relive deep memories, this technique is reminiscent of many therapy approaches. The aim is apparently to come to terms with past experiences in order to break the limitations they impose, and become able to use them rather than being controlled by them. In Don Juan's teachings, the warrior does not ever leave the *tonal*, but uses it; if the warrior can deal with the world of men, it is a relatively easy task to face the unknown.

What of 'selfish' needs and desires, passion and anger, those emotions whose illusory nature Buddhist writings stress, and which Christian morality would banish in favour of the virtues of patience, sacrifice, selflessness and charity? The implication of an immanent spirituality is that these too have a place.

Any mother who has spent hours and days taking care of her children knows that if she does not have time to withdraw, to take care of herself and enrich her sense of self, she will eventually have nothing left to give. Our 'selfish' feelings, our yearnings for pleasure and satisfaction, our daily needs for rest, affection, appreciation, help with childcare, these are not things we need to shed in order to attain spirituality. As Jane Roberts puts it in *The Nature of the Psyche*,

You will not 'glimpse eternal life' by attempting to deny the life that you have now – for that life is your own unique *path* . . .

All That Is vibrates with desire . . . The denial of desire will bring you only listlessness. Those who deny desire are the most smitten by it.

Modern 'Wicca' traditions value passion as giving depth and colour to human life. Anger is not something to detach yourself from in order to reach a 'higher' state, but is valued as a sign that action needs to be taken and changes made. Feminists have emphasised that spirituality includes every aspect of our life, including difficult feelings such as pain and anger. As Sheila Collins writes in *Womanspirit Rising*, theology starts with what we do with our time and how we feel about friends, family, bosses and money as well as with

what pains us, enrages us, saddens and humiliates us; what makes us laugh; what enlightens and empowers us; what keeps us holding on in moments of despair; . . . where we find true community and trust . . . Nothing that is of us can be alien to our theology. When did we ever get the idea that to admit to anger and rage – even in the face of injustice – is unchristian? Certainly not from Jesus . . .

Anger can be distinguished from hatred and from cruelty, which springs from unexpressed hurt and feelings of powerlessness. Anger can express the desire to prevent cruelty. Piero Ferruci in *What We May Be* has found 'something beautiful and profoundly vital about aggressive energy'. When it springs from a deep sense of the needs of oneself or others, anger can reflect one of the strongest elements of both spirituality and socialism: a sense of connection.

Spirit as Connection

The word 'religion' comes from the Latin verb *religare*, to bind or fasten together. Both the new physics and esoteric anatomy present a vision of a world interpenetrated with subtle energy movement; a world where the energy in our bodies interacts with the energy around us. An immanent spirituality suggests that we are not isolated phenomena, but exist in contact with other humans and the universe. In traditional religion, this sense of connection is expressed through the shared hymn-singing which balances the periods of individual prayer; it is reflected in the feeling of 'belonging' to a church community; it shows in the meaning and purpose that the faithful find in their lives. With the secularisation of western society, religion has lost its role as a binding force. 'New age' practitioners, themselves the products of an alienated culture, often present spiritual development as the isolated path of the individual, rather than as a quality of relationship. Socialists know the importance of connection. Labour history is full of examples of strikes which succeeded through solidarity or failed through lack of it. Collective action depends on goodwill and people's understanding of their relationship with each other. The success of any socialist project depends on the concerted will of large groups of people. And yet socialists often shun spirituality altogether and neglect those energies which can so powerfully link person to person. In the west an alienated, atomised, divided society produces an alienated and divided Left, while the mass of people search for that sense of belonging where they can: in football clubs, revivalist religions, neo-Fascist groups, or in the following of media or political stars. It is in the name of Marx and historical materialism that socialists renounce the spiritual dimension of experience, but Marx himself wrote of religion that his 'criticism has plucked the imaginary flowers from the chain not so that man will wear the chain without any fantasy or consolation, but so that he will shake off the chain and cull the living flower' (*On Religion*). Blackwell and Seabrook in *The Politics of Hope* point out that nearly all forms of socialism have drawn strength and power from this 'deeply stirring humanistic, almost mystical vision', and that when its visionary energy is dispensed with, the programme becomes lifeless and mechanistic. The living flower symbolises an existence not only with material needs met, but with the sense of belonging, meaning and connection to others that gives real nurture – as opposed to the 'consolation' of organised religion.

The sense of connection missing on the Left is not only between person and person but also between humans and the environment. Changing the relationship of human beings with the natural world, which is implied in an immanent spirituality, involves questioning the traditional identification of 'nature' with a female principle alien to the 'male' principle of intelligence and progress. A new approach to politics and spirituality needs to do more than celebrate 'nature', and rehabilitate traditional 'female' qualities associated with nurture and the earth, which is only another way of maintaining the same divisions. It needs instead to acknowledge the strong connection between 'man' himself and the earth, between nature and culture.

Raymond Williams argues that our sense of the isolation of 'man' from the environment can be sustained only by denying the real and complex interactions between humans and the natural world. We turn a blind eye to our effects on it, and its effects on us, and fail to recognise that we are part of nature ourselves:

> In our complex dealings with the physical world, we find it very difficult to recognize all the products of our own activities. We recognize some of the products, and call others by-products; but the slagheap is as real a product as the coal, just as the river stinking with sewage and detergent is as much our product as the reservoir . . . We have mixed our labour with the earth, our forces with its forces too deeply to be able to draw back and separate either out . . . It will be ironic if one of the last forms of the separation between abstracted Man and abstracted Nature is an intellectual separation between economics and ecology.
> (*Problems in Materialism and Culture*)

The separation between economics and ecology echoes our society's splits between town and country, work and play, 'man-at-work' and 'woman-at-home'. But recently the Christian image of a 'fallen' nature which man is entitled to dominate, has been increasingly questioned as the influence of eastern religions and Celtic spirituality leads to a more holistic and sacramental view of nature. There has been a growing public awareness about the dangers of pollution, and the food chain has become a familiar concept, standing as a graphic metaphor for humans' interdependence with the natural world. The recent growth of the ecology movement has begun to challenge the division between 'hard' or 'masculine' politics, and ecology.

The spiritual experience has often been described as a sense of being 'at one' with everything. Immanent spirituality suggests a series of subtle energy connections which link us not only to the natural world but also to other humans. It proposes that we are far less separate from each other than we think. As I have described in this book, it also suggests many ways in which we can attune to, heal and communicate with each other, and provides an understanding of how we do and don't harmonise when we interact with each other in small or large numbers. In short, it suggests a vocabulary and a possibility of connection of crucial relevance to a movement whose success depends on human co-operation.

Whose Revelation?

A group of women met one evening a month to meditate together and then take equal time each to talk about a recent or important dream. Without a standardised set of religious images, over several years they developed their own culture and sense of community, with their own set of guiding symbols. The group provided a supportive context for the women to articulate unconscious knowledge, and make use of dream insights and intuition to bring direction and clarity to their waking lives. 'All the information is there in the dream, but the revelation comes from physically expressing it, speaking it in the group: it becomes more conscious, it moves from metaphor to the concrete so that you can embody it in your life. The group solidifies the recognition of it.'

After the death of a young black man in a local police station, there was a public meeting. With the minimum of the formal organisation usually associated with such meetings, one person after another stood up and told their story of their own experiences at the hands of the police. Many of these people had not spoken in public before, but in the crowded hall the directness of their personal stories generated an electric sense of common interest, support and unity which seemed to envelop everyone present.

In a country community of three families living together, several members of a Goddess group organised a ritual for the sixteenth birthday of Ellie, a visiting teenager. Beth Shaw describes the occasion: 'I remember that Ellie was ceremoniously led to a throne on a dais in the hayloft meeting room. A crown of flowers was placed on Ellie's head and . . . the women present were asked to think of a quality they had within themselves that they would like to offer to Ellie. In turn they were invited to come up and speak their gift aloud to Ellie, and then light a candle which they placed at Ellie's feet. The gifts were things like enjoyment of her own beauty, and wisdom to learn. My friend Sue, a stained-glass artist, gave Colour, and seven-year-old Anna gave "a clear conscience" at which everyone laughed and said she was the only one present young enough to be able to give that. At the end Ellie's throne was surrounded by 16 candles; Ellie was very moved and asked us to write down our gifts so she would never forget them.'

Traditionally revelation, whether spiritual or political, comes from texts and leaders; the implication of an immanent spirituality, however, is that it lies within ourselves and the natural world around us. Where certain norms of behaviour and 'truths' about the world are sanctioned by religion, party or state, we need to look carefully at the vested interests involved. We always need to know what values are being endorsed and for whose benefit. Some socialist writings have almost acquired the status of sacred texts, and figures like Lenin have been elevated to a semi-heroic status; we may ask whether those texts are relevant to the lives of the people to whom they are preached, and whether they serve ultimately to reveal or to obscure. The truth looks different from different places: class, sex and race generate different inequalities and to tackle them people need to define their own arenas of struggle, develop their own strategies. A politics which validates such autonomous struggles will not attempt to pass down tablets from the mountain, but will recognise that understanding and action need to spring from the ground, from the 'grass roots'.

The members of the dream group in the example just quoted were aware that they were drawing on inner knowledge for their own guidance. I have also written in Chapters 3 and 4 about ways of using meditation, and meditation symbols, creatively to tap intuition. I explained how from this perspective some disciplines often regarded as fatalistic and esoteric can be used in an empowering and dynamic way in relation to society at large. Astrology, for example, can be seen as providing a set of symbols which stimulate intuition, and a map which leaves the individual to decide what paths to take and what to do with the information. As Martha Gold points out in an article in *Liberation*, there is fusion between change on the micro and the macro level. She recognises no contradiction between self-knowing and acting or doing in the world, and points out that staying in the dark about ourselves ultimately means depending on something else, whether it is a lover, president, science, or God. Self-ignorance helps no one. The personal revelation she is describing is thus seen as a source of strength, direction and autonomy.

Revelation also happens collectively, as in the earlier example of the dream group. Underlying the talking and sharing of ideas verbally in a group, the model of 'fine energy' suggests that unconscious exchanges of thought can take place which generate a collective wisdom and help to shape ideas which one or other member of the group may formulate. Acknowledging such processes might ease some of the deadlocked wrangling familiar in Left groups, and open paths to more productive forms of collaboration. The use of intuition can have a specifically political application. It is often at work, unrecognised, in arriving at understandings of what is happening in the political arena, and in developing theories and strategies; we speak of 'a good political nose'. It generates a creativity in tactics – for example when East London council tenants got together to create an 'agit-prop' play which imaginatively used characters from *Alice in Wonderland* to point out the dangers of a new government Housing Act. During 1989 several North American newspapers, including the *New York Times*, appeared in a 'people's edition' with mock front pages carrying news about US intervention in Central America which the press was not publishing. In the late seventies, workers at Ford's Halewood factory near Liverpool welded Coca Cola cans on to the cars to express their frustration during a work-to-rule. Recent traditions of inventive action on the Left recall groups influential in the sixties, such as the Dutch Provos, the Yippies and the Situationists. The freedom from the 'busy' mind in meditation is a fertile ground for developing lateral thinking, enabling us to imagine better ways of being and doing unfettered by the patterns and preconceptions of our present culture.

A consequence of the decentralising of spiritual power is a far greater flexibility in spiritual ideas, knowledge and practice. In organised religions, the energy changes involved in the sense of communion or grace are attained through preordained rituals and enshrined in holy laws; but people can find their own routes to achieving them, reflecting their own life experience. In *Womanspirit Rising*, Sheila Collins points out that, in her education, theology began with abstract syllogisms composed by men who had never changed nappies, waited for hours in the welfare office or sat up all night with a sick child: 'If theology is to be meaningful for us, it must not start with abstractions but with *our stories* – just as the early Hebrews and Christians of the Bible began with theirs.' Writing about theology in the politics of Appalachian women, she suggests that women

> can use that wonderful democratic tradition of 'testifying' in church to talk about how the coal and textile companies, the family planning experts, and the welfare officials are keeping women down, and how, by participating in that sit-in at the welfare office, we were able to get food in our stomach and spirit for our souls.

The same quality of 'testifying', and its power, was evident at the meeting described earlier, where black people told their stories of harassment by the police. A similar experience has been described by women attending the self-help groups set up on the basis of Robin

Norwood's book, *Women Who Love Too Much*, to help women who are addicted to painful and unrewarding relationships with men. With rotating leadership, equal time given to each woman, and a rule of 'no criticism' and 'no advice-giving', women are encouraged to tell their stories, not as a saga of personal woe or as trivial gossip, but as a way of defining their reality and validating their experience. Such telling of stories becomes a conscious, political act which can change mood, atmosphere and attitude, and has a collective impact.

The same flexibility can be applied in areas like language and ritual, which need to be continually adapted to reflect people's experience and to express the new relationships being articulated. Sheila Collins suggests that 'Subversive language . . . must be continually reinvented, because it is continually being co-opted by the powerful.' She believes that 'We can no longer afford to use some of this language: for example, the royal male language for God, nor the language of the "blood of the lamb" . . .' One of the traditional roles of religion has been the providing of rituals to mark points of transition in human life, like naming a child, marriage and death; the ritual for Ellie's birthday is a graphic example of the creativity that can develop new forms appropriate for such times of transition or celebration. Similarly, people have organised specific funeral or memorial services appropriate to the beliefs and values of the dead. An implication of an immanent spirituality is that the spiritual path has different starting points and goals for different groups, and calls for the creation or adaptation of new language and practices that are relevant to that path.

These examples give some idea of the range of possible forms that revelation can take, once it is freed from an exclusive association with ancient texts, teachers, spiritual and political leaders. Revelation is not just from above but also from the experience and inner knowledge of each individual; between person and person; and out of collective creation. The ideas, stories, symbols and rituals generated in this way constitute a flexible feast; instead of becoming reified, they can respond as situations change. As Mary Daly puts it in *Womanspirit Rising*, 'revelation is an ongoing experience'.

Away from Linear Thought

It requires a leap of imagination for us to conceive of a circle, triangle, hexagram, or sheer multiplicity as a thought pattern or model instead of the familiar dualism. In this section I will suggest how such a leap might fundamentally affect our approach to issues like science and history as well as gender.

Such a change in symbolism does not happen simply as an act of will, or by inspiration from imagined or real past societies, but is articulated in activity and struggle. Thus we might say that to a certain extent all anti-sexist work militates against these gaps in our vision. Work which decentralises the procreative act of heterosexual intercourse, and demands the recognition of a variety of sexual orientations and practices, diffuses the imagined crucial polarity of male and female. The male/female split is also undermined by anti-sexist work which encourages women to re-own 'male' qualities of strength and assertion, and encourages men to re-own 'female' qualities of tenderness, caring and sensitivity (as in men's liberation groups).

The move away from duality and towards multiplicity can also be made in models of intellectual work. In 'How Gender Matters', a paper about dualistic thinking in science, Evelyn Fox Keller has described Nobel laureate Barbara McClintock's scientific work as a 'lesson in diversity'. McClintock's research as a corn geneticist teaches us to 'count past two in our thinking about nature', as she starts not with the search for generality but with a primary interest in, and respect for, particularity: the important thing is to see one corn kernel that is different or anomalous, and make that kernel understandable. She thus offers a philosophy of science in which the fundamental ordering principle is not a cosmic division of paired opposites, but rather difference and multiplicity.

If multiplicity is one alternative to the model of duality, then circularity is another. In Chapter 7, I examine in some detail the culture of the early Cretans and put forward evidence that their prevalent symbolic view of the world did not operate with dichotomies but with a circular connection. In the late twentieth century, feminists and others interested in developing new forms of spirituality have used the circular principle in various ways. Pagans and others enjoy circular dance; witches use the 'cone of power'; healers work in a 'healing circle' to help the sick and ailing. The understanding that energy, whether psychic, emotional or physical, moves in cycles is used to release and ground intense levels of energy which cannot be sustained indefinitely without dissipating or becoming destructive. We need to recharge if we are to remain effective in personal or political activity. While many on the Left 'burn themselves out' through unremitting work, it can help to recognise the power that comes from clarity, the power that comes from resting, as well as the power that comes from using our full resources actively.

The application of the circular principle would have implications for our understanding of time. Some women have questioned the linear view of history, which sees a movement upwards in a straight line from savagery to civilisation. Instead, in writing 'herstory', women have used a circular or spiral model suggesting a kind of cyclical return to our origins, which are always incorporated from a vantage point of greater understanding in order to inform another cycle of learning in human culture. In other words, we are always starting again, but never from quite the same point. The notion of linear time has also been severely questioned by scientific developments (see Stephen Hawking's *A Brief History of Time*). Another approach which offers a circular model for human life is the idea of reincarnation. The idea that a person continually dies and then is reborn invalidates the life/death dichotomy to which our culture subscribes. The concept of the 'energy body' which can separate from the solid body (for example, during astral travel or a critical operation), and which might survive it at death, also suggests that the dead/alive distinction cannot be made as sharply as our culture makes it. In the 'Seth' books we find the idea that all our lives – past and present – are happening at once. In the 'new age' spirituality, past lives may be cited to explain a strong and immediate bond between two people meeting each other for the first time, who perhaps knew each other in a past life; or the suggestion may be that you need to learn certain lessons in this life which you failed to learn in a past life (the lesson might be, say, to recognise your own power or to choose one thing out of the many); or you may find yourself doing certain things in this life to heal traumatic experiences in a past life. Good teachers stress that the important factor is our response and actions in the here-and-now of this life.

Personally I have found the idea most useful as a tool for living if I regard it as a metaphor. It is clear that certain periods of history 'grab' certain people, whether they be historians immersing themselves in the records of an age, historical novelists who seem to breathe the air of the past time they are describing, or any individual becoming absorbed in historical facts, fiction or films. In these cases there appears to be something which attracts a person to a particular era, something which strikes a chord or has something to teach.

The circular view of history makes it easier to imagine that there may be a point at which two ages intersect, at which one may be of relevance to the other and may be fruitful to learn from. Thus an individual might look to a past era for a representation of qualities or activities which she has difficulty bringing into her present life (these might be, say, romance, taking risks, peace, investigation, aggression). While many scoff at the idea of reincarnation, the value of learning consciously from past eras like this lies in the way it reflects a feeling of connection with the whole human experience in different parts of the world and at different times in history.

Staying with the implications of a circular model of time, Jane Roberts in *The Nature of Personal Reality* suggests that we can visualise each day as an incarnation: 'In its own way, the twenty-four hour period represents both an entire lifetime and many lives in one.' In Chapter 3 I pointed out the arbitrariness of our polarised view of day and night, and the possibilities of breaking free of it by focusing on intermediary periods like twilight; taking conscious awareness into dreams, and bringing dream insights into daily life; as well as changing patterns of sleeping and waking. In *Perceiving Women*, Drid Williams suggests that in a community of the Carmelite Order, the repetition of a certain religious ritual at a regular point in the 24-hour cycle accumulates energy at that point. By being present in the same place at a certain time every day for many years, she suggests that the nuns she studied created an alternative time matrix, a point of connection like a line intersecting a number of superimposed circles: 'It is not very puzzling as to why this represents a rather different notion of space and time from that which a "secular" person might have.'

Morality or Trust?

During my early massage training, the insights gained from meditation and the massage/energy work (where I found my hands involuntarily moved in certain ways) both contributed to increasing my trust in my own unconscious. I began to recognise its role in the course of my life: the major decisions arrived at in their own time; the good things that happened not from 'trying' but from 'going with the flow' – being in the right place at the right time, being open to possibilities, acting spontaneously. This honeymoon period of trust in life came to an abrupt end when a friend was arrested. Our massage teacher often told us that the universe is evolving perfectly, and that painful or unwelcome events serve to 'teach' us positive lessons – we only have to trust. I had used this thought to weather various painful and harassing events over the months, but after the arrest I suddenly felt angry and betrayed. I reacted in panic and in frenetic, often self-defeating, activity. I felt I had lost my place in the universe, and reverted to believing that it was down to me and a few others to put the injustices of the world to rights.

In Divinity and Experience: the Religion of the Dinka, *Godfrey Lienhardt describes how the important mythological figure 'Aiwel Longar' is an ambivalent mixture of kindness and hostility to humans. His motives remain mysterious, and asking for an explanation of them '... is, to the Dinka, as pointless as if one were to ask why the sky or the river were sometimes sources of benefit and sometimes of suffering, and the answer given is likely to be the same – acie nhialic?, "is it not Divinity?" So from this point of view Aiwel is as motiveless as nature itself . . .' Lienhardt comments that 'To the Dinka, the moral order is ultimately constituted according to principles which often elude men, which experience and tradition in part reveal, and which men cannot change . . . When the word nhialic is murmured as an adequate account of accident, luck, disaster, triumph, hope, or disappointment, it often represents a type of adjustment to the uncertainties and chances of human life, a recognition of real ambiguities in experience rather than a pious aspiration towards resignation to the will of an ultimately benevolent personal God.'*

An immanent spirituality invites us to think in new ways about questions of free will and good and evil. If, as in the Christian religion, we postulate an all-powerful God, then painful events must occur with his knowledge and agreement: we must in some way deserve them, or they must form part of a higher purpose or plan. The 'new age' ideology of a perfectly evolving and didactic universe ('It was meant to happen') is not so very different, and leaves unanswered the same questions about suffering in the world: what about events like Auschwitz; what do they teach to whom, and at what price? The 'new age' attitude, as expressed by my massage teacher, is not dissimilar to the pious resignation of traditional Christian expressions: 'It is God's will'; 'These things are sent to try us'. Such ideologies, by postulating a purpose, provide consolation and some protection from the rage and anguish we might otherwise feel at the apparently random experiences of injustice and loss in human life. However, it also infantilises us, and makes us feel that people who suffer must in some way have deserved it. As Alison Leonard put it in an article about Gnosticism, 'Generalised optimism – "God/good will prevail", "We know what's good for you" – is suffused with the Will to Power. It demands submission, dependence, childish acceptance. After Auschwitz, after Hiroshima, after Lockerbie, it's essential that humankind grows up.' That traditional Christian religion is so linked with morality is a result of the soul/body duality on which it rests. The flesh is 'weak', so the spirit must keep it on a tight rein, in the same way that humans, as mortal sinners, fear the wrath or seek the grace of the all-powerful male God. The morality rests on patterns of authority and penance. A religion based on a concept of original sin makes guilty children of us all.

Twentieth-century science, influenced by Darwin, or rather, social Darwinism, has tended to concur with Christianity's view of a 'fallen' nature dominated by instinct and without any inherent 'morality' of its own. As it has been popularised, Darwin's theory of the evolution of the species through tooth-and-nail competition, culminating in the 'survival of the fittest', leaves a vacuum for an external morality to police and control nature's worst excesses. Darwin's model of human evolution is used to justify 'laissez-faire' capitalism as a true expression of 'human nature'. Writers like Desmond Morris (in *The Naked Ape*) place man at the pinnacle of an animal world motivated by territorial and aggressive instincts. If selfishness and competition are 'in our genes', then morality must be superimposed.

However, recent writers in the scientific field have highlighted some common misunderstandings of Darwin's ideas. Evelyn Fox Keller has pointed out that whether the emphasis is on 'dog-eat-dog' overt competition, or on competition over scarce resources, the

> equation of scarcity with competition serves to maintain a conception of organisms . . . as individuals capable of only one kind of interaction – win or lose . . . it obstructs recognition of and attention to the entire range of cooperative or symbiotic phenomena . . . any cooperative interaction that could lead to a more efficient use of resources, or to the *de facto* creation of new resources, would conflict with this model of scarcity.

The competition involved in evolution is actually *differential survival*, which may not involve conflict over resources at all, and may simply reflect one species' greater suitability to survive in a certain environment. Writers like Patrick Bateson have further pointed out that the image of the 'selfish gene' overlooks the dependence of each gene on the gene 'team' which must co-adapt; that there is in any case no simple relationship between genes and behaviour, which needs to be adjusted to the environment; that aggression in animals is conditional and very dependent on circumstances; and that there are many examples of highly functional co-operation between animals in activities like hunting, defence and reproduction. In short, 'If biological thinking is needed to direct attention to aspects of human nature, it should point to collective action, mutual help and trust as much as it does to conflict over resources, deceit and individual ambition' (in *New Society*). These co-operative tendencies inherent in nature have been stressed by Jane Roberts. In *The Nature of Personal Reality* she suggests that our distorted notions of morality, especially concerning guilt and punishment, have overlaid lost senses of instinctual 'biological compassion' and the more conscious 'emotional realization' of identity with those who suffer: 'So man loses full use of the animals' regulated, graceful instinct, and yet denies the conscious and emotional discrimination given him instead'. She suggests that guilt is a substitute for compassion, and that a reified morality would be unnecessary if we were still in touch with the sense of belonging and of self-regulation which are possible, but neglected, faculties in our organisms:

> . . . creaturehood, while striving for survival and longing for life, while abundant and rambunctious, is not inherently gluttonous. It follows the unconscious order that is within it even as there is a definite order, relationship and limit to the number of chromosomes. A cell that becomes omnivorous can destroy the life of the body.

This sense that creaturehood has an 'unconscious order' in it is a far cry from the notion that all matter is a potential influence for evil. It fosters a greater sense of trust in the workings of the world and human nature.

Such a sense of trust in 'human nature' is often as lacking in socialist as it is in Christian or indeed any human thought. Some socialist groups seem to derive much of their drive to action from guilt, a pressurised sense of obligation, and a judgmental attitude of moral indignation. Some seem to believe that, if we relaxed and were free from moral pressure, we would not care. Marx, however, was not making an ethical demand for the liberation of humanity. As E.J. Hobsbawm points out in his Introduction to Marx's *Pre-Capitalist Economic Formations*, Marx saw progress as something objectively definable, and at the same time moving towards what is desirable:

> The strength of the Marxist belief in the triumph of the free
> development of all men, depends not on the strength of Marx's
> hope for it, but on the assumed correctness of the analysis that
> this is indeed where historical development eventually leads
> mankind. The objective basis of Marx's humanism, but of course
> also, and simultaneously, of his theory of social and economic
> evolution, is his analysis of man as a social animal.

It is not that Marx believed the emancipation of the human race *should*
happen; it is that he believed it *will* happen. The movement towards
change in society is not fuelled by moral reasons; rather, he trusted
that it would be the inevitable result of certain processes in the human
and social arena.

If humans move towards liberation because of inherent determining
material factors, rather as plants grow towards the light, a prescriptive
morality becomes irrelevant. Here we are close to the concept of 'will'
discussed in Chapter 5. Some schools of esoteric anatomy stress the
'will' as a powerful motivating force which springs from the area of
the belly. Instead of the familiarly posed conflicts between head and
heart, or between duty and desire, this is a single unitary force which
moves strongly towards its goal. If, as both spiritual and Marxist
thought suggest, it is 'in our nature' to move towards co-operation
and survival, then selfishness takes on a different light. A definition
of 'discipline' given by the guru Chögyam Trungpa was apparently to
do *what you most need to do* at any one moment. This involves listening
closely to the body. In his courses at the Psykisk Center, Bob Moore
has talked about the difference between what is easy and what is
fulfilling, and the importance of distinguishing between wants and
needs. Much of the work of spiritual development is concerned with
contacting a sure sense of purpose and being able to bring one's best
qualities into expression in the world. In *Drawing Down the Moon*,
Margot Adler has defined 'sin' as being 'cut off from experiencing the
deep and ever-present connection between oneself and the universe'.
If we take the trouble to notice our own and others' experience, we
can recognise what nurtures us and can learn not to mistake the
imaginary flowers decorating our chains for the living flower. This is
not a morality which sets spirit against flesh, but a physical approach
to life which generates an attentive selfishness that springs from the
belly.

There remains the problem of the arrest, or the flood: the events that strike us from without and change our lives. The strength of the Dinka understanding of divinity is that such events may be accepted without guilt or blame. In the west our insidious inheritance of ideas of original sin can prompt us to blame ourselves; the concept of a superior external moral force that ensures everything in the universe is going according to plan can lead either to triumphalism ('We're right, so we must be winning') or to bitterness and despair ('How can this happen?'). Self-hatred and megalomania are two sides of the same coin. Failing to trust our own creaturehood or recognise our own power, we have illusions of omnipotence: the flight to the moon from a hungry world. It is only when we know our power that we can allow our powerlessness. The Dinka view represents a more realistic recognition of humans' powerlessness in the face of life's capricious blows; it provides a model for living with limitation, failure and loss. Although Dinka thought is based in the experience of living on the land, subject to vagaries of the weather and other natural hazards, their philosophy of a divinity 'as motiveless as nature itself' remains illuminating in our western society, where lorries can swerve, loved ones leave, jobs become redundancies, and aeroplanes drop out of the sky. Without an omnipotent God or a superhuman morality to identify such events as part of a divine plan or a divine punishment, it remains difficult for us to deal with them without guilt and self-blame, difficult both to do our best and leave it to fate.

The Point of Power in the Present

Every time a friend falls ill with cancer, the question arises: why? Conventional medicine points to smoking or bad habits, and responds with drugs to control the physical symptoms. Environmentalists write about the government's disastrous policies on pollution and carcinogenic substances. 'New age' and holistic books discuss the 'choice to live' and the 'choice to die'. Did the friend 'choose' cancer, or 'choose' not to struggle with it, or 'choose' to die?

A further implication of immanent spirituality is an emphasis on the present. If we are not expecting rewards in heaven or in an afterlife, then we will focus our attention on what is happening in this life now. As Blake puts it in 'The Marriage of Heaven and Hell', 'Eternity is in love with the productions of time.' If we are savouring the divine in the now, we will focus on the pleasure in the present, on what is wrong with it, and on how we can make it as we wish. Jane Roberts, in *The Nature of the Psyche*, describes how all our physical, mental and spiritual abilities are focused together in the 'brilliant concentration' of present experience which is our point of power:

> your power of action *is* in the present and not in the past. Your only effective point of changing any aspect of your world lies in that miraculous instant connection of spirit and self through neurological impact . . . The Point of Power is in the Present.

This idea, that the point of power is in the present, which is uncannily echoed in the theories of the new physics concerning space and time, has been articulated in eastern philosophy and is expressed in the 'new age' movement's guideline for meditation and for living: 'Be here now'. The idea is often found hand in hand with the notion, also suggested by the new physics, that the power lies with us to create our own reality. Thus in 'new age' spiritual disciplines we often find the idea that out of our beliefs we create certain events, that we 'choose' certain life experiences, both on an individual and mass scale. While this idea is to some extent empowering, it also presents some difficulties from a political standpoint and, if things go wrong, it can become yet another form of self-blame.

A very different idea is presented by socialists who understand current social situations as arising from material situations in the past, according to laws of historical determinism. Money and power are distributed unequally, individuals are born into situations of power or poverty, and the oppressed may be seen as helpless victims. This view gives a satisfying account of the important realities of property and control in our society, but we are left asking why, with the same work situation, is one person a shop steward and the other completely apathetic? Despite a recognition of the importance of education, information and consciousness, socialism fails to give a satisfactory account of the differences in awareness and capability that individuals show in dealing with what oppresses them. Why does one mother lobby the council for services while her next-door neighbour sits at home depressed? It is ultimately denigrating to see people simply as the victims of material forces unable to assume power except perhaps under the leadership of a 'party'. To see people as helpless, rather like leaves in the wind, denies their potential to take action, and fails to respect the many choices they make continuously to deal with their situation. To highlight their potential to change their situation is to grace them with power and responsibility, but also implies that they have some responsibility for being in that situation in the first place. Some 'new age' spiritual teachers even suggest that individuals choose when and where they are born in order to learn certain lessons from that life situation. The implication might seem to be that if they meet suffering and oppression on that path, it is something they have chosen rather than something they would want to change.

So are we to think that a friend has 'chosen' to get cancer? Such thinking protects us from the vision of a haphazardly cruel world, and also creates a distance from another's suffering; it is always comfortable to blame the victim. For the cancer sufferer such an idea may encourage the struggle to conquer the disease, but if this is not successful the sense of failure is even greater. Such thinking adds the burden of guilt and self-blame to an already painful situation. It might lead people to believe that a family chooses to be homeless, or that a black man chooses to be the victim of a racist murder. Are we to believe that a child chooses to be born to parents who will batter her? That a woman chooses to be exploited in her own home? Or to be raped on the street?

While the Left tends to look to external causation, and the 'new age' movement to inner causation from the self, the women's movement has long grappled with the dilemma of how much the inner and outer experiences affect each other. With its recognition of social factors as well as the importance of subjective experience and the power of internalised oppression, it has provided a middle path; see, for example, Joanna Ryan's discussion in *Feminism and Therapy*. Self-defence classes that teach us to walk down a dark road radiating confidence with a calm steady tread, rather than a frightened scurry, are really telling us that our behaviour and expectations will attract certain experiences rather than others. Is this so different from the idea that through our beliefs we create reality? Women in the movement have recognised that the strength of their gender conditioning has meant that changes in their external situation without corresponding internal changes have left them feeling as dependent and anxious as ever (see Colette Dowling's *The Cinderella Complex*). Is this so different from Jane Roberts' emphasis on the importance of beliefs? She suggests:

If you do not like the effects of a belief you must alter it, for no manipulation of the exterior conditions themselves will release you. If you truly understand your power of action and decision in the present, then you will not be hypnotized by past events. (*The Nature of Personal Reality*)

The question is a difficult one which I will not attempt to resolve here. My own predilection is to allow that external reality has some autonomy in shaping our lives. While we may create, invite, attract, collude with, or lay ourselves open to, certain experiences, we are continually crossing paths with other people, animals, germs, carcinogenic substances and so on, all equally busy making their own paths through the world; any meetings might seem to be governed by a range of causes from quantifiable social factors such as class, through synchronicity to luck or random chance. I was present when one spiritual teacher was questioned about his statement that we choose the time and conditions of our death; he finally conceded that while we do make that choice there 'may be interference from other people'. This reminds me of a stand-up comedienne joking about her fear of flying: 'I'm not ready to die, but what if the pilot is?' Thus we may choose one thing without having control of all that follows. As Engels wrote in a letter late in his life, although 'men make their history themselves, they do so in a given environment which conditions it, and on the basis of actual relations already existing' (*Selected Works*). Thus an old person who is mugged in the street may have laid himself open to the attack but cannot be answerable for the many social and personal factors which may have impelled the mugger to commit the deed. Moreover, in some situations we are quite powerless: in the light of some events we are irrelevant, unimportant, and have no control at all over whether or not they happen. In her books *Illness as Metaphor* and *Aids and its Metaphors*, Susan Sontag has described how cancer and AIDS patients suffer doubly as a result of the blame and stigma people attach to those diseases. In a television interview she suggested that we can think of some illnesses as being 'without meaning': we need to remember that 'there is such a thing as accident . . . there is such a thing as thoroughly undeserved catastrophe'.

However, if we are interested in gaining control over our lives we will want to diminish the area of accidents which make victims of us, and expand our areas of choice. While we cannot choose all that happens to us, we *can* choose how we react to any situation. The painful experience of rape, for example, may trigger a number of different responses: denial, resignation, fear, paranoia, rage, political activity, depression, helping other rape victims, a change of lifestyle. Though our response to events may be influenced by our personal history, we do not need to remain 'hypnotised' by our past and can recognise our choice of reaction as an important area of personal integrity and autonomy. Rather than turning to divine meaning or self-blame, we can see the energy we put into generating our response as a way of making our own sense of things.

Spirit in Action

In a massage training group there was a health visitor whose job involved visiting old people sick or immobilised in their homes in a block of flats, which she described as grim, depressing, and having a very bad atmosphere. On one occasion she told the group that each time she went there, she used her training in meditation and energy work to radiate positive energy into the place, but she still felt brought down by it. Other group members sympathised and recommended various meditative techniques. Then one group member suggested that she get these clients rehoused. A long silence followed; it was clear that this was the wrong thing to say. In the group, as in some other 'new age' teaching situations, this kind of practical action in the world, sometimes described as 'karma yoga', was seen as work undertaken by people who have a debt to repay to humankind because of actions in past lives; it was believed to be inferior to other more purely meditative forms of yoga.

In December 1982 women travelled from every part of the British Isles for a massive demonstration outside the American nuclear base on Greenham Common. The high point of the day was when, at the appointed hour, women joined hands to form a complete circle around the entire nine-mile circumference of the base. This action, 'Embrace the Base', was to symbolise and express the positive energy and values of the women present, in contrast to the militarism of the US army and its cruise missiles. 'Vibe them out!!' a woman near me shouted, 'Love them to death!!' Afterwards the women's liberation magazine Spare Rib No. 132 *carried a cartoon showing a row of women holding hands, one saying: 'So you hold hands for ten years . . . then this big cloud of non-violence comes down and suffocates the military . . . That's the theory anyway.'*

The gulf between politics and spirituality is not universal, but very specific to contemporary western society. Mauss points out in *A General Theory of Magic* that while religion looks to the abstract, magical traditions have stored information about the natural world, carried out experiments and developed techniques which have contributed to the growth of medicine, pharmacy, astronomy and other aspects of science: 'Magic is essentially the art of doing things.' The separation of spirituality from practical concerns, politics and struggle, is a relatively recent phenomenon in western civilisation, and looking outside Europe one can find societies where no such separation exists. In _Divinity and Experience: the Religion of the Dinka_, Godfrey Lienhardt described how Dinka 'magical' practices were a complement to and preparation for practical action. Thus a hunter would tie a stone representing a lion in a knot of grass as the prelude to serious hunting. In such cases a man 'has produced a model of his desires and hopes, upon which to base renewed practical endeavour'. Similarly Dinka religious rites prior to battle included the priest massaging the knees of the warriors with milk and butter, asking God to ease their joints and give them a brave heart. In _Guns and Rain: Guerrillas and Spirit Mediums in Zimbabwe_, David Lan has described the importance of the co-operation between religious leaders and freedom fighters in the Zimbabwean liberation war.

A practical approach to spirituality raises questions about the political role of the Christian church. In the late 1960s and early 1970s a socially conscious groundswell in Latin America gave birth to Liberation Theology. In the _favelas_ of Brazil there emerged a 'church of the people' which met in 'Comunidades de base', small gatherings of 20-50 people. By 1986 there were more than 80,000 of these small groups in Brazil alone, and the movement has spread through Catholic slum communities and rural villages from El Salvador and Chile to the Philippines. Liberation theologians like Gustavo Gutierrez have emphasised the role of Christ as a liberator concerned with earthly as well as heavenly justice; God is aligned with the poor against unjust governments, cruel landlords, corrupt bureaucrats and greedy businessmen. The movement has caused reverberations in the church hierarchy, and the Brazilian priest Leonardo Boff has been chastised for his writings, but its influence has continued to spread.

In both the practical examples given earlier, the massage group and Greenham Common, spiritual goals and methods were posed as an alternative to political goals and methods. There need be no conflict in either situation. Many spiritual disciplines stress the power of thought to help another, even at a distance; the possibility of its efficacy is recognised in colloquial speech when we ask someone to 'think of me'. However, the health visitor could _both_ send energy to her clients _and_ take practical action towards getting them rehoused if that was what they wanted. She might also find that meditation and focusing her energy before going to the local Council about rehousing would make her more effective in that situation. At Greenham in subsequent years, women launched highly successful attacks against the high circumference fence, felling the concrete posts at many points and carrying out a series of imaginative actions inside the base to draw attention to the dangers of nuclear war. It was not a question of *either* holding hands *or* taking action, but of doing both, and bringing the consciousness and collective confidence generated by the hand-holding to inform and strengthen the action. Spiritual development and practical action to change the world go hand in hand, as Jane Roberts describes in *The Nature of Personal Reality*:

> You are here to use, enjoy, and express yourself through the body. You are here to aid in the great expansion of consciousness. You are not here to cry about the miseries of the human condition, but to change them when you find them not to your liking through the joy, strength and vitality that is within you . . .

Both traditional religion and 'new age' spiritual teachers sometimes use a vocabulary which can seem remote from human problems: the language of 'enlightenment', purity, bliss, inner fulfilment, acceptance. Some 'new age' teachers suggest that when you 'resist' something, you give it energy. These words can be misunderstood and taken to advocate political passivity. It took me a long while to understand that acceptance is an active quality: when you see a situation for what it is, you respond appropriately, assisting or resisting as necessary. It is not acceptance but denial that leaves us immobilised with our heads in the sand. As Starhawk puts it in *Dreaming the Dark*:

> In Nazi Germany, it was not the resistance to fascism that allowed the spread of Anti-Semitism and led to the death camps, it was the widespread denial, the refusal to admit that such things could happen. It is not resistance to the possibility of nuclear holocaust that will bring it about, it is denial.

It is also *denial* of the failures of recent years that has left many socialists bitter, desperate and ineffective in their efforts to attract people to the movement. Much of the Left's self-righteousness is deeply depressing, because, in Alison Leonard's words, 'depression comes from knowledge denied'. Admitting mistakes and disasters –

such as the perversion of collectivism into totalitarianism in the USSR, China and elsewhere – makes it possible to start paying attention to things as they are. Accepting loss and disappointment leaves us more able to look and act clearly.

Power and Transformation

Margot Adler writes in Drawing Down the Moon: *'During my travels I came across a coven of witches living on a farm in the plains of Colorado . . . On a hot and dry day, four of us . . . were asked to go down to the river, which habitually dried up in the late summer . . . to catch the dying fish in two buckets and fill an entire small truck with the creatures, which would then be used as composting materials for an organic garden. A few of the fish were floating on the surface, but most were still quite lively and dashed away . . . It was slimy, messy, and unsuccessful work . . . It seemed an impossible task. When we arrived back at the farm, Michael said . . . that the job was possible, and that, more to the point, the fish were needed. I was skeptical . . . "Magic," he said, "is simply the art of getting results." He noted that the fish were dying and that they might as well be put to good purpose . . . Michael then began to describe how bears catch fish with their paws. He asked us to visualize ourselves as bears, . . . in the position of a hungry bear in need of food . . . In such a mood, we waded to the middle of the river, . . . and began slapping our hands together very quickly, catching the fish between our hands and throwing them over our heads and onto the beach. We continued . . . until the beach was covered with fish . . . Magic is a convenient word for a whole collection of techniques, . . . including the mobilization of confidence, will, and emotion brought about by the recognition of necessity; the use of imaginative faculties, particularly the ability to visualize, in order to begin to understand how other beings function in nature so we can use this knowledge to achieve necessary ends.'*

One evening a woman was followed home after putting up anti-fascist stickers before a local election which included a fascist candidate. Two days after the elections she entered her bedroom late at night to find a brick had been thrown through her window and there was broken glass on her bed. She felt shaken, physically violated, and overcome by a sense of her vulnerability. Remembering techniques learnt in a meditation class, she got herself to calm down, sit down and focus on her breathing. As it became less panicked, she decided to imagine tracking down the person who had

*thrown the brick and send them a beam of light. She was aware of the
irony of sending light to an enemy, but she held firm to her sense that
whoever she was sending it to needed it badly, to clear away cobwebs of
blind hatred. As she did this, fear was slowly transformed into confidence
and a feeling of her own power gradually returned. Although shaken, she
was not scared off from continuing anti-fascist activity, and her meditation
work proved a practical tool in countering – and transmuting – the
debilitating effects of malicious energy.*

Power and transformation are among the most important gifts that
religions have traditionally offered their followers: the inner strength
that comes from having the power of God on your side; the
transformation offered by the redemption of sin or triumph over fear
and death. Socialists express similar concerns: the need to take social
power; the transformation of society through peaceful change or
revolution. The religious and the socialist usually pursue their visions
separately like parallel tracks of a railway line, but bridges there are,
specifically in these areas of power and transformation, which can
provide glimpses of what a political spirituality or a spiritual politics
might be.

At several points in this book I have referred to the idea that
spirituality is the term we use to describe our experience of a fine
or 'subtle' energy which is present in our bodies and in the natural
world around us. Many diverse and confusing 'psychic' phenomena
can be reconciled and demystified with this one unitive concept. Fine
energy, which has been compared to electromagnetic energy, runs
through the body along certain paths, as described in Chapter 5. In
an article in *City Limits* magazine, I listed some of the many ways in
which we might be able to identify 'subtle' energy at work:

when pressure is applied on key spots in the circuit (*acupuncture*)
changes are brought about in the organism. We can become aware
of this through *meditation*. The energy radiates from the body and
a special method can be used to record it photographically (*Kirlian
aura photography*). We can respond unconsciously to the energy
emitted by others and this skill is developed and articulate in some
people (*intuition, telepathy, clairvoyance*). We can also draw in
energy we need from the world around us and some people have
the art of channelling this to others to a healthful effect (*spiritual
healing*). The earth emits energic forces in addition to gravity, and
some early religious and traditional customs have been able to

utilize these (*water divining, stone circles*). If the other planets in the universe also emit vibrations of particular kinds these may perhaps affect us too (*astrology*). So it goes on.

The association of all these phenomena with the 'occult' renders them suspect to many. But radio waves must have appeared magical before science quantified them. The recent interest of science in these phenomena – from using a vegetable to illuminate a light bulb to assessing the results of 'faith healing', measuring changes in brain waves during meditation and investigating the military uses of telepathy – suggest that they reflect the operations of a force as knowable (and unknowable) as other physical phenomena such as light, X-rays, and the processes of cell renewal.

Such an approach suggests that subtle energy is a neutral force which can be utilised for different ends. Like other energies in the natural world, such as sun and wind, it can help or harm humans. Electricity can be used to torture or to bring heat to people's homes. Sound can relax or grate on the nerves. As Bruce MacManaway has put it in *Healing*, 'Power is of itself neutral, it *is*. We can harness it, whatever classification of energy it may be, to heal or harm. It is our motivation and state of understanding or enlightenment which determine the use to which we put it.' 'Subtle energy' is not available only to help with fishing expeditions, as in the earlier example, but also to increase our efficacy and satisfaction in many spheres of life. One may be sceptical about whether it could assist the process of collective work and political action without denying the differential effects and power of factors like class, property, sex and race. However, it does not contradict such factors but, rather like radio waves, can be used in relation to them and can make an impact on those realities. As Jane Roberts comments in *The Nature of the Psyche*, developing an awareness of this energy is 'not to be used to supersede the world you know, but to supplement it, to complete it, and to allow you to perceive its true dimensions'.

I first became interested in subtle energy when, in political activity, I noticed things happening which did not seem explicable either on social-economic or on emotional-psychological grounds. Some people seemed to exude a lot of personal power, and to be able to control others with it, out of proportion to their material power. Subtle energy, with its vocabulary of auras that can expand, suck in and drain others, provides a means of understanding some of the effects of charm, 'charisma' and personal magnetism, which can be manipulated to sway a crowd or whip up sectarian hatred. A rather different process can be identified when people are influenced by the personal example of a figure like Gandhi, or by the example, encouragement and affection exuded by a friend during a one-to-one conversation. Jane Roberts' 'Seth' books question that hypnosis is a special magical skill, and suggest that we use it every time we have the undivided attention of another. Such considerations suggest it is all the more important to organise politically in structures which allow each person to have their say and 'take their space' rather than being drawn in to ratify leadership or toe a line. Working reciprocally in pairs (as in Co-counselling) or organising in small groups provides a framework in which people can start to reclaim some of the autonomy and dignity that has been eroded from their lives.

To increase the confidence and effectiveness of each person, some 'new age' writers recommend the practice of repeating affirmations ('I am ready to start a relationship', 'I am ready to find a job', 'I can get better'). My own experience is that such exercises, by challenging restrictive beliefs, can help to clear paths and increase confidence and determination. Like a cat preparing for a leap, you can throw your heart into something ahead and the rest of you catches up. However, what seems most important is the muscle power available for the leap. While the traditionally religious call on God to increase the amount of energy available to them, and occult traditions use spiritual hardware and power objects to draw in and focus energy, in this book I have described simpler sources of sustenance such as sound, colour and natural elements such as trees. I have mentioned ways of 'clearing the channels' within ourselves so that we can receive the maximum benefit, and operate most effectively, with the energy available. As well as harnessing power from external sources, I have also described ways of using our own body functions, such as menstruation, and activities such as dance, to raise or release energy. Much of the Castaneda literature is about increasing personal power, whether by clearing resistances, identifying 'power places' which give peace and solace, or developing the use of the will to project energy outwards into the world. Acknowledging the role of subtle energy can help people to handle their own resources better, resting when necessary and recognising the need for change of place or pace. It can also be helpful in understanding the dynamics of energy exchanges between people: why did a particular meeting leave a nasty taste in the mouth? What made a particular demonstration so cohesive? Religions and reactionary groups have long known how to use rituals and energy changes in order to hypnotise people into immobility or whip up fervour. Subtle energy is an area of human experience and a source of latent power which we can reclaim.

In the gospels, Jesus turns water into wine. To hope for a just world sometimes seems like wishing for a similar miracle. In a culture where some things – like technology – are changing so fast, we remain, in Vaneigem's words, 'unchanged, frozen in the empty space behind the waterfall of gadgets . . .' and it is hard to see how to effect any real change in transforming capitalism's relentless energy into a system which could benefit the many rather than the few. Sara Maitland has pointed out that Christianity's notion of repentance allows the possibility of some change. Even Pandora's jar contained a seed of hope. The question of how to achieve transformation for the better remains an issue on which the 'political' and the 'spiritual' approaches might seem to be most deeply divided. Do we turn the other cheek or does power grow from the barrel of a gun? Can the causes of pain and suffering, both in ourselves and in the world around, be described as 'evil' or are they the product of history, class and false consciousness?

While traditional Christianity has bequeathed us the symbol of the devil and the concept of evil, some voices in the 'new age' movement make it clear that for them there is no evil star, only energy. Sometimes the energy is in the wrong place and doing the wrong thing, sometimes it becomes blocked or distorted; in that case, it needs to be moved or released so that it can function in a more useful way. Bob Moore has pointed out that by dividing the world and our own potential into 'negative' and 'positive', we divide ourselves; much of the energy work he teaches is concerned with the transmutation of energy so that what might seem 'negative' becomes useful. In the course of giving an energy massage (described in Chapter 5), you may find yourself drawing blocked energy off into a different area of the body which can use it, or channelling the energy into the ground (like the 'earthing' of an electrical circuit) to be recycled. In the course of the work, energy may be released, and, if the process involves both thought and feeling, the release may develop into a clearance which results in a lasting change to the energy structure in and around the individual's body. In this way, the person massaging or 'healing' is effecting a transformation in the other. People can also transmute energy in their own bodies – working through fear, for example, to find their courage. As Ralph Metzner puts it in *Maps of Consciousness*, 'The capability of biological life forms, and especially man, to act as

energy transformers is one of the key concepts of esoteric philosophy.'
The implications of such an approach are both personal and
political. On the individual level, it points to a new 'alternative' route
to good health and self-knowledge which attracts growing interest as
the limitations of mechanistic allopathic approaches to medicine
become more apparent. The health and well-being of the mass of the
people are among the fundamentals of socialism; if there are
alternative methods which can improve or supplement conventional
medicine, they need to be pursued. But if healing can be seen as a
process of turning 'negative' energy into 'positive', what are the
implications writ large in the political sphere, where the issue is the
'healing' of society? One of the Greenham Common peace camp
posters showed a photograph of policemen looking in dismay and
bewilderment at some women protesters who had tied themselves up
in 'webs' of string and were lying passively on the ground. Beside the
picture was a quote from Virginia Woolf's *Three Guineas*: 'We can best
help you to prevent war not by repeating your words and following
your methods but by finding new words and creating new methods.'
Pacifists have argued that we cannot answer the state's violence with
similar violence, or combat hatred with hatred: we can never 'beat
them at their own game', and to employ their tactics undermines the
values that are being fought for. The woman with the broken window,
however, in the earlier example, continues to be active: she transforms
the hatred directed at her into something she can own, and which
will motivate her to continue her political work. The stereotype of
the pacifist spiritual life is challenged by the symbol, prominent in
the Castaneda books and current in some other 'new age' thinking,
of the spiritual person as a warrior. As Dane Rudhyar puts it in *From
Humanistic to Transpersonal Astrology*, 'Any individual seen as a
"transforming agent" is essentially a warrior – whether he or she
acts at a physical, cultural, social, religious or "occult" level . . .' The
'warrior' is involved in the world and cannot be afraid of getting
mucky hands, whether massaging someone with a serious illness or
dealing with police brutality on a picket line. The dilemma is not
between 'pacifism' and 'violent struggle'; that is a question of situation
and strategy. The question is whether we respond to our situation with
a blind reaction of 'tit for tat', or whether we can bring a different
quality into what we do.

These are not things that *might* happen, but things that can and *do*
happen, often unrecognised. Despite many difficulties and divisions
at the peace camp, such a spirit has been evident at Greenham

Common. There women, subjected to prolonged abuse, attacks and threats from military and local men, decorated the nuclear base's fence with photos of their loved ones, celebrated their own rituals, and harassed the military by numerous inventive actions, such as padlocking the military in, and going on midnight jaunts driving army vehicles around inside the base. Unarmed and ostensibly powerless, they created their own anti-military strategies to embarrass the military and raise public awareness about the nuclear issue. While Christian language speaks of transformation in terms of prayer, blessing, redemption and forgiveness, grassroots political activitists provide their own examples of returning hate with honour and humour. People involved in the ecology movement talk in terms of the redemption of the earth. And is it so different from prayer when people send thoughts, energy and telegrams or carry the names of political prisoners persecuted by oppressive régimes? A Chilean woman, Pata, who had been held in secret prisons in Chile told, after her reappearance, that while she was 'disappeared' she knew of letters and pressure on her behalf by Amnesty International groups, and it helped her very much. The transforming qualities of energy, which can infuse any activity however simple, are often experienced but rarely identified as such; as one witness described an anti-government trade union demonstration in the huge square of Terreiro do Paço, Lisbon: 'When I first saw the crowd from the platform, they were a sea of faces, like one big body, almost molecular. And they were sort of electric. I couldn't see it, but I could feel electricity coming off them.' We lack the vocabulary to chart such experiences.

In this book I have suggested how the notion of an immanent spirituality relocates authority at the grass roots and highlights humans' connection with each other and the world around. I have also described how the model of 'subtle energy' offers ways to heal, relax, replenish, to align yourself with a purpose, to prepare for and carry through a task, to deal with difficulties and to communicate. We all have the ability to act intuitively, to be in tune with the essence of our own energy and the energy of others, to heal ourselves and others through acting in harmony with forces present in the universe. 'Spirit' is simply energy present in our bodies and in the world around us. Through practice and awareness we can learn to tune in to it and recognise its workings in our lives and activities. It is a reservoir of transforming power which is there for the asking, and if we want to make a better world we cannot afford to turn our backs on it.

Book References

Page numbers relate to passages referred to or quoted, listed in most cases in the order in which they have been used. Where there are numerous references to the same text, or where the context may not be obvious, I have indicated the subject matter.

Adler, Margot, *Drawing Down the Moon: Witches, Druids, Goddess-worshippers, and Pagans in America Today*, Beacon Press, Boston, 1986, pp. 41-93 (on broken continuity of witchcraft traditions), viii (on polytheism), ix (on sin), 6-8 (catching fish) (first publ. Viking Press, New York, 1979).

Bateson, Patrick, 'The Biology of Co-operation', in *New Society*, 31 May 1984, pp. 343-5.

Blackwell, Trevor and Jeremy Seabrook, *The Politics of Hope: Britain at the End of the Twentieth Century*, Faber, London and Boston, 1988, pp. 64, 86, 94.

Blake, William, 'The Marriage of Heaven and Hell' (etched c. 1793), in *William Blake: a Selection of Poems and Letters*, edited with an intro. by J. Bronowski, Penguin, Harmondsworth, Middxx, 1958, pp. 97, 96, 109.

Boff, Leonardo and Clodovis, *Introducing Liberation Theology*, Burns and Oates/Search Press, Tunbridge Wells, Kent, and Orbis Books, Mary Knoll, NY, 1987 (first publ. Editora Vozes, Petropolis, Brazil, 1986).

Bottomore, T. B. (trans. and ed.), *Karl Marx: Early writings*, C. A. Watts, London, 1963, pp. 127, 157.

Breasted, James Henry, *The Conquest of Civilization*, Harper and Brothers, New York and London, 1938, p. 105 (first publ. 1926).

Capra, Fritjof, *The Tao of Physics: an Exploration of the Parallels between Modern Physics and Eastern Mysticism*, Shamba-La, Berkeley, 1975.

—— Speaking in a radio interview broadcast, *Minding the Earth*, produced by The Strong Center, Berkeley, CA, Spring 1981.

Castaneda, Carlos, *Journey to Ixtlan: the Lessons of Don Juan*, Penguin, Harmondsworth, Middx, 1974, p. 227.

—— *Tales of Power*, Penguin, Harmondsworth, Middx, 1976, pp. 138-9, 153, 171 and *passim* (all on *nagual* and *tonal*).

—— *The Eagle's Gift*, Pocket Books, New York, 1982, pp. 279 (precepts of the rule), Chapters 10 and 14 (on *stalking*), 236 (hanging in tree), 287-9 (on recapitulation).

—— *The Power of Silence*, Pocket Books, New York and London, 1987, pp. 69ff.

Christ, Carol P. and Judith Plaskow (eds.) *Womanspirit Rising: a Feminist Reader in Religion*, Harper and Row, San Francisco, 1979, pp. 131ff (on reconstructing Christian and Jewish traditions).

Collins, Sheila, 'Theology in the Politics of Appalachian Women', in Carol P. Christ and Judith Plaskow (eds.) *Womanspirit Rising* (see above), pp. 149-158.

Collin-Smith, Joyce, *Call No Man Master: Fifty years of spiritual adventures, in praise of teachers but wary of gurus*, Gateway Books, Bath, 1988.

Co-Counselling, see Harvey Jackins, *The Reclaiming of Power*, Rational Island Publishers, Seattle, 1983.

Country Women, April 1974 ('Spirituality' issue), publ. Country Women, Box 51, Albion, CA 95410, p. 1 (editorial).

Daly, Mary, 'After the Death of God the Father: Women's Liberation and the Transformation of Christian Consciousness', in Carol P. Christ and Judith Plaskow (eds.) *Womanspirit Rising* (see above), pp. 53-62; I quote pp. 60, 55.

Darwin, Charles Robert, *On the Origin of the Species by Means of Natural Selection: Or the Preservation of Favoured Races in the Struggle for Life*, Harvard University Press, Cambridge, MA, 1964 (first publ. Murray, London, 1859). See also Peter J. Bowler, *Theories of Human Evolution: A Century of Debate 1844-1944*, Blackwell, Oxford, 1987.

Dewey, John, Marianne S. Andersen and Louis M. Savary, *Passages: a Guide for Pilgrims of the Mind*, Turnstone Press, London, 1974, p. 33.

Dobbs, Jack P.B., *The Desert and the Market Place: a Quaker Booklet*, Quaker Home Service, Friends House, Euston Road, London, 1984.

Dowling, Colette, *The Cinderella Complex: Women's Hidden Fear of Independence*, Fontana Paperback, William Collins, Glasgow, 1982.

Einstein, Albert and Leopold Infeld, *The Evolution of Physics*, Cambridge University Press, Cambridge, 1971, p. 31 (quoted in Gary Zukav, *The Dancing Wu Li Masters* (see below), p. 35).

Engels, F., see K. Marx and F. Engels, *Selected Works in One Volume*, Lawrence and Wishart, London, 1968, p. 705.

Ferrucci, Piero, *What We May Be: the Visions and Techniques of Psychosynthesis*, Turnstone Press, Wellingborough, Northants, 1982, p. 88.

Fiorenza, Elisabeth Schüssler, 'Feminist Spirituality, Christian Identity, and Catholic Vision' in Carol P. Christ and Judith Plaskow (eds) *Womanspirit Rising* (see above), pp. 136–48; I quote p. 143.

Fishing, see under Wilson.

Garcia, Jo and Sara Maitland (eds) *Walking on the Water: Women Talk About Spirituality*, Virago, London, 1983.

Gold, Martha, 'The Dialectics of Astrology', in *Liberation*, Fall 1976.

Gleick, James, *Chaos: Making a New Science*, Cardinal/Sphere, Penguin, Harmondsworth, Middx, 1988, p. 8.

Gorman, George H., *Introducing Quakers*, Quaker Home Service, Friends House, Euston Road, London, 1981.

Goodison, Lucy, 'Soul Supermarket', in *City Limits* No 37, June 18–24, 1982, p. 55.

Gutiérrez, Gustavo, *A Theology of Liberation: History, Politics and Salvation*, trans. and ed. Sister C. Inda and J. Eagleson, SCM Press, London, 1974 (first publ. as *Teologiá de la Liberación, Perspectivas*, CEP, Lima, 1971).

Hawking, Stephen W., *A Brief History of Time: from the Big Bang to Black Holes*, Bantam, London, New York, Toronto, Sydney, Auckland, 1988.

Hobsbawm, E.J., in his Introduction to Karl Marx, *Pre-Capitalist Economic Formations* (see below), p. 12.

Hooper, Lawrence David, interviewed by Caroline Drewes in 'Dropping out from a life of spiritual quest', in *San Francisco Sunday Examiner and Chronicle*, 3 Aug. 1980, p. 2.

Keller, Evelyn Fox, 'How Gender Matters, or, Why it's so hard for us to count past two', Northeastern University and MIT, August 1985, pp. 12–14, 19–20. Now publ. in Jan Harding, *Perspectives on Gender and Science*, The Falmer Press, 1986, but see also Evelyn Fox Keller, *A Feeling for the Organism: the Life and Work of Barbara McClintock*, W.H. Freeman, San Francisco, 1983.

Lan, David, *Guns and Rain: Guerrillas and Spirit Mediums in Zimbabwe*, James Currey, London, and University of California Press, Berkeley and Los Angeles, 1985.

Leonard, Alison, 'Gnosticism and the limitations of human knowledge', in the *Guardian*, 29 May 1989, p. 25.

Liberation Theology, see under Leonardo Boff and Gustavo Gutiérrez; see also *New Internationalist* No. 155, Jan. 1986 (issue on 'The Flame of Faith: Religion, politics and everyday life').

Lienhardt, Godfrey, *Divinity and Experience: the Religion of the Dinka*, Clarendon Press, Oxford, 1961, pp. 210 (on Aiwel Longar), 54 (on ambivalence of experience), 282–3 (on 'magical' practices), 105 (on massage of warriors).

MacManaway, Bruce, with Johanna Turcan, *Healing: The Energy that Can Restore Health*, Thorsons, Wellingborough, Northants, 1983, p. 119.

Maitland, Sara, interviewed by Leonie Caldecott in 'Searching for a soul without going into retreat', the *Guardian*, 21 Sept. 1983, p. 18. See Jo Garcia and Sara Maitland (eds.) *Walking on the Water: Women Talk About Spirituality* (see above).

Marx, Karl, 'Contribution to the Critique of Hegel's Philosophy of Right. Introduction', in K. Marx and F. Engels, *On Religion*, Foreign Languages Publishing House, Moscow, 1957, pp. 41–58; I quote p. 42, (article first publ. in *Deuitsch-Französische Jahrbücher*, 1844).

—— *Pre-Capitalist Economic Formations*, trans. Jack Cohen and with an Intro. by E.J. Hobsbawm, Lawrence and Wishart, London, 1964, pp. 14, 96, 84–5 (all on individualisation).

Mauss, Marcell, *A General Theory of Magic*, trans. Robert Brain, Routledge and Kegan Paul, London and Boston, 1972, pp. 141–3 and *passim* (I quote p. 141) (first publ. Presses Universitaires de France, 1950).

Metzner, Ralph, *Maps of Consciousness*, Collier Macmillan, New York and

London, 1971, pp. 54 (on retina), 107, 109 (on transforming energy).

Morris, Desmond, *The Naked Ape*, Corgi/Transworld, London, 1968.

Newton, Isaac, quoted in *Proceedings of the Royal Society of London*, Vol. 54, 1893, p. 381.

New York Times and 'people's editions' of other North American newspapers, see *El Salvador On Line*, news summary of the Washington Center for Central American Studies, Washington, DC, 13 Feb. 1989, p. 6.

Norwood, Robin, *Women Who Love Too Much: When you keep wishing and hoping he'll change*, Arrow Books, London, 1986.

Pribram, Karl H., 'The New Neurology and the Biology of Emotion', in *American Psychologist*, 22, No. 10, 1967, p. 834; quoted in Ralph Metzner, *Maps of Consciousness* (see above), p. 81.

Quakers, see Jack Dobbs, *The Desert and the Market Place*, and George Gorman, *Introducing Quakers* (see above).

Reich, Wilhelm, *The Mass Psychology of Fascism*, trans. V.R. Carfagno, Penguin, Harmondsworth, Middx, 1983 (first publ. 1933).

Reincarnation, see Joseph Head and S.L. Cranston (comp. and ed.) *Reincarnation: an east-west anthology*, The Theosophical Publishing House, Wheaton, ILL, Madras, London, 1985 (first publ. 1961).

Riesman, Paul, 'A Comprehensive Anthropological Assessment', in Daniel C. Noel (ed.) *Seeing Castaneda: Reactions to the 'Don Juan' writings of Carlos Castaneda*, Capricorn Books, G.P. Putnam's Sons, New York, 1976, pp. 46–53 (I quote p. 49) (first publ. in *New York Times Book Review*, 1972).

Roberts, Jane, *The Nature of Personal Reality: A Seth Book*, Prentice-Hall, NJ, 1974, pp. 160–1, 234–8, 243–4, 248 (all on aggression), 431, 435–8, 444–5 (all on reincarnation happening simultaneously), 443 (on the 24-hour period as a lifetime), 160–79 (on guilt and compassion), 344, 347, 435 (all on the point of power in the present), 354 (on changing beliefs), 31 (on changing things), 77, 355, 359ff (all on hypnosis).

—— *The Nature of the Psyche: Its Human Expression*, A Seth Book, Prentice-Hall, NJ, 1979, pp. 22 (on elegance of necessary physical acts), 15–16 (on trees in a book), 216 (on desire).

Rowbotham, Sheila, *The Past is Before Us: Feminism in Action Since the 60s*, Pandora, London, 1989.

Rudhyar, Dane, *From Humanistic to Transpersonal Astrology*, The Seed Center, Palo Alto, CA, 1975, quoted in Martha Gold, 'The Dialectics of Astrology' (see above).

Ruether, Rosemary Radford, 'Motherearth and the Megamachine: A Theology of Liberation in a Feminine, Somatic and Ecological Perspective', in Carol P. Christ and Judith Plaskow (eds.) *Womanspirit Rising* (see above), pp. 43–52; I quote p. 52.

Ryan, Joanna, *Feminism and Therapy: A Lecture given in memory of Pam Smith,*

7 May 1983, Department of Applied Social Studies, The Polytechnic of North London, 1983.

Shauna, 'Book Reviews' in *Link Up*, June–Aug. 1987, p. 27.

Sontag, Susan, *Illness as Metaphor*, Allen Lane, London, 1979 (first publ. Farrar, Straus and Giroux, New York, 1978).

— *Aids and its Metaphors*, Allen Lane, London, 1988.

— talking to Michael Ignatieff on 'The Late Show', BBC2 Television, 14 Mar. 1989.

Starhawk, *Dreaming the Dark: Magic, Sex and Politics*, Beacon, Boston, 1982, p. 98.

Steward, Fred, 'New Times, Green Times', in *Marxism Today*, Mar. 1989, pp. 14–17.

Tawney, R.H., *Religion and the Rise of Capitalism*, Penguin, Harmondsworth, Middx, 1984 (first publ. J. Murray, London, 1926).

Vaneigem, Raoul, *The Revolution of Everyday Life Part* 1, no publ. or date given, p. 13 (first publ. as *'Traite de Savoir-vivre à l'usage des jeunes generations'*).

Von Dürckheim, Karlfried Graf, *Hara: the Vital Centre of Man*, trans. S.-M. von Kospoth, Allen and Unwin, London, Boston and Sydney, 1985, p. 35 (first publ. 1956).

Wheeler, John, in J.A. Wheeler, K.S. Thorne and C. Misner, *Gravitation*, Freeman, San Francisco, p. 1273 (quoted in Gary Zukav, *The Dancing Wu Li Masters* (see below), p. 54).

Williams, Raymond, *Problems in Materialism and Culture, Selected Essays*, Verso/New Left Books, London, 1980, pp. 83–4.

Williams, Drid, 'The Brides of Christ', in Shirley Ardener (ed.) *Perceiving Women*, J.M. Dent, London, Toronto and Melbourne; Halstead Press, New York, 1977, pp. 105–25; I quote p. 115.

Wilson, John, Presenting 'Go Fishing' on Channel Four Television, 30 May 1988.

Woolf, Virginia, *Three Guineas (On the part that women can play in the prevention of war)*, Hogarth Press, London, 1938, p. 260.

Zukav, Gary, *The Dancing Wu Li Masters: an Overview of the New Physics*, Rider/Hutchinson, London, 1979, pp. 199, 200, 177.

7

CRETE AND GREECE
The Story of the Separation of Heaven and Earth

If we want to broaden our sense of the possible uses and forms of symbols, it is inspiring to look to other cultures where symbols were shaped very differently from our own. This is not to say that we will want to appropriate those symbols and transplant them wholesale to our society; they grew under particular conditions and may have no organic place in ours. But the fact that someone, somewhere, used symbols in a different way throws light on the relationship between symbols and society, and opens up a possibility for their movement and change.

In recent years many women have been reading between the lines in the history books, recognising that these usually represent a one-sided version of the past which reflects the viewpoint of individuals of particular race, class and sex. Delving beneath traditional 'history', women have uncovered 'herstory', a version which reveals details of women's lives and images of female power neglected or omitted in male accounts. Very often in our indignation and excitement at rectifying the imbalance we tackle the centuries with a broad sweep of the brush, but in this chapter I am going to write a small and meticulous piece of 'herstory', based on my PhD thesis published as *Death, Women and the Sun*. I am going to look at an early period in Greek history, from 3000 to 700 BC.

I shall start on the island of Crete, set in the south of the Aegean Sea. Here a local indigenous population was thriving from around 3000 until 1600 BC in which women played very different roles, and symbols took very different forms from those we know today. Here we find a society which was in many ways unusual: a society where women predominated in religious and perhaps social life, where some settlements seem to have been communal, and where there is surprisingly little evidence of military weapons and fortifications. In investigating the available evidence for a goddess or goddesses and the images in which female power was expressed, we find not just a different symbolic framework but a completely different notion of religion and the divine.

The Early Cretans: Clearing the Ground

At around 2800 BC we find these early Cretans carrying on a centuries-old way of life, farming in villages. Over the next thousand years there was a gradual development, the culture becoming more sophisticated until we find the 'early palaces' being built at Knossos, Mallia and Phaistos from about 1900 BC onwards. It is not until about 1600 BC at the earliest that the Greek mainlanders known as the 'Mycenaeans' had any substantial influence on Cretan culture. So all the Cretan material I am discussing in this section will be earlier than 1600 BC, from that long early period over which simple farming communities gradually developed into more complex settlements culminating in the building of small palaces. For the purposes of this section we can forget the later splendid palace of Knossos whose reconstructed ruins are visited by every tourist in Crete. We can forget the famous frescoes of bull-jumping. We can forget the myths of King Minos and his craftsman Daedalus, his daughter Ariadne, and Theseus who fought the monster Minotaur. All these belong to the later period. For the purposes of this section we can forget the famous large pots with exuberant octopus decorations. We can forget the famous 'throne rooms' at Knossos and the debate about whether it was ruled by a king or a queen, a priest or a priestess.

Instead we are going back in time, to when Knossos was little more than a village. In this early period the archaeological remains are not as spectacular. The early hieroglyphic and Linear A scripts have not been deciphered, so we have no language, no written evidence, no official records, poems, prayers, sums or shopping lists. Instead we have bones and stones, pots and pans. We have wall foundations, little clay figures and tiny sealstones engraved with fascinating pictures. We have traces of fire in one place, and a loomweight in another. We have many graves; but from the early phases of our period only a handful of settlement sites have been properly excavated. There is not much evidence from which to piece together our herstory. But in Crete at this time, as on the mainland and the Cycladic islands before any invasions from the north could ever have happened, we can be sure that we are looking at a society based on different structures from those of the patriarchal Mycenaeans, a society where symbols could have been formulated and experienced in a very different way.

While we are forgetting King Minos and the bull frescoes, there are some other preconceptions we can leave behind. One is the idea that these early Cretans, or 'Minoans' as they are called, lived in some kind of golden age. It is true that in the surviving evidence they have left much to delight us and warm our hearts; but they can also show a face which is harsh and sometimes macabre. Another preconception is that Minoan society was matriarchal. If only there were enough evidence about this early period for us to state with certainty who ruled or how! We are approaching a jigsaw with many pieces lost. Great care is needed as we fill in the missing pieces to gain some picture of the society and symbols of these prehistoric people.

It is at this juncture that I feel Marx's ideas have something to offer to this exploration of the past. While some feminists have found Jung's forays into the unconscious sources of symbolism more helpful, Marx's materialist approach provides a firm path into the material evidence with which I feel any investigation must start. His model of an 'economic base' (the means of producing food and other necessaries, ownership, money systems) which to some extent shapes the 'superstructure' (such as the laws, customs, institutions, religion and culture of a society), provides us with an anchor. It helps us to connect symbol systems with the everyday reality of the people who use them. As I pointed out in Chapter 1, the relationship described is a subtle and dialectical one in which the social and the economic cannot be divorced. Thus the symbols of this early society may not be crudely 'caused' by, but can be seen in some meaningful relationship to, its means of economic survival. The best I can do here is to look at this society as a whole and to pay particular attention to those questions which are often left out of a study of symbols: questions like 'Where did the food come from?', 'Who held power and made decisions?', 'Who did what work?' and 'Who owned what?'

My main focus is on Crete, but my range of vision includes the whole of Greece and I will draw in evidence from the wider area, especially the neighbouring Cyclades, where it throws light. I will start on a sun-baked clifftop overlooking the Libyan sea where a small settlement was established for several hundred years between about 2600 and 2150 BC: it is a site called Fournou Korifi which lies a few kilometres from the village of Myrtos in south Crete.

On the high slope the criss-crossing, largely ruined, stone walls mark out the remains of over 90 small rooms or areas. There were corridors and staircases, and traces of red plaster were found on some of the inner walls. When excavations began here, it was assumed that the ruins were of a wealthy man's mansion, but after some years of detailed work the excavator, Peter Warren, concluded that what he was digging up was one settlement complex, housing about 120 people. Seeing no trace of individual self-contained houses and no larger room such as might be suitable for a lord or chief, he suggested in his book *Myrtos* that it might be some form of communal living unit: 'A settlement, then, in the form of a single large complex without separately defined houses suggests a social organisation based on a single large unit, a clan or tribe living communally and perhaps not differentiated into individual families, and quite without any chief or ruler'.

From the evidence he unearthed, Warren estimated that these people had up to 1000 olive trees, cultivated over 12–15 acres, and grew barley, wheat and grapevines. Cereal was probably a large part of their diet and they seem to have made wine. They also kept sheep, goats and a few cattle. They ate some shell-food. They stored oil, olives and cereals. The discovery of eight potter's turntables suggests that they made pots, mostly turning them by hand. Spindle and loom equipment tells us that they spun and wove. They may also have undertaken dyeing, in red and possibly purple. They must have traded in from elsewhere their metalwork and obsidian (a hard stone used for cutting). The surviving number of weapons and implements do not suggest a warlike way of life.

So much for what we think of as 'economic' in a narrow sense. What else happened in the lives of these people? There are several eating rooms scattered throughout the settlement, recognisable by the high concentration of animal bones and limpet shells found in them. Some rooms seem to have been used for ritual: one contained a little human figurine as well as an unusual hearth, an unusual pottery ring and fragments of a human male skull. Another room held some little models of bulls' heads (which are often found in ritual contexts). Another, which has been described as a shrine, contained a strangely shaped small clay figure of a woman holding a jug in her left arm. She is really a pot in the shape of a woman. Warren calls her a 'household goddess'. This raises the big question about the most central symbol of the female: the 'Goddess' – or was she?

What Kind of a Goddess?

From the earliest times in the Mediterranean area, model figures of women far outnumber those of men. The female figurines from the early Aegean belong to a long line of women who reach back way before the neolithic time, and who are also spread far and wide over many areas of the prehistoric world. Their obvious significance has led people to see them as representations of a goddess, or even 'the Goddess'. Books like Erich Neumann's *The Great Mother* and, more recently, Marija Gimbutas' *The Language of the Goddess*, have lent weight to the idea that she was a universal phenomenon. But what kind of goddess was she? Was she really a goddess? And are these figures literal representations of her in the way that we imagine?

The Aegean figures, made out of bone or shell, stone or pottery, certainly take on many different shapes and qualities: sometimes they are lifelike, sometimes schematic; sometimes they are austere and angular; sometimes they are basically circular. Some are hardly more than rounded stones. Sometimes they are oblong and waisted, sometimes they wear a bell-shaped skirt. Sometimes they are pregnant, though they hardly ever hold a child. Sometimes they appear in joined pairs; the archaeologist Jürgen Thimme has suggested these may represent mother and daughter. Whatever the style in which these female figures are portrayed, their sex and reproductive functions are usually clearly emphasised. Sometimes the 'slit' or 'hole' of the vagina is strongly featured, sometimes the inverted triangle of the pubic area dominates the body. Sometimes breasts and belly grow until the whole figure becomes like a pregnant ball, with a strange look of the unborn foetus about it. In some cases what we see is actually a pot made in the shape of a woman. Sometimes little legs taper away beneath the all-important belly or pubic area, sometimes they disappear altogether. The emphasis on the sexuality and fertility of these female figures is unmistakable, and some historians have been quick to suggest that they played a central role in a religion concerned with the fertility of vegetation. We often find generalised statements like this one, from B. C. Dietrich's *The Origins of Greek Religion:*

The majority of idols from shrines and sanctuaries representing the figure of a Mother Goddess are quite explicit in their significance . . . From at least the later periods of the Stone Age, ideas of fertility of vegetation and men [sic] were current in the settlements about and near the Aegean. This religious concept may have been universally shared by primitive cultures but more probably took its origin in the Near and Middle East . . .

But are these figures actual representations of a goddess? Here we have to tread very carefully and beware our own prejudices and the preconceptions created by our culture. These prejudices may be expressed in various ways. Some historians discount these images and the idea of a goddess altogether. They play down the social implications of such clear evidence of respect for women. Some writers try to argue the figures away as 'secular' or treat them dismissively as the objects of 'primitive' or 'superstitious' practices. Some traditional historians reveal their prejudice by referring to these figures as 'idols' or 'fertility symbols' which were used in 'cult' or 'nature' worship, for 'magical not religious purposes' (in Nilsson's words) – as if the early Greeks made such distinctions! It is not until the clear appearance of the male god Zeus that the word 'religion' is thought suitable. The assumption is that a religion which emphasises the spirit and centres round a male god is superior to one centred around plant-growing, crop abundance and female fertility: the latter apparently deserves only the name of 'cult' or 'superstition'.

Other writers, however, respect the clear evidence of the significance of women in religion, and feminists in particular have been quick to pick up the idea of a 'Great Goddess' similar in stature to, and a direct counter to, the male 'God' who is the focus of western religion. But once again we have to beware our preconceptions. Because of our experience of the religions current in our own society, we tend to assume that the object of a serious religion has to be a monolithic figure, a 'capital G' Goddess. We assume that if she was worth anything she must have been *one* figure; we assume she must have been imagined in *human form;* we assume she must have been seen as an *abstract*, an all-embracing and all-powerful entity, separate from the material world and the lives of human beings. Even to formulate the notion of a 'Mother Goddess' is a concept. We tend to assume that deities worth their salt are larger than life and, like the Christian God, in possession of some superior moral power.

We have to abandon these preconceptions and go back to the drawing board. From what is known of primitive religion, it seems its objects of worship do not usually take the form of anthropomorphic gods imagined in the shape of human beings. More often there are beliefs which envisage spirits or numinous forces living in plants, animals, stones, streams, stars, the wind, the sun and moon, and other natural elements. It was the anthropologist Tylor who first gave currency to the word 'animism' to describe such beliefs; the word 'naturism' has also been used of such religions which addressed themselves to the phenomena of nature (see Durkheim's discussion in *The Elementary Forms of the Religious Life*). These spirits or forces immanent in the natural world are often seen as affecting fertility in farming, the weather and other aspects of human life. Ideas about the decay and revival of nature often exist before they are developed into a complex schema of characters. Divine characters emerge only as natural forces gradually become personified. This process may reflect the changing relationship of human beings to the natural world: perhaps their growing sense of importance in relation to it as they increasingly master natural forces; perhaps a change in values which leads them to see everything in human terms. As the archaeologist Jane Harrison has pointed out in *Themis*, at first a thing is regarded as sacred, and then out of that sanctity a god or goddess emerges. From a plant a person grows, a plant deity in human shape who may carry a branch as her or his attribute.

Now, like the phenomena of nature which they inhabit, these original spirits are not one but many. The idea of one all-embracing Mother Goddess existing in the distant past is appealing in its neatness and simplicity, but the roots of religion are just as likely to be found to lie in pluralism as in monotheism. These early people did not necessarily have the social or political experience of centralisation and hierarchy which we have. The idea of one 'Nature Goddess' or 'Mother Nature' depends on the concept of 'Nature' being one entity – a concept which, as Raymond Williams points out, is itself the product of a particular culture and moment in history rather than being a self-apparent or prior truth. In *Problems in Materialism and Culture* he points out that this singular formation of the term 'Nature' is based on certain assumptions in its description of the world. One function of seeing nature as a unified entity has been the search for an 'essential principle' behind and distinct from her physical manifestations. Another result has been a growing sense of separation and alienation between 'Nature' and 'Man', which Williams traces not only from the domination and exploitation of nature by recent industry and urbanism but also from the growing complexity of our interactions with the natural world. There is no evidence that this abstraction of the idea of 'Nature' as a divine principle, separate from its physical manifestations, was part of Early Bronze Age religion in Greece.

Take, for example, the place of worship. We are used to specially built churches and cathedrals. In Crete at this time the evidence suggests that many religious rituals took place outside – in groves, caves, beside tombs and on mountains. Indoor shrines are found tucked away in corners of homes and settlements, and there is debate among historians as to whether there were any separately constructed shrines at all. This may have implications for the organisation of religion. If shrines were in homes, what would be the role of an institutionalised priesthood? Perhaps the divine, like other concerns and activities, was only just beginning to become the preserve of a specialised minority. Religion was clearly much more part of the natural world and the everyday life of the worshippers than that which we think of as religion today. There are no huge temples, and none of the surviving figures which could represent a divinity are larger than life size. The dead are buried with figurines of a small, companionable size. Whatever divine spirits were at the centre of the cult, they clearly were not inflated in such a way as to dwarf or terrify their worshippers. Even our vocabulary, with words like 'worshippers' or 'the faithful', may be inappropriate. The surviving pictures of religious scenes do not suggest that these people approached the divine on their knees; we cannot assume that they humbled themselves, proclaimed their own worthlessness or prayed for forgiveness in the manner of Christian religious worshippers. In fact they seem to have carried out their religion mostly on their feet, often dancing, making free use of plants and other natural elements which had a religious significance for them.

We need to consider the possibility of a different kind of relationship between humans and divinity, and to imagine a divinity immanent in the natural world rather than authoritatively resident in the upper reaches of the heavens. A divinity embodied in the earth, birds, sea, plants, animals and weather is present, palpable and more familiar. People could love her or them as sometimes we now find ways of loving nature. Fear there may be, awe and wonder, but nature offers more accessible faces too. There is a difference between feeling yourself tiny in a huge cathedral and the experience of looking into a flower or even being caught in a storm. As humans we can perhaps sense a kinship between ourselves and other elements of the physical world to which we belong; a kinship which is lost once a divinity becomes an institutionalised disembodied spirit with a power which is elevated and divorced from our physical experience.

So we have to be open to the idea of a divinity linked with physical nature and natural processes rather than with moral sanctions. We also have to be open to the possibility of many rather than one. The anthropologist Peter Ucko has pointed out the assumptions which led scholars to identify the many female figurines from the earlier, neolithic, period as representations of a 'Mother Goddess', and asks why the many animal and few male figurines have not equally been considered as possible divinities. He stresses the diversity of the neolithic figurines, and suggests that they might have had various uses as dolls, initiation figures, or for sympathetic magic. The neolithic Cretans may have seen the divine only in the phenomena of nature, and not in human form at all.

How then are we to think of the many beautiful female figurines which have survived from the early phases of the Aegean Bronze Age? Are they representations of a goddess, goddesses, or some other kind of divinity? Or did they have a completely different significance? The figurines are mostly found buried with the dead, but the fact that several show signs of repair suggests that they had a long and valued period of use by the living before they went to the grave with their owner. Many historians believe they are images of deities, others have suggested that they are votive offerings to a deity, or represent a kind of divine protectress or nurse who cares for the dead on their journey. Let's look briefly at what we know about them. Most of the evidence comes from graves on the Cycladic islands, where in any one grave we find varying numbers of figurines, ranging from none to 14. This suggests a variety of different ideas and religious practices rather than one unified concept. The paired figures also argue against a single Goddess: a monotheistic divinity does not come in pairs. Another interesting feature is that in the Cycladic graves the figures often bear traces of red paint. Many of them are made with pointed feet and cannot stand. In graves they are often found lying on their front or back. Very occasionally they seem to have lain in a dish or 'cradle', a posture reminiscent of the 'sleeping lady' type of figurine from contemporary Malta, where incubation may have been part of a 'goddess' cult. A horizontal deity is very different in quality from a vertical one, potent but not dominating. Whether they lay, were strung, held or carried, it is clear that these figures did not stand up to be worshipped. It also seems that they had a close relationship to the individual. They were perhaps kept about the person as a protective amulet, and placed in the grave as a precious and personal possession of the deceased which should not be separated from her or him. As such they were perhaps images not of a deity but of the individual concerned, as George Thomson suggested in his book, *The*

Prehistoric Aegean: 'As a representation of the worshipper they were dedicated by her in order to place her under the goddess's protection. This was done in both times of actual danger, sickness or childbirth, and in times of imaginary danger, such as initiation, marriage or bereavement.' The strongest argument for this view seems to lie in the way the figurines were placed in the grave. They were not generally placed reverentially, but mixed with other items or even pinned beneath them. Sometimes they were wedged between the stones of the grave walls and sometimes they appear to have been ritually broken before they were placed in the tomb. One excavator, Doumas, suggests in his book on Early Cycladic art that as the idol was a source of power to a person during lifetime, so at death it had to be buried with that person and at the same time neutralised in some way (by breaking?) to remove its power, which could be frightening in the hands of a dead person. What he does not explain, however, is why in this case so few male figures have been found. We would have to think of the figure not as a literal representation of the dead person but as a symbol of some life principle, vital force or essence associated with the individual, like a genius or spirit-figure, perhaps approximating to what we call the 'soul', which may have been regarded as female in both men and women.

Ultimately none of these theories is convincing, but what is clear is that these figures had some religious significance. Moreover they strongly suggest that the religious formations of these early people took a predominantly female shape. Whether these figures are goddesses, priestesses, guardian spirits, worshippers, or just women, they all indicate how women and female fertility were viewed. Some may be divine, but all are important and most are strongly sexual. What strikes us most is the sense of substance and significance they convey. Adrienne Rich's book *Of Woman Born* includes a general discussion of prehistoric figurines. She describes the deep impression they make on a modern viewer:

> they express an attitude toward the female charged with awareness of her intrinsic importance, her depth of meaning, her existence at the very center of what is necessary and sacred. She is beautiful in ways we have almost forgotten, or which have become defined as ugliness. Her body possesses mass, interior depth, interior rest, and balance. She is not smiling; her expression is inward-looking or ecstatic . . .
>
> Let us try to imagine for a moment what sense of herself it gave

a woman to be in the presence of such images ... they told women that power, awesomeness, and centrality were theirs by nature, not by privilege or miracle; the female was primary.

Whether or not the early Cretans had a goddess or goddesses, it is clear that the female principle was central to their religion: it was central to the ideas and rituals through which they attempted to make sense of the world and their place in it. Whether or not that principle was venerated in human form, it seems to have imbued the landscape, linked with the plants and animals of the natural world. I will now explore how it manifested itself, which creatures and phenomena were seen as the carriers or symbols of that female power. While our society sees cuddly creatures like cats as essentially female, I will investigate which elements of nature this very different society saw as expressions of the female spirit.

In this investigation, we will find symbols which have become discredited as 'bad', like the snake, appearing as positive manifestations of female power. We will find some symbols which we use with a female connotation, like earth, appearing in an entirely different context. And we will find some symbols which are surprising to our stereotyped twentieth-century western notions of the female: symbols which we know overwhelmingly as attributes of men. The most striking of these is the sun.

A Female Sun?

There has been a general assumption among classical scholars that the sun and the moon were never very important in the religion of the ancient Greeks. Perhaps these scholars do not like anything which smacks so overtly of primitive paganism as sun worship to be associated with the founders of western civilisation; and this particular blind spot of theirs casts a shadow which blots out evidence as far back as the early period I am studying. Thus Martin Nilsson, in his huge volume on Minoan-Mycenaean religion, juxtaposes a long list of pictures of the sun and moon, many in significant and religious contexts, with his conclusion that 'In the Minoan world there are consequently no certain traces of a cult of the heavenly bodies'. Scholars accept that a sun deity figured large in the religion of the Near East, and that the sun was important in the religious ideas of the Egyptians at this early time. But they have perhaps regarded such ideas as too primitive or barbarian to be imputed to any inhabitants – however early – of Greek soil.

There is another prejudice operating here. For us, the sun is generally thought of as masculine and the moon as feminine. We have images such as 'the man in the moon' but in general the moon with its pale, changeable, subtle light is thought of as a woman, while the bold, bright sun is masculine. In later classical Greece too the sun was male, connected with a male charioteer Helios or with the archer god Apollo. If scholars look at all for a sun deity, they are looking for a male sun god. Surprisingly, feminists too tend to look to the past for evidence of a moon goddess and a sun god. Following Jung, writers like Esther Harding have encouraged us to identify the moon with 'the feminine principle'. Emphasis is laid on the moon's cyclical pattern of appearance, its wateriness, its qualities which are said to have affinity with our supposedly sensitive, emotional and cyclical 'eternal female nature'. Little reference is made to the fact that the moon is also essentially reflective rather than the creator of light, and that it is patently the less powerful of the two heavenly bodies. Nor is the moon alone in being cyclical: the sun too has its own cycles and subtleties of phase. In a culture like ours where women are valued chiefly as the sensitive reflectors of others' energy, it is perhaps not surprising that they are associated with the reflective qualities of the moon. But in a different society where women held more patent power and probably inspired more awe and respect for their ability to *create* (life through childbirth, as well as artefacts), the sun/moon symbolism may not have been the same as ours. We certainly cannot assume that it was. Indeed, George Thomson has described how the moon was often thought of as masculine in early societies, governing the waters and women's menstrual periods on a complementary principle. Some societies have apparently believed that women conceived from the moon, impregnated by swimming in the fertile waters which the moon governed. The anthropologist Lévi-Strauss, in 'The Sex of the Heavenly Bodies', has listed many examples from South American mythology where the moon is masculine and the sun feminine. The earliest Greek word for moon (far later, of course, than the period I am discussing) was masculine in gender. Perhaps prejudice and assumptions formed by our own society have created a mammoth blindness to early Greek evidence which has been staring scholars in the face. This evidence, which we will now investigate, suggests not only that the sun was important but also that it was female.

Thus a close look at early Cretan art suggests that the sun may have been one of the most common symbols. Many sun-like designs appear on seals (including motifs like the swastika which were used in other cultures to represent the sun) but scholars have been reluctant to connect these designs in any way with the sun. One problem is that it is hard to be sure which circular and radiant designs were actually intended to represent the sun, but we can get an idea from comparisons with contemporary Egyptian and Near Eastern solar symbols – which the Cretans knew – and from later Aegean pictures of the sun and moon together.

In several instances in the early Cretan material the sun appears to be playing a part in a cult scene, and in almost every case it is linked with a woman or women. In one seal engraving two women appear to be dancing to the sun; it is hard to find any other convincing interpretation of the scene shown in Figure 4. An interesting clue is that the position of the arms on this seal is identical to the contemporary Egyptian gesture of sun worship. In his huge book, *The Palace of Minos*, the archaeologist Arthur Evans actually described Figure 4 as depicting 'long-robed women . . . adoring a rayed solar symbol', but he never incorporated such activities into his explanation of Cretan religion as a whole.

A diadem from the Cyclades has been recognised by the archaeologist Colin Renfrew as showing two sun discs next to 'adorants with arms raised' (*The Emergence of Civilisation*). Another archaeologist, Christian Zervos, has also identified the scene as showing 'the adoration of the solar disc' (*L'Art des Cyclades*). A connection between women and the sun is clearly suggested by these and other representations. We might imagine the women to be female priestesses of a male sun deity, were it not that a much closer relationship is hinted at by the evidence of some strange objects which have been found in dozens, mainly on the Cycladic islands.

The use of these objects is completely obscure, and puzzled archaeologists have nicknamed them 'frying-pans'. They are made of stone or pottery and are shaped something like frying-pans with a very short handle, although they certainly were not used for frying. Their weight and shape would make them unwieldy for daily use. They are found mainly in graves, and a number of ritual uses have been suggested for them. For example, scholars have suggested that hides were stretched across the top as drums in the funeral procession, or that they were filled with water to symbolise a sea deity or to serve as mirrors keeping away evil spirits and protecting the dead in a manner common to other cultures. Whatever their use, a study of the decoration on the outside of these mysterious objects reveals a tell-tale feature: just above the handle can often be seen a clear delineation of the female pubic triangle. And on the belly of the vessel in several cases there is a clearly depicted sun. (See Figure 5).

Archaeologists have recognised the pubic triangle, and have recognised the sun. But they have lacked the breadth of vision to put the two together and recognise the possibility that on these objects the generative power of the female belly is symbolised by the sun.

They have generally ignored the archaeologist Zschietzschmann's identification of the handle as legs and the whole object as an idol, and equally Reynold Higgins' suggestion that the 'frying-pan' was a 'fertility charm in the form of a womb' (*Minoan and Mycenaean Art*). The appearance of the sun on these objects strongly suggests that it had a religious significance; while the juxtaposition of sun and pubic triangle suggests that the sun was not only saluted by women but was also more closely linked or identified with the fertile sexual female body. The designs on the 'frying-pans' combine with the designs on the seals to strengthen the evidence that in this early society the sun was holy and was also female.

In looking at these designs, we need to remember that these objects are not simply practical, everyday items but are among the most enduring, the most skilfully produced, the most significant craft products of this culture. Not only were the 'frying-pans' probably cult objects, but the seals also had a special importance. They were not purely decorative jewellery, nor was their practical and commercial application (for example, in sealing containers) the full extent of their use. Hanging perhaps round the neck or at the wrist of its owner, the sealstone served as an amulet providing magical protection and carrying particular information about her or him. As such, it went with the wearer to the grave. As the archaeologist Branigan writes in *The Foundations of Palatial Crete*:

> the designs on the seal-stones were probably the equivalent of a man's [sic] signature, and . . . the seal-stone was in a way a representative of its owner. This being so, the seal was probably identified with its owner and regarded as part of him. Its ritual significance could thus be quite considerable.

The identification of a stone and its symbols with the human being who wears it, this perception of the stone itself as magical and the symbols as having some deep affinity with the individual, goes beyond

Figure 4. 'Sun-dancers' on prism seal from Crete. The high collars indicate a ritual scene.

Figure 5. Pubic triangle and sun on 'frying-pan' from grave on the Cycladic island Syros. Drawing by Lucy Goodison.

Figure 6. Priestess or goddess beneath a tree with sun and moon above, on a gold ring from Mycenae.

Figure 7. Ritual boat scene: mourning figure with a tree and perhaps a shrine on a seal from East Crete. Drawing by Lucy Goodison.

Figure 8. Ritual of tree touching and bending over boulder or vessel (perhaps indicating mourning) on a gold ring from Phaistos, Crete.

Figure 9. Boat journey as part of the vegetation cycle on a ring from Crete.

our generally more mechanical and restricted use of symbols. The symbolism of early people can carry an intensity and power which is unfamiliar to us except possibly in the experience of poetry, mysticism or dreams. It is not simply that for an agricultural people living closely with nature, perceptions of the natural world and the connections experienced between different elements of it, and between them and humans, would have carried more acuity and impetus than for our jaded, predominantly urban, western culture. It is also that the surviving pictures from this early culture show that those elements of the natural world were central to ideas of religion and the sacred. Sun, moon, boughs, rocks, animals, were part of religious ritual and carried their own quality of numinousness or magic. They may have acted as the window for deeper meanings which we can only guess at.

Back to the Womb

If we followed the assumptions of our culture, we might suppose that the 'female' sun I have described would have been counterpoised in the Early Bronze Age Aegean by a 'male' earth. We might imagine an inverted version of our own system, with women superior and in the sky while men were lower and identified with the earth. Some cultures *have* seen the earth as male, but this is not one of them. As far as we can tell from the evidence, the relationship between sun and earth is not one of contrast, or even complementarity, but one of affinity. The ground was female too.

At many religious sites in Crete, we find offerings wedged into the ground, often stuck into cracks in the rock. Some vessels appear to have been designed especially so that libations or liquid offerings could be poured through them into the earth. Some early shrines, for example the peak sanctuary on Mount Juktas, centred on a chasm in the ground. Many of the early female figurines had no feet, suggesting that they were commonly stuck into the earth, as if emerging from it. The sanctity of the earth is clearly implied, and these examples suggest it was a female sanctity.

Historians have noticed that caves were used for burial and ritual many centuries after communities had stopped living in them, and some have taken this to indicate that the cave was in some way sacred in itself. They have also noticed that for many centuries the prehistoric Aegeans built burial places which recreated the shape of the cave. The *tholos* tombs of early Crete have been described by the historian Friedrich Matz in *Crete and Early Greece* as 'reproductions in architectural form of caves used for burials'. The main feature of the *tholos* is its circular domed or roofed cavity, with an entrance so small in many cases that it would need to be crawled through; and one explanation for the use of this shape is that it recreates not only the cave but the internal female anatomy with round womb and narrow birth canal. Although many graves in the Aegean area do not follow this pattern, and some are square, there is a tradition of graves with a passage leading to a circular cavity in the Cyclades and on the mainland too. The recurrence of circular and passage-shaped graves in different variations throughout the Aegean area seems to mean something, and if we look at the posture of the bodies in them we get another clue about what that meaning was.

In the *tholos* tombs he excavated in the Mesara area of south Crete, the Greek archaeologist Xanthoudides reports that the dead were generally placed in the first instance in a contracted position direct on the ground or in coffin-like cists of wood or clay. In the Cyclades, too, bodies were generally buried in a severely contracted position with legs bent up and forearms against the chest. In some burials the body is extended, but this contracted position is so frequent (even when the grave has plenty of space) that it calls for an explanation, and here the similarity to the position of the unborn foetus is hard to avoid.

Let us consider for a minute the practical day-by-day existence of these early Aegean people. From the time when gathering wild plant foods developed into planting and harvesting them, their survival depended on agriculture. It is generally thought that women were the first farmers and tillers, and it is possible (though by no means certain) that they were still responsible for this activity in the period I am discussing. What is certain is that crop growing depends on a seed being deposited in the earth, germinating, and growing forth with a new life. The earth is the fertile storehouse. We have noted the emphasis on fertility and pregnancy in the figurines of this culture. The link between the woman who bears children and the earth which bears trees, crops and life-sustaining fruits is a link often made in early societies. Such societies sometimes have the idea that the human body returns to the earth in death to await rebirth just as the vegetation retreats back into the earth in winter to await spring. At the prehistoric site of Çatal Hüyük in Turkey, the excavator James Mellaart found red ochre on bodies buried in the shrine, which has been interpreted as symbolising the possibility of rebirth from death, apparently on analogy with the blood-covered state of the newborn child. We cannot be sure whether corpses were painted red in the Aegean, though remains of red pigment in many Cycladic graves suggest that they may have been. For the Aegean, a series of clues build up, including tomb shape, the foetal position of the dead and perhaps the use of red pigment, which in isolation make no sense but taken together could outline a coherent scheme of belief concerning rebirth from the earth of the human dead. We will find another clue in the tomb doorways.

Archaeologists have noticed that many tombs in the Cyclades have prominent doorways, some of them too small for any practical use and therefore probably carrying a symbolic significance. The body was usually placed with its back along the long side of the grave facing the entrance, which often looked over an open horizon, for example over a valley or towards the sea. Why was it important what the dead body looked towards? Why might it have been important for it to be provided with a symbolic doorway or an open view? The archaeologist Christos Doumas, in *Early Bronze Age Burial Habits in the Cyclades*, is clear about the answer, through ultimately sceptical: 'Such suggestions imply that the early Cycladic people believed in an After Life.'

If the grave is a womb, and the dead person is prepared in one way or another as an embryo, the implication is that the doorway is there for it to re-emerge through. As Branigan points out in *The Foundations of Palatial Crete*, the burial of the dead with belongings and victuals, combined with

the subsequent disregard for their skeletons, and the continuing practice of offerings to or on behalf of the deceased, taken together can only imply that the Early Minoans possessed beliefs which were mature enough to envisage a spiritual after-life which was not necessarily dependent on the survival of the physical body.

The physical body commanded respect, and perhaps awe, for a limited period during which it lay safely contained in the tomb behind the heavy door slab. Then the person was imagined in some way to move on, and so the body became irrelevant. The bones could be swept aside, or reused in ritual, as we shall see later. But what kind of afterlife did the dead move on to? What kind of rebirth was imagined?

Here the *tholos* tombs of the Mesara again offer illumination. Almost all the *tholos* tombs were built to face east. In some tombs it seems that the heads of the dead, when they were laid out, also pointed east.

Branigan, in *The Tombs of Mesara*, suggests that this reflects a connection with the rising sun and comments, 'In a funerary context it may clearly be related to a belief in the revival of the body after death'. The sunrise evidently had some significance for the process which the dead person was believed to go through. The implication is of revival, of the reappearance or resurrection of what had previously disappeared, as the sun rises from the night in the east after disappearing in the west.

Such ideas about rebirth linked with the sun have parallels in other contemporary societies. The prehistoric Egyptians believed that the dead could travel through the underworld with the sun to be reborn in the east, an idea linked with the regeneration of vegetation in the new year. And at Newgrange in Ireland, excavators have found a 'passage grave' of the third millennium BC which is constructed in such a way that once a year, on the shortest day, the dawn sunlight beams straight down the 70-foot-long passage and into the burial chamber. The passage graves, like the *tholos* tombs, are circular, and inside them they carry circular symbols which may be sun symbols. Andrew Fleming, writing in the journal *World Archaeology*, identifies the principle of orientation to the sun as so significant that he suggests that if 'a simple primary idea . . . or . . . initial spiritual unity' exists behind the megalithic structures of Europe, 'it must be searched for first amongst the Passage Graves', in which 'One possibility is that sun-worship was involved'.

However, if the evidence of the graves and their easterly orientation were not enough, we have the independent evidence of the seals and 'frying-pans'. The seals and diadem suggest the possibility of sun worship. The 'frying-pans', those enigmatic objects with a sun motif on their decorated face, so often found in graves, tell their own story of the link between the sun and funerary beliefs. If the grave was indeed seen as a womb for the rebirth of the dead, it is significant that the sun on the 'frying-pans' is placed on the circular area above the female pubic triangle, that is, in the womb area. If both 'frying-pan' and circular grave symbolically represent the womb, we can comment that both are round, while the 'frying-pan' has a sun on it and the *tholos* has its doorway facing east to the rising sun. There is an emphasis on circular forms: circular graves, circular funerary vessels, circular movements of the sun, and, perhaps, a circular vision of rebirth of the dead.

The most plausible explanation of this early Aegean evidence is that people believed that the body of a deceased person remained her home for a short time only; that some part or essence survived independently, and that after its disappearance in death it could be reborn, just as the sun survives the night out of sight underground and eternally reappears in the east, as the sun survives the diminution of winter and returns to full strength in the spring, and as the vegetation dies and then eternally regenerates from the earth. The east-facing doorways show that the sun was more than a symbol: after life the dead person apparently entered a process which was in some way literally identified with the sun's journey.

A Sea Goddess?

We are so used to our binary division of the world into earth and sky that it is hard for us to imagine any other. But it seems that for the early Cretans three was a favourite number, just as the triangle representing the female genitals, was a very significant shape. Thus the early Cretans had a third element: the sea. Feminists have long had the intuition which Adrienne Rich expresses in *Of Woman Born*, that:

the female principle . . . was originally personified both in darkness and in light, in the depths of the water and the heights of the sky. Only with the development of a patriarchal cosmogony do we find her restricted to a purely 'chthonic' or tellurian presence, represented by darkness, unconsciousness, and sleep.

In early Crete we find concrete evidence to corroborate this intuition, evidence that what Erich Neumann describes in *The Great Mother* as 'the circular, life-generating ocean above and below the earth' was indeed another aspect of the female principle, the third pin which stakes out and completes a world view perhaps as triangular and inclusive as ours is binary and oppositional.

The importance of the sea in religion is reflected by the sacredness of shells. They are found in sanctuaries and placed next to the dead in graves; conch shells may have been sounded on ritual occasions. The frequent proximity of shells to female figurines in graves has given rise to talk of a 'sea goddess'. Moreover some 'frying-pans' show, above the pubic triangle, not the sun but a spiral sea often carrying a boat and suggesting a clear link between the salt waters and the fertile female belly. The appearance on the 'frying-pans' of both sun and sea in exactly the same position next to the pubic triangle, and evidently to some extent interchangeable, suggests that both referred to the same aspect of experience. But how exactly did this (apparently female) sea link with the earth and the sun? How did it belong to the circular theme of the recycling, the regenerating, of life? Archaeologists have been puzzled: Renfrew in *The Emergence of Civilization* concludes of the 'frying-pans': 'The significance of symbols in this context is not clear; nor do we know why sun, sea and the female sex should be linked in this way.' Perhaps we can track down the connection if we combine what we have discussed so far with an exploration of the symbolism of fish and boats.

The first clue is the discovery in graves of model boats. These might mean only that the deceased was a fisherman, but John Betts has argued that there are very few literal representations of everyday boats. Many of the pictures engraved on seals show boats associated with vegetation, and Betts suggests, in 'Ships on Minoan Seals', that they may be 'cult objects or . . . symbols of some sort in stylized forms' with a 'symbolic, semi-religious or occult significance'. The boats on 'frying-pans' may also be decorated with boughs and with a fish emblem. The context of these finds (in graves) and the bough decoration suggest a link with death and with fertility.

The next clue comes from those seals and 'frying-pans' which in their decoration link the sun clearly with the fish. The implication might be that the sun was imagined as making part of its journey by sea. Some other seals show a sun-like disc linked with a boat. Now the later Greeks imagined that the sun travelled in a horse-drawn chariot, but these early islanders did not know the horse. The daytime sun may have been linked to a flying bird, but in the evening the islanders' most common experience would have been to see the sun set into the waters of the Mediterranean. It appears that, like many other peoples, they may have imagined it plunging into the sea like a fish or travelling in a boat for this part of its journey.

Similar beliefs were held by the Egyptians, with whom we know the early Cretans had some contact. The Egyptian imagination saw the sun travelling in a boat across a female sky. As the sun passed through the underworld it illuminated the deceased. The goddesses Isis and Nephthys were responsible for mourning and tending the dead god Osiris, whose passing away and rebirth in the growth of fertile vegetation provided a model of hope for the rebirth of the human dead. These Egyptian ideas and pictures are well documented and undisputed. But few scholars have paid attention to the Aegean parallels which link the sun with fish and boats; associate boats with the dead and with fertility or regeneration; and depict the sun alternating with a boat, on female waters, as on the 'frying-pans'.

Even without the Egyptian parallels, this Aegean material provides enough evidence to suggest that the sea was significant, not only in itself, but for the part it was believed to play in a cycle of rebirth, regeneration and fertility on which the continuity of life depended.

So we have an accumulation of evidence: the pregnancy of the female figurines, the contracted corpses, the east-facing tombs, the sea symbolism, the female sun . . . It seems to add up to a coherent world view based on conceptions completely other than our own. The regenerative power of the womb had resonances with the regenerative power of nature, in particular the fertilising forces of earth, sun and water. We could speculate that the associations were to the crop-bearing role of the earth, bringing fruit from within itself out into the world; to the regenerative power of the sun, sparking and recreating life with its heat in a cyclical fashion; to the fertilising and dissolving quality of water, the element into which the sun disappears before it is reborn, and the element out of which (as amniotic fluid) a baby appears literally to emerge. All three elements seem to have been believed symbolically to play a role in the regeneration of human life, as indeed they do play their role practically in the regeneration of plant life. The female sea may have been the third and final pin in a tripartite world view: land, sea and sky, a female matrix from which springs everything that is. Instead of an antithetic world view we have an integrated unitive one. In *The Unwritten Philosophy*, the philosopher F. M. Cornford has pointed out that as late as the classical period the Greeks saw space not as a continuum but as spherical, and time not as a straight line but as circular; perhaps here we have the first appearance of that view. The notion of time as circular has recurred in the new physics (see Chapter 6). In this early Aegean material, the theme of circularity seems to prevail: the roundness of the female belly is often emphasised; the *tholos* tombs are round; the sun moves round the earth with a circular motion, and is itself a sphere. What goes down, comes up; what goes in, comes out, possibly in another form. While we do find some sharp edges, this is not primarily a schema of splits and rigid divisions but rather one of inclusion, cycles, continuity and regeneration.

The Creative Stone and the Active Vessel

The circle was apparently associated with creation, and one symbol of its power and fertility was the plain round stone. In *The Mycenaean Tree and Pillar Cult* Arthur Evans has described the stone in Bronze Age Aegean religion as the embodiment or home of the divine spirit, although he does not specify the sex or role of the divine spirit in this particular manifestation. Along with figurines, many round stones or plain pebbles have been found in Crete accompanying the dead body in graves. Natural pebbles were the most common, and probably the original form of, amulets. Some of the female figurines which have been found are little more than rounded stones. Some surviving Cretan pictures show figures pouring liquid on to stones, and rocks putting out plants. Both stone and vessel can represent the female form; moreover, both stone and jug are shown in these pictures as producing the fertile bough interchangeably.

Now in reality nothing can grow out of a stone; in fact for us the stone is a symbol of everything heavy, mute and inanimate. The idea that this very dense form of matter has its own life and energy, a living expression of a living earth, arises for us only in imaginative flights of fiction, as when Henry Miller in one of his purple passages in *The Colossus of Maroussi* describes the pathway to the sanctuary of Eleusis near Athens:

> The rocks themselves are quite mad: they have been lying for centuries exposed to this divine illumination: they lie very still and quiet, nestling amid dancing coloured shrubs in a blood-stained soil, but they are mad, I say, and to touch them is to lose one's grip on everything which once seemed firm, solid and unshakeable.

It seems that the early Cretans, too, saw the stone or pebble as possessing a power and an active energy, whether as an amulet to protect, a divinity to bless or as a root source of fertility. One is reminded of esoteric traditions about the healing powers of precious stones. However, all that seems clear for the early Cretans is that, while the earth was seen as sacred and female, the stone or rock was part of this divine entity's flesh or embodiment. Especially if it was round and bulbous like a pregnant woman's belly, it was perhaps another version of the 'womb' of mother earth from which new human and plant life might grow. Far from being a passive 'dead weight', the stone was an active carrier of fertile power. We perhaps need the affirmation of modern atomic physics that matter is simply energy vibrating at a slower rate to help us grasp a vision in which matter is not dead but is alive and numinous.

We also need to rethink our ideas about jars and vessels. Sometimes in this early society, when the dead were not buried in caves or rock hollows or in *tholos* tombs, they were buried in jars. In one cemetery in Crete over 300 such jars were found, standing on their heads. In the Cycladic islands it was often children who were buried in this way, in large vases placed under the floors of the houses or elsewhere inside the settlement. The connection with the womb is not hard to make here, not only from the foetal position of the corpse and the inversion of the jar (making the entrance from below): there are also many small vases, jugs and other vessels whose rounded sides explicitly represent the shape of a woman. Their impractical shape and their discovery in grave or shrine contexts has led some scholars to call them 'vessel-goddesses'; at the least we can be sure that they had some religious significance. Some of them have heads and faces, some arms, some breasts which they may hold, while some bear a genital triangle; they were personified and their symbolism was clearly linked with human sexual activity. There is no jar made in the shape of a man.

This line of discovery may suddenly become uncomfortably familiar to a twentieth-century woman. It is not uncommon now for women to be symbolised as containers, whether 'old bags', 'old boots', ships or other vessels. The comparison is not usually complimentary. The implication is of a passive object you can put things in, overload, steer where you want: our picture is of a receptacle without power or locomotion of its own. The first thing we need to do is to lose the assumption that the jar had the same associations for these early people as it has for us. Then we need to remember that we are looking at a period when the making of pottery was a relatively recent invention: when the transformation by fire of ordinary clay into a creation which could be beautiful, durable, and important for survival in practical ways, was still a marvel, still a process inspiring awe and mystery to an extent we can only guess at.

For these people a jar was not the result of assembly-line production but the fruit of a process of creative handiwork and transformation. It has often been suggested that women, who ran the settlements, were in most places the first potters and even the inventors of this process. Woman's mysterious power to produce a child was perhaps paralleled by her skill and ability to produce pots, which in themselves carried an imprint of the sacred and numinous. Pots not only played a crucial role in the storage of oil, grain and other foodstuffs, but were also needed for the transformation of raw food into cooked. A jar containing grain for storage was literally a 'bearer of seed', a storehouse from which new life would grow. Some feminist writers have speculated that the making of vessels was symbolic of the shaping of life and that rebirth was seen as 'we are as fresh-baked pots' (in the words of Monica Sjöö). Fire serves as a transforming agent, not only in cooking but also in pottery making: perhaps the evidence of unexplained fires in the Mesara *tholos* tombs was connected with some parallel process of transformation believed to be undergone by the dead person. The jar symbolised the body, perhaps the womb, of the woman: the foetus-like corpse buried in the inverted jar was apparently not perceived as a static collection of bones in an inanimate vessel, but as human remains in process, in change, involved in a cycle of movement between life, death, and life.

It is therefore perhaps not surprising that we often find jars or vessels engraved on the amuletic sealstones which the early Cretans used. They appear next to other religious symbols like the double axe, and there are many engravings of scenes in which they appear to be ritually touched by a standing or seated figure. These do not seem to be any old containers, but vessels with a magical or cult significance. The jar here is not a passive or purely utilitarian object but an active transforming agent with a special power and meaning. Perhaps the only vessel which still holds, in a symbolic sense, a trace of such power for us is the witch's cauldron.

We are not talking here about any 'natural' or 'universal' symbol of the woman as vessel in the sense that many male writers have expressed it. For example, Erich Neumann in *The Great Mother* asserts:

> Woman as body-vessel is the *natural* expression of the human experience of woman *bearing* the child 'within' her and of man entering 'into' her in the sexual act . . .
> The *basic* symbolic equation woman=body=vessel corresponds to what is perhaps mankind's . . . most *elementary experience* of the *Feminine* [my italics].

Does the woman 'bear' the child or make and create it in its perfection from a tiny fusion of two cells? Does the man enter 'into' her or does she encompass the man? Do we stress her 'receiving' the man or 'producing' the child? These questions show the effect of cultural bias and prejudice. What we find in early Crete is a particular set of associations which perhaps arose out of women being the first potters and from their being seen as having particular kinds of power. Such power was not to dominate others but to transform and regenerate: through the making of pottery, the preserving and cooking of food, possibly healing by the mixing of herbs, and the creation of human life through birth. By imaginative extension the female element was also linked with the earth's creation of new plant life from seed, and the rebirth of the dead. As Adrienne Rich puts it: 'The transformations necessary for the continuation of life are thus, in terms of this early imagery, exercises of female power.' The pot or jar which is involved in many of these processes is, contrary to our society's symbolism, a very active vessel.

Where Did Men Stand?

I have written about sun, sea and earth. If female energy inhabited the firmament, where did men stand? Were they as denied and downgraded in a female-orientated world view as women are now in a patriarchal world view? Did this go hand in hand with a social system where the majority of men were denied effective political power as women are now in our patriarchal and capitalist societies? Did female power emasculate men? As Bachofen commented, 'It would be easy to jump to the conclusion of cowardice, effeminacy and lack of dignity resulting for the men from female domination'. Looking back from our twentieth century to these early periods of history, this may be what men fear and what some women longingly fantasise in a spirit of sweet revenge. But it does not correspond with the evidence which has survived from the communities living on these early Greek islands in the third and early second millennia BC.

Men are depicted frequently in this early art. They bend over jars; they play a flute or harp; they sit under trees; they carry staffs; they touch or hold animals; they dress up as animals and dance. These illustrations belong to a tradition of male representations, sometimes graceful, sometimes funny, which stretches back into the neolithic period. The models of men which have survived do not usually appear to be deities or even priests, but votive figurines, perhaps dedicated to a deity by a male worshipper. They do not hold their hands up in the air in the gesture of a goddess or priestess; they hold their hands to the chest in what is perhaps a gesture of display or clasp their hands

together in a gesture of respect. They are depicted, however, with an
enormous dignity. These are men who look tender, calm and peaceful,
but who are by no means castrated: their genitals are strong,
emphasised and sometimes erect. Some are perhaps carrying a knife
but are not using it. While the men of classical statues hurl things,
these are men who 'have balls' and yet who appear gentle and
sometimes even meditative. In the anti-sexist men's magazine *Achilles
Heel*, Paul Morrison described the impression that these male images
made on him:

> Their bodies are lithe, but not musclebound. They are usually in
> attitudes of upright prayer or contemplation. Their hands are
> folded over their hearts, or reaching upwards. They look outwards;
> and they are at peace with themselves. They don't look like men
> who would be afraid of . . . holding children.

Between two of the Mesara *tholos* tombs the excavator Xanthoudides
found six clay objects shaped like phalluses which, like other finds
at that site, probably had a ritual significance. From the Cyclades we
see phallus-shaped necklace beads. This raises the question of whether
the celebration of the phallus implied the celebration of 'macho'
values. Did it conflict with a religion focused primarily on female
elements? Perhaps only to our twentieth-century eyes. In a pre-
patriarchal society the phallus could have been seen not as a contrast
or in opposition to, but as a complement or adjunct to, the female
divine power. In a society where it was not a symbol of masculine
supremacy, of male violence against women, of misused political and
military power, it could be celebrated for its part as the fertilising agent
in the procreative process. In this religion, which was so different from
the Christian religion, it is perhaps possible that the genitals of both
sexes were respected for the power and pleasure they carried. The
phallus was clearly celebrated and appears to have taken a harmonious
place in a woman-orientated world view. There are no scenes showing
male fighting or violence, or suggesting conflict between the sexes.
Although we more often see a woman with another woman or men
with men, we also see pictures of a woman and man together:
sometimes they are holding hands, sometimes the contact seems to
be more sexually explicit.

None of these symbols speak of polarisation between the sexes.
What we seem to see is a correspondence between an economic and
social system which was relatively non-hierarchical and egalitarian

(both in terms of wealth and between the sexes) and a symbol system which reflects with equal dignity both woman and man, human and beast. In western society we experience sharp divisions between rich and poor, between man and woman, and these are reflected in the symbols we generate; in early Crete a more equal and collective social organisation seems to tally with a more circular and inclusive symbol system where there is little polarisation between woman and man or, as we shall now see, between humans and nature.

The Sacred Bough

So a female spirit inhabited the prime creative principle, the backdrop against which life took its course: the earth beneath your feet, the sun that shines on you, the water you sail on. The basis of the symbolic system was a female matrix. But that was only the basis from which things grew multifariously. Within that framework all the creations of nature flowered, and there is nothing to suggest that these were seen as more female than male, or even that as much significance was attached to the process of 'sexing' as in our world of furry kittens and butch dogs, phallic steam trains and cars that respond to a man's touch.

I have mentioned creative principles, but for these early people the focus of religion appears not to have been the contemplation of such principles in an abstract sense but rather their practical application or embodiment. They appear to have embraced a material spirituality. Their interest seems to have been not speculation about eternity, or morality, or the purity of spirit when it is separated from the weight of matter, but rather the celebration of the physical forms of plant and animal life which filled daily needs and made survival possible. Religious scenes are full of plants and animals. We distinguish the spiritual from the material, and see the former as the proper subject matter of religion. These early islanders celebrated the material, apparently retaining a stronger sense than we of the mystery of life, of the spiritual force immanent in all living things. They revered the miracles that you can see and touch and eat.

At the centre of life and religion was the living plant. It was crucial to food and survival. Cereals were central to the diet of the community. Wheat and barley were grown in Crete from neolithic times; the early Minoans probably also grew vegetables, as well as eating fruit and nuts. They apparently grew (and pruned!) olive trees,

made olive oil, and grew grapes for wine. In ancient times Crete had
very large forests which have long since disappeared; wood played an
important part in building houses, boats and maybe making spears.
We know they had pine and oak trees, possibly pear and almond too.
The richness and variety of plant life, and its importance for human
beings, is reflected in the pictures of Cretan cult. Scholars have
recognised this, but by inference from other cultures they have tended
to look in the Cretan material for 'a cult concerned with trees and
celebrations in honour of a male deity symbolic of the growth and
decay of vegetation', and to postulate that 'the tree was symbolic of,
or in some way represented, the divinity – the goddess as we gather
from the gems' (in the words of B. C. Dietrich in *The Origins of Greek
Religion*). Scholars have identified a fertility goddess and her
son/consort on the model of Near Eastern religion. Historical novels
have woven thrilling yarns about the year-king who must die. But,
although there are other parallels with near eastern symbolism, one
personified earth/tree goddess and her son who dies each year are not
figures apparent on this early Cretan landscape. There is little evidence
that personified deities were part of the thinking at all. Many varieties
of plant life are shown and it appears that different plants were vividly
perceived for their different qualities, and each figures differently in
cult in its own right. It is possible that each species was thought to
be inhabited by its own spirit and needed rituals individual to it. Thus
some boughs are carried; others grow out of stones and jugs and have
libations or water poured on them. Sometimes boughs accompany
people dressed in bird heads or people in animal costume. Trees grow
out of rocks, they are touched or sat under. Sometimes plants are a
significant feature in outdoor rituals involving dance. We have seen
that a frond or bough is often shown associated with a ship, suggesting
a link with the funerary or other rituals concerned with boats.
Sometimes boughs are incorporated into radiant or sun designs,
providing another link between solar symbolism and the fertility of
vegetation. The scenes we see on the seals may show festivals focused
on plant life at different times of the year, reflecting the planting and
reaping of crops, the harvesting of grapes and fruits. There are few
scenes where a divinity, or a priest figure representing a divinity, takes
the centre of the stage. The attention, the focus, the reverence, the
worship or whatever we should term it, is most often clearly directed
towards the living bough itself.

A breathtaking example of how this kind of religion has been
misunderstood can be seen in the case of the double axe, one of the

hallmarks of Cretan symbolism from the early days. Arthur Evans, in *The Mycenaean Tree and Pillar Cult*, wrote about '. . . the Cretan Zeus, whose special symbol was the double axe'. He sounds so certain that it is surprising to find that the double axe is never once found in the hands of a male thunder god such as Zeus, and hardly ever in the hands of a male figure of any kind. It does appear, later, in the hands of a female figure, as we shall see. The historian Nilsson argues that it originated as a sacrificial axe used for killing animals, although in this early period it is never shown with an animal or animal's head. More than a thousand years after this early Cretan society, government officials in Rome carried the same axe symbol called *fasces*, and in this century it was resurrected by Mussolini and has given its name to Fascism. Beside the swastika, this is the most painful example of how early women's symbols have been taken over and degraded under patriarchy. In early Cretan pictures the association of the double axe seems to be with fertility and plant life, and George Thomson in his book on the prehistoric Aegean suggests that its origin lay in the early and important women's task of felling trees. The archaeologist Grumach, writing in the journal *Kadmos*, saw it as a symbol of blessing, fertility from the underworld, and resurrection. Links with animal sacrifice or a male god are unproven and there is absolutely no evidence of any connection with violence, authority, or punishment. It has been hard for later centuries to recognise a religion which seems to have celebrated the natural world in its own right, rather than exploiting its phenomena to gain social and political control over others.

The Insect and Animal Queendom

The creatures of the land and air also held a place in the early Cretan pantheon: not exclusively or even predominantly those which contributed to the survival of humankind, but apparently those which could be seen as beautiful, unusual, strong, funny, sexual, graceful, dangerous, or which fired the imagination. They take pride of place in early engravings, and are shown accurately and affectionately. Sometimes they get a humorous treatment. They also appear with amuletic significance on sealstones and are depicted at the centre of religious scenes. Somewhere below the surface lies a magical network of connections between each creature and other aspects of the natural world and human experience. It is not always easy to pick out the threads, but those we can find are often surprising compared to the ways we lace together our twentieth-century symbols.

Birds seem to appear with the sun, and are incorporated into radiant motifs. We also find people, usually women, dressed as birds; sometimes the costume even includes wings. These scenes show that birds were linked with vegetation and sun cults. Perhaps birds were seen as flying like the sun, or like the soul, as Arthur Evans suggests; their association on seals with plant cult, and with sun worship on the Cycladic diadem, suggests that they were linked with fertility and with solar ideas of regeneration.

The snake has been variously understood as a symbol of the household, of death and rebirth, or of the phallus as an adjunct of a female deity; I find the evidence inadequate to justify one theory rather than another. The one thing which is clear is that it usually appears with women.

The wild goat appears with men and with plants, and has been described by Branigan in *The Foundations of Palatial Crete* as a symbol of strength and virility. We can only puzzle about the meaning of the many pictures showing people touching a goat alive or dead; but we cannot fail to be struck by the impression of respect which such scenes give. Over time the goat seems very slowly to have been replaced by the bull as a central symbol of Cretan religion.

Lions offer us a surprise. While Jung links the lion with the sun and the king as archetypal symbols of the self, it is interesting to find that here it is the *lioness* who appears as representative of the species. Contrary to our 'King of the Jungle' image, it is women who are shown as lions. The dog apparently had some special significance, and there is a picture of a bee-woman.

The discovery of models of creatures like beetles apparently used as offerings to a deity has troubled some scholars. Surely a beetle is not a suitable offering to a deity? And Dietrich puzzles how to explain the fact that other 'pests' or 'such lowly creatures as pigs and stoats or weasels' were dedicated as part of religious ritual. Models of hedgehogs, tortoises and hares were also found. Here we have to make a leap of imagination and accept that the early Cretans had a classification system radically different from our own, in which there was perhaps no such value system separating off some animals as 'lowly' or 'unworthy'. Pigs were carved in marble and ivory, toads were made in gold; both were placed in tombs among the few precious objects carefully chosen to accompany the dead body. Scorpions and spiders are carved on ivory. The whole relationship of these early people with the animal and insect world seems to have differed from our hierarchical approach, and was apparently not rooted in the superiority of one creature over another, nor in the superiority of humans over animals, but rather in some sense of identity or kinship with them.

We do find a sense of closeness to, and identification with, animals in the religious scenes which have survived. The animal may have been sacrificed and eaten; we know that goats were ritually touched; and, if we are to believe some clay models which have survived, people leapt on to the horns of the bull. Certainly snakes were handled, and we have seen that people dressed up as birds, identifying with them to perform rituals and dances. What we see appears to be participation with, rather than objectification of, the animal world. The theme is affinity with, rather than dominion over.

Apart from those portrayed gathering round the figure of St Francis of Assisi, animals are largely absent from the Christian religion. Even when they are referred to affectionately, their animal nature is seen as lacking a soul and they are therefore sharply divided from humans. Perhaps for this reason, western scholars have proved themselves imaginatively inept at grasping the significance of animals and plants in early Greek religion. Their view tends to be dominated by the humanised personalities of the later Greek Olympian gods, who each have different animals and plants as their attributes. Thus in later Greece the owl and the olive and the snake were sacred to the goddess Athena, Poseidon reigned over the bull and the sea, and so on. However, a close look reveals that this later process of association tends to happen in an inconsistent way from one part of Greece to another. Thus the horse is linked with the goddess Demeter in her cult at Phygalia, but nowhere else, while it is usually associated with Poseidon. Zeus is the god of the sky and the weather, while the sun itself is more closely identified with the god Apollo (though there is also a separate sun god called Helios). Both Apollo and Dionysus are seen in different ways as the dolphin god . . . These confused patterns show that it is in some cases fairly random which natural elements were later connected with which Olympian label, and that approaching the history of Greek religion from these later personalities is like looking through the wrong end of a telescope. The Olympian deities are not heaven-born archetypes, but are rather of inconsistent man-made construction, often jerry-built from the building blocks of an earlier era. The raw materials from which they are made are the 'largely localised vegetation figures' (in Dietrich's

words) and animal deities or spirits of our earlier period. Thus Athena
could be seen as the amalgamation of an olive-tree deity, an owl spirit
and a snake spirit, who each had their own cults and recognition in
earlier times. We could recognise that the horse was in prehistoric
times associated with fertility and death, and that this connotation was
basic and fundamental whichever Olympian deity the horse was later
linked with. The early symbolic system gets fed into, and subordinated
to, the later official Olympian god system. In the early days, these
animals and plants were not *attached to* any god or goddess with an
anthropomorphic form; they were not necessarily even personified
themselves. The spirit of the olive tree may not have been visualised
as having a human shape, but rather the shape of an olive tree. The
pictures of early Cretan rituals suggest that these natural elements
were themselves the focus of reverence and ritual, were themselves
seen as the seat or manifestation of a divine spirit. The animal was
a magical creature whose likeness you adopted so as to experience
its power and qualities. The earth was itself a divine female spirit. The
sun was not abstractly perceived as a divine character but was
celebrated as the hot burning ball which brings and takes away light
and life day by day and season by season, closely linked to other aspects
of physical experience: the sacred bird which flies like it through the
air, the woman's womb, the eclipse of life in the dead person – a set
of resonances which spread out from it like ripples in a pond. The
divine was not separate but immanent in the physical realities of daily
life.

The Magic Body

If the physical was divine, this included not only animals and plants
but also the human body. That object whose wayward lusts and desires
the Christian religion has seen as the source of evil, appears to have
been a source of awe in early Crete. The sexuality of animals and
humans was celebrated in Cretan pictures; it is hard to imagine such
sexuality explicit scenes appearing in Christian iconography. I have
described how the female vagina and womb were celebrated on ritual
figures and vessels, how models of the male phallus appeared in a
religious context. The body in Christian religion figures largely in a
context of punishment and mortification (the wracked body on the
cross, the bleeding heart, the crown of thorns . . .) and religious
services themselves traditionally emphasise the humbling of the body

through kneeling, its denial through long periods of immobility. It is hard for us to imagine a religion where the body was actively used and dance was part of the act of worship. These early Cretans seem to have known that the body is for fun. And at the same time, without any apparent contradiction, they experienced it as a pathway to the divine.

Models of parts of the human body also seem to have been used as offerings to the gods. For example a clay lock of human hair, a leg, an arm, a trunk, and the right half of a body halved from crown to crutch, were found in the ashes of the Petsofas mountain peak sanctuary fire in Crete. Branigan in *The Foundations of Palatial Crete* suggests that they 'were thrown . . . so that the "prayers" that they carried would be raised to the deity in the sacred smoke'. Again we see the religious significance of fire. The prayer may have been for the healing or protection of that part of the body. In the Mesara graves models of body parts, especially legs, were found buried with their owners, leading Xanthoudides to suppose that 'these stone legs were credited with prophylactic powers when worn as amulets', with a function of giving strength to the limb in question. The predominance of legs and feet seems compatible with a religion whose focus was so much 'on the ground' rather than 'up in the sky'.

After death the body seems to have had a religious significance which for us verges on the gruesome. Excavators examining the piled-up bones from the Mesara *tholos* tombs have noticed an overall shortage of bones and a striking absence of skulls. In his excavations of a series of tombs used for generations, Xanthoudides found only eight skulls. What happened to the others? In some tombs in Crete and the Cyclades, the skulls were stacked separately from the other bones. At the cemetery at Archanes in Crete, excavators found nearly 200 skulls in heaps; and some were found specially placed in jars or vases. Parts of a human skull were found in a ritual room at the settlement of Myrtos in South Crete, as described by the excavator Peter Warren. So what were they doing with these different bits of skeletons? There is one telling clue. At two Mesara sites Branigan found evidence that at the secondary burial stage, when the skeletons were moved aside to make room for the next burial, bones from previous burials were chopped up and also ground on a quernstone such as was used for grinding corn. For what role in ritual or other purposes such ground bone was intended, we can only wonder. The parallel to the 'Jack and the Beanstalk' folktale where the giant wants to 'grind his bones to make my bread' seems macabre to us. However, within the context of early Cretan religion such bone-grinding may not have carried such sinister associations, and is at least consistent with other beliefs and practices. Animals were sacred and were ritually handled alive and dead as well as being eaten; plants were sacred and were carried, watered and possibly consumed as part of ritual; the human body was sacred and, in its very fabric, had an important part to play in religious activity, both before and after death. It is only because we fear the human body in death as in life that we find the idea of handling a corpse so repugnant. The numinous and magical significance attributed both to the living body in its joyful religious dances and to the dead bones in their *post mortem* handling is something we can recognise but perhaps will never fully understand.

A Golden Age?

The writings of J. J. Bachofen (*Mutterecht*/'Motherright', 1861) and Robert Briffault (*The Mothers*, 1927), as well as Frederick Engels' *The Origin of the Family*, 1884, have inspired a generation of feminists eager to believe that women once held power. Among their best-known writings are Helen Diner's *Mothers and Amazons* and Elizabeth Gould Davis's *The First Sex*. Prehistoric Crete is often offered as an example of a matriarchal society. But the kind of evidence I have reviewed is all that we have about this early period in Crete. And, as we have seen, none of it proves that we are looking at a society which is matriarchal in the sense of a society run by women. None of the arguments advanced for the existence of such a matriarchy are conclusive.

While the matrix of the universe was apparently seen as female, and women figured predominantly in religion (whether as personified deities or as priestesses), we simply do not know how this religious pre-eminence related to other kinds of political or social power. That women predominated as the symbols and administrants of divine cult at a time when religion was integral to the rest of social life is not in itself certain proof that women held overall social power. Women's assumed control over the main means of food production at this early stage of agriculture is in itself a tenuous argument by analogy from the development of other primitive societies, and in any case does not prove that they held social power. There are cases where such economic control does *not* go hand in hand with political power. The feminist anthropologist Hermione Harris pointed this out in a paper called 'Women in Precapitalist Societies'; she has for many years been a valuably stringent voice reminding us that the evidence for matriarchy is woefully inadequate. Later survivals of matriliny or inheritance through women are also inconclusive evidence, for contemporary anthropological studies have shown that property or power so inherited may still be administered largely by male relatives. It is clear that women in Crete at this early time held more power than in our society, but we remain uncertain about what sort of power it was.

All we have to go on is the kind of evidence available from sites like Myrtos and the Mesara tombs, and this suggests autonomous communities lacking in highly developed hierarchies of specialisation or administration. The evidence seems to point to a collective organisation, a relative equality of wealth and status within the community, rather than to hierarchy of either sex or class. There is no reason to believe that a 'matriarchy' which was the inversion of patriarchy ever existed in the Bronze Age Aegean. It is possible that what power women may have held in an earlier period was already in decline by the period I have been discussing; perhaps what we are looking at here is a society which had already started on a slow transition to patriarchy.

Nor do we have here an example of a golden age, an early society to which we might hope to return, even if such a return were possible. As I mentioned earlier, there is a tendency, among some classicists and feminists alike, to idealise ancient Greece, to look in it for confirmation of our ideals and aspirations in the present. As George Thomson pointed out in *Aeschylus and Athens*, 'Our view cannot be wholly objective, and the professed impartiality of some modern scholars is an illusion . . . We must become conscious of our prejudices in order to correct them. The historian of the past is a citizen of the present'. Thus the Victorians looked to classical Athens for a heroic vision of an imperialist society, Sir Arthur Evans visualised the palace of Knossos as a kind of paradise ruled by a peaceful benign aristocracy, and feminists have tended to look to this earlier era in Crete for a vision of a matriarchal society worshipping an all-embracing mother figure, the Great Goddess. A unifying and reassuring vision, but one which has perhaps more to do with our needs and struggles today than with life in Crete in the third millennium BC. It is hard to accept the possibility of ambivalence, complexity and difficulty in our most cherished corners of history, but the evidence offers a patchy picture of a society in change, variously organised, with a multiplicity of divinities perhaps all lacking the personal touch of the perfect divine mother whom we might hope to find. There was probably much in the society which we would consider brutal and cruel; female symbols may have been ferocious as often as nurturing, although those value judgments of ours might be totally meaningless to a member of that early community. As Adrienne Rich points out,

> To acknowledge a cyclic change of aspects (that birth is followed by death, death by reincarnation; that tides ebb and flow, winter alternates with summer . . .) is to acknowledge that process and continuity embrace both positive and negative events – although, as parts of a process, events are less likely to become stamped as purely 'positive' or 'negative'.

We cannot enter the minds and lives of those early Cretans. I have pointed out the limitations in the understanding of other writers, but my own view is just as surely blinkered and filtered as I try to throw my gaze long-sightedly across those many centuries. Their world remains a mystery, to be approached with a combination of stringent accuracy, imagination, and humility.

All that we have here for certain is a society very different from our own. It was differently organised; women held different status; and the symbols attached to women were very different.

It has been claimed that a gynocentric view of the world prevailed over Europe and beyond throughout prehistory, over vast cycles of time compared to which our twentieth century is like one April day at the end of a long spring. My contention is more modest. I have set out to show only that a different system did seem to prevail in one small pocket of time and in one small place. That in itself is enough to show that our twentieth-century beliefs and symbols are not valid for all time, as so many theorists would have us believe. They are not pearls of archetypal truth which humanity has been labouring to articulate since the beginning of time.

This is the crux of my argument: the dreams, the fantasies, the images of women which dominate our twentieth-century consciousness are not universal; they are not a web on to which we are pinned inevitably for ever. Rather, we see that people can weave their own symbols. A radically different society and consciousness can and did give birth to a whole other family of symbols, symbols radiant with female power. That power is ours to claim. But in that claiming it may help to understand the process we have to reverse: the slow and relentless transition whereby patriarchy usurped, co-opted and discredited those symbols of female power in early Greece and transformed them into symbols of powerlessness.

Enter the Mycenaeans

I have suggested that the symbols current in early Crete reflect conditions very different from our own: a society with a different economic organisation, no sign of the subordination of women and some evidence of less authoritarian and more communal social structures. There has been much debate about the historical processes whereby the subordination of women came about. It has often been associated with the emergence of private property, the state and a class society (see Stephanie Coontz and Peter Henderson's summary of the issues in *Women's Work, Men's Property*). What concerns me here are the associated changes in the symbol system. Suffice it to say that from the early centuries of the second millennium BC the society I have described embarked on a process of transformation which was quickened by a new influence in the Aegean population, the so-called 'Mycenaeans'. However these people arrived or developed, we find them at about 1500 BC living on the Greek mainland, using different graves and other new cultural features like the battle chariot and the long sword. They seem to have survived on a rather different economic basis, and the status they accorded to women was low.

The name 'Mycenaean' derives from one of the larger citadels which these people built, at Mycenae, although the term is arbitrary as they had many other centres, for example at Tiryns, Pylos, Thebes and Gla. There is much exciting 'schoolboy' reading available about the excavation of Mycenae by Heinrich Schliemann: about the gold treasure, the gigantic stone walls, the monumental tombs which these people left to the archaeologist.

Unlike the earlier inhabitants of Greece, these may have been a pastoral people, depending for much of their subsistence on herding livestock. Because of the physical mobility required for such work, it has been suggested that in pastoral societies men rather than women were responsible for the herds and thus in control of the main source of food and wealth, as well as the political power which such control may bring. Thomson presents this argument clearly in *Aeschylus and Athens*. Unlike the long-haired, clean-shaven men of Crete, these men had short hair and wore beards. At first they were greatly influenced by the more developed civilisation of Crete, learning its techniques and crafts. But from about the middle of the second millennium BC they became the dominant force in Greece. The trade routes they developed took them to Sicily, southern Italy, Egypt, the Near East and perhaps even further afield. At least part of their growing wealth probably came from piracy, raiding and booty from wars. They made great technical progress in cutting and lifting stone, and building roads. By the fourteenth century BC they were raising their famous heavily defended citadels, epitomised for the tourist by the great 'Lion Gate' at Mycenae. Their flowering took place during the Late Bronze Age.

As might be expected, these people developed very different social structures and customs from those of the earlier population. Combining elements of their own Indo-European language with the Cretans' language and knowledge of writing, the Mycenaeans developed a written script known as 'Linear B' which has been deciphered as an early form of Greek. In some of the palaces, stacks of tablets in this script have been found; translation of them reveals a detailed picture of a very complicated and bureaucratic palace life. The findings have been summarised by historians including John Chadwick and T. B. L. Webster. At Pylos, for example, the palace staff is listed as 669 women, 392 girls and 281 boys, who may mostly have been slaves from the eastern Aegean. Excavations unearthed nearly 3,000 cups in the palace pantries. There was one bath in the household; drains were found, but nothing like lavatories. The tablets refer to many specialised craftspeople such as woodcutters, bronze-smiths, shipbuilders, unguent-boilers. Bath-pouring, carding, spinning and weaving were clearly occupations of women.

The Pylos palace seems to have controlled much of the surrounding area. One hundred and sixty place names are mentioned on the tablets, each place probably a small village whose citizens contributed goods such as linen and bronze to the palace, and may in turn have drawn rations from it. The systems of land ownership are not easy to understand, but land ownership was clearly hierarchical. Each village had its mayor or headman, and tablets from other sites also suggest the existence of various privileged classes of military personnel. At Pylos 443 rowers are mentioned and a list of military groups, the role of some apparently being to guard the coast. We can only speculate about the effect militarism may have had on the position of women, representing as it did an activity and a source of wealth apparently controlled mainly by men. Grave customs confirm the impression of an unequal society, revealing different grave types of widely varying size and quality, apparently used by different groups according to their wealth and status. At the head of the whole complex it is perhaps no surprise to find a powerful king, or *wanax* as he was called. M. I. Finley summed it up in *Early Greece:*

> The picture that emerges from . . . an analysis of the tablets and the archaeology combined is one of a division of Mycenaean Greece into a number of petty bureaucratic states, with a warrior aristocracy, a high level of craftsmanship, extensive foreign trade in necessities (metals) and luxuries, and a permanent condition of armed neutrality at best in their relations with each other, and perhaps with their subjects.

Wars, hierarchies, slaves, powerful kings . . . all this is a far cry from the earlier Cretan life I have described. It was not long before Mycenaean influence began to be felt in the Cycladic islands and then in Crete, and for the last part of this period the Mycenaeans were probably ruling in Knossos. So how did the Cretan society I have described change during this period? At this time the palaces of Knossos, Mallia and Phaistos were, briefly, at their height before earthquake and perhaps invasion brought them down. The final fall of Knossos was probably about 1400 BC. While they stood, the palaces were splendid: huge labyrinthine complexes with grand stairways, splendid courtyards, and whole quarters for storage or for workshops. 'Linear B' clay tablets found at Knossos record a system of tribute and exchange of goods as complex as that at Pylos, though the relationships behind these exchanges are hard to ascertain. For example, was the Knossos palace primarily a temple to which people brought religious offerings? Or was it a storehouse or central clearing house which served to recycle and redistribute goods among the population, rather like an early 'social security' or 'welfare' system? Does our label 'palace' distort the fact that this was primarily a town or living complex with a religious area at its centre? The historian Paul Halstead has recently suggested that it combined the functions of Buckingham Palace, Whitehall, Westminster Abbey and perhaps even Wembley Stadium.

Did a king or queen, high priest or high priestess, rule from the stately 'throne rooms'? Many male archaeologists have favoured the theory that the complex was ruled by a priest-king with semi-divine status. The fact is that there is only one existing picture from Knossos which seems to show a man, wearing a crown, in what might be a position of authority; this picture is endlessly reproduced on postcards, book covers, and archaeological conference posters. The picture is, however, reconstructed from several small fresco fragments, which are actually found some way apart. The archaeologist W.-D. Niemeier has recently shown that the crown does not belong with this figure: another piece of reconstituted history, glued together by prejudice, has crumbled back into the dust. Helen Waterhouse, in her paper 'Priest-Kings?', has carefully dismantled all the supposed evidence for a male ruler at Knossos. Almost every surviving authentic picture of an elevated personage, celebrating or receiving offerings, is of a woman.

However, whether a queen or high priestess ruled at Knossos, we have come a long way from the earlier communal structures of Cretan life. The tablets afford a picture of a highly stratified society and much power may have lain in the hands of specialised groups. Helen Waterhouse suggests that 'Male hierarchies no doubt co-existed with the palace priestesses, some in charge, perhaps, of trade and maritime affairs, others serving as priests, of native Minoan deities as well as of the oriental gods . . .' Knossos was not fortified, but the figure of 400 chariots itemised in the tablets suggests that by the fifteenth century BC it was already militarised. It is to this period that most of the famous bull-leaping pictures belong. What about the legend of the tyrannical Cretan king, Minos, whose tribute of young people from Athens included Theseus, famous for his adventures with Ariadne against the monstrous Minotaur? It belongs to this period or (perhaps more likely) slightly later, when the Mycenaeans held sway at Knossos. Whatever the factual basis of that myth, archaeology shows clearly that many of the characteristics which had made early Cretan society so remarkable have been lost by this period of the palaces' heyday. Among other evidence, we see a move away from collectivity towards individualism in grave customs, with the growing use of 'pithos' jars and clay coffins called *larnakes*. Helen Waterhouse comments on the shift of emphasis from collective to individual well-being, reflected perhaps in the number of stately private villas built in Crete during this time. After the collapse of the palaces, social conditions were very different in Crete, but I will take this period as one, right through until the destruction of the Mycenaean palaces themselves and the disappearance of the whole culture, at about 1100 BC, into the Greek 'Dark Age'.

The Tenacity of the Woman Symbols

Religion and its symbols adapt slowly and are not transformed overnight by social developments. In this changing era, the beliefs of the earlier time were retained to a surprising degree. This is true not only in Crete but also on the islands and on the mainland, where it may have been a result of the surviving traditions and conservatism of the pre-Mycenaean population, or of the influence which Crete exerted on the Mycenaeans during the early centuries of their emergence. Mainland Greece, Crete and the other islands all offer similar evidence of religious activity during this period, and it shows many of the forms and structures of the earlier religion still going strong. Important changes did take place, but before I chart them I will describe these survivals, the symbols which held their power and significance intact in the face of an increasingly male-orientated society.

Seals and gems continue to provide the main evidence about religious practice, and one element which clearly maintains its religious significance is the sun. Whereas for the earlier period I could only suggest tentatively that some scenes showed women dancing to the sun, this later period has a virtual deluge of Cretan sun-dancers. We also have some rather larger-scale religious scenes from the mainland, centred on a female figure (whether she is a goddess or a priestess) with the sun, or sun and moon, in attendance (for example, Figure 6). And we can see the sun linked with bird and fish, as well as with fertile vegetation, in religious scenes. Birds were clearly important in religion, and we find many dancing bird-women, some perhaps with suns. We also find lions linked with the sun and still find them closely associated with female figures.

You could present a good case that not all these motifs are suns, but some of them certainly are. It is hard to understand how they have either passed unrecognised as suns or unnoticed as a significant religious feature by the generations of scholars who have turned their eyes on the Bronze Age Aegean. This disregard is perhaps even more surprising since the ruins of Cretan buildings provide independent evidence for the importance of the sun. The large courts of the palaces are all on a north-south-east-west axis, and the archaeologist Shaw has pointed out that they seem to be deliberately aligned for maximum sunlight, especially during winter. Perhaps the rituals performed there were related to the sun. Many shrines and sanctuaries of this period, not just in Crete but over the whole Aegean area, face east.

Preoccupation with the sun's movements evidently continues, and new possibilities are opened up for our understanding of earlier Cretan religion. Again a link is suggested between women, the rising or setting of the sun, rebirth from death, and the regrowth of fertile plant life.

Evidence for the religious significance of the sea also continues and is amplified. Shells are found in graves and in shrines, in one case at Knossos even paving a sanctuary floor. What of the fish? I suggested that in the earlier period it was associated with the nightly journey of the sun and therefore of the dead. This later material offers further evidence of links between the fish and the sun, a female deity, the dead, and ideas of fertility and rebirth: fish on sarcophagi (the terracotta tubs used as coffins), fish engraved on seals with suns, with boughs, and with an imposing female figure sometimes described by scholars as 'goddess with fish'.

The evidence about boats tells an even fuller story. Model boats are found in graves and boats are painted on sarcophagi. A famous sarcophagus from Aghia Triadha in Crete shows a boat being presented as an offering to the deceased. Evidently a boat was regarded as useful for the dead, perhaps for their journey. For a wealth of further evidence, there is a fascinating series of boat scenes engraved on seals and rings. The boats hold a female figure or figures, priestesses or possibly divinities, as in one case the figure is flying in the air. Suggested by various scholars to be the epiphany of a goddess, or even 'the departure of the goddess', we may wonder whether these scenes in fact show a sun deity taking her leave by boat for her westerly journey. Sometimes she has a little structure (an altar?) on the boat; in one she has a hand raised to her head in a formal gesture of mourning (Figure 7). As in several cases she takes vegetation with her, perhaps it is actually her departure for the winter which we are being shown.

I am reminded of the earlier material, especially the boats on the belly of the 'frying-pans'. The evidence of this later period too suggests that boats were linked with the journey of the dead, of a female priestess or divinity and perhaps of the sun, and that all were linked with rebirth and with the regeneration of vegetation.

However, there are signs that the horse may have been replacing the boat as the means of departure for this deity. For an island people like the Cretans who did not know the horse, a boat may have seemed the most suitable vehicle for the sun and for the dead. For a mainland people who prized the horse highly, the horse might have appeared a more appropriate method of transport. This may be why the boat was gradually replaced by chariots drawn by the horse, and other more fabulous creatures, in funerary pictures during this later period. A special connection between the horse and death is also suggested by some unusual bony evidence: the skeleton of a horse (sometimes cut up) has been found in some Cretan tombs, and at Marathon on the Greek mainland the skeletons of two horses were found laid out in the *dromos* or entrance passage of a *tholos* tomb; perhaps these too were for the dead's journey. The evidence suggests that both boat and horse-and-chariot were imagined as transport for the dead, linked with vegetation and with female attendants or a female deity. These mysterious women are still around, still linked with sun, sea, death and fertility, still retaining the same associations, but now sometimes also drivers of horses.

Earth continues to be celebrated in cult, whether in a female-orientated cave cult or in her mountain aspect. The celebration of Earth and her products remains a recurrent theme in the pictures. Again we see plants growing from stones; we also see plants appearing between the sacred 'horns of consecration', evidently the objects of worship. Vessels continue to play an important role in cult, again shown with vegetation growing out of them. Again the sun is linked with vegetation cult; so are the fish and bird. The people we see in these scenes are involved in ritually touching boughs or a tree, or they dance in bird costume beside a tree or at a tree shrine.

What did these people believe they were doing in such scenes? The actual form of the vegetation ritual appears in a far clearer and more crystallised way, unravelling what was enigmatic in the earlier pictures and making explicit connections which were implicit before. The scanty evidence of the earlier period showed that the cult involved not only watering and touching vegetation but also dance. There were also unexplained scenes of people bending over to touch a jar or vessel. Now from this later, fuller evidence we can see clearly that on the one hand there is a joyful aspect, involving touching or shaking vegetation during an energetic dance, while on the other hand there are figures bending over boulders, jars or stone altars as if in mourning. These may have been burial jars and tombs, or jars storing seeds or grain, or sacred stones. Perhaps all were in some way interchangeable and equated as womb symbols. Jars were still identified with the female belly, and the naked bodies of the people bending over the stones suggest that human and plant regeneration were linked. A series of fascinating scenes, carved on to rings and tiny sealstones, show these activities of dancing or bending in progress (see, for example, Figure 8). The historian Persson, in *The Religion of Greece in Prehistoric Times*, has suggested that what we see is ecstatic mourning such as commonly appears as part of a vegetation cult. In winter the lost vegetation is mourned, and is joyfully greeted on its return in spring.

Persson traces several stages of the ritual, which help us to piece together an order or cycle in the cult scenes. The first stage involves death, departure, the sun going, and associations with the sea and boats which were imagined as transporting away the dead, the sun and the vegetation. The second stage involves mourning, bending over jars, boulders or graves which literally or symbolically contained what was dead: whether the inert seed, the buried body, or a symbol of either. Persson suggests that there was a simultaneous ritual of calling on divine power to aid regeneration, attracting the attention of the divinities 'by shaking the tree . . . or by conjuring up the heavenly powers through an ecstatic dance . . . or by gifts'. Then Persson identifies a stage which perhaps involves the use of fire, lamps and mirrors to re-spark and revitalise what seems to be lost and dead. Then, in spring, the return of life may be celebrated by dancing and perhaps acrobatics. The double axe, in the hands of a woman, appears to be part of the vegetation cult; you can see it in the intricate procession scene shown in Figure 6; this ring may show some kind of 'harvest festival' with offerings celebrating the fruits of the earth later in the summer. The poppies which appear in this picture and elsewhere suggest that opium could have contributed to the ecstatic quality of the rituals, and, with greater likelihood, wine may have played a part. Figure 9 seems to show several different stages of the whole process, including the boat journey.

This cyclical process can be seen as applying to the sun (which undergoes both a daily and a yearly 'death'); to the vegetation; and to the dead person. From the links and overlaps in the rituals we can see that these three elements were somehow linked in the minds of the worshippers, but we cannot tell how they were combined practically in cult. Perhaps the whole cycle of ritual (mourning, revitalising, celebration) was performed together on one occasion in the funeral rites of the dead person; or perhaps the regeneration of the dead was believed to coincide with a phase of cult concerned with the regeneration of vegetation; we cannot tell. What we do know is that by this later period personified deities were now involved. In describing the earlier period I was careful to talk about the 'spirit' of the dead, the 'divinity immanent in' the sun and plants; but for this later period the Linear B tablets, inscribed in a decipherable language, reveal that we are dealing with deities with personal names, and it is probable that the sun or vegetation were now symbolised as a person. Traditionally scholars have tended to assume that the figure at the centre of the cult was a 'male vegetation god', but as we have females departing by sea, females at the centre of mourning and celebration, there is equal reason to think that the divine element involved was female. Nilsson in *Minoan-Mycenaean Religion* is rather surprised at the evidence that the mythical figure Ariadne may originally have been such a deity. He comments:

> It appears . . . from . . . legends that her death is the salient feature in the myths of Ariadne . . . No other heroine suffered death in so many ways as Ariadne, and these different versions can only be explained as originating in a cult in which her death was celebrated.
>
> The Naxian rite gives us the clue. It closely resembles a type of vegetation-festival, well known from the Oriental religions but foreign to the true Greek religion. The death of the god of vegetation is celebrated with sorrow and lamentations: his resurrection with joy and exultation. In these cults it is a god who is worshipped: here it is a goddess, and this seems to make the originality of the cult certain. As far as I know, the death of such a goddess is unique . . .

(Note his surprise at finding a female figure in this role, and his assertion of the foreignness of all this business to the 'true Greek religion'.)

Here then we find a complex of ideas around the issue of death and regeneration which may provide the structure for rituals focused on several different deities: we can see in it the raw materials for the development of a sea deity, a sun deity, a vegetation deity, a fish deity and so on. Archaeology has revealed evidence of other more specific aspects of cult (a goddess concerned with childbirth located in a particular cave here, an animal sacrifice there), just as many different stories, characters and rituals cluster around the fundamental theme of birth/death/resurrection in Christian religious belief. What is striking is that so many of the symbolic identifications of the earlier period continue to hold their power in this later period. We even find the same animals appearing in similar associations: for example, snakes and birds with women, goats with men and in a sexual context, a dog or fox in a ritual scene, the scorpion still popular, and so on. Many of the pictures of people with real or imaginary animals still show a symbiotic relationship in which participation and communication are suggested. We see some survival of identification with the divinity, either by dressing up in animal or bird costumes, or by using dance and frenzied movement to enter what William Taylour in *The Mycenaeans* has called a 'mystic union' with the deity. We can still only speculate whether during such 'mystic union' the deities were believed to respond with gifts of healing, illumination or prophecy to their entranced followers. All we can securely comment on is the continued importance of the female element, a sense of participation with the natural world, and a cyclical world view. Circular and threefold symbolic forms – such as the tripartite altar – continue to hold force.

Moreover, we no longer have to wonder whether we are dealing with one all-embracing monolithic deity, or with a number of local deities, based in nature and with specific roles. The Linear B inscriptions, found on a series of clay tablets and seal impressions at bureaucratic centres both in Crete and on the mainland, have thrown dramatic light upon the issue. They record offerings (for example, of oil, honey, barley) being made to no fewer than 26 divinities, and maybe as many as 70. The most commonly used name 'Potnia', which means 'lady' or 'mistress', is often preceded by a place name perhaps indicating the locality of her shrine. We also find mention of goddesses with completely different names, such as 'Dapuritojo', ('Lady of the Labyrinth'); 'Atanapotinija' ('the Lady Athena'); 'Sitopotinija' (who may be an agricultural deity as *sitos* means 'corn'); 'Eileithyia' (worshipped in the Cretan cave of Amnisos); and 'Divine Mother'. Sometimes deities are grouped together in the records as 'the gods'; or as 'the thirsty ones'; the 'Omirijoi', who may be rain spirits; or the 'Pakijanijoi', who may be local deities of Pakijanes, a site near Pylos. Whether any of the deities cultivated were in fact spirits of the dead is a matter of heated controversy. Some of the names in the tablets are of Olympian deities (Hera, Poseidon, Artemis, Athena, Hermes) who later end up in the classical period as part of the select group at the centre of organised Greek state religion, headed by Zeus. It is evident that the number of deities acknowledged in this period was subsequently whittled down. Fewer deities are mentioned on the mainland tablets than the dozens mentioned at Knossos. There is a trend from the many to the few. A centralised hierarchical divine pantheon with fewer deities would seem to be more compatible with, and supportive of, the palace hierarchies than would the multiplicity of deities created by the earlier more egalitarian and autonomous settlements. We might imagine that the divine family of Olympian gods better reflected the élite ruling the palace centres. The all-subsuming Zeus is nowhere found in early Crete and was apparently invented, or at least promoted, by the Mycenaeans; perhaps he provided a more effective divine sanction for their earthly king or *wanax*. But here we are turning our eyes to what happened in Aegean religion after the tide had turned.

The Tide Turns

I have described some of the elements which survived into this Late Bronze Age period from the earlier period of women's religion. There was, however, much that changed. Gradually, on a seal here and a frieze there, a vase decoration here and a cult scene there, we begin to see unmistakable signs that religious ideas were creaking under the strain of social change. The symbol system is bending, adapting, transforming. Alongside the older traditions, sometimes even on one and the same seal, we see new features appearing.

I have mentioned the larger part played by men in the running of society, and the evidence of growing militarisation. In line with this, we start to see men appearing more prominently in pictures. We also see scenes of violence between men and men, men and animals, one animal and another, such as were hardly ever found in early Cretan art. Artists of this period show more aggression than symbiosis in the animal world. New too is the glorification of hunting (especially the moment of kill) and of the military. We even find items of military equipment celebrated in isolation and sometimes personified as if they had a life of their own.

We see ramifications of this in the realm of religion. One is perhaps the sharper segregation of women and men in cult scenes and festival audiences, easy to distinguish through the convention of painting women with white skin and men with brown. Another new feature is the appearance of divinities carrying weapons; another is the appearance of men playing a larger part than hitherto in religious scenes. The Linear B tablets list religious offerings, to both male and female deities, which were evidently centrally sanctioned and large in size – more in the nature of a tribute. They also record a hierarchy of religious personnel and make it clear that priests and priestesses could now be a sect of influence and wealth. The ruler of the palaces may even have been a high priest or priestess claiming to derive secular power from religious connections. The way is open for religion to become a tool in the acquisition and maintenance of social power and control.

It is generally assumed that the religion of this time was focused on the epiphany, or appearance, of the deity. Whether this appearance was manifested in some visionary experience or realised in the person of a priestess or priest is unclear, but in pictures we can see that the deity or priest figure starts to assume positions of greater status and command. They are brought things, they are honoured by formal processions, as in Figure 6, and sometimes they tower over their celebrants in a way that is not found in the earlier material. The personified deity or priest figure not only assumes larger than human proportions, but we also start to see little divine figures floating in the sky, perhaps revealing a trend by which divinities became elevated, cut off from their roots in the natural world and more abstract in conception. Divinities seem to be both fewer and superior. Although the scale of religious objects is still very small when compared with, say, the Near East or Egypt, large cult objects start to appear more frequently. Shrines and sacred buildings become more grandiose and for the first time we find that they can dwarf their attendants. It seems that as the relationships between humans change, so does their relationship with the divine.

While many of these inflated deities are female, it is clear that male gods are increasing in importance; they start to lay claim to some of the main religious symbols previously associated with a female divinity. The process starts with the sun, a process which would have taken place very differently in different parts of the Aegean, but which resulted at the end of the Bronze Age in a male sun god. In this era also it first becomes common for women to be represented accompanied by a male child. Scholars suggest that a son-consort of the goddess, joined with her in a holy marriage or *hieros gamos*, became the centre of a fertility cult, dying and being reborn with the vegetation. Some, like Robert Graves in *The Greek Myths,* have linked this young god with other cultures' traditions of a 'year-god' who was sacrificed at the end of his reign. Though there is no firm evidence for such a cult in Greece, we do start to find a personified god or gods of vegetation. We find him apparently growing out of the 'horns of consecration' where we sometimes saw a plant growing. We also see a dramatic development in his relationship with the fabulous creatures called 'genii', whose traditional role was to pour water or libations on the plant. We find the young god grasping his fabulous attendants by the forelock in a gesture of command. Fertility is apparently becoming less of an issue than authority. Divorced from his plant roots, he asserts his control over these traditional attendants of the vegetation rites.

We seem to see the development of a plant spirit into a dominating personified male deity. We might detect some Mycenaean influence here: vegetation cult may not have been so relevant for a people who depended more on stock breeding, trading and raiding, and this shift of emphasis in social organisation perhaps parallels the process whereby the plant fades and a strong male figure grows in significance. Meanwhile the jar or vessel, in earlier Crete associated with the fertility of plants and human erotic activity, can now be decorated with grotesque faces. While the jar, still visualised as female, is attributed sinister qualities, the column is celebrated. The transition from womb to phallus, from creative fertility to man-made institution as a source of power, could hardly be more graphically expressed.

In the animal world we see the same process as that which can be traced with plant life. In the earlier period there was rarely a gesture of domination over animals. The goddess linked with animal life and known as the 'Mistress of Animals' in this late period generally continues to show a symbiotic relationship with the creatures who accompany her. She feeds them or touches them gently, although she sometimes grasps them or commands. The more lately arrived 'Master of Animals', her male counterpart, takes this a stage further: his gesture usually appears as one of control over, rather than affinity with, the creatures who accompany him. Scenes of hunting, killing and sacrificing animals are also more common in this later period.

I have discussed some of the changes in the organisation and practice of religion, and the changes in symbolism, which seem to have coincided with the Mycenaean impact on the Aegean. But the woman symbols were not finished yet. The Mycenaean civilisation was itself to fall, and the battle between the female and the male world view was to be carried on at more sopisticated levels in the making of epics, poetry and myth, before the symbols of female divinity were finally disempowered and the great sky god Zeus could look down from his throne with complacency.

The Slumber before the Dawn of Patriarchy

Historians are not sure how the Mycenaean civilisation came to collapse. It is thought, as G. S. Kirk puts it, that 'signs of increasing economic pressure and social disintegration . . . are to be seen in the series of aggressive enterprises of which the long and costly attack on Troy was the most important' (*Homer and the Epic*). The mainland citadels were divided against each other, probably by petty dynastic quarrels such as those reflected in the later myth of the Seven Against Thebes. They were probably also weakened by unsuccessful expeditions abroad, as in the story of Troy. The later myth of Jason and the Argonauts also dates back to this time and may reflect efforts to travel even further to the north-east in the search for gold and booty. All that archaeology tells us clearly is that from about 1200 BC many of the great Mycenaean palaces began to get burnt and destroyed, and at the same time a new dialect appeared in Greece, known as the Dorian dialect. Were the Dorians, as the old view held, a new people who invaded from the north? Or, as the historian Chadwick has suggested, a local and previously subdued population rising against the Mycenaean masters? All we know is that the Mycenaean culture collapsed and its carriers seem to have fled to obscure parts of the Peloponnese and to Athens, from where they departed in successive migrations to Cyprus and to Asia Minor. There followed what is known as the 'Dark Age'.

The 'Dark Age' appears to us a period of deep slumber in Greek culture. Its people have left few weapons and fewer enduring buildings. Population declined and many technical skills were lost. Communication between different parts of the country was fragmented. People did not use money and lost the art of writing. However, what appears 'dark' to us is largely a lack of records. People still ploughed and sowed the fields. They continued to use many of the old Minoan and Mycenaean sites, and even objects, in religion. We know that rituals relating to agricultural life can survive and hold their ground while rulers change. The historian Snodgrass in *The Dark Age of Greece* has referred to the many surviving traditional festivals which were not linked with official worship. People wove textiles which have long since perished. They saw friends and told stories which were to carry memories of the past Minoan and Mycenaean eras into the great myths and epics of later Greece. Clan structures survived and preserved traditions. Some people still used jars, or *pithoi*, for burial of infants. Innovations, such as the partial introduction of cremation, were few, and the pottery traditions that emerge at the end of the 'Dark Age' show familiar motifs such as birds, goats and snakes. Moreover, the continued use of female figurines and bell-shaped idols in many parts of Greece shows that the goddesses of earlier times were still alive and ready to fight another round.

The Geometric Age and the Institutionalisation of Misogyny

The curtain rises on Greece again about 300 years later, around 900 BC, to reveal a relatively settled society, consisting mostly of small, isolated communities ruled, not by an individual king, but by an oligarchy or sect of aristocrats. The Bronze Age is over: we now find iron in general use. The majority of the population make a living from mixed farming with little to spare, while there are also some specialised groups such as potters, metal-smiths, builders and minstrels. Settlements are grouped round central towns run by the oligarchs, who have been compared to the Old Testament judges. Differences in housing suggest distinct social classes, as the archaeologist Nicolas Coldstream has pointed out in *Geometric Greece*. Though land could be bought or sold, and labourers hired, there is also a group of house-serfs or slaves. The general picture of a static and relatively immobile society, with a sharp division between peasants and nobles, led the historian Burn to compare it with the medieval European feudal system.

Within this hierarchical world, women held a circumscribed place. It seems that they were excluded from legal processes and could not hold property; nor could a woman be head of a family or conduct family sacrifices or religious rites. The poets make it clear that women's work is at the loom and the spindle, their place indoors, their duty to obey their menfolk. When a Homeric hero wants to insult another for weeping or showing weakness, he calls him a 'woman'. So between women and men we now have a clear division of labour and a division of roles. The language of mythological genealogies is revealing: poets tell us that before bearing his child the female is 'tamed' or 'mastered' sexually by the man, a vocabulary derived from the taming of animals. The historian Marylin Arthur, in an essay on early Greece, suggests that control over the woman, and especially her sexuality, was felt to be essential – and at the same time problematic – because of the man's dependence on an heir to maintain family rights over land. She also suggests that the woman's very exclusion from political responsibility, and her liability to be transferred in marriage from one family to another, made her loyalty to her social order and family dubious. Linda Sussman, in the same essay collection, suggests that the need to control population growth caused changes in attitudes towards female sexuality, while growing urbanisation, and the specialisation of what had been women's household industries, led to a devaluing of women's work. Whatever the social causes, this period shows, as the historian Chester Starr puts it in *The Origins of Greek Civilization*, a 'hardening of masculine claims to superiority'. We will see what effect this had on the symbols, pictures and stories which this period produced.

The many large and densely decorated vases whose 'Geometric' patterns give their name to this age, show a convention-bound formalism which contrasts strongly with the flowing style of earlier Crete; it is these vases which show us the pictorial symbols and images being shaped in the consciousness of this re-emergent culture.

From around 800 BC there is a quickening: the Olympian Games are founded, drawing together people from different parts of Greece. Trade increases, and the growth of population leads to expansion and the founding of colonies. Renewed contact with the Near East provides a revitalising influence. Towards the end of the eighth century BC writing comes back into use and written poetry is produced for the first time.

Some mystery surrounds the two first large-scale works of Greek literature, those of Homer and of Hesiod. Who was Homer? Did he exist? Or does the name stand for a number of anonymous oral poets? No one is quite sure who first wrote down the Homeric epics, the *Iliad*, about the Trojan War, and the *Odyssey*, about the hero Odysseus' journey home from that war. However, it is agreed that these epics are based on an oral tradition preserving stories from the Mycenaean age seen through later, Geometric, eyes and reflecting the values and everyday life of this later period. Little more is known about the life of Hesiod, apparently a small-scale owner-farmer living in Boeotia, who wrote (or had attributed to him) a series of poems on practical living and on traditional mythological subjects. There are also the so-called 'Homeric Hymns', traditional poems of uncertain authorship, written down from the eighth century BC onwards. The rediscovery of the alphabet and the creation of literature means that we can see the struggle for the control of symbols played out in a whole new area: that of mythmaking and poetry.

In this period I will trace the continuation of the trend away from a symbolism reflecting the power of the female towards a symbolism reflecting male power. As the social systems of patriarchy become increasingly entrenched, we will see the male deities take control of the sky, allowing female deities a place in 'heaven' only in male-specified roles, and banishing the rest to the lower regions of earth. The old Cretan female symbols are either co-opted, or become discredited: a familiar process whereby the gods of the old religion become the devils of the new religion. The process reflects a historic shift, begun in the Mycenaean age, towards a society in which one half of the population, the women, are politically inferior to the other half. The repercussions of this shift in the symbolic plane can be seen not only in the division of male gods from female gods, but also in the separation of sky from earth, of mind from body, of spirituality from sexuality. Incorporated into the mainstream of Greek thought and later crystallised in the philosophical writings of Plato, these ideas then pass via Neoplatonism into Christian theology and contribute to the symbolic world view which is still dominant in western society today. From this early Greek Geometric period onwards, European culture ceases to offer the imaginative vocabulary for any human being, female or male, to experience themselves as whole and undivided.

By this age we find a specific and articulate theology. Homer and Hesiod both offer a clear picture of a set of gods dwelling on the heights of Mount Olympus, who preside over the world of men in much the same way as the nobles of the Geometric age presided over the rest of the population. This Olympian line-up of deities was headed by the ill-matched couple of Zeus and Hera, and included Athena, Aphrodite, Apollo, Poseidon, and other names familiar from Greek mythology. They, and the stories and values they carry, represent an organised and institutionalised aspect of Greek religion, projecting a view of the world which we may guess was in the interests of a dominant class of Greek society. The Homeric poems, as epic poetry orientated towards an aristocratic audience, seem to reflect a class bias in their emphasis on the Olympian gods; the more popular elements of religion seem to slip in as if by oversight. Poetry designed to entertain aristocrats will not tend to promote the world view of the peasant. Hesiod, though not a peasant, is closer to the soil, and his poems are full of what scholars call 'magical' or 'superstitious' ideas. He pays lip service to Zeus and the Olympians, but dwells far more on observances of a very different kind, concerning the sun, streams, the natural world, the dates of the month, and daily life. He probably reflects more accurately than Homer the preoccupations of men working the land on a day-to-day basis. I say 'men' rather than 'people' because his misogynism is blatant, and he will not tell us anything about the work, activities, myths or rituals specifically concerning women. None the less, Hesiod's poems, together with the vase decorations and what slips through the net in Homer, provide enough evidence to show that earlier beliefs were not forgotten.

Alongside the religion of the Olympian gods, we can trace the survival of some Bronze Age traditions and 'animistic' ideas of divinity immanent in nature. In the Bronze Age we saw that plant life had a central place in cult. Hesiod's instruction to pray before ploughing shows that agricultural activity was still the stuff of religion. Homer lets slip only a few mentions of plant magic, but surviving pictures from this period suggest rituals celebrating plant life which involved dancing and athletics. Whenever a divinity appears in these scenes, she is female. Moreover, one of the 'Homeric Hymns' gives us the full story of Demeter and Persephone, in which plant life is central. This story is one of the most important early myths and was to survive until the classical era at the centre of the popular mystery cult known as the Eleusinian Mysteries. The origin of this mystery religion is debated, but it does have Bronze Age parallels. In the story, Persephone is picking flowers when Hades, God of the Dead, snatches her in his chariot and takes her down to the underworld. Her mother Demeter's desperate grief causes the earth to become barren (winter?) so that Hades is obliged to let Persephone return (spring?), but only after she has eaten a pomegranate which will ensure her return to the underworld for a third of each year. The story is closely linked with the cycle of vegetation, and the strength of the relationship between the two women recalls the female pairs common in Bronze Age art. The parallel between Persephone as a disappearing vegetation goddess and the female figures departing with vegetation by boat on Bronze Age seals might also suggest that this story grows out of older traditions of fertility cult. We can see two main differences in the way she disappears: the boat is replaced by the chariot, and, whereas the Bronze Age females left of their own accord, Persephone is kidnapped by a male god.

Other symbols are changing too. What is happening to them?

The Rising Gods of the Geometric Age

Confronted with the symbols inherited from the Bronze Age, the Olympian gods adopt one of two strategies: they encroach and co-opt; or they downgrade. Among the first elements to be co-opted, to become male, were the sky and the sun. Among the first to be downgraded was the earth.

It is revealing to read Hesiod's account of the creation of the world in his poem, the *Theogony*. He starts:

Now in the beginning Chaos came to be, but next broad-bosomed Earth, the ever-sure foundation of all the gods . . .

So Earth came first, but a few lines later she gives birth to 'starry heaven, her equal, to cover her on every side . . .' Now Heaven, who is male in gender, takes exception to some of the children he fathers from Earth and forces them to hide in 'a secret place' inside her, away from the light of day. Eventually she, groaning within, gives one of the children, Kronos, a sickle. The story comes to its climax as follows:

And Heaven came, bringing on night, and stretched himself full out all over the Earth, longing for love. Then the son from his ambush . . . took the huge long sickle . . ., and swiftly sliced off his own father's genitals.

The son castrates the father, and war between the sexes is declared.

Many of the themes of patriarchy are already present in this early account: the conflict between father and son reminiscent of the later Oedipus story; the deceitful and potentially castrating nature of the female; even perhaps a primordial allusion to the man's place in love-making: on top, enveloping the woman below. Although Hesiod points out Heaven's wrongdoing in confining his children, the result of the story is to put Earth in a bad light. We are left with a self-righteous, superior and desexualised Heaven and an irreparable breach between sky and earth. The separation of a male Heaven from a female Earth speaks of changes in the symbolism of up and down, male and female, light and dark. The cosmos is divided.

The poets seem aware that the Earth they know is a shadow of her former self, and has been stripped of powers she held in ancient times. In his *Theogony* Hesiod tells us that thunder, the thunderbolt and lightning had been hidden by Earth before they were given to Zeus.

Now they are used against her: Homer tells us that the earth groans beneath the battering of Zeus the thunderer when he is angry. What of the earth-womb's power of procreation, so celebrated in Bronze Age times? Even that is pre-empted by the male. The very same sickle-wielding son of Earth, Kronos, who castrated his father Heaven, grows up to swallow his own children (born of the goddess Rhea, another earth figure) so that no son of his could usurp his ruling position. Zeus is the only son who escapes, by being raised secretly. This is the same story reduplicating: Heaven forced the babies back inside, Kronos swallows them himself as soon as they are outside. In both cases, the father interferes with childbirth. We have, if not 'womb envy', certainly disregard for, and disempowerment of, the workings of the womb. The succession problems of the divine royal family are not solved until the next generation, when Zeus settles the matter once and for all by swallowing his wife Metis whole; he then gives birth himself to Athena, an 'honorary male' goddess lacking in female sexual attributes. The myth could be interpreted as showing the attempts of male divinities, over three generations, to deny and appropriate the procreative power of the earth-womb in the vocabulary of myth.

Of the few places where religious observances continued unbroken from the Mycenaean Age right through the 'Dark Age' to the Geometric Age, Coldstream lists no fewer than four major sites (including Delos, Delphi and Olympia) where a male god replaced a female one during the 'Dark Age'. Divine attributes were changing hands. So it is no surprise that the most prominent occupant of the heavens, the sun, is by now indisputably male. It is known as Helios, a chariot-driver, attributed a traditionally male occupation (herding). What is different about Geometric solar symbolism is not only the male sex of the sun, but also the emphasis placed on his power of sight. Homer tells us that Helios' eye misses nothing in the world, and he sometimes acts as a spy for the gods. On the Early Bronze Age 'frying-pans' (Figure 5) the sun was placed on the female belly; now the part of the body associated with the sun is the eye. From female belly to male eye, from source of regeneration to supervising role, is quite a shift. Paul Friedrich, in *The Meaning of Aphrodite*, suggests there is a symbolic link between sight and male sexuality. In the Geometric material we find that the absence of light, the invisible and blackness are described as bad and unpleasant. And Helios is not the only deity attributed with this overseeing role. Zeus has an Eye which sees everything, and Apollo also spies on the deeds of men: again, a complex picture suggesting not the direct transmission and continuity of one tradition, but the collision of different religious traditions which results in the scattering of different solar associations to different divinities.

The archer god Apollo, more significant than Helios in the Olympic pantheon, was responsible for purification and healing. There is a very revealing poetic account of how Apollo gained control of the important oracular shrine at Delphi. Sources state that the site at Delphi was originally a shrine of Earth, where a dragoness, or snake held sway. The shrine centred on a sacred round stone called the *omphalos*; the word means 'navel', recalling the importance of the stone-belly connection in the Bronze Age. The *Homeric Hymn to Apollo* tells how he wiped out this shrine:

> Whoever met [the dragoness], the day of doom carried him away, until Lord Apollo, who shoots from afar, fired a strong arrow at her . . . and darkness covered her eyes. And the holy power of Helios made her rot away there, from which the place got its present name of Pytho; and people call Lord Apollo 'Pythian' after it, because on that spot the power of piercing Helios made the monster rot away.

If myths are thought to epitomise political trends, a clearer metaphor of the male takeover could hardly be found. The new male sky-and-sun authority (expressed in the combined efforts of Helios and Apollo) violently defeats the old earth-based, female-centred religion based on the 'belly-stone' and symbolised by the dragoness or snake. The snake, previously revered, becomes monstrous, a symbol of everything in the old religion which has to be rejected, one of the first major symbols to be thoroughly discredited. From the role it plays in Greek history it is clear that control of the Delphic oracle was an important political weapon, too powerful and influential a weapon perhaps to be left in control of women, and it is likely that the transition from female to male control of prophecy was a period of struggle, expressed poetically in the battle of Apollo with the snake.

The Death-bringing Earth

Monique Saliou has pointed out that the exclusive identification of 'woman' with 'earth' happened at the time when women were removed from work on, and ownership of, the land, and actually represents the opposite of the valuation of women. The symbolism of this exclusively female earth offers, as we have seen, many new elements. The Earth which suffers under Heaven, which is defeated by Apollo, has remained female but is taking on qualities not only of passivity but of the sinister. Instead of being revered as the source of life, her vegetative and animal creations celebrated, Earth becomes in Hesiod's *Theogony* the home of sinister hybrid creatures. The dog, the snake, the lion, the very creatures who appeared as motives revered in the earlier religion, are now selected for inclusion in a nightmare hotch-potch of flesh-eating monsters.

This new conception of earth goes hand in hand with different ideas about death. Whereas the earth in the early Cretan belief system was a womb for regeneration, and the grave a stage in a cycle of rebirth, it is now seen as a dead end, a cold dark place where people go when they die, never to return. In her article, 'Death in the 8th Century and After', Christiane Sourvinou-Inwood points out that changes in funeral practices, such as the shifting of the funeral feast away from the grave, the use of more individualised grave markers and purification rituals to cleanse death-related pollution, all suggest fear and revulsion towards death, and growing anxiety about personal survival which sems to outweigh the earlier sense of death 'as a collective phenomenon, part of the world's life-cycle'. Now those who die are believed to go into the ground and stay there; their disembodied ghosts cross the ocean to the gloomy realm of Hades from which they do not return. In Homer's *Odyssey*, Book ii, Odysseus visits this realm of the dead, and finds ineffectual disembodied ghosts who flutter to and fro with 'a moaning that was horrible to hear'. The ghost of the hero Achilles tells Odysseus, 'Put me on earth again, and I would rather be a serf in the house of some landless man . . . than king of all these dead men.' The shades of the Trojan war heroes are all there, battle wounds gaping, still nursing anxieties and resentments, with all the cares of the living and none of the joys. Homer's epic battle scenes show vainglorious personal ambition and a male-orientated individualism; we might wonder how much these values would have eroded an earlier vision of a soul or life force which could shed a particular body or personality and reappear vitalising another life form. Achilles is so entrenched as Achilles, so obsessed with Achilles' fame and Achilles' glory, that any idea of regeneration or survival which is not completely personalised is out of the question. The patriarchal hero Herakles (Hercules) is embattled against the underworld as well as the animal world. However, what mainly concerns us here is how this new gloomy vision of earth and of death is linked with a changed attitude to women and to the body. Let's look at the Greek account of the creation of the first woman.

Blaming the Body

Feminists have recently been examining the Old Testament's patriarchal version of the creation of the world and its story about Eve and the snake. They have pointed out the misogynism of a story which blames the Fall of humanity on women. The Greek version of the creation of women succeeds, like the Bible story, in attributing to women the destructive power of sexuality and the responsibility for bringing all ills on to humankind. As told in Hesiod's *Works and Days* and *Theogony*, the story starts when Zeus tells the Titan Prometheus that, as a punishment for his stealing fire,

'. . . I will give men something bad, in which they can all delight while they are embracing their own destruction.' And he coommanded . . . Hephaistos to quickly mix water with earth and place it in a human voice and human strength, and to shape it into the sweet and lovely form of a young girl, with a face like the immortal goddesses; and he told Athena to teach her skills, the weaving of the delicate loom; and golden Aphrodite to shed over her grace and cruel desire and crippling cares. And he ordered Hermes the guide . . . to place in her the mind of a bitch and a deceitful character . . . And he called the woman Pandora . . .

Because before this the human race lived on earth quite isolated and free from troubles and hard labour and serious illnesses . . . But the woman's hands lifted the great lid off the jar and scattered all these, causing suffering and misery for humankind. Only Hope remained inside, in its impregnable home under the lip of the jar, and did not fly out into the open . . . But the rest, countless miseries, wander amongst men; for the earth and sea are full of evils . . .

For she was the founder of the race of women . . . who live among mortal men as a source of misery to them . . . As in the covered hives the honey bees feed the gangs of drones who are up to no good, . . . in the same way Zeus who thunders on high set women among mortal men as a source of problems, a confederacy of troublemakers. And he gave a further evil to offset the good: the man who, shunning marriage and female mischief, refuses to wed, reaches wretched old age without anyone to take care of his declining years . . . And whoever chooses the lot of marriage and has a conscientious wife well suited to his temperament, for him the bad still continually offsets the good . . .

Beneath the blatant misogyny of this story, and the overt stereotyping of women's roles in the division of labour, there lie a number of complex symbolic threads and tensions, as earlier positive connections are turned to negative. Pandora is a creature of earth and her name in origin was an epithet applied to Earth meaning 'all-giving' or 'bounteous'; but in this story all she gives is bad. The celebration of the creativity of the earth is replaced by mistrust of its workings and fear of the woman and the womb with which it was associated. Like the earlier earth and nature deities celebrated in the fertility rituals of Crete, Pandora is linked with a jar. But in the Bronze Age the jar was touched reverentially or put forth fertile vegetation, while now the opening of the jar is a disaster and all that emerges is evil. The attitude to sexuality and fertility has changed dramatically. Longing or desire is now 'cruel'. We have come a long way from those earlier female figures, sure and whole in themselves and proudly celebrating their sexuality. Now the woman brings both delight and destruction at the same time; Pandora looks beautiful but she has a deceitful nature. Now that woman is separated off as a second-class citizen, the sexual feelings of desire which draw a man to her are ambivalent, discreditable, suspect, regrettable. Women, as social inferiors, taint what they carry, and sexuality becomes something potentially harmful or degrading. By creating an enemy in his home, man has also created an enemy within his heart: his sexual feelings. There is a tension between sex and sense, between beauty and an untrustworthy nature, between appearance and reality. Nothing is any more what it seems; no person is any longer whole but rather torn and divided within. Somewhere behind this story, and perhaps behind the Eve story, lies an intuition that there has been a price to pay for the path towards knowledge and progress which patriarchy has chosen (fire, the apple). That price for the men who create the dominant culture has been the loss of innocence, the loss of the body, the learning of shame about sexual feelings and of hatred for the woman who arouses those feelings. The advance of the spirit has been at the expense of the body.

We can notice too a changed attitude to reproduction and childbearing. No longer a magical vessel swollen with power, the

pregnant woman is seen in the Pandora story only as a vehicle for the
man to have heirs to tend his ageing years. Monica Sjöö has speculated
on the implications of discrediting the female role in reproduction:

> . . . when the cult of the male god was firmly established, there
> must have been great difficulty in explaining how he could be the
> giver of life to all creation, since the man, unlike the woman,
> cannot produce from his own body either the child or the food
> for the child. The whole attitude of human beings toward god had
> to be altered; there could never be that vital link between the child
> and the father that there is between the child and its mother; this
> meant from the reliigious point of view a separation between the
> human and the divine . . . [The father] is *not* of the same substance,
> and the relationship becomes abstract and alienated. That is why
> the creation can then be thought of as evil and the idea of original
> sin becomes possible. This lays the basis for all further alienated
> relationships.

The body, instead of being openly celebrated *as a link with the divine*
as in earlier Crete, becomes that which marks humans down as *less
than divine*: it becomes that which brands them as inferior. As the gift
of the 'bad' woman, sexuality must be viewed with suspicion. These
are the values which lead to the body's needs being denied, its
impulses discredited, its activities strictly controlled.

As with all these symbolic changes, a connection can be made to
the changed social conditions of Greece which I described earlier: the
new formations of class, wealth and power, economic forces and social
structures. The anthropologist Mary Douglas has elaborated on this
parallel between social organisation and attitudes to the body. In
Natural Symbols she suggests that a concern to preserve social
boundaries will be reflected in a concern with the definition of bodily
boundaries. The more value a society sets on social constraints, the
more value it will set on bodily control:

> The human body is the most readily available image of a system
> . . . the body tends to serve as a symbol of evil, as a structured
> system contrasted with pure spirit which by its nature is free and
> undifferentiated . . .
> . . . along the dimension from weak to strong pressure the social
> system seeks progressively to disembody or etherealize the forms
> of expression; this can be called the purity rule . . .

. . . the more the social situation exerts pressure on persons involved in it, the more the social demand for conformity tends to be expressed by a demand for physical control . . .

Here in Geometric Greece we have what is usually described as a static and hierarchical society with a sharp division between the ruling oligarchs and other sections of the population. I have also commented on the social control of women. And sure enough, in line with Mary Douglas' hypothesis, we find specific instructions about a bizarre series of controls to be exerted on both the sexual and excretory functions of the body. These controls are listed in Hesiod's *Works and Days*. Their emphasis on right living and religious observance through strict bodily control (over talking, excretion, timing, cleanliness) contrasts dramatically with the glimpses of energetic and ecstatic religion in earlier art. We gain a clear sense of a body hierarchy in exactly the sense Mary Douglas describes. Women and what they touch (for example their washing water) is impure and dangerous to men. Death apparently carries a feminine influence, for sitting on tombstones can make a male 'unmanly'. The discrimination of women from men, and of earth from sky, brings fear of what is now suppressed. In the earlier religion, death was significant in ritual activity, closely linked with human fertility and rebirth, and integrated to the extent that the remains of the dead were used in cult. Now, however, Hesiod suggests that funerals and even tombstones are anathema and dangerous to the whole process of religion and procreation. Women's association with funerary ritual, previously important and empowering, now appears contaminating.

Overall, a circular model incorporating the ebb and flow, waxing and waning of day and night, life and death, seems to have been replaced by a polarised one with purity on one side and impurity on the other; spirit on one side, matter on the other; male on one side, female on the other; sun gods and the male principle on one side, genitals and body products on the other.

There are many different levels on which these precepts and myths like that of Pandora can be apprehended, and I would not like to reduce them simply to masculinist propaganda. However, it is clear that stories and images which we tend to set in a world apart as 'archetypal myths' or 'timeless poetry' can be interpreted as operating on one level as polemic in a specific social struggle. As Sarah Pomeroy has put it in *Goddesses, Whores, Wives, and Slaves*, 'Myths are not lies, but rather men's attempt to impose a symbolic order upon their universe'. Mythic stories can thus be seen as tools in a propaganda war whereby those involved in the perpetuation of the mythic tradition shaped it to reflect their interests, and to give a divine sanction to the subordination of women. One would not call this a conspiracy any more than one could apply that term to the mother-in-law jokes we see on the television, or press coverage which is based on the side of the police. It is simply that those in power like to hear the 'truths' which validate them and reflect their interests as a race, as a sex, as a class. Inevitably, therefore, these are the truths which are sponsored, encouraged, repeated and held in circulation. In Geometric Greece, which had no newspapers or television, the carriers of those values were pictorial motifs, rituals, sayings, oral poetry, and in particular mythic stories.

Such, then, is the fate met by the female symbols which were so powerful in the earlier period. The symbols of sun, bird, horse and fish are more or less totally co-opted: they become male symbols. At the same time the symbolic associations of earth, sex, death, darkness, snake, dog and lion become negative. They are discredited and relegated to a murky (female) world inferior to that of the Olympian gods. To the two fates of co-option and discrediting is added a third: silence. Some of the early symbols, and the beliefs and customs linked with them, are simply not mentioned. We know they survived because of later evidence. The technique of undermining by silence is harder to chart but cumulatively the omissions make themselves vividly felt as page after page of the Homeric epics pass with barely a mention of, for example, the fertility goddess Demeter. Magical practices and customs of tending the dead, to which archaeology testifies, pass unmentioned in book after book of heroic poetry, the medium through which the aristocracy of the period perpetuated its own vision and attempted to consign any conflicting traditions to oblivion.

Suppression and Survival: the Heritage of Classical Greece

The process of symbol transformation and takeover is complex. Here I have been able only to pick out a few threads and strands in a dense fabric. Moreover I have looked only at the first few hundred years of a process of writing, mythmaking and philosophising which continued right down to the Greek classical period of the fifth century BC. I can do no more than to mention that the use of symbols to discredit women continues consistently throughout that time. In 'Law, Custom and Myth', John Gould has pointed out that in Greek myth 'male attitudes to women ... are marked by tension, anxiety and fear'. Perhaps one of the most painful aspects of this process is the way in which the very same symbols which were important in the women's culture become used against them. Thus, in the sixth century, the poet Semonides compiles a list of undesirable stereotypes of women, which includes the sow (who is fat and dirty), the bitch (prying, talkative), the earth (stupid and gluttonous), the mare (fastidious and unprepared to work), the sea (too changeable), and so on. There is clearly some survival of the tradition which linked those symbols to women, but now they are used to reinforce male values of hatred and contempt towards the female. In *Sowing the Body*, Page duBois charts the continued stripping of power and dignity from symbols of the female body, like the jar and earth: from 'fruitful inside' it becomes seen as 'mere receptacle'.

What we see over the centuries is not just the continuing derogation of women in myths and symbols. We also see what inevitably ensues: the widening split between mind and body, between spirituality and sexuality. As the power of women and of sexuality became associated with physical blindness, men developed the mind's eye. Bruno Snell in *The Discovery of the Mind* has suggested that Greek art and literature, during the Geometric period and later, reflect a view of the body which changes from an assemblage of articulated parts, each possessing relatively autonomous life energy (so that the concept of the spiritual is not divorced from the corporeal), to a synthesised body occupied by an abstract spirit which is polarised and separate from it. In Homer's view of the body, the life force is still seen as occupying the body *passim*, and death can be expressed by phrases like 'his knees sank' or 'darkness covered his eyes'. This changes to a picture where death is expressed as a non-physical spirit or life force leaving the physical body, and where 'psyche', or soul, is seen as a centre of self 'which is not body and which is related to body as master is to slave', (as David Claus has put it in *Toward the Soul*). In the centuries after the Geometric era, poets tell us that their mind can be where their body is not; that the spirit and the internal contrasts with what is external; that they love and love not. Themes of nostalgia, separation, longing, bitter-sweet love, contradiction, ambivalence and emotional tension flower in verse. While in the earlier period love had evidently been seen as one of the great delights of life, like dancing, wine and sleep, it now becomes in poetry a source of misery, making the lover 'dead with desire'. That appearances deceive, that virtue is an abstract, internal, invisible quality, become oft-repeated clichés as substance is vanquished by idea and spirit. E.R. Dodds in *The Greeks and the Irrational* has shown how at the same time the concerns of religion move steadily away from physical action (such as the performing of 'public' rituals) towards interiority, morality and guilt. He has described this as the transition from a 'shame' culture ('shame' being a public or social notion externally expressed) to a 'guilt' culture (where the burden of moral responsibility is carried *internally*). The divine, from being a source of joy, gradually becomes a source of fear and the punitive role of the supernatural is emphasised.

The most well-known period in Greek history is the classical era between approximately 500 and 400 BC: this is the age famous for Athenian 'democracy', the Parthenon and Greek tragedy. By this time patriarchal values had become deeply entrenched and reached their acme of militarism and imperialism in Athens, while the position of women remained subordinate. Society's dependence on slavery had increased the division between mental and physical labour. Only a small proportion of the population actually participated in the running of the 'democracy' from which women, slaves, immigrants and many peasants were effectively excluded. The process of propaganda continued its work, and that most esteemed of Greek artistic products, the tragedy, is sometimes clearly a vehicle for reaffirming the inferiority of women and the authority of the civic religion of the Olympian gods. One of the most poignant examples is the defeat of the female principle in Aeschylus' famous *Oresteia* trilogy.

By the late classical era, dualism is so established that in the fourth century BC the philosopher Aristotle in his *Metaphysics* reports a current theory that divides the world into opposing pairs, including right and left, male and female, straight and crooked, light and darkness, good and evil. He also remarks that the soul rules the body like a master, and that the male is by nature superior, the female inferior, the male ruler and the female subject (in his *Politics*). The philosopher Plato, born in the late fifth century BC, describes the soul as imprisoned in the body, and material reality as a pale shadow of a higher spiritual reality which is ethereal. Over the centuries that follow, this division between spirit and matter is propagated by Neoplatonism, the dominant philosophy of the pagan world from the third to sixth centuries AD. Via teaches like St Augustine and

Boethius, it is in turn inherited and perpetuated by Christianity with its doctrine of the pure white soul alien from, and mastering, the dark 'animal' instincts of the body. Plato's theory of the 'Idea' as more real than the physical-material (epitomised in his fable about the Cave) has in turn influenced many twentieth-century thinkers from Jung to Lacan.

Zeus had won the victory, then, on paper and in marble. Literature, public buildings, official cults, quality statues and pottery, all the media of power and prestige, carry the same message. But the evidence available to us from classical Athens is, as Gould has put it, 'almost without exception the product of men and addressed to men in a male dominated world.' It shows only one side of the picture. If the victory was won on paper, oral traditions continued. If the Olympian gods were officially victorious, their opponents went underground and survived. As Jane Harrison comments in *Themis*,

> The Olympian gods . . . seemed to me like a bouquet of cut-flowers whose bloom is brief, because they have been severed from their roots. To find those roots we must borrow deep into a lower stratum of thought, into those chthonic cults which underlay their life and from which sprang all their brilliant blossoming.

The former women's customs were too deeply rooted in popular life to be killed off altogether. As Dietrich puts it in *The Origins of Greek Religion*, 'the aspects of the gods revered in [public] cult . . . seemed to appeal only to a section of the city-state: the ruling classes'. Wherever one group of the population is subordinated, wherever its beliefs, traditions and symbols are suppressed and discredited, that group will resist the process: 'where there is oppression, there is resistance'. So it seems to have been in ancient Greece. Thus we find that a women's culture, perpetuating aspects of the old religion and the old symbols, continues to survive. It lacked access to the channels of communication which preserved male traditions, and thus we know of it mainly through hints about what we have lost. We hear of women poets: Corinna who allegedly beat the poet Pindar at a contest and was called a 'sow' by him; Telesilla; Praxilla who apparently told local myths in simple language. Their work is almost entirely lost like so much of popular ancient Greek culture. We know that in one fragment ascribed to Corinna she claimed to sing 'for women'. We know from a passing contemptuous reference in Semonides that there was much 'women's gossip about venery'. From what we can gather piecemeal, it seems that women did get together, talked, sang, and preserved many of their ancient traditions and rituals.

Homer may banish any mention of 'magical' practices from his epic verse, but we know they existed and continued. Mostly from passing and sidelong references we hear, for example, about the goddess Hecate, the witch Circe ('daughter of the Sun'), about the continuing importance of the nymphs in country religion, and of allied cults in which plants and the spirits which occupied them were sacred. There is a continuing tradition of sacred stones. Although they never receive the full official blessing of the state, traditions of ecstatic religion continue, as in the cult of Dionysus. And although the earth and fertility goddess Demeter was never fully accepted as one of the Olympian deities, her cult at Eleusis was one of the most powerful centres of religious life in classical Athens. With a snake attendant, a sustained focus on the mother-daughter relationship, and based around cycles of vegetation and fertile plant life, her cult recalls earlier, woman-based prehistoric religion. Nor does it seem a coincidence that one of the main Athenian religious festivals of the year, the Anthesteria, included rituals of opening jars, celebrating seed and addressing the dead, activities reminiscent of early Cretan religion; this festival has been described by Jane Harrison in *Themis* as 'a feast of the revocation of souls and the blossoming of plants, a feast of the great reincarnation cycle of man and nature'. Every so often in myths and poems, a mention slips in of 'witches' who 'sing spells', brew herbs in cauldrons, charm snakes and use fire and birds to take part in other 'magical' practices, suggesting that the older rituals of the women's religion were not forgotten and perhaps remained most strongly preserved in the countryside.

Nor have those traditions ever been completely lost since. In *Zeus*, Cook describes how as late as the nineteenth century the story was still told at Eleusis about 'St Dhimitra' whose daughter was carried off by a Turkish magician. Although mainstream Christianity perpetuated the divided world view of patriarchy, yet on its underbelly, at its fringes, sometimes underground, sometimes surfacing, alternative symbolic systems have survived. We can look for them in Gnostic Christianity and other heretic sects or mystical teachings such as the Cabbala; we can look for them in the traditions of astrology, alchemy, the Tarot, witchcraft and other esoteric or occult bodies of knowledge which can be traced back over thousands of years and linked to ancient women's traditions in Greece and other parts of the Mediterranean. Forgotten, resurrected, buried, influenced by patriarchy, often distorted by suppression, these alternative symbolic systems have survived into the twentieth century.

In this book I have looked at the ways in which we can work with our dreams, our fantasies, our bodies, to dismantle the dominant symbolism which we have all internalised, and allow the surfacing of new symbols which reflect a different experience and values. In this process we may find it useful to draw on some of the alternative symbolic systems which have survived from the past. If we do, the legacy of the women of Crete is in some form still there for us to reach towards.

Book References

Page numbers relate to passages referred to or quoted, listed in most cases in the order in which they have been used. Where there are numerous references to the same text, or where the context may not be obvious, I have indicated the subject matter. I have also pointed out which are the most suitable books to start on.

Aeschylus, *The Oresteian Trilogy*, trans. P. Velacott, Penguin, Harmondsworth, Middx. 1956.

Aristotle, most accessible in *The Metaphysics, Books I-IX*, trans. H. Tredennick, Loeb Classical Library, Heinemann, London; Harvard University Press, Cambridge, MA, 1956 (first publ. 1933). See Book I. V. 6, 986a for the list of oppositions.

—— *The Politics*, trans. H. Rackham, Loeb Classical Library, Heinemann, London; Harvard University Press, Cambridge, MA, 1932. See Book I, II, 1254b, 11–12, for the soul mastering the body and men being superior to women.

Arthur, Marylin B., 'Early Greece: the Origins of the Western Attitude Toward Women', in John Peradotto and J.P. Sullivan (eds.) *Women in the Ancient World: the Arethusa Papers*, State University of New York Press, Albany, 1984, pp. 23–6.

Bachofen, J.J., *Myth, Religion and Motherright*, trans. R. Mannheim, Routledge and Kegan Paul, London, 1967 (*Mutterrecht* first publ. Stuttgart, 1861).

Betts, John H., 'Ships on Minoan Seals', *Colston Papers* 23, (Proceedings of the 23rd Symposium of the Colston Research Society, University of Bristol, 1971), Butterworths, London, 1971, pp. 325, 334.

Boardman, John, *Greek Gems and Finger Rings* (Photography by Robert L. Wilkins), Thames and Hudson, London, 1970. Provides a history of Aegean seals with many illustrations.

Bossert, H. Th., *The Art of Ancient Crete*, Zwemmer, London, 1937.

Branigan, Keith, *The Foundations of Palatial Crete*, Routledge and Kegan Paul, London, 1970, p. 97 (seal-stones), 175–6 (after-life), 112 (goat), 107 (peak sanctuary fire). This book provides a compact and handy guide to Crete before the palaces, and lists archaeological sites which can be visited.

—— *The Tombs of Mesara: a Study of Funerary Architecture and Ritual in Southern Crete 2800–1700 BC*, Duckworth, London, 1970, p. 185. This accessible book is an excellent source of information about the Mesara *tholos* tombs.

—— 'The Tombs of Mesara: New Tombs and New Evidence', *Bulletin of the Institute of Classical Studies*, 22, 1974, pp. 200–3.

Briffault, Robert, *The Mothers: a Study of the Origins of Sentiments and Institutions*, Allen and Unwin, London, 1927.

Burn, Andrew Robert, *The World of Hesiod*, Benjamin Blom, New York, 1966, p. 1 (first publ. 1936).

Chadwick, John, *The Mycenaean World*, Cambridge University Press, 1976, pp. 80, 151–2 (on Pylos). Basic book on Mycenaean society.

—— 'The Mycenaean Dorians', *Bulletin of the Institute of Classical Studies*, 23, 1976, pp. 115–16.

Claus, David B., *Toward the Soul: an Inquiry into the Meaning of 'psyche' before Plato*, Yale University Press, New Haven and London, 1981, p. 1.

Coldstream, J.N., *Geometric Greece*, Methuen, London, 1979, pp. 308, 329–31. A very informative guide to the period.

Cook, Arthur Bernard, *Zeus: a Study in Ancient Religion, Vol. I*, Cambridge University Press, 1914, pp. 173–5.

Coontz, Stephanie and Peta Henderson (eds.), *Women's Work, Men's Property: the Origins of Gender and Class*, Verso/New Left Books, London, 1986; see 'Introduction'.

Cornford, F.M., *The Unwritten Philosophy*, Cambridge University Press, 1950, pp. 43–5.

Davis, Elizabeth Gould, *The First Sex*, Penguin, Harmondsworth, Middx., 1972 (first publ. G.P. Putnam's Sons, USA, 1971).

Dickinson, Oliver, *The Origins of Mycenaean Civilization*, Studies in Mediterranean Archaeology No. 49, Paul Aströms Förlag, Göteborg, Sweden, 1977.

Dietrich, B.C., *The Origins of Greek Religion*, Walter de Gruyter, Berlin and New York, 1974, pp. 110 (Goddess), 8 (ideas about fertility), 79–81 (caves), 105 (red ochre), 74, 91 (both on tree cult), 292 ('lowly creatures'), 28 (localised vegetarion figures), 2.

Diner, Helen, *Mothers and Amazon: The First Feminine History of Culture*, Anchor Press/Doubleday, New York, 1973 (first publ. 1965).

Dodds, E.R., *The Greeks and the Irrational*, University of California Press, Berkeley and Los Angeles, 1951.

Douglas, Mary, *National Symbols*, Penguin, Harmondsworth, Middx, 1973, pp. 17 (body as image of a system) 12 (social pressure and physical control).

Doumas, Christos, *The N.P. Goulandris Collection of Early Cycladic Art*, J. Makris, Athens, 1968, pp. 81, 92. A clear and beautifully illustrated general account based on the collection, recently republished by the British Museum as *Cycladic Art* (1983).

—— *Early Bronze Age Burial Habits in the Cyclades*, Studies in Mediterranean Archaeology No. 48, Paul Aströms Förlag, Göteborg, Sweden, 1977, p. 55.

duBois, Page, *Sowing the Body: Psychoanalysis and Ancient Representations of Women*, University of Chicago Press, 1988, pp. 106–7, 39ff (both on changing symbolism of earth and jar).

Durkheim, Emile, *The Elementary Forms of the Religious Life*, Trans. J.W. Swain, Allen and Unwin, London, 1926, pp. 48–86.

Engels, Friedrich, *The Origin of the Family, Private Property and the State*, trans. A. West, Lawrence and Wishart, London, 1972 (first publ. in German 1884).

Evans, Arthur J., *The Mycenaean Tree and Pillar Cult and its Mediterranean Relations*, Macmillan, London, 1901, pp. 21ff, I.

—— *The Palace of Minos Vol. I*, Hafner, London, 1921, p. 125. Along with Volumes II-IV this makes up Evans' classic report of his excavations at the palace of Knossos.

Finley, M.I., *Early Greece: the Bronze and Archaic Ages*, Chatto and Windus, London, 1981, p. 53.

Fleming, Andrew, 'The Myth of the Mother Goddess', *World Archaeology* 1 (2), 1969, pp. 247–61; I quote pp. 249, 257.

Friedrich, Paul, *The Meaning of Aphrodite*, University of Chicago Press, 1978, p. 41.

Marija, Gimbutas, *The Language of the Goddess*, Thames and Hudson, London, 1990.

Gnostic Christianity, see Elaine Pagels, *The Gnostic Gospels*, Random House, New York, 1981.

Goodison, Lucy, *Death, Women and the Sun: Symbolism of Regeneration in Early Aegean Religion*, Institute of Classical Studies, London, 1989. This is the published version of my PhD thesis, which provides fuller evidence and argument for most of the ideas developed in this chapter.

Gould, John, 'Law, Custom and Myth: Aspects of the Social Position of Women in Classical Athens', *Journal of Hellenic Studies*, 100, 1980, pp. 38–59; I quote pp. 57, 58.

Graves, Robert, *The Greek Myths*, Vols. 1 and 2, Penguin, Harmondsworth, Middx, 1955. Informative about Greek myths, but remember that many of the sources he cites come from much later periods of Greek history, and cannot be used as evidence for the religion of the Bronze Age. The Introduction is fanciful.

Grumach, Ernst, 'The Minoan Libation Formula – Again', *Kadmus* 7, 1968, pp. 7–26; I quote p. 23.

Halstead, Paul, 'From Determinism to Uncertainty: Social Storage and the Rise of the Minoan Palace', in Alison Sheridan and Geoff Bailey (eds.) *Economic Archaeology: Towards an Integration of Ecological and Social Approaches*, BAR International Series 96, Oxford, 1981, p. 201.

Harding, M. Esther: *Woman's Mysteries: Ancient and Modern*, Harper and Row, New York, 1976 (first publ. C.G. Jung Foundation for Analytical Psychology, 1971).

Harris, Hermione, 'Women in Precapitalist Societies', talk given at the Institute of Race Relations in London, 25 April 1977.

Harrison, Jane Ellen, *Themis: a Study of the Social Origins of Greek Religion*, Merlin Press, London, 1977, pp. 63, xi, 294 (first publ. Cambridge University Press, 1927).

Hesiod, *Theogony*, most accessible in *Hesiod, the Homeric Hymns and Homerica*, trans. H.G. Evelyn-White, Loeb Classical Library, Heinemann, London; Harvard University Press, Cambridge, MA, 1982 (first publ. 1914). See especially pp. 87–93 (lines 116ff) for the story of Earth and Heaven; p. 117 (lines 504–5) for Earth hiding thunder; pp. 101–3 (lines 295ff) for the earth-born monsters; and pp. 121–3 (lines 561ff) for the Pandora story.

—— *Works and Days*, most accessible in *Hesiod, the Homeric Hymns and Homerica*. See especially pp. 5–9 (lines 421ff) for the Pandora story; and pp. 55–9 (lines 719ff) for the injunctions about bodily activities.

Higgins, Reynold, *Minoan and Mycenaean Art* (revised edn), Thames and Hudson, London, 1981, p. 55 (first published 1967).

Homer, *The Odyssey*, trans. E.V. Rieu, Penguin, Harmondsworth, Middx, 1946.

—— *The Iliad*, trans. E.V. Rieu, Penguin, Harmondsworth, Middx, 1950. Although Rieu has not kept the formulaic, repetitive character of Homer's (originally oral) poetry, these translations are my favourites for a racy read.

—— *Homeric Hymns*, most accessible in the Loeb edition of *Hesiod, The Homeric Hymns and Homerica* (see under Hesiod). See especially 'Homeric Hymn II to Demeter', pp. 289–325 for the Demeter and Persephone story; 'Homeric Hymn III to Pythian Apollo', pp. 349–363 lines 356ff) for the account of Apollo founding the oracle at Delphi.

Hood, Sinclair, *The Arts in Prehistoric Greece*, Pelican History of Art, Penguin, Harmondsworth, Middx, 1978. Systematic and informative, with many illustrations.

Jung, C.G., 'The Psychology of the Child Archetype', in *Collected Works*, trans. R.F.C. Hull, Routledge and Kegan Paul, London; Bollingen Foundation, New York, 1959, Vol. IX, Part I, Par. 267.

Kirk, G.S., *Homer and the Epic: a Shortened Version of 'The Songs of Homer'*, Cambridge University Press, 1955, p. 54.

Lévi-Strauss, Claude, 'The Sex of the Heavenly Bodies', in *Structuralism: A reader*, ed. Michael Lane, Jonathan Cape, London, 1970, pp. 330–9.

Marx, Karl, *Pre-Capitalist Economic Formations*, Lawrence and Wishart, London, 1964, pp. 68, 69–81.

Matz, Friedrich, *Crete and Early Greece*, Methuen, London, 1962, p. 46.

Mellaart, James, 'A Neolithic City in Turkey', *Scientific American*, 210, 1964, pp. 94–104; I quote p. 103.

Miller, Henry, *The Colossus of Maroussi*, Penguin, Harmondsworth, Middx, 1987, p. 48 (first publ. Colt, San Francisco, 1941).

Morrison, Paul, 'Pregnant Fatherhood Two Years On', *Achilles Heel*, 3, 1979, publ. Achilles Heel, 79, Pembroke Road, London E17 9BB, p. 14.

Neumann, Erich, *The Great Mother: an Analysis of the Archetype*, trans. by R. Mannheim, Routledge and Kegan Paul, London, 1955, pp. 222, 42, 39.

Niemeier, W.-D., 'The "Priest King Fresco" from Knossos: a New Reconstruction and Interpretation', in E.B. French and K.A. Wardle (eds.) *Problems in Greek Prehistory*, Bristol Classical Press, 1988, pp. 235–44.

Nilsson, Martin P., *The Minoan-Mycenaean Religion and its Survival in Greek Religion*, C.W.K. Gleerup, Lund, 1950 (first publ. 1927), pp. 290–1, 420, Chapter 6 passim (on the double axe). Though dated by now, this is the classic and fullest source-book on Bronze Age Aegean religion.

Persson, A.W., *The Religion of Greece in Prehistoric Times*, University of California Press, Berkeley and Los Angeles, 1942, pp. 89, 88.

Plato, most accessible in the Loeb Classical Library editions: see *Plato's Republic II, Books VI-X*, trans. P. Shorey, Loeb Classical Library, Heinemann, London; Harvard University Press, Cambridge, MA, 1942 (first publ. 1935). Read from the start of Book VII for the 'Cave' fable. He discusses the relationship between soul and body in many different texts, but see, for example, the dialogues *Phaedo* 64Cff and *Phaedrus* 246Aff in *Plato: Euthyphro, Apology, Crito, Phaedo, Phaedrus*, trans. H.N. Fowler, Heinemann, London; Harvard University Press, Cambridge, MA, 1966 (first publ. 1914).

Pomeroy, Sarah B., *Goddesses, Whores, Wives, and Slaves: Women in Classical Antiquity*, Schocken Books, New York, 1975, p. 1.

Renfrew, Colin, *The Emergence of Civilization: The Cyclades and the Aegean in the Third Millennium B.C.*, Methuen, London, 1972, p. 421.

Rich, Adrienne, *Of Women Born: Motherhood as Experience and Institution*, Virago, London, 1977, pp. 93–4 (prehistoric figurines), 109 (female principle), 98 (transformations necessary for life), 116 (cyclic changes) (first publ. W.W. Norton, USA, 1976).

Saliou, Monique, 'The Processes of Women's Subordination in Primitive and Archaic Greece', in Stephanie Coontz and Peta Henderson (eds.) *Women's Work, Men's Property: The Origins of Gender and Class*, Verso/New Left Books, London, 1986, pp. 169–206; I quote p. 204.

Schweitzer, Bernhard, *Greek Geometric Art*, trans. P. and C. Usborne, Phaidon, London, 1971 (first publ. 1969). A large source-book with many illustrations.

Semonides, most accessible in *Elegy and Iambus with the Anacreonta*, ed. and trans. J.M. Edmonds, Loeb Classical Library, Heinemann, London; Harvard University Press, Cambridge, MA, 1954 (first publ. 1931). See pp. 217–225 (Section 7) for the diatribe against women.

Shaw, J.W., 'The Orientation of the Minoan Palaces', in *Antichità Cretesi: Studi in onore di Doro Levi, Vol. I*, Università di Catania – Istituto di Archeologia, Catania, Sicily, 1973, pp. 47–59.

Sjöö, Monica, *The Ancient Religion of the Great Cosmic Mother of All*, self-published, Bristol, 1975, pp. 2, 5. See also revised edition, Monica Sjöö and Barbara Mor, *The Great Cosmic Mother: Rediscovering the Religion of the Earth*, Harper and Row, San Francisco, 1987, pp. 16, 50.

Snell, Bruno, *The Discovery of the Mind*, trans. T.G. Rosenmeyr, Blackwell, Oxford, 1953.

Snodgrass, A.M., *The Dark Age of Greece*, Edinburgh University Press, 1971, p. 399.

Sourvinou-Inwood, Christiane, 'A Trauma in Flux: Death in the 8th Century and After', in Robin Hägg (ed.) *The Greek Renaissance of the Eighth Century B.C.: Tradition and Innovation*, Paul Åströms Förlag, Stockholm, 1983, pp. 33–48; I quote p. 45.

Starr, Chester G., *The Origins of Greek Civilization 1100–650 BC*, Jonathan Cape, London, 1962, p. 315.

Sussman, Linda B., 'Workers and Drones in Hesiod's Beehive', in John Peradotto and J.P. Sullivan (eds.) *Women in the Ancient World: the Arethusa Papers*, State University of New York Press, Albany, 1984, pp. 79–89.

Taylour, William, *The Mycenaeans*, Thames and Hudson, London, 1964, p. 61.

Thimme, Jürgen, 'Die Religiöse Bedeutung der Kykladenidole', *Antike Kunst*, 8, 1965, p. 79.

Thomson, George, *Studies in Ancient Greek Society: The Prehistoric Aegean*, Lawrence and Wishart, London, 1949, pp. 211–2, 247, 251. A readable, illuminating and wide-ranging book on the early Aegean.

—— *Aeschylus and Athens*, Lawrence and Wishart, London, 1973, pp. 2, 13.

Todd, Ian A., *Catal Hüyük in Perspective*, Cummings, Menlo Park, CA., 1976, pp. 67–71 on ochre burials.

Ucko, Peter, *Anthropomorphic Figurines of Predynastic Egypt and Neolithic Crete with Comparative Material from the Prehistoric Near East and Mainland Greece*, Andrew Szmidla, London, 1968.

Warren, Peter, *Myrtos: an Early Bronze Age Settlement in Crete*, British School of Archaeology at Athens/Thames and Hudson, London, 1972, pp. 87, 267, 39. Gives a very detailed, and readable, description of the excavation.

364 *Moving Heaven and Earth*

Waterhouse, Helen, 'Priest-Kings?', paper presented at Mycenaean Seminar, University of London, 23 January 1974. Summarised in *Bulletin of the Institute of Classical Studies*, 21, 1974, pp. 153–5. An excellent paper, which should be published in full.

Williams, Raymond, *Problems in Materialism and Culture, Selected Essays*, Verso/New Left Books, London, 1980, pp. 67–85.

Xanthoudides, Stephanos A., *The Vaulted Tombs of Mesara*, trans. J.P. Droop, University Press of Liverpool/Hodder and Stoughton, London, 1924.

Zervos, Christian, *L'art des Cyclades du Début à la fin de l'âge du Bronze, 2500–1100 avant notre ère*, Editions 'Cahiers d'art', Paris, 1957, p. 258.

Zschietzschmann, W., 'Kykladenpfannen', *Archäologischer Anzeiger*, 50, 1935, pp. 663–4.

INDEX